Gregory Kwater.
Tasty Comix No. 2.

A History of Underground Comics

Rand Holmes. The original wraparound front cover of this book. Holmes, a talented artist in his own right, skillfully copied the characters of many other underground artists in those artists' own styles, interspersing them with caricatures of some of the cartoonists themselves. Parlor game: find the characters in the art elsewhere in this book, and find the artists in this book's photos. Holmes's cover underscores historical influences on the underground comics in some subtle ways. For instance, the collection of cats at the bottom right includes not only underground characters but also Felix the Cat. And *Mad* mascot Alfred E. Newman, having dropped his "What? Me Worry?" trademark in favor of a more underground undershirt, stands in front of a hulk of the type favored by the E.C. horror comics that spawned *Mad*—while *Mad* and the horror comics both helped spawn the undergrounds.

A History of
Underground Comics
BY MARK JAMES ESTREN

Copyright and Legal Notices

A History of Underground Comics
20th Anniversary Edition

ISBN: 978-1-57951-156-2

Published by
Ronin Publishing, Inc.
P.O. Box 22900
Oakland, California 94609
www.roninpub.com

Dedication
For Merri
O, quantum est hominum beatiorum,
Quid me lætius est beatiusue?

Production

Cover Design	Brian Groppe	briangroppe.com
Cover Image	Robert Crumb	

Library of Congress Catalog Card Number: 2012940456
Printed in the United States of America
Distributed to the book trade by PGW/Perseus

Acknowledgments: Copyright notices not on this page appear adjacent to illustrations. The author also wishes to thank the following people and organizations for permission to quote from selected written material: *Love and Death* by G. Legman, © 1949 G. Legman, by permission of G. Legman; *R. Crumb's Head Comix,* introduction by Paul Krassner, © 1967, 1968 Robert Crumb, by permission of The Viking Press, Inc., by Nancy Schafer; *Understanding Media: The Extensions of Man* by Marshall McLuhan, © 1964 Marshall McLuhan, by permission of McGraw-Hill Book Co., by Marjorie Mitchell; "Color and the Comics" by Jack E. White, from *Columbia Journalism Review*, Vol. VIII, No. 4, Winter 1969-70, © 1970 Columbia University Graduate School of Journalism, by permission of *Columbia Journalism Review,* by Alfred Balk; *Seize the Time* by Bobby Seale, © 1968, 1969, 1970 Bobby Seale, by permission of Random House, Inc., by Gerald Summer.

Table of Contents

Robert Crumb. *Motor City Comics* No. 1. © 1969 R. Crumb Productions. By permission of R. Crumb Productions, by Robert Crumb.

Preface: Beyond the Bizarre

The original underground comics scene was a wild delirious dream in American culture. Fueled by drugs, hippie politics, and countercultural rebellion, it raged for a few years before burning itself out, undergoing endless reinvention, and forging a path for generations to come.

I read my first underground comic when I was about 13 years old. In the beginning, the sci-fi and horror titles were my favorites: *Slow Death, Insect Fear,* and *Fantagor*, with their fabulously detailed artwork by the likes of Greg Irons, Richard Corben, Spain Rodriguez, and S. Clay Wilson. But my underground tastes were expanding as quickly as my consciousness, and I soon found my way to *Zap*. The first couple of issues that were all by Robert Crumb are some of the definitive works of underground comics, but when the rest of the gang shows up, *Zap* truly reaches its zenith as the best underground comics series ever published. The hallucinogenic visions of Robert Williams are rendered with Old Masters brilliance. S. Clay Wilson's insanely detailed pages blur the boundaries of hyper abstraction and hyper-realism. But when I first saw the comics of Victor Moscoso and Rick Griffin I felt I had truly discovered the music of the spheres. Their comics didn't make any sense. They didn't need to, because instead they had found a perfect visual language. These were flawless poems told purely in metaphorical images open to numerous interpretations. I could stare at them for hours, having finally found perfection in the comics form.

"The first underground comics were very abstract in nature, and this abstraction wasn't practical for telling a narrative story," Williams explains. "S. Clay Wilson's influence on me was enormous. He made it underground and he made it gnarly. The core group of *Zap* artists was bitchin'. It was an amazing artistic team. Being involved with underground comics was one of the best experiences of my life." Williams continues, "We were doing a nonsensical form of graphics. But as time went on, more story-driven narratives started to evolve. Then in '70 to '71 the audience got huge and the nonsensical element faded away. In the beginning the comics were half art, half literature. All the early cartoonists had formal backgrounds in art. We wanted to keep things as experimental as possible, but as time went on the audience demanded a story and the narrative took over. Shelton, Crumb, Wilson, and others started to go this more traditional route. Griffin, Moscoso, and I tried to keep it abstract, but we were fighting against where everyone else was going."

Where did these comics come from? That is what *A History of Underground Comics* is all about. And the cartoonists themselves have a keen sense of history. According to Williams, "Underground comics were a direct result of a drug culture that had been building in America since the '50s. It had evolved through various subculture movements like the beatniks and be-boppers and then busted wide open during the Vietnam War. Underground comics were part of that cultural resistance to authority."

Crumb agrees. "All those old characters of the '60s all came from LSD trips. I'd see the vulture demonesses on LSD, these red old deaconesses with bird beaks. I think they're all archetypal, lurking in my subconscious or something... Mr. Natural, the bearded sage. Guess I interpret people through my cartoon mind, you know?"

Underground comics were a vibrant and tumultuous art form filled with vividly expressed delirium and drug-filled madness. As readers of this book will see, some comics, like those by Rory Hayes, were raw and primitive, while others, such as those by Williams, showed flawless technical skills. Underground comics had no one defining style; they were all over the map, outside of the box, experimental, challenging, bedazzling. They were one of the best places to see creativity in its most inspired and purest form. Many of them give the impression that the comics came directly from the artist's soul to the reader.

According to Williams, "Another point that needs to be made is that in the beginning underground comics were flagrant pornography. Now these comics were being distributed through the mail all over the country, so as time went on the FBI began to look into it. They started to put the squeeze on publishers and other people involved in underground comics. At one point they were putting pressure on The Print Mint. The FBI went to the owner and said, 'You're probably

Don Dohler. *Mark Estren Comics*, drawn especially for this book. In typical underground-comic style, Dohler imagines the author's response to the capitalist pigs without whom *A History of Underground Comics* would not exist.

going to jail.' So he panicked and just gave the company to this guy Bob Rita who was working there in the back and left. The Vietnam War was raging and the government was moving further to the right. Everyone knew the FBI was watching us and we all thought we were going to be rounded up and sent to internment camps any day. The FBI was watching Big Daddy Roth trying to get him on racketeering charges because of his connections with the Hell's Angels. I was a draft resister, so between that, my underground comics connections, and working for Roth, I knew I was on multiple FBI watch lists. It's hard for me to overstate the paranoia that was involved with that early underground comics scene. We really thought the shit was gonna come down. But then the country mellowed after '72. In the beginning there were like ten underground cartoonists and the FBI knew who they all were, but by the early '70s there were thousands of underground cartoonists and I don't know if they ever really appreciated the dues we had to pay to pave the way for them." It seems hard to believe today, but the comics did get taken to court, sometimes successfully. [See Chapter 10.]

At one point in the '60s, Crumb took a drug thinking it was LSD, but it was something different, much stronger. "It made me fuzzy for several months. The fuzz was cleared up the next time I took LSD. Fwish! Something, the fuzz was lifted, it was like clearing the picture on a TV screen, all of a sudden everything would be clear. But it was during that fuzzy period that I was able to perceive this bizarre world and understand the mechanics of it. It was very inspiring. The rational part of my brain was shut off. Almost completely. I could not function rationally, I was crazy. It was very... very inspiring. I really got into drawing in that wacky big foot style. Keep On Trucking, all that stuff came out of that period. That rational part of the brain that was usually in control was really like damaged, seriously damaged."

During this time period, Crumb filled his sketchbooks with new drawings. "The whole thing just suddenly started coming out in my brain, I couldn't control it, I couldn't stop it. All these what I'd call horror squeaky big foot characters, with these third-rate 1940s funny comic book styles, low stupid drug humor, wacky duck cartoons for adults. During that period I had a bunch of these books that I had gotten at a secondhand magazine store in Chicago that had all the titles torn off. And I just sat there gazing at those things. And I just started coming out with drawings attuned to that whole vision. It lasted all through the hippie period and then seemed to peter out after I stopped taking LSD in the mid-'70s."

This savage drug experience sent Crumb careening in a whole new creative direction through a political landscape and counterculture that seems as mad as the effect of the drug itself. Crumb's comments are almost like a metaphor for the whole tenor and chaos of underground comics in the '60s and '70s.

Underground comics were about sex and drugs [see chapters 5 and 8] and taking it to the extremes. Marvel and DC were about the good things in life, the bright, sunny, optimistic side of mainstream heroics, but underground comics were always about the dark side. Unclean thoughts and even more unclean deeds: where Sigmund Freud met Hieronymus Bosch. This could have been the back cover description for *Snatch Comics*, which depicted people having sex until their genitals went flying off. And *Snatch* was just the tip of a sperm-covered iceberg. I'll never forget the first time I saw the issue of *Bizarre Sex Comics* that screamed: It came from Alpha Centauri looking for love… and depicted a gigantic space vagina being penetrated by the Empire State Building. Poontang was dripping

Denis Kitchen. *Fourth Estate Funnies*. © 1974 Magazine Management Co., Inc. Mark Estren, the author, becomes a character as this book gets sucked into its own content.

Charles, I'd never done that with another artist. And I liked his work, you know. His work was a real eye-opener to me. So we started talking about doing a comic together and... He had played around with comics before that but, having gone to art school where they belittled comics and made comics seem like dirt, he lost his confidence in that. But then when he saw my stuff he kind of was re-inspired to do comics. And then Moscoso and Griffin had been talking about doing a psychedelic comic at the same time. But we didn't know them, I didn't know them, I had just seen their posters. But somehow, I forget who it was, maybe Moscoso, contacted me about doing comics, after he saw *Zap* comics, about getting together on something. So then the four of us got together. And Shelton came along. And Spain came along. I met Spain in New York in '68. He was doing comics for the *East Village Other*. They were really great, those Trashman strips [see pp. 182-3]. Really liked his stuff. Then he moved to San Francisco and he got in on it. Then Williams came along."

It wasn't the artists that made underground comics available to a wider audience—it was the publishers, like Apex Novelties, Last Gasp, Rip Off Press, and The Print Mint and stores like Gary Arlington's San Francisco Comic Book Company. [See Chapter 11] Crumb confirms, "Donahue (of Apex Novelties) was a very important person in those days in the underground comic world in the late '60s. He was really connecting people up a lot in those days. He was significant. A really interesting character, Donahue. Gary Arlington was too. He was very significant. A lot of people met at Arlington's store. There was this place over on Valencia Street I used to hang out at a lot. Hayes lived there for a while, and the Deitch brothers hung out there in the early '70s and the late '60s. It was a pretty crazy time. Pretty crazy."

Spain Rodriguez also expresses fond memories of those days. "It was one of the greatest times in history to be a cartoonist," he said. "Artists lived in the same neighborhoods. There were all these guys and women like Trina Robbins doing amazing work. People would come up with an idea and you all would collaborate on a comic. It was a magical time."

S. Clay Wilson was also a major force during those formative times. A lot of the underground comics scene was about peace and love but not all of it. Wilson always displayed a punk attitude, even in the middle of the most placid hippie scenes. Wilson's effect on the *Zap* artists and other cartoonists around him was immeasurable: he got them to really push the boundaries. It was the '60s and it was all about going FURTHER. Wilson always took things as far as they could go.

Mainstream comics had their superheroes with their cut-and-dried morality and the black-and-white certitude of truth, justice, and the American way. Underground comics, on the other hand, had Mr. Natural and the ambiguous mysteries of the universe. Like *Superman, Zap* was decidedly American, but its caricatures of '50s era uptight morality exposed cruel, greedy, and sadistic realities. The artists didn't always have all the answers to universal mysteries, and they frequently chased down some dead ends, but they always seemed to be trying to find out what it all meant.

This general searching for the hidden truths of existence was one of the common themes of the classic undergrounds. Griffin's comics are filled with Christian mysticism while Moscoso's strips seem to reach for universal absolutes. Williams' beautifully surreal works are often lowbrow scenes violently mashed up with visions of the infinite. Flakey Foont would scream out, "What's it all mean, Mr. Natural?" and even if it didn't mean shit, it still had moments of true revelation and pure bliss. Hippie minds everywhere were being opened by drugs and flooded with rivers of new truths. Underground comics were part of this great consciousness expansion.

All of this led to some of the best fine art that has ever been produced. Artists such as Crumb and Williams have already been recognized as some of the best artists of their generation. And they are just two of many great cartoonists that left an indelible mark on their time. The cultural and artistic effects of underground comics have expanded outwards in ever increasing waves that reverberate to this day. They took *Mad* magazine's concept of questioning authority and elevated it to trampling authority. Their anarchy of concept and design still echoes in the media all around us. They were like a huge tab of LSD dropped in the cultural reservoirs of the American mind. As Rodriguez eloquently recalled, "San Francisco was like Paris in the early part of the century –the center of a major art movement. We thought we were pioneers, breaking molds, and it was something we did with a great deal of joy."

Jon Longhi is the author of *Wake Up and Smell the Beer, The Rise and Fall of Third Leg, Flashbacks and Premonitions*, and *Bricks and Anchors*. His writing has also appeared in *San Francisco Noir* and *Retaking the Universe: William S. Burroughs in the Age of Globalization.*

Foreword: Backward!

Return with us now to those thrilling days of yesteryear.

So said the 1930s radio serial and, later, the 1949-1957 television show, *The Lone Ranger*. But a look back at the heyday of underground comics is quite different from an adventure-packed cowboys-and-Indians (or, as we would now say, European-settlers-and-Native-Americans) entertainment program. The underground cartoonists were very much of their era, but the best of their work transcends the time in which it was created, as the best art invariably does.

This is *a* history of underground comics, not *the* history; it partakes of the author's viewpoints, prejudices and interests. Among those is the book's title: "comics," not the more-often-seen "comix," because the notion here is that these works, for all their unique characteristics, are part of a continuum dating back at least to Richard Outcault's The Yellow Kid (1895; see page 25). Another bias here is a strong belief that the underground cartoonists had (and the surviving ones still have) a unique approach to their medium—one strongly grounded in history, true, but one that transcended all the work that had come before their time. These cartoonists' intention was to break barriers, and they did; but to break something, one must first know what it is, acknowledge its existence and find its weak points. They did that, too. This book tries to show how.

A History of Underground Comics is a snapshot in time, devoted primarily to the 1960s and 1970s, when underground comics flourished. Much had changed by the 1990s, when the Ronin edition of this book first appeared; much more has changed in the 20 years since. Of major importance is the reality that the survival of the undergrounds became in large part a matter of printing and distribution agreements. Make no mistake: there is still more to these comics than the marketplace — artists self-identifying as "underground" or as strongly influenced by the undergrounds are driven to do what they do, sometimes demon-ridden by their own ideas and needing to bring them out. Thus, underground comics, for all the changes in the world around them, have remained a means of intensely personal expression. And some of the same comics are still around: reprints of *Zap* and *The Fabulous Furry Freak Brothers* have persisted alongside new work by "established" underground cartoonists (is that a contradiction in terms?) and comics by altogether new voices. Yet economic realities affect the underground comics and cartoonists whether they want them to or not.

So where does one find undergrounds these days? A tough question, and an important part of the undergrounds' story in the decades after the time chronicled here. Jay Kennedy (1956-2007), author of *The Official Underground and Newave Comix Price Guide*, explained:

"Underground distribution all started changing in 1982 because of the emergence of an alternative distribution system of comic-book specialty retail shops. The undergrounds originally sold through head shops and hip joints, but all those dried up in the mid-Seventies, and from 1975 to 1980 there was really no outlet except mail order for these books.

"In the late Seventies, though, [establishment publishers] Marvel and D.C. agreed to sell their comics at big discounts to comic-book retailers on a non-return basis. This established a pattern for later deals that helped the undergrounds. Stores could get discounts that newsstand distributors get, but could not return the books. These stores sold only comics, and people objecting—to comics in general or undergrounds in particular—didn't go in much. Comic-bookstore customers might start out reading superhero books, but graduate beyond adolescent fantasies and look for alternative materials that were more meaningful."

The best undergrounds are certainly meaningful, or try to be, and some of their characters, such as Gilbert Shelton's Wonder Wart-Hog (see pages 59, 123 and 194), use the superhero genre to take adolescent fantasies a step or two beyond the largely sanitized worldview of D.C. and Marvel.

So comic-book stores helped build a new audience for undergrounds in the United States. The audience grew in other countries, too, notably in France, where comics have always been taken far more seriously than in the U.S. This is one reason that Shelton moved to Paris and Robert Crumb, the best-known underground cartoonist of all, took up residence in an 800-year-old farmhouse near Nimes.

German rights attorney Manfred Mroczkowski, executive director of Interlicense Ltd., understands the lure of markets outside the U.S. By the 1990s, his firm, established in 1982, was well on the way to helping cartoonists get distribution outside North America: "Overseas has become very important for underground artists—in Europe they remain extremely popular."

Indeed, Shelton's overseas distribution has long surpassed his sales in the U.S. His work appears in French, German, Italian, Spanish, Dutch, Portuguese, Danish, Norwegian, Swedish and Finnish. Shelton relocated to France, according to Mroczkowski, because "you need freedom of expression plus a marketplace. If you express yourself freely and don't make a buck out of it, it's really worthless."

Hmm. Perhaps that was true in the 1990s and beyond—but making a buck wasn't always a priority, certainly not in the years portrayed here. Crumb used to sit on the street in the San Francisco Bay area, to which many underground cartoonists gravitated, drawings his cartoons and selling them. And not for much.

"The whole excitement [at that time] was something unique," says Mroczkowski. "I saw my first Crumb cartoon when I was a law student in Germany in 1968. It was a little guy in a box, trying to get out of the box. The visual image was so strong, so right for what was going on at that time, that I just thought, hey, here's one guy who really knows what's going on.

"Now it's changed. It's an art form. It's history now."

Well, maybe. If "it" (the original flourishing of underground comics) is history, then this book is a history of a history. Not *the* history, remember, but *a* history—being, by design, as personal and quirky and occasionally wrong-headed as all histories are, even if few of them admit it.

So much has changed since the days chronicled here that the temptation to revise, review, re-edit and rethink has been almost overwhelming. By and large, though, I have resisted it, preferring to let *A History of Underground Comics* stand as a chronicle of its times, written in the style and language of those times (although I certainly think I could polish it quite a bit today). There are a few corrections and updates in this edition, but by and large, what you are now reading is a 20-years-later reprint of a snapshot of history taken while the history was being made—the literary equivalent of a self-taken photograph from the days before digital cameras and Photoshop. In those long-ago times, if you can envision them, pictures one took oneself might come out fuzzy or poorly composed; and if they did, it was reasonable to blame the photographer. So *mea culpa* for anything here that is not as it should be. I thought it was, when I and the world were younger.

To get the most out of *A History of Underground Comics*, readers should try to visualize the pre-Internet, indeed pre-personal-computer, social and political climate that spawned the comics and inspired the cartoonists. Some call these years the undergrounds' Golden Age. But that is a fossilizing term, and these comics deserve better. A golden age? Wrong metal. Brassy, perhaps—brash and brittle and brilliant, glowing with a luster that is hard to recapture from the vantage point of today.

Luckily, a few people preserved in themselves the spirit of the time, such as Ron Turner, owner and publisher of Last Gasp, which celebrated its (gasp!) 40th anniversary in 2010. Turner is "probably the guy who most upholds the image and the idea of the underground comic," according to Mroczkowski and others. Right into the 21st century, Turner continued to look pretty much as he did in the 1960s ("and still sticks his head out just as much"—Mroczkowski again). Turner believes that underground comics arose and flourished when they did because "things were unleashed. Every 30 or 40 years, things kind of come together—political unrest and political awareness at the same time, a shift in who controls what the culture is, how the culture defines itself. The images that have established what culture is no longer fit. It happened in the Twenties and into the Thirties—and then in the Sixties and into the Seventies. Underground comics, along with psychedelic posters, were the most significant new American art form to develop during that time."

Mroczkowski seconds Turner's analysis: "What very few Americans realize is that the underground cartoons were a totally unique art form that went way beyond what the cartoon really was. And they were an extremely powerful medium of communication."

So they were, and so they still are, as you will discover (or rediscover) herein. What the underground cartoonists did was to start with the inherent communicative power of cartooning, build on the most visually striking and effective work that had gone before, and take the cartoonist's art to a new level of visual impact. "The core of the undergrounds is personal expression," said Kennedy. And by the 1990s, "the hardest thing [became] to decide what is underground and what is not, because boundaries are so blurred that there is no longer a clear distinction. It always comes back to motive. In most cases with undergrounds, the artists need to say something—often without a great deal of concern with remuneration—something they have chosen to spend time on. Some graphic novels extend that urge."

Graphic novels, in fact, are but one newer branch on the family tree on which underground comics themselves grew. One of the most famous and celebrated graphic novels of all, Art Spiegelman's two-part Holocaust survival tale called *Maus* (published in 1986 and 1991), had its roots in an underground comic from 1973 that Spiegelman credits in the first *Maus* book (see pages 149, 171 and 300). The second part of *Maus* thanks the John Simon Guggenheim Memorial Foundation for its financial backing—a long trip for Spiegelman from his underground days.

And Spiegelman is not the only one who has made the trip. Perhaps because Bill Griffith "was never really part of the underground, but learned a lot from the way these guys did it" (Mroczkowski), he moved successfully into syndication with his character Zippy—and in 1992 created a series explaining how his more

Robert Crumb, *Zap Comix*, No. 5.

Gilbert Shelton. *Hydrogen Bomb and Biochemical Warfare Funnies.* © 1970 Rip Off Press. By permission of Rip Off Press, by Gilbert Shelton.

"undergroundish" Mr. Toad (in Zippy's words) "represents th' unresolved anger in [Griffith's] relationship with [his] father." (For Mr. Toad and Zippy together in their underground days, see page 236.)

In the decades after the underground comics' heyday, there was some flowering of syndicated cartoonists whose styles and themes had an "underground" flavor, even though the artists themselves were never underground cartoonists. Examples include Gary Larson (*The Far Side*), Bud Grace (*Ernie*) and Berke Breathed (*Bloom County* and, to a lesser extent, *Outland*). But "I don't think the underground comics have really had much influence on syndicated newspaper comic strips," said Kennedy—who, as a comics editor for King Features Syndicate for almost 20 years, including a decade as editor-in-chief, was in the right position to know. "Even when the rare syndicated cartoonist acknowledges Crumb, he is only one of the many influences. If the sensibilities of some syndicated strips align with those of the undergrounds, it's generational change, a zeitgeist. There is an evolution in humor simply because people become accustomed to old humor and you need something more to get a laugh out of them. Syndication is always entertainment-driven, and in general humor entertains best. On the whole, undergrounds are not funny, though of course some are."

Underground influence may never have become highly significant in syndicated comic strips, but it did have an important influence on films. Underground-style animation was perhaps most notorious in Ralph Bakshi's *Fritz the Cat* (1972), the first animated film ever to receive an "X" rating, the equivalent of the later "NC-17" (see page 258). There was also a sequel, *The Nine Lives of Fritz the Cat,* in 1974; and *Dirty Duck* appeared in 1977 (see pages 27 and 28). There was underground influence as well in the animated version of *The Lord of the Rings* (1978) and the bizarre *The Forbidden Zone* (1980), in which the zone of the title is reached when actors, transformed into cartoon characters, pass through intestines and are excreted—a sequence strongly paralleling one in a Crumb strip (see below and page 20). The continuing popularity of *Monty Python's Flying Circus* also represents an extension of the appeal of the humorous side of underground-comic-style art.

But there was certainly nothing funny about the times some of these comics and their creators went through. Aside from the notorious obscenity trial of *Zap No. 4* (see chapter 10), economic realities hit the undergrounds hard, even if the comics had not been drawn for economic reasons. "1974 to 1975 almost killed off everyone," Turner remembers. "Business was off 80 percent for a while. I assumed $40,000 in debts. It took years and years to pay things off and make them stable. We're affected terribly by the business cycles, just like everybody else."

Yes, business factors became as important, in a way, as the art of the cartoonists itself, and the thoughts behind it. Those who care about the underground comics' roots were not happy with that reality: "I think the only difference between a businessman and a criminal is that the businessman is on better terms with the IRS," says Turner. But, comfortable or not, Turner and other longtime supporters of underground comics made the necessary adjustments.

Why? Because the artists had so much to say and were so determined that it be heard. "I think they found a way to really look inside themselves and bring it out and put it on paper and look at it," says Turner. "They love it. It's therapy, but I don't mean it's like basket weaving. It's necessary for their growth."

It's good for the growth of the rest of us, too. "Cartoonists can give you the inner canyons of the human psyche that you wouldn't ever be able to probe in any other humans," says Turner. "Writers do it too, but I can't see the picture—I have to imagine it. Some avant-garde filmmakers do it, but they have to have cameras and technicians and lighting and actors—they can't do it themselves. These cartoonists can actually show me.

Robert Crumb. *Hytone Comix.* © 1971 R. Crumb. By permission of Robert Crumb.

Gary Grimshaw. *Slow Death Funnies* No. 1. © 1970 The Visual YoYo Tribe. By permission of The Visual YoYo Tribe, by Ronald E. Quinn.

"Cartoonists add the power of vision to that of cognitive thought. The eye has its own nerve net, its own ability to organize material.

"It's powerful stuff on all levels. They're dealing with the future all the time. Some day maybe the rest of the mass will catch up. But these artists are always ahead of their time. They're visionaries."

That is one compelling set of reasons for delving into this history. Mroczkowski offers another: "There's one thing you can't repeat. The Sixties happened here. The excitement of it was everywhere in this country, and that was unique. What is happening overseas now is esthetic play—in this country, there was wildness. The raw energy was here, not over there.

"But, ironically, America has not come to terms with that yet. Now maybe it's time. Perhaps now America will find a historic view of that period. The late Sixties still need to be culturally digested."

There's a lot to digest, even after all these years, as you will see. Not all of it will go down easily. Your sensibilities, even in the 21st century, may be offended by some of what you will find here. If so, good: the artists' intent was often to offend. Your gorge may rise at some of the panels. If so, good: better that kind of lump in the throat than the sort artificially created by mass-media manipulators of emotion, the cartoonists would say. Many underground comics are still as powerful as they were when Ronin's first edition of this book appeared. Mroczkowski understands the value of leaving that earlier edition, even the inelegantly written parts (for which, again, *mea culpa*), essentially unchanged: "It stands as a frozen drop of time, and to fiddle with that is to destroy it."

Yet time, of course, does not freeze: it moves ahead inexorably, with the result that many of the creators of the works you will see here have passed on; only their art endures. Joel Beck, Vaughn Bodé, Roger Brand, Rick Griffin, Rory Hayes, Greg Irons, Willy Murphy, Dave Sheridan—they, among others, are gone. So are Wally Wood, a seminal influence on so many cartoonists; Will Eisner, one of the giants in the field; and Harvey Kurtzman and Bill Gaines of E.C. Comics and *Mad*—two of the most far-reaching influences of them all.

But what the cartoonists did, or tried to do, has not died. It may have refocused, developed, progressed and moved on—but in one form or another, it still lives. Crumb's Lenore Goldberg put it simply: "Well, y'know…life goes on an' things change…" (see page 131).

For the cartoonists still working, what is here represents the solid foundation on which their work rests. For those who are no longer with us, *A History of Underground Comics* freezes, and I hope preserves, what they tried to do but will do no more. To each of them, *ave atque vale* and *in pace requiescat.*

Mark James Estren
Fort Myers, Florida &
Oakland, California

Gilbert Shelton. *Gothic Blimp Works* No. 6. © 1969 Gilbert Shelton. By permission of Gilbert Shelton.

O The Phantom Psychiatrist

Robert Crumb. *Zap Comix* No. 5.

In an attempt to gain some special insights into the minds of the underground cartoonists, based on their comics, I interviewed the head of psychiatric training at a major New York hospital. His comments will be found sprinkled through the present volume, in which he is referred to as *The Phantom Psychiatrist* because he has refused to let his name be used. Born in 1931, *The Phantom Psychiatrist* was in private psychiatric practice for ten years before moving to his present position. He sports sideburns, a beard and mustache, and is balding on the top of his head. In another ten years or so he'll look remarkably like Freud himself.

The Phantom Psychiatrist said his name could not be used because statements by officials at his hospital could not be publicly released until they had been cleared by the entire chain of hospital command ("which I'll do for you," he said, "but you'll be an old man before it happens"). But another doctor associated with *The Phantom Psychiatrist's* hospital thought the business about clearing his comments was "bullshit," and that *The Phantom Psychiatrist* was playing politics—and was perhaps a little worried about being associated with underground comics.

Ah well, it's a terrible thing to subject a psychiatrist to analysis, so we'll let it go at that. If nothing else, the situation shows the faintly sinister air which seems to hang around underground comics in many people's minds. We have too many problems with dirty air to worry much about sinister air. I hope this book will at least help clear the air, if not clean it.

Joel Beck. *The Profit.* ©1966 Joel Beck. By permission of Joel Beck.

Robert Crumb. *Big Ass Comics* No. 2.

1 An Attempt at Definition

"Given three strikes, the truth will out."
—Walt Kelly

From the four corners of America—and the lands across the sea—they come, looking like the most innocent and garish reminders of childhood gone by, but with cryptic warnings on the covers: "For Adults Only," or sometimes "For Adult Intellectuals Only." From Los Angeles and San Francisco they come, and from Chicago and Milwaukee, and from New York, even from Texas.

It's the titles which first alert you to the fact that these are not mere juvenilia, not for frustrated subteens who want to ogle Millie the Model's swelling but fully-clothed bosom. *Zap, Yellow Dog, Spiffy Stories, Death Rattle, Gothic Blimp Works, Baloney Moccasins, Mom's Homemade Comics, Bijou, Fat Lip Funnies, Moonchild, Big Ass, God Nose (Snot Reel), Feds 'n' Heads, The Alienated War Baby Report, Tasty, Googiewaumer, The Kingdom of Heaven is Within You, XYZ, Motor City, Ghost Mother, Quagmire, Skull,* and on and on to the point of inaccuracy, so quickly are the new underground comics springing up.

Once you make it past the title —and even the innocuous sounding *Smile* may not be what you expect—you're confronted with

Right: Skip Williamson. *Bijou Funnies* No. 4. ©1970 Bijou Publishing Empire, Inc. By permission of Bijou Publishing Empire, Inc., by Jay Lynch.

Opposite: Foolbert Sturgeon. *The New Adventures of Jesus.* ©1969 Foolbert Sturgeon. By permission of Foolbert Sturgeon.

Middle R: Robert Crumb. *Zap Comix* No. 1. ©1967 R. Crumb. By permission of Robert Crumb.

Bottom R: Robert Crumb. *Motor City Comics* No. 2. ©1970 R. Crumb. By permission of Robert Crumb.

Right: Dave Sheridan. *Motner's Oats Comix* No. 1. ©1969 Sheridan and Schrier. By permission of Dave Sheridan.

Right: Dave Sheridan. *Motner's Oats Comix* No. 1. ©1969 Sheridan and Schrier. By permission of Dave Sheridan.

STORIES FROM THE GOOD BOOK
THIS REALLY IS A GOOD BOOK!
BY FOOLBERT STURGEON
AND DID YOU EVER REALLY MEET THE DEVIL, MR. CHRIST?
INDEED, YES! AND A DRAMATIC ENCOUNTER IT WAS. WHEN I WAS ABOUT THIRTY YEARS OF AGE, (THIS WAS OF COURSE SOME TIME AGO) I WAS LED BY THE SPIRIT INTO THE WILDERNESS...
I'M OFF TO THE DESERT WILDERNESS TO BE TEMPTED. GOD, IT'S HOT!
ALL I HAVE TO DO IS STAY OUT HERE FORTY DAYS WITHOUT FOOD OR WATER. JEEZ! I'LL STARVE TO DEATH!
SHIT! IT'S HOT. NOBODY TO TALK TO, NOTHING TO DO, NOTHING TO EAT. WHAT I'M REALLY TEMPTED TO DO IS GO HOME.... IN ORDER TO SURVIVE I'LL HAVE TO TURN MYSELF INTO A STINKING CAMEL.
WELL, I'LL BE DIPPED IN SHIT! THE SMELL IS SO BAD I CAN'T HARDLY STAND IT!

HERE COMES MY ARCHENEMY THE PRINCE OF DARKNESS NOW!
HA! YOU CAN'T FOOL ME WITH YOUR SILLY CAMEL DISGUISE, J., YOUR HALO GIVES YOU AWAY! I GUESS YOU KNOW I'VE COME TO OFFER YOU THE POWER AND PLEASURE OF THE WORLD.
GET THEE BEHIND ME SATAN!
BEHIND A CAMEL! YEKK! PERISH THE THOUGHT!
WELL! WHAT ABOUT IT! DO YOU WANT THE POWER AND PLEASURE OF THE WORLD OR DON'T YOU?
COME ON! COME ON! I'M NOT GOING TO WAIT ALL DAY!
DID YOU SEE THAT? THE PRINCE OF DARKNESS WAS BACK THERE OFFERING THE POWER AND PLEASURE OF THE WORLD TO A CAMEL!

Nicola Cuti. *Moonchild Comics* No. 3. ©1970 Nicola Cuti. By permission of Nicola Cuti.

the price: sometimes only twenty-five cents, but usually at least fifty cents per comic, and sometimes as much as one dollar. For this, you normally get inside pages printed only in black and white (though full-color underground comics started appearing in summer 1971).

Okay, by now you realize these aren't like ordinary comic books.

Let's assume the unenlightened type (not the present reader, of course) gets past the color cover to the black-and-white, high-priced insides. The first thing he or she notices is that these comics deal with "taboo" subjects: drugs, sex (including accurate drawings of penises, vaginas, and other necessary evils), shit, religion, snot, politics, etc. Worst of all, notes this hypothetical person, these topics are Right Out In The Open, and the evildoers who screw and take drugs and mock God don't necessarily die of gonorrhea, overdoses of speed, or a bolt of lightning from Olympus.

Marcus Welby it ain't.

So the unenlightened one walks away, vowing never to patronize any place which would carry such monstrosities again, and forgets the whole incident—or perhaps calls the local chapter of Morality in Media to start yet another campaign to drive out the evil influences which are eroding everything sacred.

I'd like to assume that you, dear reader, are a little more enlightened than that, and aren't looking at this book just to have something new to complain about at the next church bingo night. In fact, I'll make that assumption from now on.

Defining the underground comics by their appearance is really impossible. The most striking thing about them is their startling variety of styles. Almost as striking is the difference in quality of draftsmanship, which ranges from amateurish to expert (often within the same comic) and which encompasses everything from stick drawings of people to complex, posterlike metamorphoses which are closer to traditional concepts of "art" than to anything previously seen in what looks like a comic book.

The artistic styles are so varied that some have suggested defining the medium by simply calling it "comix." That helps a little in writing, but not in speaking (it sounds the same as "comics")—and besides, while some

Opposite: Foolbert Sturgeon. *The New Adventures of Jesus.* ©1969 Foolbert Sturgeon. By permission of Foolbert Sturgeon.

Far Left: Robert Williams. *Tasty Comix* No. 2. ©1970 O.D. By permission of O.D.-Tasty Comix, by Robert Friedman.

Below: Denis Kitchen. *Mom's Homemade Comics* No. 2. ©1969 Denis Kitchen. By permission of Denis Kitchen.

Top: Hak Vogrin. *Yellow Dog Comix* No. 16. ©1969 Hak Vogrin. By permission of Hak Vogrin.

of these creations do call themselves "comix," others prefer "komiks" or even "karmix," or simply "funnies" or "stories." And in still other cases, the traditional spelling "comics" is retained. Besides, trying to incorporate the newness of these books into the single word "comix" makes about as much sense as defining a hoop as a three-dimensional circle: that doesn't tell you much about the hoop.

Underground comics are truly three-dimensional, at least figuratively. (There's also one that is *literally* three-dimensional: *Deep 3-D Comix.*) The dimension of depth, as lacking in Mary Worth soap operas as in Archie antics, is present in the underground comics to an astonishing degree. Most of the underground strips can be read and enjoyed on several levels—indeed, *must* be read that way in order to make complete sense (in some cases, to make any sense at all).

Realizing that there are bound to be exceptions to any set of criteria used in defining so varied a field, it's still worthwhile to point out that there are some things which most of these books have in common. It would seem logical for underground comics to emerge through underground newspapers, and in fact this is where the term "underground comics" comes from. Various underground papers still do print comics, either by artists now established in the field or by ones just getting started. Allen Katzman, former editor of the *East Village Other,* speaks for many editors of underground papers when he says that he likes the comics because they are so immediate and direct. *EVO* was the jumping-off point for several underground cartoonists, notably Bill Griffith *(Tales of Toad),* who also contributed to not-quite-underground-press publications like *Screw* and *Other Scenes;* and Kim Deitch, who became editor of *EVO*'s comics supplement, *Gothic Blimp Works.* Indeed, of all underground papers, only *Yarrowstalks* in Philadelphia has been as committed to underground comics as *EVO*.

Of course, the next logical request is for a definition of underground newspapers—which puts us perilously close to being back where we started. You don't have to go to Tijuana to buy either the underground papers or the underground comics—though even in many large cities, such as Buffalo and Baltimore, the comics are extremely difficult to come by. In the tra-

Denis Kitchen. *Snarf* No. 3. ©1972 Denis Kitchen. By permission of Denis Kitchen.

Robert Crumb. *The People's Comics.* ©1972 R. Crumb. By permission of Robert Crumb.

Opposite: Willy Murphy. *San Francisco Comic Book* No. 4. ©1973 Willy Murphy. By permission of Willy Murphy.

AUTOMATIC TRANSMISSION
SO THEN THE SONOYABITCH HAS A BIG PRESS CONFERENCE THE NEXT DAY, SEE...
PIGS... PIGS!
HNN...
SNNF
SO I KEEP TELLING HER LIKE THAT HE'S CRAZY, RIGHT? BUT SHE DOESN'T PAY ANY ATTENTION...
HA HA HA HA HA HA HA
(CHUCKLE)
YEAH... DIDJA EVER GET LAID IN ONE A THOSE SAUNA TRIPS? ... LISSEN...
SO ALL FIVE OF US HAD OUR CLOTHES OFF, AND WE'RE REALLY RIPPED...
I GOT THIS BLOWJOB ONE TIME IN A SUPER MARKET...
YEAH... ONE TIME IN PHILADELPHIA, MY OLD MAN BRINGS THIS CHICK HOME, SEE...
13+ 27 40
SO THEN, LIKE AFTER THAT, IT WAS REALLY VERY BAD...
GODDAM LIONS LOOKED TOUGH IN THAT GAME DIDN'T THEY?
OK.. BUT THEN MY OTHER AUNT USED TO ONLY SHOP AT BAMBURGERS
RIGHT... YEAH... RIGHT...
HNN...
©1975 • WILLY MURPHY •

ditional sense of "underground" literature, these things aren't really "underground" at all.

Yet the availability of the comics *is* restricted, and it's usually easier to buy them by mail from their publishers than to try to find them wherever you happen to live. They're emphatically *not* sold on newsstands, and aren't even available in most bookstores.

Robert Crumb. *Hytone Comix.* ©1971 R. Crumb. By permission of Robert Crumb.

Limited availability alone, however, does not an underground comic make. There are other characteristics which are also part of the field. These comics are produced in the tens of thousands (or less) rather than the hundreds of thousands. Their artists are mostly young and politically aware, and their subject matter is usually contemporary and satirical. Each artist is responsible for his own contribution to a book—there's none of the "straight" comics' division of labor between writer and artist. Nor is there any of the deadline pressure (at least in most cases) which straight cartoonists experience. Even the underground comics which have been published two dozen different times have come out at thoroughly irregular intervals, and the artists in one issue have often been completely different from the artists in the preceding and following ones. In fact, underground cartoonists may contribute at the same time to half a dozen different books published by three or four different companies—and this too is something special about the field.

Another important point is that these comics emphatically do *not* abide by the censorship of the Comics Code Authority of America. Thus, they are not aimed at the sort of "family audience" which is supposed to attend "G"-rated motion pictures. The artists in these comics really care about what they draw and the way they draw it—something which cannot matter much to those straight cartoonists who willingly submit all their work for pre-publication censorship according to a set of arbitrary standards. In fact, the underground cartoonists are amused when, for instance, the New York *Times* of February 4, 1971 devotes a long article to a single "straight" comic which was published by the Marvel Comics Group without that Comics Code seal of approval. The article goes on at length about *Spiderman* No. 96, which treated (and heavily condemned) the subject of drug use by teenagers—a subject totally banned by the head-in-the-sand administrators of the Comics Code. The underground cartoonists are amused because they've been doing that sort of thing for years—and have even dared to present some pro-drug arguments. But by and large, their sort of courage doesn't make headlines in the New York *Times*—which is one reason they're still "underground."

Bill Griffith. *Funny Aminals* [*sic*] No. 1. ©1972 Bill Griffith. By permission of Bill Griffith.

Not every strip in the underground comics uses words like "fuck" and "shit," and not every strip deals with subjects deemed taboo by the comic-book bluenoses (sex, religion, the victory of criminals, the *visible* portrayal of blood and gore, etc.). But if someone *is* shot in an underground comic, he bleeds—and it's not pretty. The underground comics deal with whatever subjects their artists wish, in uncompromising visual and verbal terms. Hence the "Adults Only" designation which most of the comics carry voluntarily on their covers—and the inside-cover warning to dealers on a few of the books: "Dealers are instructed not to sell this book to minors."

The underground cartoonists are acutely aware of the general censorship of American comic books (ninety percent of those in this country abide by the Comics Code)—and they come down hard and directly on the censors. *Zap* No. 1 bears a seal resembling that of the censorship board but saying, "Approved by the ghost writers in the sky," and *Zap* No. 2 bears a similar seal, this one with the words, "Approved by the united geeks of

Above Left: Justin Green. *Binky Brown Meets the Holy Virgin Mary.* ©1972 Justin Green. By permission of Justin Green.

Top Right: Larry Todd. *Tales of the Armorkins.* ©1971 Larry S. Todd. By permission of Larry Todd.

Left: Spain. *Gothic Blimp Works* No. 8.

THE UNDERGROUND CARTOONIST

By Denis Kitchen

The Underground Cartoonist holds a unique role among the intellectual and cultural forces that shape our destiny. It is not enough that he be well-versed in the technique of "cartooning," that peculiar form of story-telling that has evolved only in the last seventy-five years. He must also have a firm grip on our entire artistic heritage, from the classic beauty of ancient Greece to the neurotic scribblings of modern Bohemians. In addition, he must be well versed in fine literature, for cartoons rise above both art and literature in that they are a hybrid of the two. By their mid-twenties, most cartoonists, if properly schooled, have mastered the basic elements. At this point the cartoonist faces what has best been described as a massive fork in the road of his future. He must grapple at this point with the great social questions of our era. Most succumb to the harsh demands of capitalist economics and are swallowed up by the giant maws of faceless industry or the

Illustration A

mass media, where their talent is soon exploited and drained. The others, through superior genetic chains (or perhaps divine guidance) choose the smaller path and become Underground Cartoonists. The rewards are small and the glory is never what they deserve, but this band of hardy libertarians assume their role with Spartan dignity. It falls primarily on their shoulders to lead the masses against the corrupt bourgeois institutions that oppress all mankind. The first comic strip on this page (Illustration A) could have been drawn by a hack of the first category described above. Its insipidness alone condemns it; but, beyond that, it reinforces the sexist and anti-working class attitudes that have curtailed our growth for so long. Contrast this cartoon with Illustration B, which was drawn by an Underground Cartoonist. Feel the vigor and forcefulness that mark it as a classic of the genre. If you cannot grasp its innate genius, you are probably a turd.

Illustration B

America." Even more overtly, *Gothic Blimp Works* No. 8 contains a strip in which "Dr. Lester Prong" (Les. Prong, you see, as in Perry Mason's arch-rival Ham. Burger) of the Comics Code Authority is destroyed, in front of the symbol of his organization, by the huge horde of demons and goblins which he has censored from old comic books.

Most underground comic books have certain other things in common. They are almost always true cartoons, not mere illustrations, and therefore go against the trend in straight comics over the past twenty years. A cartoon, unlike an illustration, stands almost entirely on its own: words and pictures together make an effect which neither words nor pictures would make alone. By contrast, many straight strips really don't need drawings: these are there only to interest readers in the story. Think of "Terry," "Mary Worth," "Rex Morgan," "Juliet Jones," even (in a slightly different way) "Dick Tracy." The pictures add something to the words; and sometimes, as in Hal Foster's "Prince Valiant" strips, that something is very fine. But the words could exist without those pictures, with at most a few minor changes (usually descriptive) in the story line.

Straight comics have absorbed a very superficial part of the television influence: people like to watch dramatic shows with punchy stories, so the comics conclude that still pictures with punchy stories are as good as moving ones. Hence the upsurge in various dramatic types of comics, and the trend of established books and strips (even in the superhero vein) to seek more "contemporary social drama." New nondramatic strips are increasingly scarce, and at least some of those that appear are pure imitations of television programs (such as one syndicated strip based entirely on "Laugh-In").

The underground comics exist in a world which has absorbed the television influence to much better advantage. Most of the creators of the underground comics have grown up in a television world, and have not been forced to change print-and-radio minds to accommodate the new influence. Thus, the underground cartoonists create works with a highly visual orientation, sometimes without coherent story lines. The visual impact of the works is striking, showing an acute awareness (usually unconscious) of the special capabilities and limitations of the print medium.

Another point about the underground comics is that they're *funny.* People around America are suddenly beginning to wonder why there is no humor in their lives—to the point where even the sensationalist *National Enquirer* ran an article (Vol. 45, No. 2, September 13, 1970) in which three psychiatrists discussed the subject. One of the psychiatrists, Dr. Jean Rosenbaum of the New Mexico Psychoanalytic Association, was quoted as saying, "Well over ninety percent of the people I talk to don't have a favorite joke anymore. Most of them can't remember any joke at all."

The laughter provoked by the underground comics is that of irreverence, of amusement (often mixed with anger) at human foibles and failures. But the laughter is genuine (a rare thing in these days of television laugh tracks)—and this too helps explain why the comics are "underground" (though the laughter of live audiences at TV shows like "All in the Family" and "Maude" sometimes approaches the sound of laughter at the underground comics). Mike Barrier, an *Arkansas Gazette* columnist and comic-book/cartoon scholar who publishes *Funnyworld* magazine, explains, "The newspaper syndicates, with rare exceptions, don't peddle strips that provoke laughter, since syndicates are established institutions that have every reason to fear laughter's effects. Instead, they peddle strips that embody accepted ideas about what is 'funny,' even though it's been a long time since anyone cracked a smile at 'Henry' or 'Blondie' or any of a host of such zombies. A strip like 'Peanuts,' innocuous as it is, is

Bill Griffith. *Tales of Toad* No. 1. ©1970 Bill Griffith. By permission of Bill Griffith.

Opposite: Denis Kitchen. *Snarf* No. 4. ©1973 Denis Kitchen. By permission of Denis Kitchen.

Will Eisner. *The Spirit* No. 1. ©1969 Will Eisner. By permission of Will Eisner. Here an underground comic was put out by a "straight" cartoonist who has had a good deal of underground influence (see Chapter 2).

dangerous to the syndicates because it calls into question what we have been told for years is 'funny' . . . [Underground comics,] with their complete disregard for syndicate conventions, are an even greater threat, which is why you'll never see those cartoonists on a newspaper comics page."

Well, the way things are going these days (see Chapter 11), you *may* see the comics in a straight newspaper eventually—in a watered-down version. You're already seeing their influence everywhere from straight comics to television commercials . . . and just about anything else is possible. But the unique vitality and irreverence of the comics, their limited and selective distribution system, and their uncompromising visual and verbal approach to their material are not likely to make their way into the straight mass media—at least not on any regular basis. And the cartoonists wouldn't have it any other way. They may eventually co-opt the system; but they're fighting hard so it won't co-opt them.

Will Eisner. *The Spirit* No. 1. ©1972 Will Eisner. By permission of Will Eisner. Here the "straight" cartoonist takes a new, more "underground" look at his own work.

Whence They Cometh

2

Richard Outcault's Yellow Kid. Courtesy Mad Peck Studios.

1. Ancient History

Like it or not (and many underground cartoonists might like it very little indeed), underground comics are but the latest step in a process which dates back some five thousand years, to the days when Egyptians were amused by cartoons of animals circulated on limestone flakes and papyrus. In America, cartoons had already emerged by 1747, when Benjamin Franklin did a woodcut illustration for his pamphlet "Plain Talk." Seven years later, in the Pennsylvania *Gazette*, Franklin invented the cartoon "balloon" in a panel called "Join or Die," which later turned up on patriot banners during the Revolutionary War.

The modern comic strip is generally agreed to have begun with Richard Outcault's "The Yellow Kid," which first appeared in Joseph Pulitzer's New York *World* in 1895. The Kid was an accidental success, having been started in connection with an attempt to develop a new kind of yellow printing ink. Ugly, almost Mongoloid in appearance, communicating through messages written on his nightshirt rather than through "balloons," wildly sarcastic and satirical, the Kid stands as the first direct ancestor of today's underground comics.

(His later history is interesting and not irrelevant: Outcault was hired away from Pulitzer during the circulation war with William Randolph Hearst, so Pulitzer hired another cartoonist to draw the Kid for him. There were then two Kids, and in following years there were many more. As time went on, the face aged and the clothes changed, but the gaptooth smile and enormous ears remained—until the Kid was finally made an American institution by Harvey Kurtzman in early issues of *Mad*. You now know him as Alfred E. Neuman.)

If the Yellow Kid's satirical bent made him the first direct ancestor of an underground-cartoon character, the extremely odd character of the first comic ever published in book form made it the first direct ancestor of an underground comic book. The book, now impossibly rare, was a collection of twenty-five strips by an amazing and little-known artist named Gustave Verbeek. Verbeek produced sixty-four extraordinary comic strips on a weekly basis between 1903 and 1905, for the New York *Herald*. The comic-book collection appeared in mid-1905, but has apparently disappeared completely: even the Library of Congress has reportedly been unable to locate its copy, and has said that no other library has ever reported *having* a copy of the book.

Verbeek's work was extraordinary in that it pushed far beyond even the nominal bounds which existed for comic strips in 1903-5. Verbeek, like all others at the *Herald*, was limited to a six-panel sequence each week. Unsatisfied, Verbeek developed stories that were first read in the traditional way, then turned upside down and read once more. Every portion of every strip had to be meaningful when rotated 180 degrees—and the whole thing had to maintain a sequential narrative!

The whole project is so farfetched as to be impossible; but Verbeek managed to produce these strips sixty-four consecutive times before abandoning the upside-down format for more conventional comic strips. (A serious artist, Verbeek eventually quit newspaper work for painting; several exhibitions of his work were held in New York before his death in 1937.)

George Naimark, writing of Verbeek, quotes Martin Gardner (who does mathematical puzzles and games for *Scientific American* magazine) as saying, "How Verbeek managed to work all this out without going mad passeth all understanding." The remark might also stand, in somewhat weaker terms, for the work of many underground cartoonists today—though none of them has ever mentioned Verbeek as a stylistic influence, and some people have been known to suggest that the minds of today's underground cartoonists *have* snapped.

Incidentally, most studies will tell you that the first comic book was *Famous Funnies*, published in 1934 (twenty-nine years after the Verbeek collection). This comic too was an ancestor of today's undergrounds, for it was an instant financial failure. But *Famous Funnies* continued to appear, and by the seventh issue had moved well into the black (a pattern also followed by some, though by no means all, of the modern underground comics).

Only a few years after *Famous Funnies*, a very direct ancestor of today's underground comics appeared. The *Eight-Pagers* (also called *Tijuana Bibles*) were crude wallet-sized comics, mainly sexual in content and never available on the open market. No one knows exactly where they came from, though their name implies the source was Tijuana, Mexico, where liberal sexual attitudes supposedly awaited the American tourist.

The *Eight-Pagers* presented quite a number of characters: famous American outlaws, movie actors and actresses, even copies of "straight" comic characters. The artwork varied widely, and the best samples of the genre conveyed a real feeling

Gustave Verbeek. *The Incredible Upside-Downs of Gustave Verbeek.* ©1969 The Rajah Press. By permission of The Rajah Press, by George Naimark.

Artist unknown. From one of the *Eight-Pagers.* Courtesy Mad Peck Studios.

of watching the well-known person or comic character offstage, as it were. But in general, these comics were carefully tailored to adolescent sexual fantasies, and were no more the expression of the artists' own feelings than are the Marvel and DC Comics of their creators' feelings today. The *Eight-Pagers*, however, accomplished the not-inconsiderable feat (for pre-World War II America) of promoting nihilistic, anti-authoritarian points of view, not exactly satirizing the forces of goodness so much as placing them on the same level as the forces of evil. And the comics often contained little details worthy of much more sophisticated creations of later years: in the "Dillinger" strip, for instance, note the car's hood ornament in the second panel.

Once in a while, the artists of the *Eight-Pagers* would hit on a sarcastic, anarchistic idea which, thirty years later, would be independently thought up by an underground cartoonist. The best example: one eight-pager revealed that Superman, the epitome of clean-cut superheroism and asexuality, actually had a tiny penis. This revelation is exactly the one provided by Gilbert Shelton about his Superman parody, Wonder Wart-Hog, in *Zap Comix* No. 4.

Time passed the one-dimensional *Eight-Pagers* by—though when Krupp Comic Works put out a catalogue in 1970, it did so in the size and style of the old *Eight-Pagers*. A series of new cartoon-style influences appeared. The importance of movie cartoons, especially the ones featuring Bugs Bunny, Daffy Duck, and like characters, can scarcely be underestimated. It sounds less true than it is to say that these cartoons (which your children may be watching on television even today—beware!) had a lot to do with molding the anti-establishment feelings of many young people today. If you laugh at that statement, your sense of humor is misplaced: these cartoons invariably preach the cause of the underdog, support the little man against the big society around him, and often make telling comments (not necessarily knowingly) about the state of that society. In one Bugs Bunny cartoon, for instance, the entire audience at a movie theater runs to the lounge whenever Bugs lights up the "Intermission" sign and runs back whenever he turns it off—even though he does so time after time. Has there ever been a more telling comment on man's slavery to his machines?

Even political consciousness, including anti-police feelings, emerges from these remarkable cartoons. In one of them, Bugs is being pursued by Elmer Fudd (the prototypical small, property-owning conservative), who in this production is a Royal Canadian Mounty. The "Wanted" posters we see say that the rabbit is "Wanted Dead Or Alive—Preferably Dead." Bugs doesn't know he's Wanted, but Elmer finds him and reads a list of the charges against him: resisting arrest, disturbing the peace, being a public nuisance, jaywalking, "conduct unbecoming a wabbit," etc. (shades of the Chicago Seven, the Gainesville Eight, and *1984!*). Bugs ridicules Fudd, makes a fool of him, even strips his uniform off, piece by piece—but finally gives himself up. He is promptly led off to be executed by a firing squad. There is a copout ending: granted one last wish, Bugs starts to sing "I Wish I Was in Dixie" and the whole cast (Bugs, Elmer, and the firing squad) suddenly appears in blackface in the American South. But the basic message of the cartoon, that the law is arbitrary, harsh, and foolish, is crystal clear (maybe clearer than the cartoon's producers ever intended).

It's interesting to realize that Charles M. Jones, who directed Bugs Bunny and many other Warner Brothers cartoons for almost a quarter of a century, completely misses this aspect of Bugs' character. In an interview in *Funnyworld* No. 13 (Spring 1971), Jones comments, "Actually, Bugs was a counter-revolutionary, not a revolutionary at all. He didn't go out to bug people, people bugged him and then he fought back. And I think that counter-revolutionaries are a damned sight more intriguing than revolutionaries." By such a definition, perhaps all underground cartoonists who feel "bugged" (and whose telephones maybe *are* bugged) by American mores are counter-revolutionaries. Or perhaps the influence Jones put into the cartoons isn't the one the underground cartoonists took out. In any case, Bugs Bunny's influence can certainly be seen, extended and distorted, in the political and social anarchism of so many underground comics.

Also ancestral to the underground comics are the Road Runner cartoons, in which the bird himself is irrelevant and all attention is focused on the coyote, whose clever, systematic attack on the problem of catching the bird only fails because of extraordinarily rotten luck. (According to cartoonist/comic-book scholar The Mad Peck, one rumor has it that the Army had a cartoon in which the coyote finally caught and ate the bird—a cartoon shown to combat

Below: Bobby London's Dirty Duck, ca. 1970. Drawn especially for this book. ©1974 Bobby London. By permission of Bobby London.

Below Left: The Mad Peck's reinterpretation of the Road Runner and Coyote of Warner Brothers cartoon fame.

Below: Gilbert Shelton's Wonder Wart-Hog. *Zap Comix* No. 3.

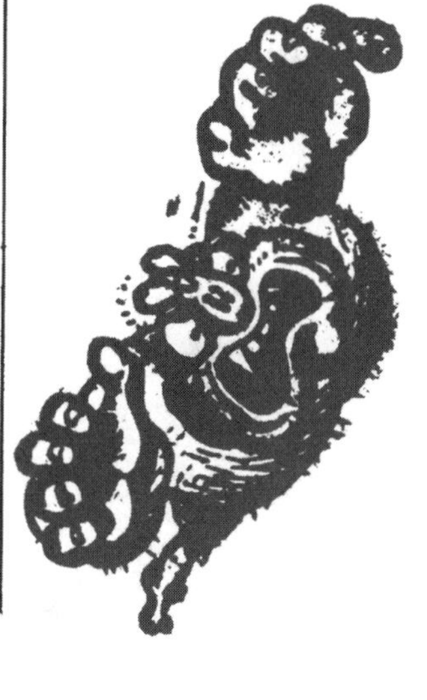

BIG NIGHT TO-NIGHT, EH WEEVIL?
IT CERTAINLY IS, MR. DUCK!
YOU HAVE BEEN WAITING FOR THIS GIRL A LONG TIME, NO MR DUCK?
YES
'DIRTY DUCK'
MY MAMA DONE TOLE ME
THERE SHE IS! QUICK!! MY WIG!!!
HERE IT IS MR. DUCK!
COME IN, MY SWEET, COME IN..
HOWDY.
NOW THE FIRST LESSON OF MY PRIVATE MUSIC METHODS INVOLVES THE 'SOUL'. TO PRACTICE CORRECTLY WE MUST GO UPSTAIRS, TAKE OFF ALL OUR CLOTHES AND 'MEDITATE' FOR ONE HOUR!
MIND IF I TAKE M' VIOLIN OUT FIRST???
WHY NO..
KIK
BOP
SAY, 'SLEAZY', YER PRETTY CUTE — WADDYA SAY WE GO OUT AN' TRIP SOME LIGHTS FANTASTICALLY? EH?
WHO? ME?!! OH YAS! YAS!! AHAAHAHAA!!!
'TIME WOUNDS ALL HEELS!'

troops the night before they were shipped off to Korea.) The coyote is the product of mechanized society, even more directly victimized by machines than is the audience in Bugs Bunny's movie theatre.

All these influences are more of the spirit than of the printed page; and family trees being what they are, today's underground comics bear little resemblance to their remote ancestors from Tijuana and the straight world. Many underground comics spring from a single mind, and are as unique as that mind is unique (which can be pretty strange, indeed). Other underground comics look exactly like pop posters, generally containing one-panel pieces instead of sequential stories (though an occasional continuum will be developed, usually by metamorphosis of one panel into the following one).

Those one-person and poster-oriented comics have no direct relatives among straight comics or cartoonists. But in general, underground cartoonists are influenced by certain straight strips, either of the present or of the recent past. The late Walt Kelly, one of the most overtly political of the straight cartoonists, often wrote words which the underground cartoonists put into effect. Thus, of *Pogo's Sunday Punch:* " . . . this is not exactly a podge of pieces about the Nevernever or even about the Maybemaybe. In a flimsy disguise that would not get past the border at the far end of the table this lopsided slab of life is about the Now." Or, speaking more directly of the underground cartoonists than he knew, in *Potluck Pogo:* "Give us power and we will turn and destroy. . . . It will be necessary to show there's a touch of the tar brush in us, a bit of the slop along the river, some of the scum that floats in with the tide from another land."

Many underground cartoonists freely admit their debt to Kelly, and their admiration for what he was able to do within the confines of straight newspapers. Kelly, however, was so severely hampered by his readers and editors that he had to offer alternate strips to papers on days when his political messages became more overt than usual. Here the underground cartoonists parted company with Kelly.

The major influence Kelly had was that he let the underground cartoonists see just how far the straight media allow political and social satire to go. This gave them a definite idea of which fields still needed to be explored. Or perhaps that analysis is entirely too sober: Kelly also showed the way to be irreverent and amusing at once, and that is something for which underground cartoonists are often striving. One major difference: Kelly worked entirely with anthropomorphic animals, while the underground cartoonists often prefer to draw people, showing the people's animalistic personalities in the process. It's sort of like turning Pogo inside out, while keeping his heart in the same place.

Jules Feiffer is another "overground" cartoonist whose work has had some influence in the underground comics. Yet the direct imitations of Feiffer—of which there have been quite a few—are not generally successful, for Feiffer's gently acerbic wit just cannot be imitated, however simple his drawings may appear. The Feiffer imitations tend to be more complex in style and less subtle in writing than the original article. Feiffer's major influence, like Kelly's, lies in the fact that he shows how far non-underground artists can go in locking horns with every politician and social reformer who makes a fool of himself (which is to say, all of them).

Some underground cartoonists have begun to be influenced by certain mass-market comic

Opposite: Bobby London. *Air Pirates Funnies* No. 1. ©1971 Bobby London. By permission of Bobby London. Probably the single most successful imitation of "Krazy Kat" humor, wordplay, etc.

Adams. *Rat*, January 26, 1970. A typical Feiffer imitation.

strips, such as "Doonesbury"—but those strips themselves show influence *from* the underground comics, and it's getting much harder to tell who influenced whom and when.

Another important influence on underground cartoonists is the old "Krazy Kat" comic strips—which, as a matter of fact, have been picked up and quite directly imitated in an underground-comic series called "Dirty Duck." Here, as in the Feiffer imitations, the magic of the originals is lost in the imitations—but the influence of "Krazy Kat" goes far, far beyond overt copying.

"Krazy Kat" looms large above anyone who does cartooning today. An hilarious strip with unique language, perpetually changing backgrounds, and stock characters with enough twists to give the plots true philosophical import, "Krazy Kat" is as fresh and funny today as it was when its creator, George Herriman, died back in 1944.

"Krazy Kat" has provided fuel for many recent cartoonists, most notably the aforementioned Walt Kelly, who several times paid homage to Herriman by interpolating bits of Krazy Kat's Coconino County into Pogo's Okefenokee Swamp. At the end of one especially extended tribute, in which Howland Owl was constantly trying to bean Churchy La Femme, the turtle, with a brick (using the logic that what was funny in "Krazy Kat" will be funny in "Pogo"), Kelly actually showed a brick being thrown from offstage left, and hitting a kat offstage right.

The underground cartoonists' tributes to "Krazy Kat" are, outside of "Dirty Duck," less direct but more deep-rooted. Some artists, like Denis Kitchen *(Mom's Homemade Comics)*, openly acknowledge a major debt to the strip; others, like Paul Buhle (general editor of *Radical America* magazine and guiding spirit behind *Radical America Komiks*), are more concerned with denying "Krazy Kat" its importance: Buhle calls an allegation that Herriman's strip is poetic (which it is), "bullshit, unless we redefine the word 'poetry.'" But love Krazy or hate him (or her, depending on Herriman's mood that day), the underground cartoonists cannot escape Krazy's influence. If they don't openly admit their indebtedness to the strip, someone else is likely to admit it for them, as in Paul Krassner's introduction to the Viking Press edition of *R. Crumb's Head Comix:* "If R. Crumb was the illegitimate offspring of Krazy Kat, now . . . he is responsible for turning good old Charlie Brown on with LSD."

The influence of the Herriman strip on the underground comics occurs on several levels—a fact which may become clearer after a brief description of the plot of "Krazy Kat" itself. Simply, Krazy loves the mouse Ignatz, who hates the kat and lives only to throw bricks at him/her. Offissa Pupp, self-styled representative of "law and order," himself loves Krazy and constantly tries to stop Ignatz from throwing the bricks. When he fails, as he usually does, he arrests and jails the mouse.

There is a special twist to the strip which gives the whole thing an underlying philosophical meaning: to Krazy, the bricks Ignatz throws are evidence of love, not hate; hence Krazy conspires with Ignatz, not with Offissa Pupp. There is a whole mythology built around the throwing of the brick (dating back to ancient Egypt, when Herriman postulates that the brick bore a message of love upon it); this helps explain the different meanings kat and mouse give to the act. The twists to this plot are endless—or, at any rate, gave no signs of ending when George Herriman died in 1944 and took his marvelously personal, gently surrealistic world with him. That world then seemed as fresh as it did when he first created it thirty years earlier.

Herriman's inspired sense of nonsense has led to further flights of fancy on the part of the underground cartoonists. The unusual depth of his characters, making it a necessity to read his strips on several different levels, gave the underground cartoonists a prototype for their multilayered work. (Just how deep Herriman's thoughts went is an extremely debatable question. In a 1946 essay reprinted as an introduction to Grosset and Dunlap's 1969 collection of "Krazy Kat," the poet e.e. cummings has suggested, tongue only slightly in cheek, that Krazy represents the Democratic ideal and that the strip is an extend-

Below Right: Jim Pinkoski. 1973 Berkeley Comix Convention program. ©1973 Jim Pinkoski. A very accurate updating of Winsor McCay's "Little Nemo in Slumberland," both in style and in content. Note that "Omen" is "Nemo" spelled backwards.

Below: Denis Kitchen. *Mom's Homemade Comics* No. 1. ©1969 Denis Kitchen. By permission of Denis Kitchen.

ed parable about democracy.)

Herriman's personal art gave the underground cartoonists a concept of backgrounds as an independent part of a cartoon panel—since in "Krazy" the backgrounds were always surrealistic, generally unrelated to the foregrounds, and constantly metamorphosing into things for no reason other than Herriman's desire to have them change. And Herriman also planted some special seeds of irreverence, of disrespect for convention both in drawing and in language. When Krazy contends that a glass eye should be able to see if made of looking glass ("lookin'-gless," as Krazy says it), or rushes to catch the shades of night when they fall, we have the seeds of the humor of the underground comics.

Certain other strips have had their influence on specific cartoonists. The Katzenjammer Kids, of whom the Captain once said, "For them kids reality is nix," have done their part; so have the absurdities of strips like "Barnaby" and "Little Lulu." A number of cartoonists say they were influenced by Carl Barks, who or-

DOONESBURY by Garry Trudeau

Left: George Herriman. A "Krazy Kat" strip from 1935. ©1935 King Features Syndicate. By permission of King Features Syndicate, by Mary V. Kelly.

Above: One of Garry Trudeau's "Doonesbury" strips. © 1973 Garry Trudeau. By permission of Garry Trudeau. When it was published in Spring 1973, this strip caused the greatest uproar Trudeau had faced up to that time, and led a number of newspapers to suspend or cancel "Doonesbury." The strip seems mild in the aftermath of Watergate, but raised many hackles *during* Watergate—even though the character Mark, shown here, was a *satire* of campus radicals, not Trudeau's mouthpiece.

YES, DEAR READER! THAT'S HOW THE STORY ENDS! AND THIS MAY BE THE VERY MAGAZINE THOSE CREATURES WILL FIND WHEN THEY LAND ON THE EXPLODED FRAGMENT OF EARTH! - THE END

iginated Scrooge McDuck and some of the other early Disney characters and whose style is especially clever and skillful. There has also been some influence from the brilliant strip called "Little Nemo in Slumberland," which presented the daily dream adventures of a boy in a beautifully drawn world of the imagination – a world which, over the years, he controlled more and more, only to be snatched from it by the calls of his mother. Just about anything can be read into "Little Nemo," including the idea that it was an overtly Freudian strip, in which the mother represented the Reality Principle to which we must all accommodate ourselves.

Some underground cartoonists pay tribute to Al Capp—not the Al Capp of today, but the Al Capp of twenty-five years ago, who was the first cartoonist to adapt the satirical element of the *Eight-Pagers* to the family-type format which was needed to get along in the straight world. Capp carried out his famous statement of purpose ("to create suspicion of, and disrespect for, the perfection of all established institutions") by dragging real-life types into the town of Dogpatch, and later by subtly altering other cartoonists' characters and then satirizing them. The best and most famous example was Fearless Fosdick, who looked more like Dick Tracy than Dick Tracy did and who gained such popularity in his own right that he began appearing in hair tonic ads and eventually wound up the object of satire himself, being parodied by Bill Elder in *Mad.* But Capp did not age gracefully, and his recent hatchet jobs against everything even slightly progressive have caused the underground cartoonists to disown his influence. Denis Kitchen now calls Capp the "sex symbol of the D.A.R."

For all that has been said, the most direct influence on the underground cartoonists has not even been mentioned. This is the old line of E.C. Comics, which, until underground comics began, were by far the best-written, most original and intelligent things ever printed in comic-book form. E. C. originally stood for Educational Comics, an outfit which, during the 1940's, published a variety of educational comic books under the direction of M.C. Gaines. These educational books presented picture stories from the Bible (Old and New Testaments), from American and world history, and from science. At the same time, M.C. Gaines developed a line of Entertaining Comics, aimed mostly at very young children and sporting titles like *Animal Fables, Dandy, Fat & Slat,* and *Animated Comics.*

The E. C. influence really begins, however, after the death of M.C. Gaines and the takeover of the business by his son William M. Gaines. Then, in the late forties, E.C. Comics began to develop the special style which made a lasting impact on all their readers, including today's underground cartoonists. New titles began to appear under the imprint of various publishing companies—companies which were actually named after no-longer-published M.C. Gaines comics: Fables Publishing Company (after *Animal Fables*), I.C. Publishing Company (after *International Comics*), L.L. Publishing Company (after *Land of the Lost*), and Tiny Tot Comics,

Al Feldstein. Originally published in *The Haunt of Fear* No. 17 (actually No. 3), Sept.-Oct. 1953. ©1974 William M. Gaines. By permission of William M. Gaines.

Opposite: Al Williamson. Originally published in *Weird Fantasy* No. 17, Jan-Feb. 1952. ©1974 William M. Gaines. By permission of William M. Gaines.

Below Left: Wally Wood. Originally published in *Weird Science* No. 21, Sept.-Oct. 1953. ©1974 William M. Gaines. By permission of William M. Gaines.

Below: Denis Kitchen. *Mom's Homemade Comics* No. 1. ©1969 Denis Kitchen. By permission of Denis Kitchen.

Inc. (after *Tiny Tot Comics*). A trend toward crime and adventure comics was developing, and E. C. was in the forefront—staying in the field of love comics and Western stories as well. But the special E.C. style was emerging fast as the forties waned. It was a style that never took itself completely seriously: when an adventure comic did not make it after three titles were tried (*Moon Girl and the Prince*, then simply *Moon Girl*, then *Moon Girl Fights Crime*), the book was changed to a love comic with completely different settings and characters, but with an oddly familiar title: *A Moon, a Girl . . . Romance*. (*Moon Girl* No. 5, by the way, had a story with a title that looked forward to the great horror comics of a

Right: Al Feldstein. Originally published in *War Against Crime* No. 10, Dec. 1949-Jan. 1950. ©1974 William M. Gaines. By permission of William M. Gaines.

few years later: "The Corpse with Will Power.") When another love comic was scheduled to be dropped from the line, a young cartoonist named Al Feldstein drew a final story, for the final issue, in which he and publisher Gaines appeared as characters working for a mythical "T. Tot" (the comic was published by Tiny Tot Comics, Inc.). The story, written by Paul Krassner, was a series of in-jokes about the publishing business, on top of a satire on the whole concept of love stories in comics. Rival publishers and writers popped out of almost every panel, and the story ended with a friend of Gaines and Feldstein (pictured as an office boy) taking over "T. Tot's" business because everyone else had committed suicide after losing millions of dollars in investments—all this in a comic called *Modern Love*, August-September 1950!

Clearly, the E. C. line was something unique in the comic-book field and a force to be reckoned with. As the crime comics grew in popularity during 1949, E. C. introduced something new: "Tales of Terror," also by Feldstein, in *War Against Crime* No. 10 and *Crime Patrol* No. 15. The former tale was said to be from "The Vault of Horror," the latter from "The Crypt of Terror." Neither story had supernatural elements, but each was introduced by an eerie, monstrous being lurking somewhere just out of sight. A comic-book classic was straining for birth—and sure enough, in early 1950, the E. C. line shifted its focus from crime to out-and-out horror stories, as *The Vault of Horror*, *The Haunt of Fear*, and *The Crypt of Terror* (soon renamed *Tales from the Crypt*) sprang full-blown and mouldering from the collective head of E. C.

The E. C. horror books flourished for approximately five years, by the end of which time the earlier numbers were already highly-prized classics. They coupled superb storytelling with grotesque and often truly horrifying artwork, using plots that were just close enough to reality to send chills up readers' spines

Far Right: Al Feldstein. Originally published in *Modern Love* No. 8, Aug-Sept. 1950. ©1974 William M. Gaines. By permission of William M. Gaines. The opening panel and a four-panel sequence from the satire on comic-book publishing, written by Paul Krassner (later of *The Realist*).

in the dark hours of the night. The stories left a lasting impression on everyone who read them—and among their fans were almost all the present underground cartoonists, then just reaching the age at which comics became appealing reading material. There is no way to convey the impact of the E. C. line by the few panels on these pages, because those comics (unlike the present underground comics, in which every panel may give a capsule picture of the mood, if not necessarily the plot, of the entire story) were very carefully conceived and often read like fine short stories. Indeed, E.C. several times adapted short stories by Ray Bradbury to the comic-book form, and it was remarkable to see how well the E.C. writers' tales stacked up against those of the master storyteller himself. In regard to these last couple of sentences, I invite you, dear reader, to turn to Appendix B, where I hope you'll find a pleasant surprise.

Wally Wood. Originally published in *The Crypt of Terror* No. 18, Jun.-Jul. 1950. ©1974 William M. Gaines. By permission of William M. Gaines.

The E.C. Comics contained many of the themes which today's underground cartoonists are obsessed with—especially that of violence, often tinged with horror and involving innocent people. The E. C. line even undertook an occasional foray into the political arena, as in one story of a newspaperman who is gunned down by thinly disguised members of the Ku Klux Klan. But social and political involvement were not looked upon kindly during the era of Joe McCarthy, and the violence in the comics provided a convenient point of attack for a variety of censors, vested interests, and just-plain-nuts.

The Senate Subcommittee on Juvenile Delinquency investigated the comics scene, and one Dr. Frederic Wertham published a book called *Seduction of the Innocent* in which he virtually attributed all crime and evil to the influence of the comics. Censors have votes; children do not. The E. C. editors fought back, publishing editorials condemning the Senate investigation and asking that their readers—or their readers' parents—write the Subcommittee and support the right of the publishers to put out their work. But it was all in vain. Publishers depend on distribution, and the constant cries against the comics cost E. C. its newsdealers. Just as a fourth horror title was

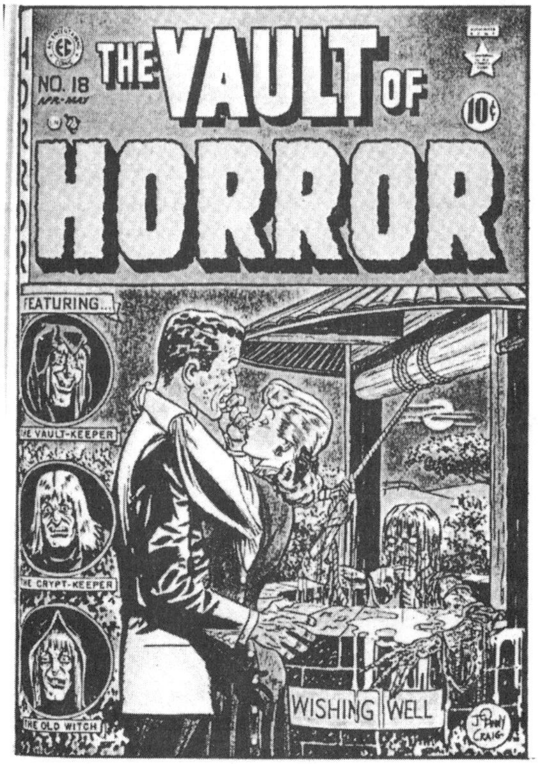

Far Left: Johnny Craig. Cover of *The Vault of Horror* No. 18, Apr.-May 1951. ©1974 William M. Gaines. By permission c William M. Gaines.

Left: Johnny Craig. Cover of *Crime SuspenStories* No. 17, Jun.-Jul. 1953. ©1974 William M. Gaines. By permission of William M. Gaines.

to be added to the E. C. line (reviving the title *The Crypt of Terror)*, an editorial appeared on the inside front cover of *Tales from the Crypt*. It said, in part, "As a result of the hysterical, injudicious, and unfounded charges leveled at crime and horror comics, many retailers and wholesalers throughout the country have been intimidated into refusing to handle this type of magazine. . . . Economically our situation is acute. Magazines that do not get onto the newsstands do not sell. We are forced to capitulate. *We give up*. WE'VE HAD IT!"

Strong words—but not strong enough to prevent the E. C. line from degenerating into a series of supposedly "adult" magazines

Jack Davis. Originally published in *The Vault of Horror* No. 25, Jun.-Jul. 1952. ©1974 William M. Gaines. By permission of William M. Gaines.

Jaxon. *Skull Comix* No. 5. ©1972 Gore, Spain, Todd, Sheridan, Jaxon, Deitch, and Dallas. By permission of Messrs. Gore, Sheridan, Jaxon, Deitch, and Dallas.

("picto-fiction," they were called), plus a series of comic books whose conventional titles reflected their contents: *Impact, Valor, Extra!, Aces High, Psychoanalysis*, and *MD*. None of these titles lasted more than five issues, and the E. C. line was reduced to a single publication: *Mad*.

The underground cartoonists never forgot the lessons of the ruin of E. C. They developed an unremitting hatred of the Comics Code Authority of America, which was set up in the wake of the Senate Subcommittee investigation to censor all future comic books. They later tried direct imitation of E. C. Comics (one underground comic actually bears the title *Extra!*, as an unsuccessful E. C. one did, and

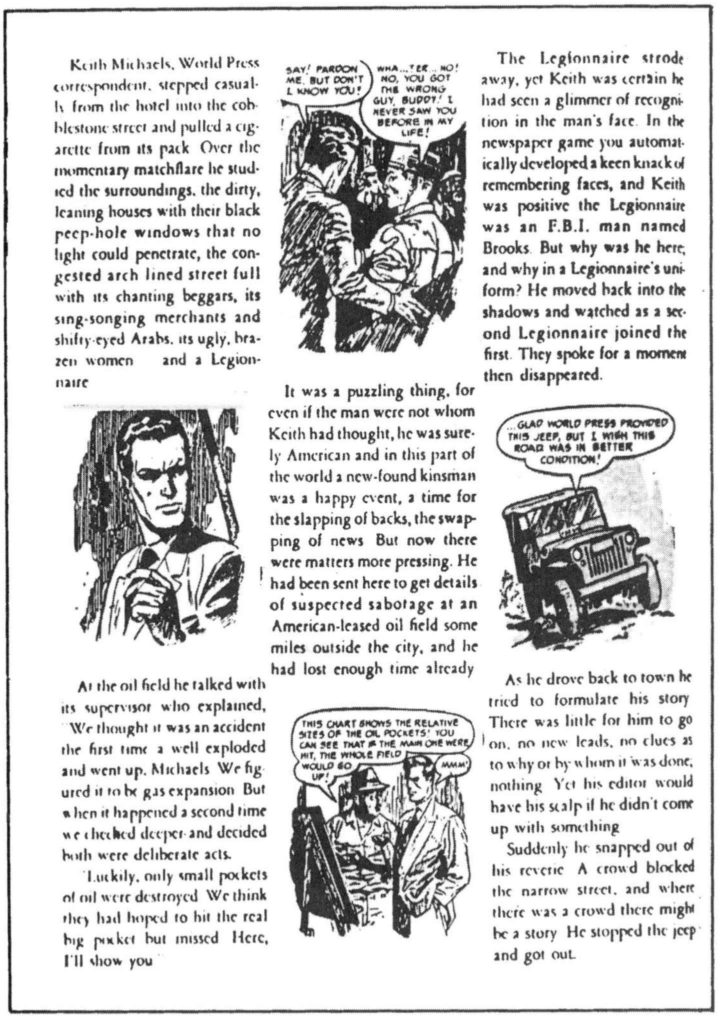

Keith Michaels, World Press correspondent, stepped casually from the hotel into the cobblestone street and pulled a cigarette from its pack. Over the momentary matchflare he studied the surroundings, the dirty, leaning houses with their black peep-hole windows that no light could penetrate, the congested arch lined street full with its chanting beggars, its sing-songing merchants and shifty-eyed Arabs, its ugly, brazen women and a Legionnaire.

The Legionnaire strode away, yet Keith was certain he had seen a glimmer of recognition in the man's face. In the newspaper game you automatically developed a keen knack of remembering faces, and Keith was positive the Legionnaire was an F.B.I. man named Brooks. But why was he here, and why in a Legionnaire's uniform? He moved back into the shadows and watched as a second Legionnaire joined the first. They spoke for a moment then disappeared.

It was a puzzling thing, for even if the man were not whom Keith had thought, he was surely American and in this part of the world a new-found kinsman was a happy event, a time for the slapping of backs, the swapping of news. But now there were matters more pressing. He had been sent here to get details of suspected sabotage at an American-leased oil field some miles outside the city, and he had lost enough time already.

At the oil field he talked with its supervisor who explained, "We thought it was an accident the first time a well exploded and went up, Michaels. We figured it to be gas expansion. But when it happened a second time we checked deeper and decided both were deliberate acts.

"Luckily, only small pockets of oil were destroyed. We think they had hoped to hit the real big pocket but missed. Here, I'll show you."

As he drove back to town he tried to formulate his story. There was little for him to go on, no new leads, no clues as to why or by whom it was done, nothing. Yet his editor would have his scalp if he didn't come up with something.

Suddenly he snapped out of his reverie. A crowd blocked the narrow street, and where there was a crowd there might be a story. He stopped the jeep and got out.

Far Left: Johnny Craig. Originally published in *Extra!* No. 3, Jul.-Aug. 1955. ©1974 William M. Gaines. By permission of William M. Gaines.

Left: Harvey Kurtzman. Cover of *Mad* No. 1, Oct.-Nov. 1952. ©1952 E.C. Publications, Inc. By permission of E.C. Publications, Inc., by William M. Gaines.

Bogeyman was started as an overt imitation of the E. C. horror line), or at least paid homage to the E. C. line by the topics and approaches of their own stories.

The E. C. line had another direct influence on the underground cartoonists—and of all the influences, this was the most important of all. The most successful E. C. comic of all time, and the only one to survive, was *Mad*—now known, of course, as *Mad Magazine*. But the underground cartoonists usually cite the earliest *Mad* issues as the most important molders of their own styles and attitudes. This means that they cite Harvey Kurtzman, editor of the first few dozen *Mads*, of two E. C. war comics (*Two-Fisted Tales* and *Frontline Combat*), and of some E. C. science-fiction comics as well. It is Kurtzman that the cartoonists think of first when they are

Far Left: Harvey Kurtzman. Originally published in *Two-Fisted Tales* No. 19, Jan.-Feb. 1951. ©1974 William M. Gaines. By permission of William M. Gaines.

asked whose influence was longest lasting and strongest.

It's not hard to see why the cartoonists remember Kurtzman so favorably. The early *Mad* comics were a forum for crazy plotting and crazier drawing, where artists like Wally Wood, Bill Elder, Jack Davis, and Kurtzman let their imaginations and their drawing tools run wild. *Mad* institutionalized "eyeball kicks," humorous effects jammed into a panel in some way or another, supposedly secondary to the story line but often funnier and more telling than the main plot itself. Eyeball kicks, which Kurtzman calls *chochkes,* were actually a trademark of Bill Holman ("Smoky Stover") years before *Mad* come into existence, but even underground cartoonists who know Holman's work associate the eyeball kicks specifically with *Mad. Mad* very early developed the Shadow's power to cloud men's minds, to such an extent that another E. C. comic, *Panic,* folded after only twelve issues—even though it was as wild and funny as *Mad* itself (though under the editorship of Al Feldstein, who took over *Mad* after Kurtzman left the E. C. organization). Combining a willingness—even eagerness—for nihilistic, irreverent, topical satire with drawings heavily influenced by the work of such fine artists as Will Eisner ("The Spirit") and Jack Cole ("Plastic Man"), *Mad* was unique in its time for its willingness to come to grips with other comics (including those in the E. C. line), politicians, the communications media, even the Comics Code Authority itself (slyly, in *Mad* No. 16). Despite its popularity with teenagers and subteens, *Mad* was an *adult* comic book—a publication virtually unique to the present day.

Underground cartoonists almost all call themselves *Mad* fans, and more specifically Kurtzman fans ("Kurtzmaniacs," as one cartoonist puts it). Jay Lynch (*Bijou Funnies*) is especially proud to have a complete collection of *Mad.* For others, *Mad* itself was less important than Harvey Kurtzman—for Kurtzman, though he left *Mad* after only some two dozen issues had come out, remained an idol in his own right. Kurtzman left *Mad* to edit a humor magazine called *Trump* for the then-budding empire of *Playboy's* Hugh Hefner. When that failed, he co-published an excellent but financially

Basil Wolverton. *Mad* No. 11, May 1954. ©1954 E.C. Publications, Inc. By permission of E.C. Publications, Inc., by William M. Gaines.

Bill Elder. Originally published in *Panic* No. 3. Jun.-Jul. 1954. ©1974 William M Gaines. By permission of William M. Gaines.

Harvey Kurtzman. Originally published in *Weird Fantasy* No. 16, Nov.-Dec. 1950. ©1974 William M. Gaines. By permission of William M. Gaines.

disastrous magazine called *Humbug* with Arnold Roth. Then, heavily in debt, he tried once more to publish an independent *magazine, Help!* (with Jim Warren). *Help!* existed for only two years and depended more on text and photographs, and less on artists' work, than *Humbug* had; but *Help!* also provided the first major outlet for such cartoonists as Robert Crumb, Skip Williamson, Jay Lynch, and Gilbert Shelton.

From *Help!*, Kurtzman returned to Hugh Hefner, for whom he and Bill Elder (also once of *Mad* comics) now produce *Playboy* magazine's "Little Annie Fanny." Short, balding, middle-aged, shy, nervously introspective, with the large family and attractive house in the suburbs which so many underground cartoonists disown as goals, Harvey Kurtzman remains very much in touch with underground comics and the people who draw them. He suffers somewhat from the expected Generation Gap (see Appendix A), but remains one of the most sympathetic middle-aged ears the underground comics and cartoonists have. Kurtzman thinks he knows why the underground cartoonists admire him so fervently: "I'm tortured by the same devils. I can talk about them [the cartoonists] to a certain extent because I identify with them. By profession I regard myself as a professional *noodge*, a troublemaker. I'm sure I'm driven by my own internal acids and frustrations, and I justify it to myself by . . . well, I think that troublemakers are necessary. You have to keep *noodging*, pointing out the bad things. Although I certainly don't believe in the violence that I think is so fashionable today, I certainly subscribe to change—and to serious thinking."

A few underground cartoonists think Kurtzman has become a sellout, but most of them are willing to forgive him anything, even working for *Playboy*, because of what he used to do and because he does have a certain feel, a certain sympathy, for them and their work. Writes Paul Buhle (*Radical America Komiks*), "Harvey Kurtzman says my political judgment of him fails to recognize that we all get old and

Whence They Cometh

Harvey Kurtzman. *Mad* No. 7, Oct.-Nov. 1953. ©1953 E.C. Publications, Inc. By permission of E.C. Publications, Inc., by William M. Gaines.

Will Eisner. Wraparound cover of *The Spirit* No. 1. ©1973 Will Eisner. By permission of Will Eisner.

support a family, etc. In reality, I forgive him many times over: his achievement stands, no matter what he does now to make money." And according to Wendel Alan Pugh *(Googiewaumer Comics),* "Harvey Kurtzman's effort with *Help!* and *Mad* and all those others is one of the keys to the whole revolution—we all grew up with *Mad* as a teacher . . . I think Kurtzman blew his mind out on his earlier publications and deserves the rest he's taking with 'Annie Fanny.' It's okay, nothin' like ol' *Mad* stuff though. Really wish someone would put something like that together. FAT CHANCE."

Despite all the foregoing, it would be a mistake to assume that Harvey Kurtzman alone continues to blow the minds (even the retrospective minds) of today's underground cartoonists. At least one other cartoonist of Kurtzman's generation has continued to make his impression on underground comics—and has, unlike Kurtzman, actually drawn a series of underground comics himself. This is Will Eisner, whose creation of a mysterious crime fighter called The Spirit caused a bit of a sensation back in 1940 and had a lasting impact even on cartoonists who weren't born until about the time The Spirit had his last adventures, in 1952.

What was unique, and influential, about The Spirit is succinctly noted by comic-book scholar Maurice Horn in an underground comic which revived some of the old Spirit stories and introduced Eisner's newer views on his own character: "The Spirit, in his eternally elusive search for justice, in his ironic probings into the very values he is supposed to uphold, is a tragic hero much closer to Raymond Chandler's Philip Marlowe or Dashiell Hammett's Sam Spade than to Superman or Batman, whose childish motivations and grotesque self-righteousness provide the necessary contrast to the Spirit's disabused philosophy."

While not being quite that philosophical about it, many underground cartoonists cite Eisner's ironic detachment from his character and occasional touches of black humor as influences on their own approach to cartooning. As for Eisner himself, he feels the underground comics have provided a new and valuable outlet for cartooning talent—an outlet with which he himself is glad to be associated: "Freed from the economic constrictions, from the dictatorship of a publisher enslaved by a mass audience, [the underground cartoonist] could talk to a segment of the audience with freedom from fear. The audience too was able to split into small pockets of common taste, being freed from having available to them only those publications that would survive, because they catered to the broadest audience with wide common-denominator editorial material. . . . There is even a place for old talents looking for more elbow room, a place to keep on expanding. And that is why I am trying to make The Underground."

Of course, some of the character of The Spirit has rubbed off on Eisner (or is it the other way around?), and he is well aware that there are bound to be problems in *any* system, however free —indeed, he finds the very freedom of the underground cartoonists a kind of problem, though not an unconquerable one: "True, like any frontier, charlatans and frauds were along for the ride; but gradually the great talents, the sincere artists surfaced. The significant thing was that the comic-book cartoonist was free to do what he wanted, what he thought was good, even if it appealed only to a limited audience."

To add to Eisner's comments, there are certain things in his work which the underground cartoonists found influential. Aside from his general attitude toward his characters, there was the down-playing of the whole "secret identity" bit (The Spirit wore a simple eye mask, and no costume at all); the occasional bursts of sheer exuberance which led Eisner to break into rhyme in the middle of some stories; and even the choice of a location for his character's secret headquarters: The Spirit operated out of a cemetery. Add to these characteristics dry (and wry) humor and clever plotting, and you have a product which actually fits quite nicely into an underground-comic format, as enthusiasts found when *The Spirit* No. 1 appeared early in 1973.

Herewith are offered, as postscripts to this section, selected lists of influences cited by various underground cartoonists, followed by two historical overviews by two appropriate historical overviewers:

"Nauseous," identified by underground cartoonists as a D.C. Comics artist moonlighting. *Gothic Blimp Works* No. 6.

Compendium of Cartoonists' Comments (Selected)

Nicola Cuti (*Moonchild Comics*): *Moonchild* is a combination of Girls, Gadgets, and Gargoyles. It is a liberal burlesque on the old-time science fiction of Buck Rogers and the famous line of E.C. comics of the Fifties. It contains philosophy because most men fantasize themselves as philosophers, but it exists mainly to verbalize my fantasies.

Denis Kitchen (*Mom's Homemade Comics*): I really dig 'Pogo,' 'Krazy Kat,' and some other commercial strips. My first art hero (when I was younger) was Al Capp. However, the discovery that Frank Frazetta ghosted much of his stuff, and his recent politically oriented tripe have succeeded in turning me off. I missed the E.C. Comics when they were current. I guess I was a bit too young to realize they existed. But when I finally did discover them, I couldn't find enough to satisfy me (by this time they were already incredibly rare). I still assiduously seek them out. No one today is turning out anything to compare with the stuff Wally Wood, Jack Davis, Bill Elder, *et al.* were doing in the early Fifties . . . The language of comics is probably underestimated. Walt Kelly again comes to mind. Or George Herriman's 'Krazy Kat' and currently Tom K. Ryan's 'Tumbleweeds.' These commercial strips are often poetic. Or, at the very least, clever prose.

Jay Lynch *(Bijou Funnies):* I like Carl Barks' 'Scrooge McDuck' comics cause Barks really knew how to tell a story. I have copies of everything Kurtzman, Elder, Wood, and Davis ever did, although it's hard to keep up with Davis who has kind of been overexposing his work lately. The original guys who started *Mad* started a whole new school of what I think of as insane comic art. It's not merely funny stuff, but it really conveys the attitude of anxiety caused by tricks the mind plays on yer perception when you're tense. It's hard to put yer finger on what these guys got, but I really like their stuff, and the stuff that guys like Eisner and Jack Cole did. They have the same insanity about their work. I also like the old Mutt 'n' Jeff—Krazy Kat school of comic art. Herriman and Fisher knew how to convey that same insane feeling, but they only used it once in a while when the plot called for it. In *Mad* comics it was on every page, in every panel. The core of what I like in comic art is *Mad* comics . . . . I dislike the slick modern treatments of comic strips like 'Snuffy Smith' and 'Mutt 'n' Jeff.' The guys who draw these strips today have gotten too slick. Billy DeBeck's original 'Barney Google' strip was great, but the guy who does it today is too fuckin' neat. I hate sloppy comics like 'Miss Peach' and 'B. C.' They remind me of packaging.

George Metzger *(Moondog):* I was a big E. C. Comics freak, still have most of those I originally owned—indeed still have lots of strips—the E. C.'s blew my mind, mainly the S.F. and Kurtzman's great war comics and his *Mad* . . . . Also Wyeth, Alex Thoth, *Webster's Dictionary,* Chester Gould, Caniff's Terry, Stan Lynde, 'Little Nemo,' Dali, Jean Cocteau, the S.F. poster artists, Bogart, Bacall, Lorre, Cooper, Jules Verne, Christ, Baba Ram Dass, Black Elk, Chief Joseph, Einstein, Macomber's apple boysenberry juice, Ray Bradbury, Sherlock Holmes, Hairy Who (maybe), ENERGY, It, I threw out my t.v., Betty Boop, Hieronymus Bosch, rain on my tin roof.

Wendel Alan Pugh *(Googiewaumer Comics):* When I was a kid I read mainly what fell into my hands. Carl Barks—Donald Duck, Uncle Scrooge were favorites. *Mad, Humbug, Help!,* which were all Kurtzman gigs. He deserves credit for the comic-book revolution. Everyone working

Whence They Cometh

Bill Pearson and Tim Brent. *witzend* No. 7. ©1970 Wonderful Publishing Company, Inc. By permission of Wonderful Publishing Company, Inc., by Bill Pearson. Though not truly "underground," *witzend* often gave "straight" cartoonists a chance to satirize the work of other "straight" cartoonists. This story, for instance, is a careful and elaborate satire of Steve Ditko's "Mr. A."

seems to have used his inspirations as a jumping-off place. I personally feel he more than anyone else started the whole thing! Al Capp early childhood influence, Walt Kelly later when I figured out what he was doing. Missed most of adventure things and never could get into war or horror gigs. 'Wonder Woman,' dug her. Read some Superman. Also really liked 'Super Duck'—who did that stuff? . . . Walt Disney animation of course—blew my mind (then) visually and (now) technically. Will Eisner—'Spirit.' Basil Wolverton.

Skip Williamson *(Bijou Funnies):* The E.C. stuff, and practically everything done before 1962 influenced me. Most of that stuff was better technically than anything we're doing.

Historical Overviews

By **Bill Pearson,** *commercial artist and co-editor of* witzend *magazine:* Harvey Kurtzman is generally acknowledged as the father of underground comics, first with *Mad*, then *Humbug* and *Help!* He encouraged experimentation with styles (his own style is very exciting and unique, but was prematurely weird for the fifties), and he was an iconoclast of the first order. Also, of course, he had a fantastic sense of humor and of sequential panel pacing. . . . In short, Underground Comix are a direct descendent from reg-'lar comics, movies, TV, Radio, Wheaties, Charles Atlas, Miss America, Gen-U-Wine Atom Bombs and every other Super stamped-out product stuffed into the consciousness of a generation of freaked-out Americans.

By **Harvey Kurtzman,** *who should know:* Fifteen years later you start running into these people who read your stuff, and you find they have been deeply affected by your stuff, they *have* been. But in what way you don't know. They haven't run out and hung Richard Nixon as a result. But I think that's the way art—if I can put that designation on my stuff—that's the way art will affect people. It will open up new attitudes which don't necessarily do anything specific, but nevertheless make for a more sensitive or sensitized world. I was very serious and very worried about living and life and politics, very involved in 'reality' humor in my work and in the material of others. I think all of us collectively helped to sensitize the young people. I still don't know whether it's good or bad. I like to think it's for the eventual good: a sensitive society is capable of so much more.

2. Modern History

We have already seen that many underground cartoonists got their first exposure through underground newspapers, and they existed (eight issues), they provided a clearing house for many underground cartoonists, a chance to experiment with larger pages than comic books provided, and a certain number of very unusual stories: one in which "Dr. Lester Prong" of the Comics Code Authority is destroyed by the creatures he has censored (see page 21), and

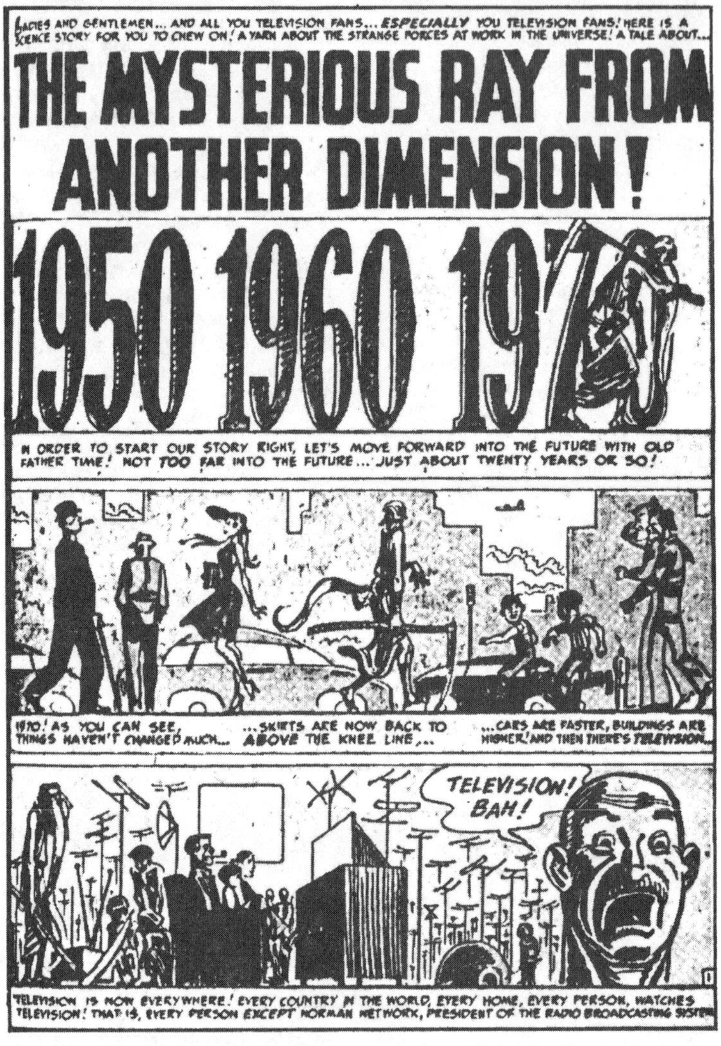

Harvey Kurtzman. Originally published in *Weird Fantasy* No. 16, Nov.-Dec. 1950. ©1974 William M. Gaines. By permission of William M. Gaines.

many in fact continue to appear in those papers. In some cases, underground comic books have actually appeared in newspaper form and size, rather than in comic-book format. The best-known comic in this format is *Gothic Blimp Works* (the first issue was called *Gothic Blimp Works Presents: Jive Comics*); other examples are the original *Yellow Dog*, S. Clay Wilson's *King Bee*, and *The Collected Trashman* by Spain Rodriguez.

The *Blimp Works* gradually declined in quality, took to reprinting material from other underground comics, and finally disappeared altogether. But while one in which Kim Deitch offers his interpretation of the "cosmic laugh" around which Hermann Hesse's *Steppenwolf* is centered.

Although the *Blimp Works* finally failed, all the artists found other places which would print their work (Bill Griffith: "Now that I'm out West, it's strictly the BIG TIME for me").

The *Blimp Works* would never have existed without the commitment of the underground press to the comics form. In line with this, *Radical America* ("An SDS Journal of American Radicalism") put out a very fine comic book, *Radical America Komiks*, in 1969, as Vol. III, No. 1 of the magazine.

Soon afterward came the fragmentation of SDS, however, and after that only the Weatherman faction made any use of cartoons—but that comic book is still around and still selling.

All in all, the fanzine route has been more important in producing underground comics than the underground press, for many underground cartoonists were very interested in comics before the Great Comic Book Cleanup Campaign of the McCarthy era, and the pap produced under the Comics Code virtually drove them into the fiercely energetic world of comics fandom.

Fanzines are small-circulation magazines produced by amateur cartoonists with particular interest in certain aspects of the comics world. The more creative fanzines include cartoon strips by the editor, his friends, other fans, and occasionally by a professional cartoonist. There are science-fiction fanzines, superhero fanzines, funny animal fanzines, and satire fanzines; there are even fanzine fanzines. Hard-core fandom is a sort of amateur elite, a rigid system which can take years of publication and correspondence to break into. But on the fringes of fandom, in the smaller and more unusual fanzines (such as one called *Odd,* which originally published Dave Herring's study of the frustration of a would-be suicide), the budding underground cartoonists thrived.

Far Left: Kim Deitch. *Gothic Blimp Works* No. 7.

Left: Don Dohler's *Wild* staff. *Wild* No. 7. © 1962 Don Dohler. By permission of Don Dohler.

A microcosm of the fanzine world—and a story with purpose, because the publication made waves that are still being felt—is the tale of *Wild,* a dittoed fanzine which almost made it through eleven issues before expiring for the usual reason: lack of money.

Wild was the 1959 product of the combined minds of Don Dohler and Mark Tarka—more or less. Actually, the two met then and, in Dohler's words, "We found we enjoyed drawing insane comic strips together, and a partnership, of sorts, was formed." Five hand-drawn copies of something called *Wild* were produced by this partnership in 1959 and 1960.

"Great oaks from little acorns," and all that. Maybe not a large tree, but a respectable bush eventually took the name *Wild.* In 1961, the Dohler-Tarka partnership actually started to ditto a fanzine of that name. This was not the world's greatest production, says Dohler: "In fact, *Wild* No. 1, although it might be considered 'camp' by today's standards, was probably the worst fanzine in history." Other issues, equally successful, were distributed in press runs of about fifty or sixty each. Then, between issues No. 3 and No. 4, Dohler got a letter from one Jay Lynch, enclosing a cartoon. (The letter arrived through a mutual friend, but this story sounds nepotistic enough without going into *that* kind of detail. Still, that's what fanzines are all about.)

Jay Lynch thus broke into print through *Wild.* In later issues, Dohler began to receive contributions from other soon-

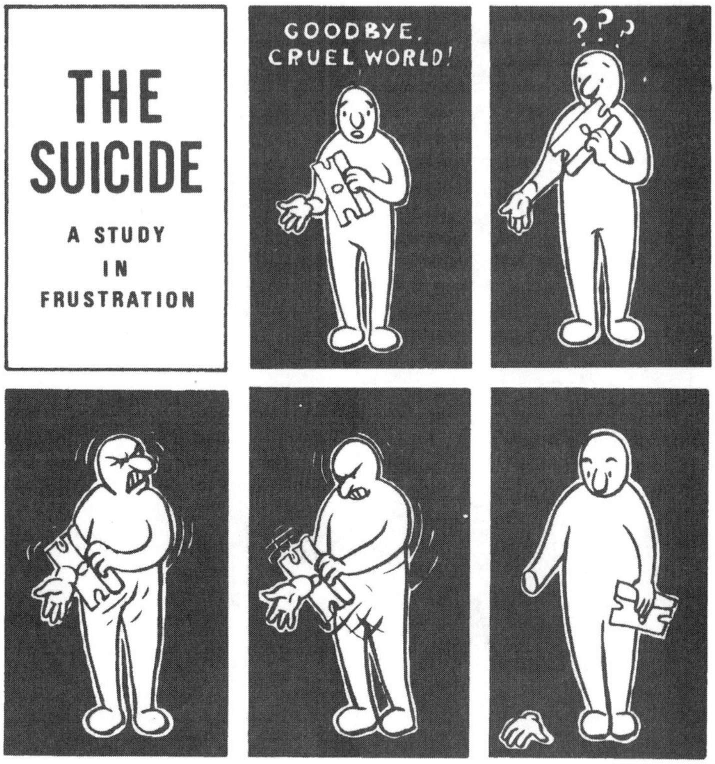

Dave Herring. *Bijou Funnies* No. 1. © 1968 Jay Lynch. By permission of Jay Lynch.

to-become-underground cartoonists, most notably Skip Williamson and Art Spiegelman. And since fanzines feed on themselves, and the artists feed on all of them, Lynch and Williamson also appeared in a fanzine called *Smudge*, by Joe Pilati, and Williamson started his own fanzine, *Squire*, which lasted only a few issues but which Dohler says "was probably the best satire fanzine put out on a consistent basis." Art Spiegelman also did a fanzine, *Blasé*.

The topics in the satire fanzines tended to get wilder as production problems were overcome. *Wild*'s Tarka did a piece on cleaning a stuffed toilet, and another called "Bat Kid" (never published, but scheduled for *Wild* No. 8) which dealt with a school strike (in *1962!*). As time went on, the fanzines ran into typical publication burdens, like money and time. *Wild* No. 11, which was printed before No. 10, never got officially "published" —mailed out—because it was just too much of a hassle. *Wild* No. 10, the most ambitious issue of all (seventy pages, including several by pros), was ruined by a flood in Dohler's garage—the straw, says Dohler, which broke the camel's back. At about the same time (late 1962), similar fanzines created by similar proto-underground-cartoonists also stopped being published. The people who had put them together while in high school, at the age of fifteen or sixteen, were going off to college or were eager to move from wherever they were to somewhere else. And the better artists were working to get directly into the professional world: Lynch and Williamson, as noted earlier in this chapter, were being published in Kurtzman's *Help!* at about this time.

So *Wild* died just as it was becoming interesting. Says Dohler, "*Wild* would have, without a doubt, become a very comic-book-like publication had we lasted another five or so issues. Near the end, I got wrapped up with the *Mad* comics and had desires to turn *Wild* into a fully cartoon kind of thing with little or no editorials, written articles, and like

Far Right: Jay Lynch. *Wild* No. 5. ©1961 Don Dohler. By permission of Don Dohler.

Right: Mark Tarka. *Wild* No. 8. ©1962 Don Dohler By permission of Don Dohler.

Below: Jay Lynch. *Chicago Seed*, Vol. V, No. 13. Originally published in the fanzine *Squire*.

that. In fact, *Wild* No. 11 (which never got published) contained only one page of written material (an editorial) and nine pages of comic-like stuff. This would've been my trend had we gone on."

Though *Wild* stopped publishing in 1962, it left behind an interesting legacy. The ruined-by-rain No. 10 was to contain a rejected cover for *Mad* by Kelly Freas, a six-color foldout, and a free comic—perhaps the first modern more-or-less-underground comic. Not only that: the comic even contained a crude but very real 3-D story, something which had not been tried since E. C. put out two 3-D books seven years before (and was not to be tried again until *Deep 3-D Comix* in 1970). And, most important of all, *Wild* was the birthplace of a character still used by several underground cartoonists: Projunior.

Projunior originated as something Don Dohler sketched in his school notebooks when he was in fifth grade in 1958. Herewith, The Genesis of an Idea: "He caught on in those days too, and it wasn't long before my fellow classmates started doodling him also. But I *was* the creator. (Christ, that almost sounds like 'I *am* the President'!! 'Scuse me.)"

The original character created by Dohler had no name and was used only as a mascot on the five hand-drawn issues of *Wild* which he and Tarka produced in 1959 and 1960. When the "general distribution" *Wild* was being started, says Dohler, "I racked my brain for a week before remembering the white-eyeballed character I had done in school and the homemade *Wilds.* But I wanted him more human, so I eliminated the 'absurd' characteristics: the jester's hat, the corks in the ears, the double eyebrows, the two sideway teeth, and of course the long, rectangular head."

Thus was born a character who has survived to the present day. Dohler says he thought of the name when he began thinking of himself as a "junior professional editor." After repeating that phrase to himself a few times, he decided to call the mascot "Junior Pro." Then, says Dohler, "After staring at those two words on paper for an hour or so, it just seemed more catchy and less hackneyed to switch the words around. Thus Pro Junior was formed. It had a nice ring to it—and was easy to say and easy to remember. And somehow, it fit my '58-born character beautifully."

The character, whose name was eventually changed by other cartoonists to one word, Projunior, never really died. Jay Lynch and Robert Crumb modified him, each in his own way, and used him in various stories (Crumb even gave him a girlfriend, Honeybunch Kaminsky). Oddly enough, Dohler himself dropped the character from *Wild* after issue No. 6 because friends and readers kept telling him they hated mascots in general, if not Pro Junior in particular.

Projunior is a "living" link of the underground comics with their immediate past, and as the subject of *Projunior Comix* (published in late 1971) he has the distinction of having been drawn by more underground cartoonists, in more styles, than any other comic-book character, with the possible exceptions of Richard

Whence They Cometh

Jay Lynch. *Wild* No. 9. ©1962 Don Dohler. By permission of Don Dohler.

Below, Far Left: Skip Williamson. *Wild* No. 7. ©1962 Don Dohler. By permission of Don Dohler.

Below Left: Pro Junior's debut, as drawn by Don Dohler for *Wild* No. 1. ©1961 Don Dohler. By permission of Don Dohler.

Below: Don Dohler's two versions of Pro Junior, especially re-created for this book. ©1974 Don Dohler. By permission of Don Dohler.

Nixon and Spiro Agnew.

While the *Wild* story was developing, scores of other fanzines were being born and dying (usually at about the same time). To take just one example, Robert Crumb, probably the nation's best-known underground cartoonist, did a horror-and-parody fanzine called *Foo* which lasted three issues. Crumb and his brother Charles (with whom he often collaborated on cartoons) sold the fanzine door to door for fifteen cents a copy, saying they were working their way through college.

Unfortunately for later historians, even the underground press and fanzines do not tell the full story of the rise of underground comics. For instance, before producing *Foo*, Crumb and his brother Charles had done an amateur comic called *Funny Friends* for six-and-a-half years in the fifties. Only one copy of each issue was produced (as Dohler and Tarka put out only one copy of each issue of the first version of *Wild*), but Crumb took the opportunity to develop one character, Brombo the Panda, from 1952 to 1958.

Robert Crumb. *Bijou Funnies* No. 4. ©1969 Bijou Publishing Empire, Inc. By permission of Bijou Publishing Empire, Inc., by Jay Lynch.

Opposite: Joel Beck. *Projunior Comix.* ©1971 Denis Kitchen. By permission of Denis Kitchen.

PRO JUNIOR COMIX!
BY JOEL BECK
IN "HIS CHILD HOOD"!
HONEY! HE WON'T EAT HIS DINNER!
NOW, JR. MIND YOUR MOTHER!
AAAARG!
JR., STOP THAT!
YOU KNOW THAT'S BAD TABLE MANNERS!
I TELL YOU. THE KID'S ROTTEN!
HE'S JUST LIKE HIS AWFUL UNCLE HARRY!
HE! HE! HE!
NOW SAY YOUR DINNER PRAYERS- YOU "ROTTEN KID"!
MAW! I'LL DO EVEN BETTER! I'LL TURN INTO AN ANGLE AND FLY AWAY!
...DID YOU HEAR THAT?
...ALL HE NEED'S IS A GOOD SPANKING!
OH. DEAR!
...LOOK AT HIM! HE'S CHANGING!
PING
UH- LOOK. SON....
JUST SAY YOUR PRAYERS AND-
GOOD GOD!
NOW, SON! DON'T ....
SOB-
...HE LOVES TO TORMENT ME THIS WAY!
THAT'S ODD-
JUST LIKE HIS......
..HIS UNCLE HARRY NEVER DID DO THAT!
THE END!

PROJUNIOR
in "TOO MUCH TOO SOON."
HIS SIXTH PERIOD BIOLOGY CLASS IS OVER AND OUR HIGH SCHOOL HERO IS IN HIS USUAL DAZE.
DUKE DUKE DUKE DUKE OF EARL DUKE DUKE DUKE OF EARL DUKE DUKE DUKE OF EARL DUKE DUKE...
HAW HAW HAW!
HEH HEH!
HAW HAW!
CHUCKLE!
HA HA!
TEE-HEE!
HAW HAW!
HO HO!
TEE-HEE!
HA!
YUK YUK YUK!
HAW!
ISKY
Doris
Ron + Sally
JAYZEY LYNCH
SOMETHING FUNNY IS GOIN' ON TODAY. I GET THE FEELING EVERYBODY IS LAUGHING AT ME BEHIND MY BACK.
HAW HAW!
!
1

Robert and Charles Crumb. *Zap Comix* No. 5.

Obviously, the seeds of the underground comics are a bit hard to find under the tree roots.

A few cartoonists got their start through campus or off-campus humor magazines, notably Gilbert Shelton and Jaxon (then Jack Jackson), who worked with each other on *The Texas Ranger* as the fifties were ending. As far back as 1959, Shelton was creating strips featuring Wonder Wart-Hog, the best-known and funniest underground anti-superhero (or super-antihero) yet.

Who deserves the dubious distinction of producing the first thing that resembled today's underground comics is an open question and a moot point, all at once. Dohler's 1962 giveaway comic never got into circulation, and it was part of a fanzine rather than an independent comic book. Probably the first recognizable modern underground comic (and certainly the earliest one still available) was Jaxon's *God Nose (Snot Reel)*, which appeared in 1963—though Jaxon himself cryptically says he was influenced by "a mimeographed Adventures of Jesus mini-comic." That Adventures of Jesus comic had been drawn by Foolbert Sturgeon (real name: Frank Stack) and published by the cartoonist in Austin, Texas. Texas was the home ground for most of the earliest underground cartooning (pre-1964 or so), with Shelton, Jaxon, and Foolbert Sturgeon being the best-known and most talented of the tiny group of underground cartoonists. But there were rumblings in California at the same time: Joel Beck, an artist for the University of California satire magazine *The Pelican*, drew a small, crudely-printed book called *Lenny of Laredo* about the same time the Texas cartoonists began their work. In later years, it would be California, and particularly the San Francisco-Berkeley area, that would attract most of the underground cartoonists.

To Jaxon, 1963 was an eternity ago: "Those were the days of homemade peyote, before 'hippies' were created by the mass media and being stoned was like being drunk." (Come to think of it, that *was* a long time ago.) Three years after Jaxon's *God Nose*, Spain Rodriguez did a comic newspaper called *Zodiac Mindwar*. But it was not until

Opposite: Jay Lynch. *Teen-Age Horizons of Shangrila* No. 1. ©1970 Denis Kitchen. By permission of Denis Kitchen.

Skip Williamson. *Chicago Mirror* No. 3. ©1968 Jay Lynch. By permission of Jay Lynch.

Opposite: Dave Sheridan. *Tales from the Leather Nun.* ©1973 Dave Sheridan. By permission of Dave Sheridan.

1967 that the underground comics began to coagulate, as it were, into a recognizable medium of their own. In that year, Jay Lynch and Skip Williamson got together in Chicago and published a magazine called the *Chicago Mirror*. According to Lynch, "We called it that since we couldn't think of a better title." The *Mirror* contained written pieces, most of them rather juvenile, and a few pages of cartoons; it was magazine-sized, lasted three issues, and contained a few cartoons that are still reprinted occasionally in underground newspapers, plus some cartoon pages that eventually found their way into later underground comics. All in all, says Lynch, "It was pretty tame stuff, but quite a few crazy folks really got irritated by the *Chicago Mirror*."

Underground comics, even before they really existed, were beginning to show their insidious mind-warping potential.

Meanwhile, on the West Coast, one Don Schenker was failing to get into the picture-framing business. Schenker, who knew Harvey Kurtzman in the Bronx before moving to Berkeley, had opened a shop on Telegraph Avenue in September 1965, planning to do picture framing and sell fine prints. In 1966, as a sideline, The Print Mint, as the place was called, published two comic-type stories—first *Lenny of Laredo* by Joel Beck, then *The New Daisy Duck*. Then, says Schenker, "It wasn't to be that I was going to be a picture framer and sell fine prints, because posters started coming in, and we were the first to get them, and we started getting known as a poster place."

It was Robert Crumb who united the West Coast with the Mid-

Right: Joel Beck. *Lenny of Laredo.* ©1965 Joel Beck. By permission of Joel Beck.

Far Right: Skip Williamson. *Chicago Mirror* No. 2. ©1968 Jay Lynch. By permission of Jay Lynch.

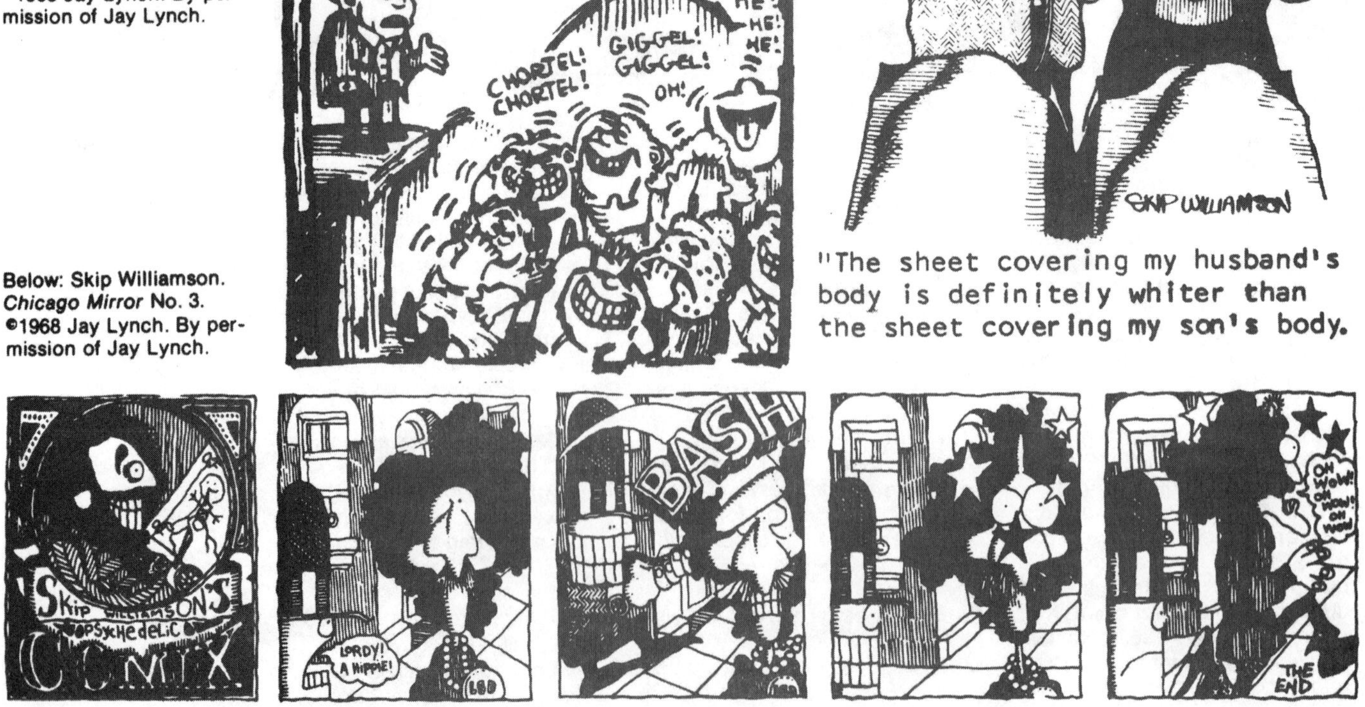

Below: Skip Williamson. *Chicago Mirror* No. 3. ©1968 Jay Lynch. By permission of Jay Lynch.

BRO. LINGUS WILL NOW BRING US...
CHAPTER ONE
TALES OF THE
LEATHER NUN
Once upon a time...
© SHERIDAN '73

west, at least spiritually and temporarily. In 1967, his *Zap Comix* No. 1 appeared. (There was an even earlier *Zap* scheduled for publication, but the person who was supposed to publish it left the United States with the artwork and never returned. Crumb later, around the time *Zap* No. 3 went to press, found Xerox copies of the art work for this first *Zap*, drew new covers, and printed the whole thing as *Zap* No. 0.)

In Chicago, Lynch and Williamson were preparing to change the name of the *Chicago Mirror* to *Bijou*, after Lynch discovered an old magazine called *Savoy* and decided that movie theatre names also work well as magazine titles. Lynch was drawing a comic strip for the *Chicago Seed* (a local underground newspaper) at this time, and he and Williamson decided to make their new magazine at least half comics. As Lynch tells it, "Then *Zap* #1 came out, and we figured that Crumb really had balls to publish something like that. We weren't sure if it would sell, 'cause hippies in them days were very snobby about taking drugs, and took the whole thing very seriously. Hippies seemed to lack a sense of humor. But Skip and I decided if that's what hippiedom is coming to then fuck it, so we put all the

Skip Williamson. *Chicago Mirror* No. 2. ©1968 Jay Lynch. By permission of Jay Lynch.

Jay Lynch. *Chicago Mirror* No. 1. ©1967 Jay Lynch. By permission of Jay Lynch.

Jay Lynch. *Chicago Mirror* No. 3. ©1968 Jay Lynch. By permission of Jay Lynch.

comic material together, and added more, and published it as a comic book called *Bijou Funnies.*"

While *Bijou Funnies* No. 1 was being put together, Gilbert Shelton came out with *Feds 'n' Heads Comics,* which was mostly reprints of things Shelton had done for the *Austin Rag,* that Texas city's underground paper (just as *Bijou* was mostly taken from the *Chicago Seed*). By this time, underground comics were beginning to take shape as a movement—but aside from Crumb's *Zap* and Jaxon's very early *God Nose,* they had yet to emerge as a truly creative medium rather than a vehicle for reprints.

While Crumb, Shelton, and Lynch and Williamson were working on their comics, one of the great E. C. figures, Wally Wood, began to publish *witzend* magazine as "an occasional public service." At first it appeared that this professionally printed and professionally drawn magazine might become, like Kurtzman's *Humbug* and *Help!,* a forum for new cartoonists. That was certainly the original intention, or at least part of it, according to *witzend's* later co-editor, Bill Pearson: "*witzend* was created to serve as a forum for professional artists to establish copyrights on properties they didn't wish to give away to the giant companies for the standard (low) page rate—and to introduce new cartoonists who couldn't get into the reg'lar comics either because their rendering wasn't 'professional' (indistinguishable from the house style) or because their material was too controversial (intelligent, funny, shocking, or particularly . . . different) to pass the editor's desk." But perhaps the time for this sort of assistance to budding cartoonists was past. In any case, *witzend* was a disappointment to the Maddicts among the underground cartoonists, for the magazine's artists seemed more interested in drawing women's naked breasts than in the hard-hitting satire of the old E. C. series. Given what was supposedly a chance to express themselves, free of the restrictions imposed by "straight" cartooning assignments, the professional artists produced little more than slightly exaggerated versions of what they had already done for the kiddie trade.

Yet *witzend* too had its influence on the underground comics, partly because it cut the cartoonists from the mental umbilical cord which still joined many of them to Kurtzman's early sixties magazines, and partly because the economic attitudes of *witzend* came to be the attitudes of the underground cartoonists as well (whether or not the influence was an overt one in every case). According to Bill Pearson, "*witzend* doesn't claim to be an underground comic or any other kind of comic, but of course we are just as underground as any publication could be, which simply means that we have no professional distribution arrangement, and therefore very few people ever manage to see it. It's not a money-making project—the work is contributed

Jaf. *witzend* No. 5. ©1968 Jaf. By permission of Wonderful Publishing Company, by Bill Pearson.

Below: Wally Wood. *witzend* No. 6. ©1974 William M. Gaines. By permission of William M. Gaines; and Wonderful Publishing Company, by Bill Pearson.

free by the creator for a one-time-only printing, after which the copyright and the material go back to the kat wot did it . . . a revolutionary concept. Usually the publisher feels he should own and be able to reprint a picture a thousand times after paying his artist what little he can get away with in the first place."

A while back, I mentioned that Crumb's *Zap* united the Midwest with the West Coast. So it did, though the publication

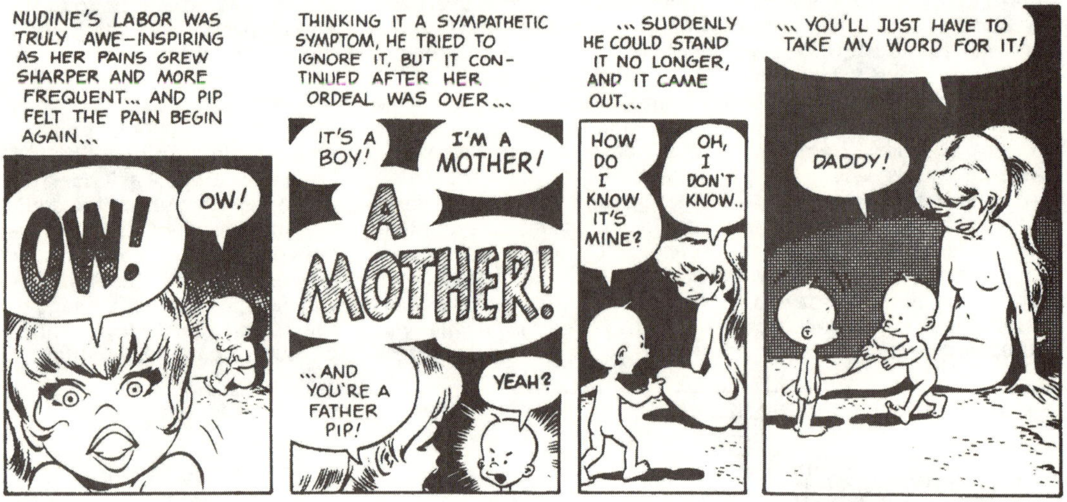

Wally Wood. *witzend* No. 5. ©1968 Wallace Wood. By permission of Wonderful Publishing Company, by Bill Pearson.

of *Feds 'n' Heads Comics* and the first *witzend* intervened in the coagulation process. It was in early 1968, according to The Print Mint's Don Schenker, that he first saw a copy of *Zap* No. 1. "I was deeply moved," says Schenker, "and I decided that since the posters were going down, we had to do something that was really good, and I said that we should start a comic newspaper, like the old inserts in the New York newspapers. So my wife, who controls the money, gave me $75, and she said, 'You can't have any more until you make it back.' Nobody believed me, but I went and made the first *Yellow Dog*—for a lot more than $75, but that was essentially all I had to work with."

(It's worth pointing out that Schenker is not the only one who takes credit for the creation of *Yellow Dog,* the longest-lived underground comic book. According to cartoonist John Thompson, the original idea was for a comic newspaper called *Puck the Yellow Kid,* and the plan was submitted by him and Joel Beck. According to Thompson, Schenker "said no—he didn't think there was any money in comics. We coaxed him finally but he changed the name to the *Yellow Dog.*" Schenker says he originally planned to call the

Right: Masthead of *Yellow Dog,* 1969. *Yellow Dog Comix* No. 15. ©1969 The Print Mint. By permission of The Print Mint, by Bob Rita.

Below: Franz Cilensek's earlier masthead. *Yellow Dog* No. 8. ©1968 The Print Mint. By permission of The Print Mint, by Bob Rita.

publication *Puck the Yellow Dog,* but shortened the title because he did not want to make the reference to Puck, an early Hearst comic character.)

The symbol of *Yellow Dog* is a yellow dog pissing (originally on Herman Melville's Captain Ahab). The Dog is the underground answer to Alfred E. Neuman—like the *Mad*-man, the Dog traces his ancestry straight back to the Yellow Kid of Richard F. Outcault. Says Schenker, "I thought it was a great idea to have the dog pissing on Ahab, to show contempt for symbolism, which was the American rage. Yellow Dog is, you know, a coward, and instead of 'what fools these mortals be' he's saying 'piss on them.' " Schenker says that the parallel of *Yellow Dog* with Melville goes beyond the masthead: "If Melville was right when he said *Moby-Dick* was a naughty book, then *Yellow Dog* was designed to be a naughty paper."

Schenker emphasized, at first, that *Yellow Dog* was a paper rather than a comic book; but with issue No. 13-14, *Yellow Dog* too emerged in comic-book form. In the following issue, Schenker paid a special tribute to Harvey Kurtzman, leading off with a twelve-page story reprinted from Kurtzman's 1959 *Jungle Book.* Schenker is obviously very aware of the historical foundations of underground comics, and the Kurtzman reprint tied the comics even more firmly to their past.

After that time, *Yellow Dog* became extremely variable in quality, as various artists boycotted The Print Mint (see Chapter 11) and a fairly mediocre crop of newcomers replaced them. *Yellow Dog* does retain the distinction of having come out more times than any other underground comic. But it was no longer closely tied to the history of the underground comics by the time it ceased to exist in 1973. More recently, it has been Denis Kitchen's publishing outfit, Krupp Comic Works, which has taken the lead in producing comics whose roots are showing. The most notable comic of this type was an entire book drawn by Will Eisner, creator of The Spirit and one of the most admired comic-book artists of the forties. The comic combined some of the original Spirit stories with some new pages drawn especially for Krupp—and those pages took a satirical look at the old Spirit tales, which were themselves satirical! If the underground cartoonists are becoming more aware of their past, the best of the "straight" cartoonists of thirty years ago are starting to become aware that today's underground comics may be a place for their future.

So the wheel is slowly coming full circle. Under these circumstances, the words of cartoonist Justin Green are worth contemplating: "See, I don't think there's anything new. I think that there is always a dynamic force that counters dominant mediocrity and convention-ridden activity. Unfortunately it isn't revered until long after it has occurred. So labels like Alternate Culture or Underground Comics are beginning to appear slightly fallacious to me, although we have to use these terms to communicate."

Addenda:

A brief look at three cartoonists not yet mentioned seems to sum up, in microcosm, both the variety of the underground-comic field and the entire set of historical influences operating within the comics. Rand Holmes, who comes from Canada, thinks he's always been interested in drawing of some sort: "Have been drawing ever since I can remember—don't know when I began—probably as a child on

Harvey Kurtzman. *Yellow Dog Comix* No. 15 (reprinted from *The Jungle Book*). ©1959 Harvey Kurtzman. By permission of Harvey Kurtzman.

Rand Holmes. *Harold Hedd* No. 2. ©1973 Rand Holmes. By permission of Rand Holmes.

John Adkins Richardson. *Fever Dreams* No. 1. ©1972 Richard Corben, John Richardson, and Jan Strnad. By permission of Richard Corben and John Adkins Richardson.

the pot finger-painting with my shit—hah!—no real direction of course."

Holmes cites many of the same influences mentioned by other underground cartoonists—but for him, they weren't easy to come by. E.C. Comics, he says, were banned in the Canadian province of Alberta, and he never saw an original E.C. until he had long since started drawing. He wasn't encouraged to start being a cartoonist, either—because, he says, Canada is in many ways merely a northern part of the United States: "See, in Canada is no magazines, no comics, no nuthin' —only American imports—better to become a refrigerator repairman in Greenland than a cartoonist in Canada." Holmes cites Wally Wood, Will Eisner, and such other artists as Nestor Redondo and Alfred Alcala as influences on his style, and says that his first cartoon was printed in Harvey Kurtzman's *Help!* He is grateful to the Age of E.C., but not limited by it: "Eventually E.C. and the Golden Age may be put in proper perspective—seen as only a beginning to the incredible potential of the illustrated story."

If Holmes' interest in comics shows pretty much a straight line of influence from earlier works, the approach of John Adkins Richardson indicates that the underground comics also have room for people whose influence has come from anywhere *but* the earlier days of comic books. Richardson, a professor at Southern Illinois University, got into comics as the result of a research project "concerned with the relationships between the fine arts and the popular ones." He had done advertising strips professionally, he says, and "when I thought about doing comics, I thought it'd be a 'snap.'" But he found it difficult and challenging to produce "hundreds of portraits and views of characters from all sorts of points-of-view," and comics began to occupy more and more of his mind—though time problems, he said, led to his leaving strips aside for weeks or months and sometimes letting "inadvertent variations creep in."

Richardson is certainly not unaware of the styles of other cartoonists, but their influence on him has been mainly a negative one: "I wanted to avoid the slick conventions employed by all the imitators of Alex Raymond, Milton Caniff, and the other superpros."

Of course, some underground cartoonists don't even trace their development as far back as the E.C. Comics and the work of various "straight" artists. The medium grew quickly enough so that a large number of cartoonists began to appear who were influenced completely (or almost completely) by *other* underground cartoonists. Guy Colwell, who found that underground comics provided a release for the

Guy Colwell. *Inner City Romance Comix* No. 2: "Radical Rock." ©1972 Guy Colwell. By permission of Guy Colwell.

tensions he built up while serving a prison sentence for draft evasion, says, "Greg Irons and Spain Rodriguez both had a part in influencing my decision to do comics, and though my style imitates neither I was, you might say, an avid fan of both and loved it when I saw another of their books. But my comic life is intertwined with these two cartoonists in other ways than artistic influence. The friend who turned me on to doing comics was so wiped out by Trashman in the underground periodicals that made their way into our prison dorm, he would hold the strip in his clenched fist and scream 'TRASHMAN!' down the rows of beds so everyone could hear. He loved it and some of his turn-on in prison turned me on. . . . I managed to develop a feeling, however pseudo-mystical, of being connected to the underground artists, and I was there."

These three cartoonists sum up among them the relationship of the underground comics to their historical antecedents. Rand Holmes is aware of, influenced by, and to some extent molded by the past; John Adkins Richardson is aware of past comic-book art but is influenced negatively by it, if at all; and Guy Colwell is directly influenced not by the comic art of the past, but by the work of today's underground cartoonists themselves, to try his hand at producing comic books of his own.

Two samples of work by Guy Colwell from *The Inner City Romance Comic:* "Choices." ©1972 Guy Colwell. By permission of Guy Colwell.

3 A Few Hows, Whens and Wherefores

Walt Kelly, whose influence on the underground cartoonists is discussed in Chapter 2, spoke for many of them when he explained, through an anecdote in *Gone Pogo*, why he became a cartoonist himself. His father, he said, once told him "the truth which I still cherish, 'Language is the worst means of communication known to man.' He further claimed that pictures were better than words any day. 'Pictures and good luck,' he said, 'will get you anywhere.' "

That commitment to pictures is about the only thing that holds the underground cartoonists together in a group—that, and the fact that many of them know each other personally, and almost all are familiar with their compatriots' work. But at that, the commitments of the underground cartoonists make them more cohesive as a group than these few pages are as a chapter. Be forewarned: I make no pretense to completeness, and present the cartoonists pretty much in a random order. Since this book is a cooperative effort, I have gone along with some cartoonists who would rather be known by their artwork alone than by their words (and I have gone along with a few who would rather not be known at all). The plan in this chapter, even more clearly than elsewhere in the book, is to give some idea of the variety and interest of a field I personally enjoy very much. The idea is *not* to write the definitive anything.

So with that disclaimer, I hum-

Gilbert Shelton. *Zap Comix* No. 3.

Gilbert Shelton. *Radical America Komiks.* ©1969 Radical America. By permission of Radical America, by Paul Buhle.

bly invite you to meet some of the cartoonists.

Some of the very best are among the least willing to talk about themselves. **Gilbert Shelton** sums himself up in a single sentence: "I'm just an ol' 'artist' sittin' around 'doin' mah thing' and I write and draw and print and sell my own stuff, so that makes me a businessman, too." But of course there is much more to Shelton than that. A shy, soft-spoken Southerner with a gentle regional accent, Shelton has been working in the field since the early 1960's, when he was a graduate student in history at the University of Texas. He is one major underground cartoonist whose primary purpose—his only purpose, he would have it—is to entertain. Perhaps for that reason, he is extremely successful whenever he does take on political subjects. According to Harvey Kurtzman, granddaddy of the underground comics, Shelton is "the pro of the group," and an enormously skillful artist.

Shelton has created some characters who have almost become folk heroes: Wonder Wart-Hog, the brutal, lecherous pig whose adventures decimate whatever small validity the superhero com-

Robert Crumb. *Zap Comix* No. 1. ©1967 R. Crumb. By permission of Robert Crumb.

ics might still have in a few minds; and the Fabulous Furry Freak Brothers, three stoned dropouts whose strips are at once hilarious and much truer to life than some of the more "realistic" strips by other artists. Shelton's humor cuts across everyone equally, and he is virtually the only male underground cartoonist whose work is completely free of sexism. Indeed, Trina, a woman cartoonist who comes down justifiably hard on the sexism of her male counterparts, says, "Shelton is funny as hell and I have *never* seen a sexist comic by him—his comics are real, fair, and funny."

Shelton, who tends to minimize his own ability and effectiveness on all levels other than that of pure entertainment, also tends to minimize the effective communication power of the underground comics themselves: "People either dig comics or they don't." In most cases, just about everyone who likes underground comics at all seems to dig Shelton.

Shelton is often mentioned in the same breath as **Robert Crumb,** undoubtedly the best-known underground cartoonist—and probably the most elusive person in the field. When cornered, Crumb is willing to talk about himself, but no two people come away from him with the same impression—he seems to change his opinions of himself almost every hour. This both explains the perennial freshness of his work and shows why Crumb is best illuminated by studying other cartoonists' reactions to him.

Crumb is personally an anachronism. While the other underground cartoonists sprout the long hair and mustaches or beards that mark them as part of the "underground culture," Crumb walks around looking like a fugitive from 1950. In his early thirties, this tall, gangly artist looks about sixteen. He carries his art supplies in a beat-up old case plastered with the same kinds of travel stickers that middle-aged businessmen get for their luggage when they travel. He likes jazz, but not modern jazz or even swing, and he is almost unaware of comic-book art since the forties.

Almost alone among the underground cartoonists, Crumb was never especially interested in any of the E. C. Comics. But what did influence him is impossible to say. Everyone has his own observations (most of which Crumb will confirm, depending on his mood). Cartoonist Roger Brand is quoted in an article in *Cavalier* as saying that Crumb's influences were Billy DeBeck ("Barney Google"), Elzie Segar ("Popeye"), and especially one of the early *Mad* artists, Basil Wolverton. In the *Journal of Popular Culture,* Harvey Pekar names George Herriman ("Krazy Kat"), Carl Barks (early Disney characters), and Walt Kelly. Crumb's brother-in-law, Marty Pahls, told *Funnyworld* magazine that Crumb especially liked Kelly, Barks, and "Little Lulu."

Crumb comes from a lower-middle-class background (his father once worked as a chicken plucker). His family moved from Philadelphia (where Crumb was born) to Iowa to California to Delaware and then, in 1962, returned to Philadelphia. That year, Crumb went to Cleveland, where—fresh out of high school and without formal art training—he was hired by the American Greetings Corporation to do greeting cards (a job he kept until 1968). Some of his cards are still on the market, and a sample may be found on page 257.

From 1964 on, Crumb spent little time in Cleveland, mailing his cards in while traveling with his wife (whom he married in 1964) in Switzerland, Denmark, England, Yugoslavia, Bulgaria, Germany, and various parts of

Robert Crumb. *Yellow Dog Comix* No. 13-14. ©1969 R. Crumb Studios. By permission of R. Crumb Studios, by Robert Crumb.

Below: Robert Crumb self-portrait, especially drawn for this book.

Robert Crumb. *Hydrogen Bomb and Biochemical Warfare Funnies.* ©1970 Rip Off Press. By permission of Rip Off Press, by Gilbert Shelton.

America (eventually landing in San Francisco in 1966). Harvey Kurtzman published some Crumb sketches of Bulgaria, plus a "Harlem Notebook" that Crumb did in New York City, in his magazine *Help!*

Indeed, Crumb found publication everywhere. He appeared in underground newspapers (*Yarrowstalks*, the *East Village Other*), in his own comic (*Zap*), and in other comics (such as *Yellow Dog*), even doing the cover art for the Columbia Records album *Cheap Thrills*, by Big Brother and the Holding Company (featuring Janis Joplin). He later became the first underground cartoonist to have his work published in the "straight" world.

Through it all, Crumb was extremely cavalier about the uses to which his work was put. He stuck to his belief that comics are fun for both creator and reader, and he got burned (see Chapter 11). He occasionally reprinted stories he had done with his brother Charles, and he developed such unusual projects as a "cartoon novel" called *R. Crumb's Big Yum Yum Book*, which started out being about a frog who murdered some ladybugs at a medieval university, and ended up with the frog kissing a bountifully proportioned teenybopper, turning into a man, and running off with the girl to New York.

Crumb's imagination covers everything, to put it mildly. He has created such characters as Angelfood McSpade, the totally sexual, unthinking child of nature who represents all white civilization's repressed desires; Fritz, a true "hep cat"; Mr. Natural, a very capitalistic guru originally based on Master Subramuniya of San Francisco's Himalayan Academy, by whom Crumb thought many of his friends were being taken (in *Zap* No. 2, Mr. Natural is played off against one Holy Ned, who was actually a West Coast scientologist); Flakey Foont, Mr. Natural's bumbling disciple, a hopeless city-dweller who is perpetually hung up on sex and always seeking an instant answer to the world's problems; Whiteman, a sort of Flakey Foont twenty-five years later; and many more. Except for these characters, Crumb rarely uses a person more than once; but he never runs out of characters. And despite the fact that he generally draws with a Rapidograph (a pen that produces uniform lines), his style is so varied that he seems to contain the entire underground comics world within himself. If the underground comics have produced a Mozart, it is Robert Crumb.

Commenting on Crumb, other cartoonists tend to wax ecstatic.

Right and Below: Robert Crumb. Scenes from two stories in *Uneeda Comix*.

George Metzger: "When *Zap* came out it blew my mind. Eventually I went and saw Crumb. He's a weird guy, but a genius, I think. Very aware; he draws what he sees—a damn fine cartoonist." Foolbert Sturgeon: "Crumb is important as an artist who makes current pressures and feelings expressible. The world'll never be the same. That's bound to be important—probably more important really than Ginzberg [sic] or the hotshot respectable novelists as an influence." Wendel Alan Pugh: "I really envy the uncultured slant he has on the world and drawing." Justin Green: "If you have the insight and honesty of Crumb, then your personal myths tamper with the collective unconscious." Harvey Kurtzman: "Crumb really gets downright poetic with his stuff. The truest kind of art to me is the kind that really comes from deep down inside your brain. You don't quite know why you're doing an idea, but you're doing it and it's effective. Crumb does a lot of that. And he seems to love everything he's doing." Meredith Kurtzman (Harvey's daughter, and a car-

A Few Hows, Whens and Wherefores

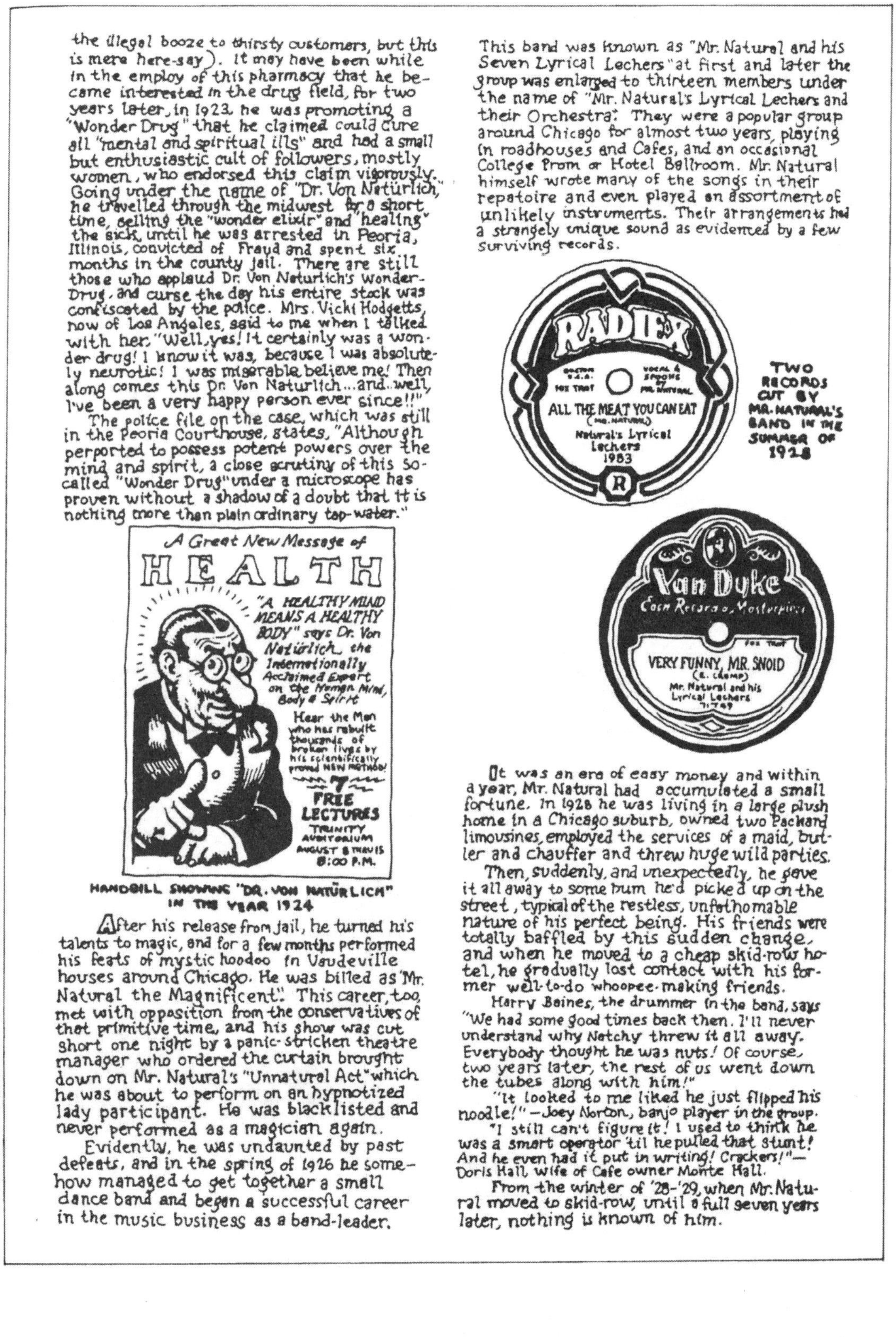

Robert Crumb. *Mr. Natural* No. 1. ©1970 R. Crumb. By permission of Robert Crumb.

toonist in her own right): "Bob Crumb is capturing things that I see on the street every day better than anyone else ever has—he's really amazing. I saw a real Snoid on the subway one night at midnight—this little solemn guy was blowin' a little razz whistle at people on the train."

The problem with adulation is that it sometimes gets in one's way. Crumb has fallen victim to his own skill. Just as the more popular "straight" comic characters receive fan mail, and just as people think the man who draws Dick Tracy *is* Dick Tracy, so people have come to believe that Robert Crumb is Mr. Natural and, as a result . . . well, here's what Paul Buhle of *Radical America* says: "Crumb makes himself scarce as possible: people think he is Mr. Natural, literally, and hang around wherever he is, asking How To Do It . . . Crumb would rather make a little bread and do *Kunt Komiks* for free than become An Artist . . . He is beautiful despite himself."

Not everyone has unqualified admiration for Crumb's work, however, and Buhle's comments hint at one reason. Crumb has put out, among other things, a series of overt sex comics, giving vent to every adolescent and post-adolescent sexual fantasy he can imagine. To John Thompson, the sex comics are just expressions of a part of Crumb's personality: "He lusts over so many girls' bodies. Great sexual energy. Bob is so animated he lives his characters." But others are not so forgiving. The women in Crumb's strips, in his sex comics and elsewhere, are usually degraded and almost always one-dimensional. If Gilbert Shelton is difficult to accuse of sexism, Crumb is anything but hard to attack—and his work is, in fact, often attacked on that ground. Crumb is certainly no woman-hater, but as Paul Buhle puts it in *TriQuarterly* magazine, "For Crumb, women remain larger than life." This can be true literally, as in his creation of an abominable snow-woman who convinces Whiteman of the emptiness of a "civilized" life. But it is *always* true figuratively: Crumb stands somewhat in awe of the female sex, possibly because of the "great sexual energy" to which John Thompson refers but possibly for less flattering reasons. More on Crumb and

Right: Robert Crumb. *Snatch Comics* No. 2. ©1968 R. Scrum. By permission of Robert Crumb.

Below: Robert Crumb. *Big Ass Comics* No. 2.

women in Chapter 5.

If Crumb's sex comics leave him open to attack, then one of his collaborators on those comics, **S. Clay Wilson** is even more vulnerable. Wilson—a fugitive from Kansas who lives in San Francisco—happens to be a fine storyteller and, when he so chooses, an excellent artist. Crumb himself says that Wilson was a major influence on him, showing him that he doesn't have to hold himself in while drawing cartoons. That may be what Wilson preaches—it's certainly what he practices. He has an astonishing preoccupation with pirates, lesbians, motorcycle freaks, and demons—sometimes all in the same story. He distorts the comics' medium, in which the drawings usually only suggest the characters' appearances, by drawing every hair, every wart, as carefully as if he were painting a mural for an art museum. Writes Mike Barrier in *Funnyworld* magazine No. 10: "Drawing a cartoon involves simplifying, leaving things out—so what you leave *in* assumes greater importance than in life. So with lips, nostrils, and teeth; to include them may amount to a distortion of reality, but not the comic distortion that a cartoonist should have in mind . . . . Wilson's is a world seen after too many days of too little sleep and too much coffee, when every person's physical imperfections loom so large that they're disgusting. Wilson's is merely the obverse [sic] of the neat, tidy, dirtless world that so many people would prefer. In each case, there is at bottom a hatred and fear of the physical, and contempt for us poor physical human beings. . . . Maybe Clay Wilson is an uptight little old lady in disguise."

S. Clay Wilson. *Snatch Comics* No. 1. ©1968 R. Cum. By permission of Robert Crumb.

Far Left: S. Clay Wilson. *Zap Comix* No. 5.

Though Barrier is too critical of Wilson's style—he calls it "crude and ugly," though its ugliness is actually the product of considerable talent—he is extremely preceptive about Wilson's view of the world. In *Funnyworld* No. 12, he states that Wilson "looks at human beings as a Houyhnhnm might. Wilson refuses to see human beings as a whole; rather, he seizes on physical imperfections and magnifies them. This may be preferable to what happens in syndicate comic strips and traditional comic books, where everyone seems to have been photographed through those Doris Day gauzes, but it's still a distorted and limited way of looking at things."

Wilson's view *is* distorted and limited, but as fellow cartoonist Buckwheat Florida Jr. says, he "has his corner down tight." And let us not forget that the Houyhnhnms who looked down on Gulliver were, in Gulliver's own eyes, a race of perfect beings.

Wilson is not really like his cartoons, though it's hard to imagine him being any other way. According to Harvey Kurtzman, "In person, you know, he doesn't go around on a motorcycle with a hook where his arm should be. But in his imagination, sure, he's very much like his cartoons—he drinks a lot of beer and swears a lot. He can affect you so you think maybe he's a pussycat when he gets drunk, but I would say he's a violent man." Keith Green, brother of Justin Green, by the way, says Wilson *doesn't* swear. Wilson remains an enigma, and a center of controversy.

(A word of interpretative caution from *The Phantom Psychiatrist:* "You have to divide up the cultural aspects of this—you know, what's politically hot at the time. I think Wilson's selling very hot products—I mean, lesbians, whew! And motorcycle gangs a couple of years ago—that was really it! You say well, okay, but it also shows something about him. Yeah, it probably does, but it also shows that he's part of the whole culture scene. And I don't think he's doing very much different from some of the Jean-Luc Godard films, which start nowhere and end nowhere, as opposed to the classic Western: horse and man ride into town, the shooting up, the woman, the kissing of the horse, and at the

MOTORCYCLE MELLOW DRAMA
YOU OUGHTA' TRY A SNORT A' COKE ANGIE
SNUK
..MAKES ME PUKE
YOU REALLY DIG THAT?
PHEW HOTCHA, LESS RIDE INTO... UK SNURF.. RIDE INTO HUCKBURG AND STOMP SOME CITIZENS
HERE COMES MERLE THE GEEK.. MAYBE HE'S GOTTA' BOSS PLAN, MAYBE HES GOT SOME TAIL LINED UP FOR US..
GUESS WHAT BOYS AND GIRLS..
BLUP BLUP
TINK
THE HOG RIDIN' FOOLS ARE HEADIN' THIS WAY AND IT LOOKS LIKE THEY WANNA' TANGLE ASS... I STOMPED ONE OF 'EM BACK THERE IN HUCKBURG
OUTTA' SITE
BITCHIN' GEEK
BLUP BUP KA-CHUFF
SUDDENLY, A SHOT RANG OUT.. TAKIN' GEEK'S HEAD OFF.
KA-THOOM
AND....
GET DOWN
ELSE WHERE, LEROY FLIRTS WITH COMELY BERNICE.
ANY MORE BEER?
YOURE SUCH A SWINGIN' PIECE OF ASS BERNICE, I COULD LICK YOUR ASSHOLE..
DOWN DOWN DOWN IN A BURNIN' RING OF FAR
SPAIN BEER

end going into the sunset. This kind of form, the kind Wilson uses in his cartoons, has become part of the culture. If you ask whether this all shows something about him, I say yeah, it does, but I'm not as impressed by it as I would be if this was Elizabethan England and he was doing this kind of stuff.")

Harvey Kurtzman talks with ye author about Wilson (excerpts):

Kurtzman: Let me be positive about Wilson. When I first saw his stuff (and Crumb was the one who pointed him out to me), I was just completely offended by it. I mean, it was just more than the mind could absorb. It moved into every fantasy of pornography that hadn't been touched yet. And so my mind automatically rejected Wilson. I refused to think about him or look at him. But I eventually came back to his stuff again and again—I kept looking and slobbering, and the guy's a *writer,* he's got a good writing mind, a literate quality that I think is better than any other underground cartoonist's. His choice of words is very fine.

M.J.E. I've noticed that his writing doesn't always match his drawings. The drawings may be bursting with degradation and violence and grotesqueries, but sometimes there's this very—not beautiful, but very literate strip with these reeking drawings underneath it, and I've never been quite sure whether he's making some point by the contrast.

Kurtzman: I think he works like Crumb. He's very close to Crumb, in that they're both guided by the gut rather than by their conscious calculations. They're "gut" artists. And they practically record their dreams—that's all daydream stuff that Wilson does.

M.J.E.: But cartoons are usually much less detailed than life—it's a characteristic of the medium.

Kurtzman: Cartoons are an enormous shorthand. People don't realize it. You get into "what is a cartoon"—it's a terrible shorthand, just says what it has to say, which is very little alongside what a photograph says or alongside what nature says when you're looking out at a scene.

M.J.E.: But Wilson draws his cartoons as if they were paintings—every hair, every wart, every bit of skin perfectly shaped.

Kurtzman: The underground cartoonists are sensitive guys. They have a lot to say about everything. And everything Wilson does is original. These aren't guys who are drawing clichés. Your average cartoonist collects a headful of clichés, thousands of little patent formulas: the bottom of a shoe with a hole in the sole, a bulbous nose on a face—you know, all the hack cartoon devices. But guys like Crumb and Wilson, these guys are sensitive—they keep seeing things, and they have things to say, so they're saying them. And everything's original—they're making new statements all the time.

Some cartoonists have as much to say in words as they do

Above: S. Clay Wilson. *Zap Comix* No. 5.

Left: S. Clay Wilson. *Yellow Dog Comix* No. 13-14. ©1969 The Print Mint. By permission of The Print Mint, by Bob Rita.

Opposite: S. Clay Wilson. *Real Pulp Comics* No. 1. ©1971 Joel Beck, Roger Brand, Leslie Cabarga, Kim Deitch, Justin Green, Bill Griffith, Art Spiegelman, and Ron White. By permission of Messrs. Beck, Deitch, Green and Griffith.

in drawings. **Justin Green,** sometimes Joshua Orange, who left the Graduate School of Fine Arts at Syracuse University to do underground cartooning, has been trying to justify the relevance of cartoons, and their validity, ever since leaving school. "No longer burdened by pretentious notions of making 'art' (I used to be an easel-painter and a darned good one), I am concerned with refining and communicating specific ideas capable of changing others' consciousness. This is still pretentious, but it's much more fun." Green also feels that "vested interests—museums, art historians, critics, patrons, even the artists themselves as P. R. men for church and state promote the inaccessibility of art." The comics, then, are an accessible form, a good way to reach into people's minds (as the underground press discovered: a cartoon is more likely to be read and remembered than is the article it accompanies). And Green does not feel that comics need be defended; like Gilbert Shelton, he is influenced by McLuhanesque thinking: "Comics demand highly abstract participation from readers. Usually the characters are finger-sized, and are just a few lines and dots thrown together but they are often more lifelike than movie actors. The kinetic experience of movement and sound (reader supplies dialect) is gleaned from a very sparse vocabulary of signs and conventions."

Some underground cartoonists are trained outside the art field, and their concerns go beyond the creation of comics. One such is **Denis Kitchen,** who has a degree in journalism from the University of Wisconsin at Milwaukee and now prints and distributes many comics other than his own *Mom's Homemade Comics.* Kitchen does comics because they "can be read quickly. And, if successful, they can have astounding impact, irony, and shock value, or whatever is intended." Kitchen started his own underground newspaper when he was in the eighth grade; it lasted twenty-five issues, to his surprise. After unsuccessful attempts to get jobs in journalism or art, he went underground. Now, he says, "I'm starving, but I love my work." Kitchen is more concerned than the other underground cartoonists with reaching a relatively "straight" audience, going further than the "straight" cartoonists can but not forgetting their accomplishments: "That there *are* some damn good syndicated strips is amazing considering the restrictions straight cartoonists labor under. First, they are forced to recognize that newspapers are read by the family and cannot contain anything offensive. This restricts their use of language and subject matter. Then, whatever would get by the family barrier must pass the economic barrier—nothing in the strip can offend an advertiser. Then there are the individual papers with their sacred cows: political, regional, or whatever (Walt Kelly was forced to do alternate strips for such situations)." Kitchen regards himself primarily as an entertainer who occasionally puts across social and political messages: "Perhaps 'satirist' is the most apt word, if

Justin Green. *Insect Fear* No. 1.

Justin Green. *Yellow Dog Comix No.* 19. ©1971 The Print Mint. By permission of The Print Mint, by Bob Rita.

Opposite, top: Self-impressions by Midwest cartoonists. From left to right: Jay Lynch, Don Glassford (with hand over mouth), Bruce Walthers, Wendel Alan Pugh. Back, left to right: Denis Kitchen, Jim Mitchell, Skip Williamson. Originally published in *Funnyworld* No. 13, Spring 1971. ©1971 J. Michael Barrier. By permission of J. Michael Barrier.

it's not too presumptuous." And he bills *Mom's* as "America's Most Wholesome Underground Comic" for the very specific reason that "I think I gain a wider audience and, in the long run, a more respectful one."

As a matter of fact, Kitchen is unusually audience-oriented for an underground cartoonist. He said, soon after he started drawing *Mom's Homemade Comics,* that he was amazed at the number of people who seemed to be reading his work: "The most fun is getting letters from all over the country. In my first issue I facetiously offered subscriptions at two dollars for four issues. I got a dozen subscribers in Oregon, Illinois, Wisconsin, New Jersey, New Hampshire, and Texas. And many more requested only single copies." In fact, it was the success of his own early work—much of which he now regards as amateurish (though in fact his basic style is unchanged after several years)—which helped make him decide to go into the distribution of underground comics, not merely their creation. Thus he founded Kitchen Sink Enterprises, which eventually became Krupp Comic Works—*the* Midwest source of underground comics, and in some ways the most consistent publisher of high-quality underground work anywhere in the country. Kitchen is the closest thing in this field to a businessman who is also an actual comic-book artist. But he is quick to disown the basic capitalist ethic. He moved out of Milwaukee onto a Wisconsin farm because he started to feel the rats were winning the city rat race, and he gives the impression more of a reluctant entrepreneur than of anyone with a strong drive for financial success. Besides, as he says, he isn't getting rich.

A Few Hows, Whens and Wherefores

Above: Denis Kitchen. Madison-Milwaukee *Bugle-American,* Vol. I, No. 7. ©1970 Krupp Comic Works, Inc. By permission of Krupp Comic Works, Inc., by Denis Kitchen.

Left: Denis Kitchen. *Snarf* No. 3. ©1972 Denis Kitchen. By permission of Denis Kitchen.

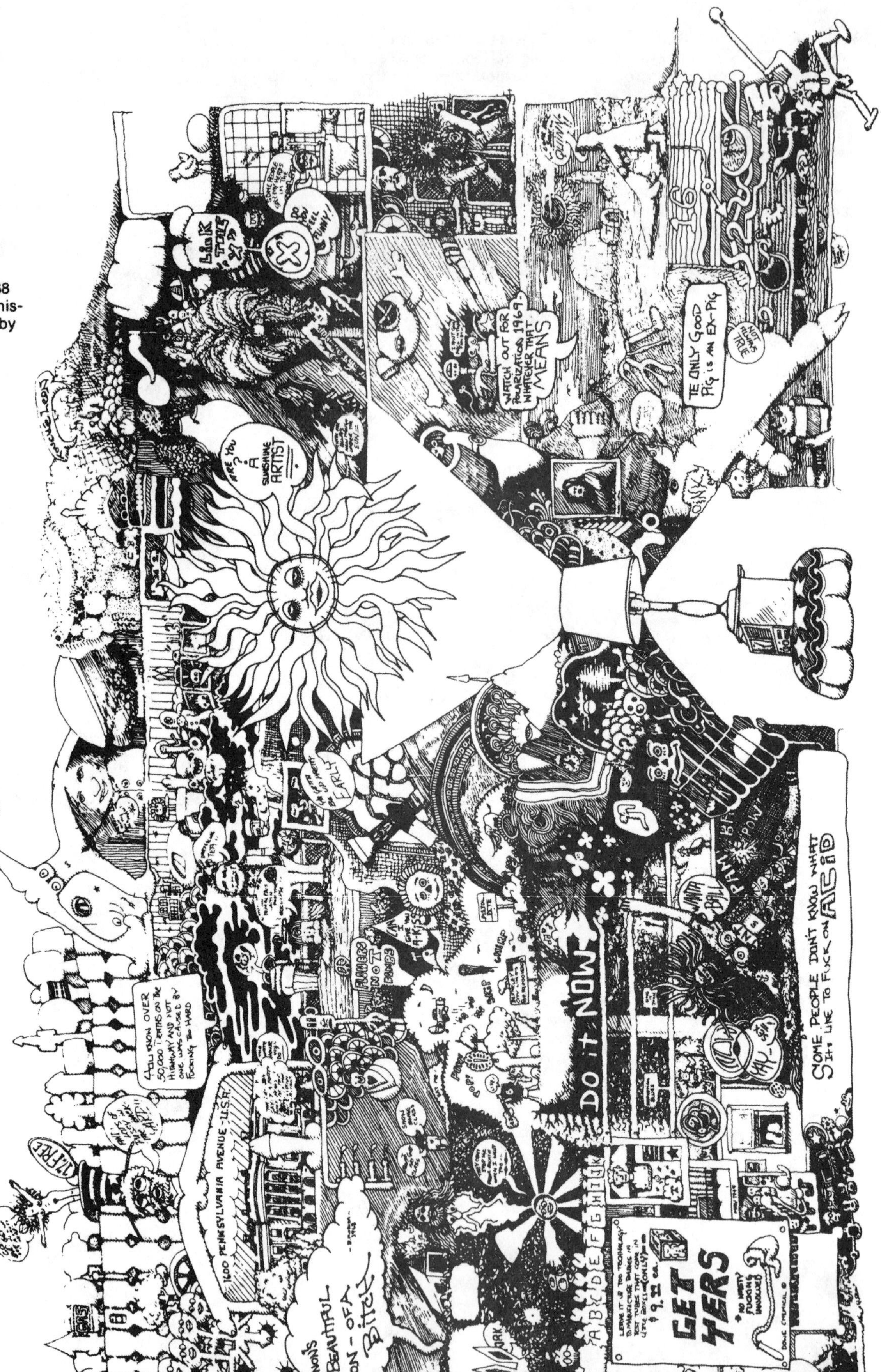

Buckwheat Florida Jr.
Yellow Dog No. 8. ©1968
The Print Mint. By permission of The Print Mint, by
Bob Rita.

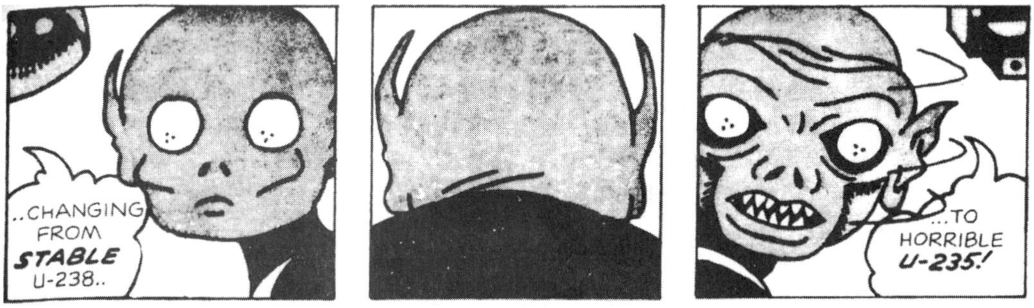

Above and Far Left: Nicola Cuti. *Moonchild Comics* No. 3. ©1970 Nicola Cuti. By permission of Nicola Cuti.

One cartoonist who well understands censorship in the "straight" media is **Nicola Cuti** (pronounced "cutty"). Cuti is on the fringes of the underground, working professionally as a contributing editor to the Warren magazines (*Creepy, Eerie, Vampirella*) and

also putting out his own comic magazine, *Moonchild.* Cuti ("I use the Italian spelling of my name instead of translating it into 'Nicholas'") started doing cartoons while a security policeman in the Air Force ("mostly out of boredom"). He stayed in the field because "my story ideas were much too fantastic for short stories, although for a long time I did try to make it as a short story writer. The primary purpose of my stories is to entertain, but there is no reason why they can't make a point. In fact, I find it almost impossible *not* to make a point." Cuti also traces his influences much further back in time than anyone else in the field: "A person who writes or illustrates comics is not a writer such as Hemingway, or an artist such as Dali. He is a storyteller. A writer is interested in characters and a situation, but a storyteller is interested only in plot. Characters may be strong but they are there *only* to unravel the storyteller's plot. By such a definition you might say that the *Odyssey* was one of the first comic-book stories."

Cuti has created two main characters: Moonchild and Pussywillow. Reflecting his commitment to both "straight" and underground production, Cuti considers Moonchild basically "overground," Pussywillow "underground." Both characters are Starbabies, space-age versions of sprites and pixies, and both are drawn in a childlike, almost child*ish* style reminiscent of the wide-eyed moppet pictures sold in most dime stores.

Some cartoonists never create any characters at all. One such is **Buckwheat Florida Jr.**, who has supported himself by running a record store and playing Gospel and Country and Western music. Like most other underground cartoonists, he never earned enough from his art to live off his own creativity (he took in five to six hundred dollars over two years, he estimates). Florida attended Florida State University, became very involved in student politics, and, in his words, "I soon saw it was a dead end, bum trip. I decided I had something to say that was more sensitive, sensible, sensational, etc." Florida never had art training, but he drew informally from the age of six on ("I spent 1966-67-68 filling up ten composition books with poetry and drawings"). Then, in July 1968, he saw a copy of *Yellow Dog* No. 2, and especially liked the more surrealistic drawings. He submitted some of his own drawings, got some printed, and soon spent over forty hours a week just drawing whatever came into his head. Florida says his work consists purely of "thought patterns," and is more an expression from his own mind than an attempt to communicate specific things to specific people. He does say he "gets a charge out of entertaining people," but that is really not his concern. And Florida has more self-doubts than many underground cartoonists, even to the point of saying, "The first printing of *Suds* sold out, but I'm not sure who bought it.

Below: Wendel Alan Pugh. Madison-Milwaukee *Bugle-American*, Vol. I, No. 9. ©1970 Krupp Comic Works, Inc. By permission of Krupp Comic Works, Inc., by Denis Kitchen.

NOVEMBER 5, 1970

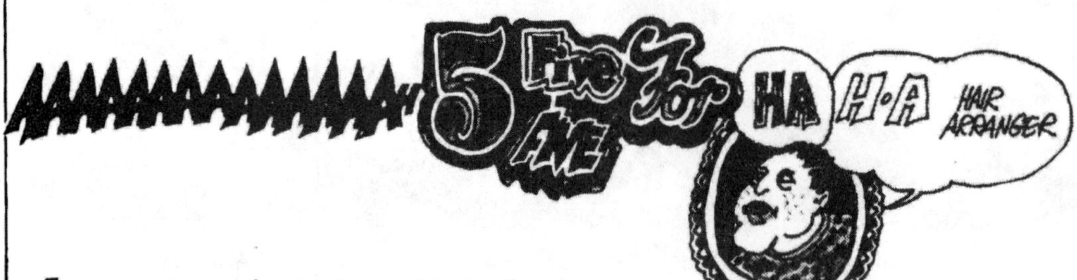

1. I AM 26 YRS. OLD/NO 27 YRS. NOW/ A GRADUATE OF SOUTHERN ILLINOIS UNIVERSITY (M.F.A & B.A) TAUGHT THERE AND THEN WENT TO UNIV. OF WISC. MILW. FOR TWO YEARS OF TEACHING. LOVE IT 'CAUSE ALL I REALLY KNOW ABOUT IS DRAWING. DISGRUNTLED ONLY IN THE SENSE THAT I FEEL THE GALLERY AND MUSEUM ART BEING DONE TODAY IS DECADENT AND MORE TALENT SHOULD BE DIRECTED TOWARD MASS-MEDIA. I.E. T.V. NEWSPAPERS, COMICS, MAGAZINES, RADIO. CAUSE LOTS A KIDS ARE LOOKIN' AND LISTENIN' TO THIS STUFF AND MORE GOOD STUFF OUGHT TO BE DONE FOR 'EM TA LOOK AT ★★★

2. WHEN I WAS A KID I READ MAINLY WHAT FELL INTO MY HANDS. CARL BARKS-DONALD DUCK (WALT DISNEY COMICS & STORIES) UNCLE SCROOGE WERE FAVORITES. MAD MAG. HELP. HUMBUG. WHICH WERE ALL

KURTZMAN GIGS

HE DESERVES CREDIT FOR THE COMIC BOOK REVOLUTION EVERYONE WORKING SEEMS TO HAVE USED HIS INSPIRATIONS AS A JUMPING OFF PLACE ★

I PERSONALLY FEEL HE MORE THAN ANYONE ELSE STARTED THE WHOLE THING!

AL CAPP EARLY CHILDHOOD INFLUENCE WALT KELLY LATER WHEN I FIGURED OUT WHAT HE WAS DOING. MISSED MOST OF ADVENTURE THINGS AND NEVER COULD GET INTO WAR OR HORROR GIGS. WONDER WOMAN BUG HER. READ SOME SUPERMAN. ALSO REALLY LIKED SUPER DUCK — WHO DID THAT STUFF?

3. I THINK KURTZMAN BLEW HIS MIND OUT ON HIS EARLIER PUBLICATIONS AND DESERVES THE REST HE'S TAKING WITH ANNIE FANNIE IT'S OKAY NOTHIN' LIKE OLE' MAD STUFF THO. REALLY WISH SOMEONE WOULD PUT SOMETHING LIKE THAT TOGETHER. **FAT CHANCE**

WALT DISNEY ANIMATION OF COURSE — BLEW MY MIND (THEN) VISUALLY AND (NOW) TECHNICALLY.

DENIS TURNED ME ON TO SOME OTHER PEOPLE WORKING THEN THAT I REMEMBER VISUALLY AND FORGOT NAMES. WILL EISNER — SPIRIT. BASIL WOLVERTON.

4. I CONFESS I NEVER. THREW THAT IN BUT MY $20,000 **FUCK ALL CENSORS** PLUS THE STORY WHICH IS WRITTEN RATHER REPULSIVELY BUT THE FACTS ARE FAIRLY STRAIGHT.

THEY CENSORED IT IN 3 WAYS AND IT COST THEM ALL THAT BREAD BECAUSE THEY DIDN'T CATCH IT UNTIL AFTER IT WAS PRINTED AND DISTRIBUTED FOR SUNDAY DELIVERY. (1) THEY TORE IT OUT (2) BLOCKED OUT FUCKER WITH SOLID ORANGE (3) LEFT IT IN. THE THIRD METHOD WAS THE ONLY ONE I AGREED WITH.

5. GOOGIEWAUMER #1 WAS THE KIND OF COMIC I WOULD LIKE TO DO BUT SALES WERE SHITTY. NO ONE UNDERSTOOD IT. I WOULD LIKE TO DO IT AGAIN. BUT NO ONE WILL PRINT IT. #2 IS WAITING AT THE PRINTER FOR FINANCIAL ASSISTANCE. IT IS MUCH STRAIGHTER AND OBVIOUSLY VERBAL RATHER THAN VISUAL. I'M STILL DOING IT BUT IN A MORE LIMITED SENSE. —▷★

LATER.

. . . I think my audience is people who aren't just limiting themselves to standardized conceptions of entertainment. They are willing to try something that's different—a small minority." And he adds, "I don't always agree with everything I say or do after I've done it."

Florida is one of several cartoonists whose work is often thought to be drug-influenced (see Chapter 8). In Florida's case this is true; but it is less so in the apparently similar work of **Wendel Alan Pugh.** Pugh received B. A. and M. F. A. degrees from Southern Illinois University, then taught there and at the University of Wisconsin at Milwaukee. Pugh has the art training which Florida lacks, but he's not happy about it: "My stuff is all fucked-up because I went to school for six years and got all involved in aesthetics and professionalism (?) which I've decided is all bullshit. Wish I'd never *learned* to draw." Pugh's love of art comes through in everything he does—even his letters. And his style is not as confused as it might first appear: "My style is not incredible; it's regressive. The only real reason I'm doing comix is 'cause some guys did some good things for my eyeballs when I was a kid and I thought I'd like to put my stuff out so someone else could see it. I got fed up with fine art galleries and gallery owners and decided to do the stuff somewhere else. I think comic freaks really

A Few Hows, Whens and Wherefores

Wendel Alan Pugh. *Googie-waumer Comics* No. 1. ©1969 Wendel Alan Pugh. By permission of Wendel Alan Pugh. No, the bottom part of this illustration isn't printed sideways by mistake. This is exactly the way the page originally appeared.

A John Thompson ad for The Print Mint.

Opposite: Actual letter from Wendel Alan Pugh to the author. Original in multiple colors.

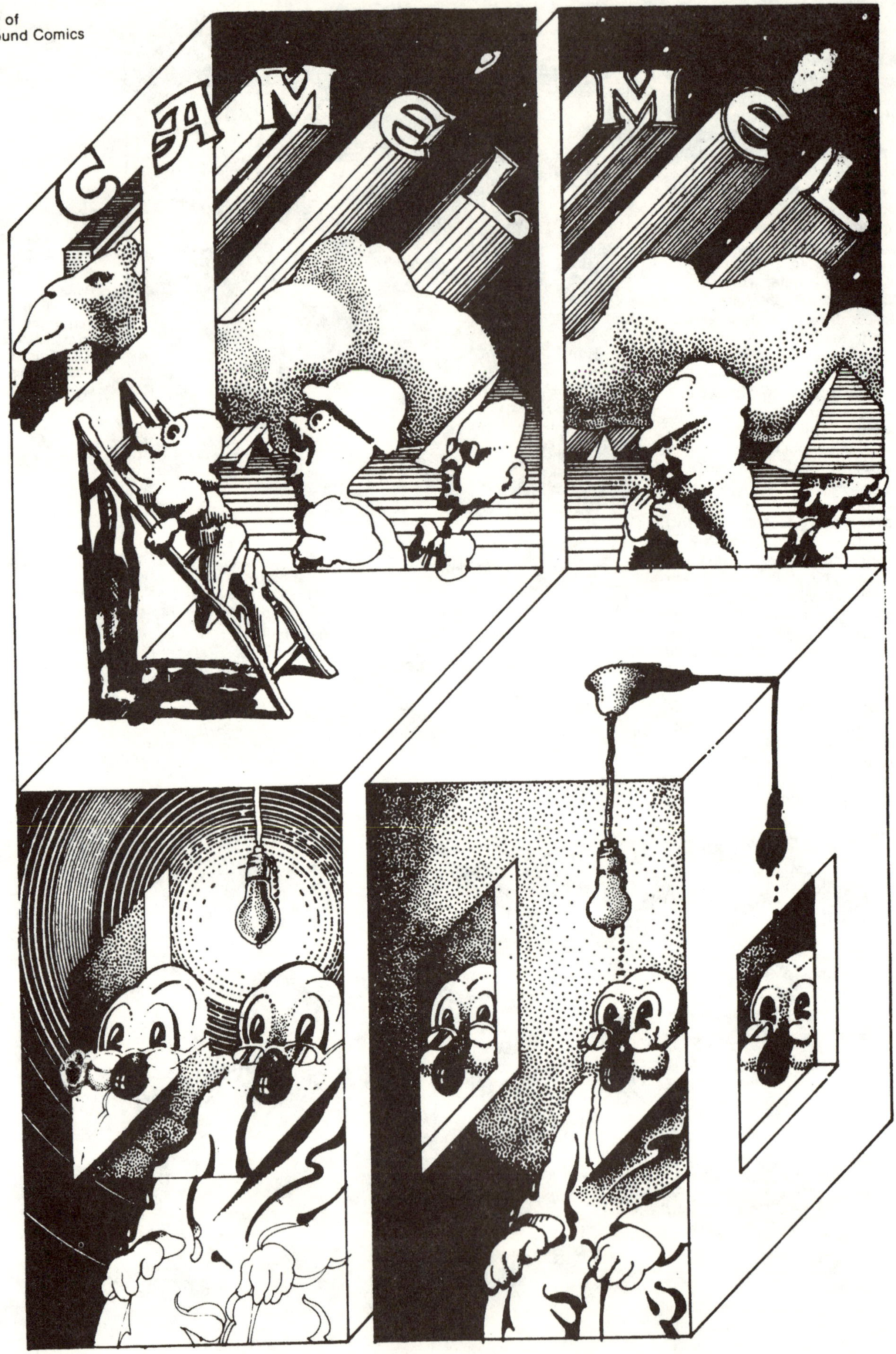
CAMEL
MEL

John Thompson. *Yellow Dog Comix* No. 18. ©1970 The Print Mint. By permission of The Print Mint, by Bob Rita.

dig the drawing more than anything else, and if those people are out there, I'm working for their visionary pleasure." And Pugh is modest about his own place among the underground cartoonists: "Crumb and Wilson seem to be the only two people who still are doing 'their' stuff with any degree of stamina and consistency. As far as I am concerned my stuff will always be second rate to really honest images like those."

Another cartoonist who is generally associated with drug-inspired drawings is **John Thompson,** undoubtedly the most important "mystical" cartoonist (see Chapter 7). Thompson's highly detailed drawings are often accompanied by captions in strange, obscure, or personal languages—his works are ones which you either get into at once, or are unlikely to get into at all. Thompson's early life was not unusual: "My parents are affluent wasp banker types whose ultimate concern is love and the symbologistical barter-flow of goods commodities and services. Born into such I gained the materialistic basis that many people spend lifetimes trying to achieve and experience." Bored with school, he began to play "mind-games," and immediately after leaving high school "began to live a post-beatnik daydream."

Thompson traces his development in language which matches the gentle curves and waves of his drawings: "drowned dead, experienced death state transformation, rebirth, drown in mother ocean in carmel during storm washed ashore deader-than-a-doornail. magic wamo came back to life. felt I had to get shit together know true nature of god truth highest perfect wisdom blah blah blah . . . had been drawing since age two had been writing and drawing since old enough to spell. I remember my first words written and illustrated were 'oh look see' from then on became evenly proportionately loquacious even though am carefree speller am experimenter at sentence structure as u can see. love poetry wrote it since old enough to hold pencil. in elementary school printed illustrated manuscripts in carbon paper editions long alchemal[*sic*] allegories tiny drawings with much secret language."

Thompson worked on high school newspaper experiments, a college literary magazine, and in the underground press. He was involved with the 1964 Free Speech Movement at the University of California at Berkeley. After a hassle with the Army ("i refuse to do my co job refuse to leave country refuse to go to jail work in ghettos with black revolutionaries all along teaching peace love harmony togetherness"), he got married and divorced, became more deeply involved with drugs and underground culture, and in 1967 published "a cyclopic comic" in a limited edition of one thousand. Thompson had close friendships with fellow cartoonists Joel Beck and Robert Crumb, and they influenced his thought, if not his drawing. "Currently i am interested in (jungian terms) the universal archypical [*sic*] symbologistics that attempt to define the processes of consciousness in terms of experiential phenomenological knowing. The Kundalini of Tibetan Tantic [*sic*], the qabbalistic linguistics of ancient hebrew, astrological and alchemal [*sic*] presentations, shamanistic science, einsteinian definitions of field, electromagnetic gravitation flow of Energy."

Although Thompson did not come to comics by drawing posters, several cartoonists whose work physically resembles his did get their start that way. One of the best is **Victor Moscoso,** who has an unusual and interesting feel for space, perspective, and shape. His technique is that of a printed cartoon motion picture, with heavy emphasis on delicate metamorphoses. Moscoso does do an occasional sequential strip, and when he does there is little plot, little action, and little "sense" in the traditional meaning of the word—characters do things and the story progresses, but there is never a real "story line." His work is always purely visual, and often seems like a series of posters reduced to comic-

Opposite: Victor Moscoso. *Zap Comix* No. 3.

book size for no particular reason. And yet the work has unusual power.

Moscoso is heavily influenced by the "traditional" art world, including Dali, Klee, and Magritte—but the influences appear to have been strongly filtered through the world of hallucinogenic drugs.

Another former poster artist is **Rick Griffin.** Like Moscoso's, Griffin's work resembles frames of motion picture films; unlike Moscoso's, much of it has a mystical quality, using some of the letters and languages that John Thompson favors, plus such cryptic comments as "Black is the coloure [*sic*], none is the number." Griffin drew Murf the Surf cartoons years before underground comics emerged. Enthusiasm for his work started in the San Francisco-Berkeley area and quietly spread along the West Coast—and beyond.

Actually, Griffin and Moscoso—whose names are often mentioned together in discussions of

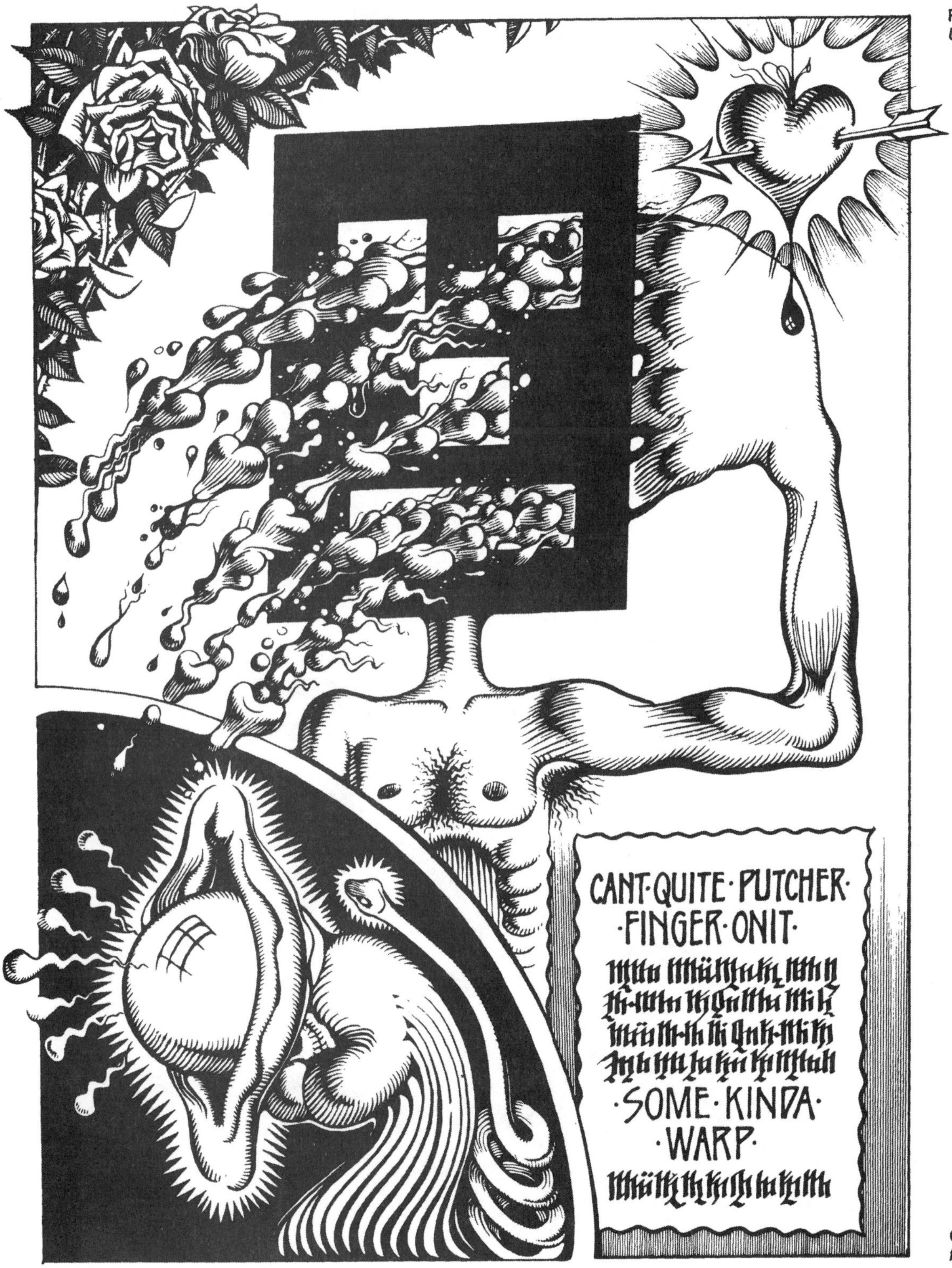

Rick Griffin. *Man from Utopia.*

Opposite: Rick Griffin. *Man from Utopia.*

ROBERT
WILLIAMS

underground comics, because their styles are superficially so similar—provide a fascinating study in the leveling effect of certain drugs on certain artists. Moscoso's influences are clearl the characters of Walt Disney Studios—but his work closely re sembles Griffin's, which comes from a different background. Even the things which differentiate the work of these two artists—Moscoso doesn't use dialogue, while Griffin often does (though admittedly only as parl of the geometry of his panels)–seem hard to pick out sometimes and the work of these two very different people seems much more similar than one would ex pect from their backgrounds.

A third poster artist—one whose West Coast followers verg on fanaticism—is **Robert Williams** whose incredible depths of per ception have led him to devote one comic page to a "model of th universe cutout"—a sort of three dimensional Möbius strip—but whose drawing style is so complex and multifaceted that his work is almost too rich for some people's blood. Williams, who writes letters on stationery bear ing the Nazi eagle and swastika and imprinted "Der Führer," moved to San Francisco from Albuquerque, New Mexico in 1963 and spent some time draw ing for Los Angeles-based moto cycle magazines. Considering the complexity of his comics, Williams' attitude toward art may sound strange: "My greatest success is as a painter. Now, when I say painter, I don't mean pictures of the style that is in vogue today, abstract expressionism! I mean pictures you can fuckin' see, 'visions' crystal clear. Not the foggy, blurred shit that art schools are pumping out." But the return-to-realism feelings Williams holds are strongly tempered by his awareness of the effects of modern technology: "The camera has freed the artist from having to duplicate reality, leaving more important images to pursue, like maybe the universe as a modest start!" Williams tries to combine expression in pictures with this pursuit of "more important things" in comics because "the comics represent the last bastion of art expression employing *pictures*, you know, the things that used to be *art*, remember? Art as we know it is dying fast. Cocktail parties, ass-kissing and mind-masturbating of a handful of wealthy people is the only thing that's held it together. But the comic, that's true art because it's a simple mirror of the times. Underground comic artists stand at the end of a line that goes back all the way to cave painters. Man is a greasy plains ape that has learned organization from killing large ungulates. The only god man will ever know is himself, when he figures out how simple everything really is!"

A fourth poster artist, **Greg Irons**, has made a rather startling metamorphosis. Irons used to produce dance-hall posters, but then moved into the straight

Greg Irons. *Yellow Dog Comix* No. 17.

Opposite: Robert Williams. *Coochy Cooty Men's Comics* No. 1. ©1970 Robert Williams. By permission of Robert Williams.

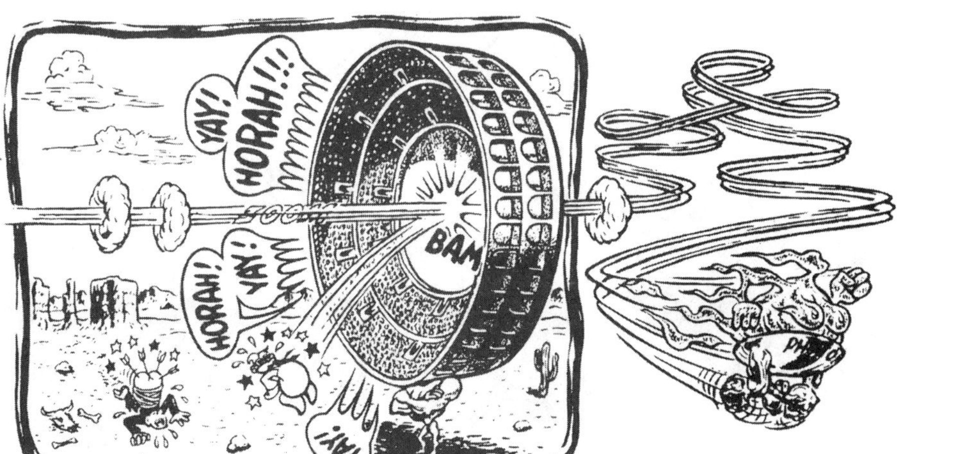

Below: Robert Williams. *Coochy Cooty Men's Comics* No. 1. ©1970 Robert Williams. By permission of Robert Williams.

FOR ALGERNON BACKWASH

comic-book field. He has become extremely concerned with ecology and horror stories (not surprisingly, the two themes can be combined), and has learned to incorporate an extraordinary amount of sentiment and expression into basically horrifying, skull-like faces. Unlike Moscoso and Griffin, Irons has become an artist who is constantly making social and political points.

Another artist who is constantly making points is **Joel Beck.** If Harvey Kurtzman is the granddaddy of all underground comics, then Joel Beck is the father. Beck was already drawing cartoons for the University of California *Pelican* in the days of the Berkeley Free Speech Movement (1964), and his *Lenny of Laredo* was the first comic to be published by Don Schenker at The Print Mint. Beck has an unusually delightful sense of the comic, and his grotesqueries are gentle, if such can be imagined. His style is simple and direct, and he somehow manages to make words like "fart" sound absolutely hilarious. His satire is always double-edged, and is as hard on ridiculous radicals as on cretinous conservatives. His friendship is cited as a major influence by John Thompson and other cartoonists and, like Robert Crumb, he has been victimized by his own skill and has made himself scarce in more recent years. His work now appears only occasionally.

Jay Kinney's satire, like Beck's, is double-edged. Kinney has studied art at Baldwin-Wallace College and Pratt Institute. He did some work for fanzines, but stopped after coming to feel that fanzines were mostly for superhero buffs. Kinney especially likes the chance to communicate ideas through the comics: "One of the nice things about working in the comics medium is that of being

Left: Joel Beck self-portrait, especially drawn for this book.

Opposite: Jay Kinney. *El Perfecto Comics.* ©1973 Jay Kinney. By permission of Jay Kinney.

Below: Joel Beck. *Yellow Dog* No. 1. ©1968 The Print Mint. By permission of The Print Mint, by Bob Rita.

able to shock people into awareness. Most people have become so accustomed to comics as innocuous Dagwood Bumstead forms of pop trash that when confronted with an underground comic they are momentarily flustered. The communication is more direct in comics than in underground papers—a fact with much potential. People will read a comic strip while they will ignore a pamphlet."

Kinney is more concerned than most cartoonists with getting his work through to an audience—though he is often rather cavalier about just who is *in* that audience. Originally, he says, he aimed his material at "fellow radicals, alienated youth, freaks, interested sympathizers, and curious suburbanites." But he admits he doesn't know whether his work "ever particularly reached them or had any effect at all." His notion of his audience later expanded to include "the stray 'straight' or middle-class person who might happen to run across my comics."

Like many of the underground cartoonists when they feel themselves starting to believe their work may actually change people's attitudes toward themselves and toward life, Kinney is quick to point out that he is not looking for a specific audience in order to start preaching. In fact, his audience may be so small as to be virtually nonexistent: "*Anarchy Comics* is a vision into two different worlds, the 'real' world and the world of the mind. The captions are all in Persian and are genuine; thus the comic only makes full sense to Persian students of Baldwin-Wallace College, of which the comic is a satire. Since this is a very limited audience, I just hoped that I might impart an uncomfortable feeling to people reading it. In other words, I was saying, 'English isn't the only language and "reality" isn't the only reality.'"

Generally, the underground cartoonists don't like to be thought of as preaching because they know only too well about the value (or lack of it) of preachers. In fact, there are some cartoonists whose main area of satire is religion. One of these is **Jaxon** (his first name is Jack,

Jay Kinney self-portrait, especially drawn for this book.

Jay Kinney. *Young Lust* No. 1. ©1970 Jay Kinney and Bill Griffith. By permission of Jay Kinney and Bill Griffith.

Above: Jay Kinney. *Conspiracy Capers* No. 1. ©1969 The Conspiracy. By permission of The Conspiracy, by Skip Williamson.

Joel Beck. *Yellow Dog Comix* No. 18. ©1970 The Print Mint. By permission of The Print Mint, by Bob Rita.

but he doesn't use it when cartooning), whose *God Nose* ("God knows," get it?) was the first widely distributed underground comic book. When posters were in vogue, Jaxon was the art director for a magazine called *The Family Dog;* he has also published a portfolio of drawings and paintings. "Comics are only one aspect of art for me. You pick the medium that will best express what you have to say, right? It just happens that comics are one of the best mediums." Jaxon feels his art has grown enormously since 1963, and he now disowns most of his work in *God Nose*—indeed, he feels his cartooning *starts* (his emphasis) with his work for *Skull Comics,* which was first published in 1970. But much of his earlier work is funny, and stylistically more unusual than his later drawings (if much less polished). Jaxon has also produced a very strange book, *Happy Ending Comics,* which consisted mainly of unillustrated or very lightly illustrated short stories—a real extension of the comic-book medium, though Jaxon now says "I tried to stretch the traditional format a little too much. I was satisfied with the book but would not do another one in that manner." (A few other cartoonists have since produced text-only stories, but not as extensively as Jaxon did in *Happy Ending Comics.*)

Another cartoonist who often satirizes religion is **Foolbert Sturgeon,** whose real name is

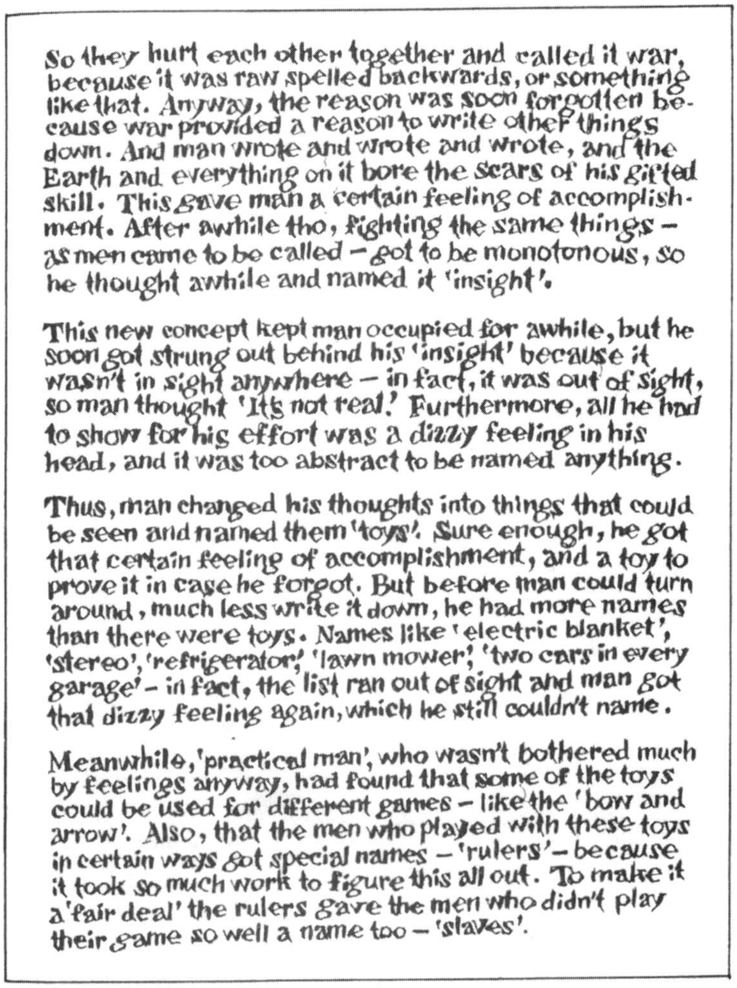

Far Left: Jaxon. *Happy Ending Comics.* ©1969 Jaxon. By permission of Jaxon.

Left: Foolbert Sturgeon. *The New Adventures of Jesus.* ©1969 Foolbert Sturgeon. By permission of Foolbert Sturgeon.

Jaxon. *Skull Comics* No. 1. ©1970 Irons, Sheridan, Jaxon, Schrier, and Hayes. By permission of Messrs. Sheridan, Jaxon and Hayes.

Foolbert Sturgeon. *The New Adventures of Jesus.* ©1969 Foolbert Sturgeon. By permission of Foolbert Sturgeon.

Frank Stack and who comes from Texas (as do Gilbert Shelton and Jaxon). Sturgeon took his art degree from the University of Texas at Austin, where he met Shelton and worked with him on *The Texas Ranger*, a monthly student humor magazine. After a stint in the Army, Sturgeon received a Master's degree and began teaching art—which he still does. He also renewed his brief collegiate acquaintance with Shelton, and they became good friends (Sturgeon even had Shelton sit for a portrait once). Each had the other to talk to, as Sturgeon says: "In college in the late fifties, no one was the vaguest bit interested in comic books and newspaper strips—most of the good ones had died out anyway, and I could hardly even get anyone to talk about it." Sturgeon says his own work—which brings more genuine laughs than almost any other underground cartoonist's—was influenced not only by the old E. C. Comics, but by such strips as "Tarzan," "Prince Valiant," "Alley Oop," "Little Lulu," "Krazy Kat," "Little Nemo," "Gasoline Alley"—mostly adventure and humor strips: "I really wasn't terribly nuts on the horror strips, or the war or romance comics. I liked *Batman, Captain Marvel,* and *Submariner* for a time, but I can't say I liked the superheroes extravagantly. I positively disliked most of the police and criminal comics—it wasn't enough escape to suit me." From those influences, and from a smattering of Jules Feiffer, Sturgeon developed the idea of a Jesus with some very human characteristics to complement his godly ones . . .

Jay Lynch, like Sturgeon, is heavily influenced by the past. His characters, especially Nard 'n' Pat, look very much like something out of a forties comic book—even though the characters often have very contemporary adventures. Lynch has drawn cartoons all his life. While in high school, he contributed to several fanzines (see Chapter 2). A few years later, in 1964, "I was kind of nuts, and fancied myself as a James Bond type of character. I was in New York City on a case—which I incidentally cracked, and it was the high point of my short career as a private eye. That case was involved in a great degree with the origin of Pat the Cat." Lynch soon realized that his amateur private eye days were over, and he started working on Nard 'n' Pat in earnest. The original models for the characters were two of his friends ("a religious nut and what Agnew would call a radical liberal"), and the first Nard 'n' Pat strips were seen in the *Chicago Seed,* a local underground newspaper. As time went on, and Lynch saw less of the people on whom the characters were based, Nard 'n' Pat began to take on new personality characteristics. Lately, says Lynch, "Nard 'n' Pat's antics have come to be based upon the adventures of me and my wife. Sometimes I'm Nard and my wife is Pat, and sometimes it's vice versa."

Lynch also began signing much of his work "Jayzey" rather than "Jay," choosing the nickname because "when I was a lad my fellow children called me Jayzey." This name change came about because, in the illiberal early sixties, "people used to phone me and threaten to kill me, and throw rocks through my windows and stuff. I'm listed in the phone book as Jay Lynch, so I sign my stuff Jayzey because stupid people look in the phone book to find Jayzey Lynch, and they don't make the connection that Jayzey is the same as Jay, so they don't call me and tell me about Jesus and that kind of stuff. I enjoy talkin' to crazy folks once in a while, but they started sendin' me death threats and throwin' rocks at my window when I was publishing the *Chicago Mirror* [see Chapter 2]. Since I've been signin' my stuff Jayzey, I haven't had any trouble from violent religious nuts and right wing fanatics."

It is strange that Lynch should have had so much trouble because of his work. Lynch says, "I just try to print what I like. I never plan out deep social or political messages in my stuff. I just sit down and draw." Quite different is the attitude of **Skip Williamson,** with whom Lynch produced the *Chicago Mirror* and later *Bijou Funnies.* Williamson is one of the most overtly political underground cartoonists, believing that the underground comics should be "both propaganda and entertainment. They're effective—the antithesis of rhetoric." Williamson's work often features well-known political figures, particularly Nixon and Agnew, saying out loud the things which usually lie hidden behind their words. Williamson did some work for fanzines when

Left: Jay Lynch. *Bijou Funnies* No. 1. ©1968 Jay Lynch. By permission of Jay Lynch.

Below: Jay Lynch. *Bijou Funnies* No. 2. ©1969 Jay Lynch. By permission of Jay Lynch.

Left: Jay Lynch. *Bijou Funnies* No. 4. ©1970 Bijou Publishing Empire, Inc. By permission of Bijou Publishing Empire, Inc., by Jay Lynch.

in high school, and was later published by a Chicago humor magazine called *Aardvark*—the art director of which, at that time, was Jay Lynch. Williamson has also worked for a variety of men's magazines: *Playboy*, *Rogue*, *Dude*, and *Cavalier*, to name a few.

Williamson (whose correct first name—let it be said and then forgotten—is Mervyn) believes that the underground comics reflect the personal life styles of the people who draw them. Thus, "I'm into a very heavy political trip, so I draw heavily political cartoons. The comics appeal to base, crude emotions—they're basically anti-intellectual on a good ol' American level. Comics can be subtle and exaggerated at the same time, so they're a valuable propaganda tool. And they're a cinematic concept, which is very effective because of the very heavy visual trip these days."

Skip Williamson. *Bijou Funnies* No. 1. ©1968 Jay Lynch. By permission of Jay Lynch.

Williamson is the best known and most vocal of the highly political underground cartoonists, but he is scarcely the only one. **Bill Crawford** reversed the usual pattern of underground cartoonist migration by working first in California, then moving to Albany, New York. He has developed only one important character, Rufus the Radical Reptile, who goes from an egg to a revolutionary in his first twenty-four panels. Says Crawford, "In summer 1969 a new underground paper in New Haven, Connecticut, *The View from the Bottom*, was about to come out. They needed a cover and maybe some comix for the back page. Got thinking about cover illustration: view from the bottom. Okay, some guy looking up—thru a manhole up at the city—then I remembered the myths (?) I heard as a kid about alligators in New York City sewers, so that guy became an alligator, and I did a story to explain how he got there, and it went on from there." Despite the overtly political theme of the Rufus strips, Crawford says, "I never got around to formulate a philosophy or any coherent analysis of what I am trying to do. I just do it and do it the way I do

Right: Skip Williamson. *Bijou Funnies* No. 4. ©1970 Bijou Publishing Empire, Inc. By permission of Bijou Publishing Empire, Inc., by Jay Lynch.

Below: Bill Crawford. *High-Flyin' Funnies Comix and Stories*. ©1970 Bill Crawford. By permission of Bill Crawford.

because I enjoy it."

The argument that the underground comics express the life styles of their creators is given fuel by the work of **Hak Vogrin.** The sole purpose of Vogrin's work is to fulfill his own being. His simple, gentle drawings of men, women, birds, and moons are an expression of a life style: "My life existence energy moves in certain ways through days-nights years [*sic*] and the drawing is part of it. . . . In my Grammar School Grad Book, under profession I filled in a cartoonist. It hits me right. . . . Generally all the young 'underground' cartoonists have a certain 'zest,' a 'spirit of living' that comes through to me . . . . I am kind of gently and precariously in touch with my comix work and would find it difficult, very, to convert into words, ideas etc. which should go into my lifeday."

Most underground cartoonists, however, react more strongly to social and political issues than does Vogrin. **Ron Cobb,** for exam-

Left: Hak Vogrin. *A Moon Book.* ©1963 Hak Vogrin. By permission of Hak Vogrin.

Below: Ron Cobb. *Raw Sewage.* ©1968 Ron Cobb. By permission of Sawyer Press, by Eric Matlen.

Hak Vogrin. *Yellow Dog Comix* No. 16. ©1969 Hak Vogrin. By permission of Hak Vogrin.

ple, is one of the most consistently acute social critics in the field. John Thompson calls him "a living tradition—for years he has produced underground comics of dynamic quality and quantity." Cobb's greatest concern is ecology; and while he has been called a "political cartoonist," he does not consider himself one: "Even though I may dip into what might be considered a political realm of human activity, I'm much more fascinated with man and his relationship to reality. This relationship intrigues me far more than man and his relationship to man, because that's too subjective. Political cartoonists are all ensnared in a lot of human assumption about what is good and what is bad and I don't like to get into that area."

Cobb is one of the few cartoonists who try to make a living from their art. His work often appears in ecology books, and occasionally finds its way into "straight" literature. He is truly an artist, unable to release a panel for publication until he is completely satisfied that it is as perfect as he can make it. For this reason, Cobb produces much less than many of the other underground cartoonists—but at the same time he is one of the few who demonstrate the real communicative power of the cartoon, and his new work is always worth waiting for.

One aspect of comics rarely dealt with by underground cartoonists is science fiction. The most important science-fiction underground cartoonist is **George Metzger,** who says, "When I was a little kid, a reasonably intelligent, neurotic asshole of a kid, I led a rather introverted life, generally due to overprotective parents, and escaped into reading science fiction, which led to comic strips and comic books. And I was interested in art from a very early age on—that is, I drew a lot." Metzger is always pushing at the bounds of the comic-strip form, and he has a fine sense of wit (not strictly of humor) to go with his deep immersion in the comic-strip field. Thus, when he produced works for *Graphic Story Magazine,* he named one of them "Master Tyme and Möbius Tripp." Metzger's art has a highly visual orientation, as everything in the panels—even the speech balloons, which are often empty—becomes part of the artistic process. This brings Metzger's work into the realm of metamorphosis, the process used in most of the work by poster artists Moscoso and Griffin.

Metzger, however, came to comics in a very different way from that of most poster artists. Born in rural Illinois and raised in northern California, he stud-

Below Right: George Metzger. *Yellow Dog Comix* No. 17.

Below: George Metzger self-portrait, especially drawn for this book.

ied art in high school (where he grew a goatee which he had to shave off for graduation in 1957), and then at a two-year junior college, where "I got good grades for utter shit." After working for two years in forestry, he found himself back in college ("College taught me a lot, tho dunno if it was worth it"). One teacher complained that all his art sketches looked like drawings for comic books ("This I benefitted by").

Metzger also developed an interest in serious graphics, and in the early sixties he discovered fanzines. He did some stories which got published in fanzines, then did a strip for a local underground paper which eventually folded. After a stretch with the National Guard (including two months' punitive duty for trying to avoid the commitment), Metzger began doing more comic-type material. In 1967 (early, as underground comics go), he began work on *Moondog*, which was completed and published in 1969. He also did several strips for *Gothic Blimp Works*, most notably one called "Mal-ig" in which all speech balloons were

George Metzger. *Moondog*. ©1969 George Metzger. By permission of George Metzger.

blank ("It had lotsa symbols for communication"). While poster artist Rick Griffin did influence his style, Metzger says that he was more heavily influenced by E. C. Comics, by woodcut artists like Eichenberg, by the prints of Escher and the paintings of Parrish and Bok, and by a whole list of science-fiction illustrators. Metzger sums himself up as "a general longhaired freak."

Metzger admits that he isn't sure just whom he reaches with his work—or just what effect his work has when it *does* reach someone: "What audience do I aim at? Cannot really answer that. My stuff is highly personalized—you gotta be oddly oriented to get into my shit it would seem—some people can't relate to my work at all. My friends say it's pretty good but I don't really know what it's like on the other side. Am I communicating anything? Can people even follow the damn story? The structure of a strip like 'Mal-ig' is such that people can relate to it in such a way as they interpret their own story—maybe. I don't much know what people think of my stuff."

Many artists give much less complex reasons for drawing than does Metzger. **Bill Griffith** says simply, "I got into comics via the jealousy path, I suppose. I'd been painting and drawing for seven years with little access to any kind of audience. The paintings were becoming closer and closer to comics anyway, so I took the leap and brought some work to various New York tabloids. Such was my humble beginning."

Other artists find in comics an outlet for pent-up emotions. **Dave Sheridan:** "I guess it all started when I was thrown out of a grammar school art class for making my cowboys too small for the tastes of my instructors. I attended the Cleveland Institute of Art for a few years, majoring in graphic design and beer drinking. There I found all the basic elements in the world of 'Art': drawing, painting, the social requirements involved in being a respectable graphic designer, which is another word for a producer of visually decadent material to be used in the Great Consumer Market. The worst, most vile sin being something that

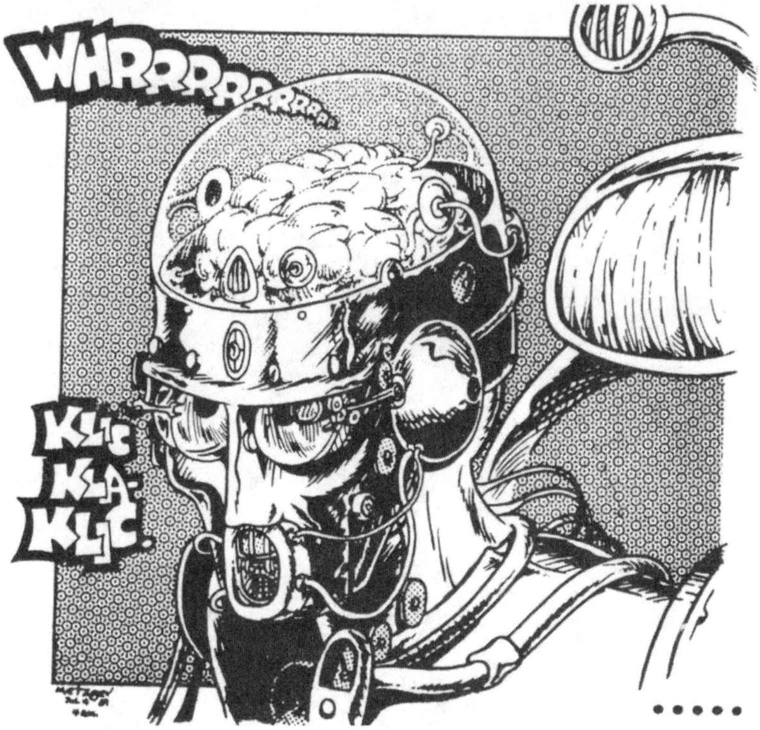

George Metzger. *Got*
Blimp Works No. 7. F
the "Mal-ig" story.

George Metzger. *Yellow Dog Comix* No. 17.

A Few Hows, Whens and Wherefores

would (Goshawful) offend the precious money-holder. I found nothing here but a few frustrated individuals who were content in talking about it but little else.

"After art school came two years in the Army where my talents were confined to painting safety strips on stairways so the fools didn't trip and break their fragile brass necks. It was here in the midst of the military reality that I realized all was not well anywhere, if you know what I mean. Caricatures paraded before me daily and I began to think of ways to get my revenge. Cartoons became an outlet for my anger. Before this period of awakening I had confined them to the margins of my books and the corners of my head. After the eternity of the military I returned to Cleveland to see if the life I left was still operating but was disappointed to find only the grim reality of 1968 waiting about. I spent a year there wondering if I were going to wake up some morning turned to stone when **Fred Schrier** (I met him at school a few years before—he was studying industrial design and

Bill Griffith. *Illuminations.*

Dave Sheridan. *Skull Comics* No. 1. ©1970 Irons, Sheridan, Jaxon, Schrier, and Hayes. By permission of Messrs. Sheridan, Jaxon, and Hayes.

Dave Sheridan. *Mother's Oats Comix* No. 1. ©1969 Sheridan and Schrier. By permission of Dave Sheridan.

Kim Deitch. *Bijou Funnies* No. 4. ©1970 Bijou Publishing Empire, Inc. By permission of Bijou Publishing Empire Inc., by Jay Lynch.

had been working in Detroit) came to Cleveland and we decided that the only thing to do was to do Something! Six months later we came up with *Mother's Oats Comix,* hoping that this would be the beginning of something a little more constructive than alcoholic political discussions and radical speculation."

Of course, what you find constructive depends on your own outlook: sometimes the mere expression of artistic interest is constructive enough. That's the case with **R. Scott Pflug,** who makes his living "partly by commercial arting, but mainly by driving Lulubelle, my 1948 Ford truck"—and who, without aiming at specific messages in his work, says he's drawn all his life but "didn't get into serious cartooning till I saw *Zap* No. 1 and got inspired." Pflug drew his first strip while working as a mailman, and he freely admits that his style isn't what it could be if he were more strongly influenced by other cartoonists: "Had a passing acquaintance with Wilson and Crumb, Spain and other cartoonists, which unfortunately, while enriching my life in general, did nothing to improve my drawing."

Though some underground cartoonists have been interested in comics for twenty years or more, others only became aware of the medium a few years before they entered it. One such latecomer is **Kim Deitch.** "The first comic stuff to turn my head was late in '65 when *Redbook* magazine reprinted two 'Little Nemo in Slumberland' pages . . . At this point I could do little else but admire, for though I had a pretty good sense of color and design, I didn't know Jack shit about drawing." At this time, Deitch was a semi-professional, semi-abstract painter "of big acrylic things"; after seeing the "Little Nemo" pages, he found his own stuff "began to become more figurative and comic-strip oriented." His brother Simon, also a cartoonist, turned him on first to Marvel Comics, and eventually to "the whole spectrum of comic-book history." Soon afterward, Deitch created a cat named Waldo, "but only for my own amusement and with no thought of publishing." Eventually, though, Waldo appeared in the *East Village Other* and, later, in *Gothic Blimp Works*, under Deitch's editorship.

Deitch failed to make money on

Below: Kim Deitch. *Bijou Funnies* No. 2. ©1969 Jay Lynch. By permission of Jay Lynch.

R. Scott Pflug. *Funnybook* No. 1. ©1971 The Almighty Publishing Co. By permission of The Almighty Publishing Co., by R. Scott Pflug.

the comics. He eventually wound up working for the Post Office, "and found peace on the side through Hatha Yoga." Once he had saved some money, Deitch planned to quit his job—but then *EVO* made him a cash offer to draw comics again, and he agreed. Then events caught up with New York's East Village, says Deitch: "By this time (Spring '68) the Lower East Side was a much different place. I soon quit Yoga, got mugged, and started packing a loaded gun to make sure it didn't happen again." Deitch eventually left New York City for San Francisco, where he still lives. His creation of happier Village days, Sunshine Girl, reappeared in somewhat more cynical form after his bad experiences in 1968. Through everything, though, Deitch's attitude toward his work has remained simple: "What I'm basically trying to do is tell good stories, and when I'm working, I give virtually everything I've got to that cause. I subscribe to the hard bop school of comicking. My stuff may look crude, but it used to look cruder."

Kim Deitch. *Insect Fear* No. 2.

Opposite: Trina. *Wimme Comix* No. 3. ©1973 Trina. By permission of Trina.

Rosie the Riveter
in RIP VAN ROSIE
ROSIE THE RIVETER WORKS AT THE PLANT IN 1943...
I'M HELPING TO WIN THE WAR ON THE HOME FRONT!
ONE DAY AS SHE TAKES HER LUNCH BREAK A SABOTEUR SLIPS A MICKEY INTO HER COKE...
AH, THE PAUSE THAT REFRESHES!
By Trina
ROSIE FALLS ASLEEP FOR 30 YEARS...
1943
1953
1963
1973
YAWN
?! JEEPERS! WHAT HAPPENED TO THE PLANT?!?
OUTSIDE...
THERE'S SOME WAR WORKERS NOW... I'LL ASK THEM!
HI! WHERE'D THE FACTORY MOVE TO?
KEEP OUT
YOU KIDDIN'? THAT FACTORY'S BEEN CLOSED FOR 25 YEARS!
1973...
YIKES! WHAT YEAR IS THIS?
JEEPERS! WHAT A CATNAP! THAT'S FUNNY, THE STYLES DON'T SEEM TO HAVE CHANGED MUCH...

Trina. *It Ain't Me Babe Comix.* ©1970 Trina, Lisa Lyons, Carole, Michele, Willy Mendes, Meredith Kurtzman, Hurricane Nancy. By permission of Mss. Trina, Willy Mendes, and Meredith Kurtzman.

For a while after moving to San Francisco, Deitch lived with another cartoonist, **Trina** (full name: Trina Robbins), one of the few women deeply involved in underground comics. Trina edited *It Aint Me Babe Comix*, the first all-girl comic and an important advance against sexism among the underground cartoonists (see Chapter 5).

Before that, Trina had been interested in science fiction, especially sci-fi fanzines. But her roots as a cartoonist go back still further: "I've always been drawing. As a kid I really dug the superheroines: Wonder Woman, Mary Marvel, especially Sheena and the Jungle comics. In about '64 I got turned on to comics once more, in the form of Marvel Comics. Being also very into Beardsley (I discovered him in 1957), I started drawing very decorative abstract art-nouveau comics. My work has slowly gotten less and less abstract as I've gotten more into it." When Kim and Trina had a daughter on June 2, 1970, they announced the event with a joint comic panel, which was published as a poster and also appeared in underground newspapers around the country. And other cartoonists wrote in "congratulations" in some of their own strips!

There are many, many other underground cartoonists contributing panels and strips to the field.

There is **Rory Hayes**, counterman at one major comics distribution center, the San Francisco Comic Book Company. Hayes has appeared in a wide variety of books, including Crumb's sex comics and *Bogeyman Comics*, among others. In fact, Hayes was the sole artist in the first issue of *Bogeyman*, which was begun by the head of the San Francisco Comic Book Company, Gary Arlington, as an overt imitation of the old E.C. horror comics. Hayes' work shows little of the polish of the best underground cartoonists, but he has a special following of his own (mainly on the West Coast) and is well thought of by some *because* of the simplicity, even crudeness, of his style.

There is **Vaughn Bodé** (pronounced Boh-dee), who works

Trina. *Gothic Blimp Works* No. 7.

A Few Hows, Whens and Wherefores

Rory Hayes. *Insect Fear* No. 2.

Kim Deitch and Trina announce the birth of Casey. Published as a poster and in many underground newspapers.

Rory Hayes. *Skull Comics* No. 1. ©1970 Irons, Sheridan, Jaxon, Schrier, and Hayes. By permission of Messrs. Sheridan, Jaxon, and Hayes.

on as many as sixty strips at a time. Bodé, a Syracuse University dropout, has illustrated children's books and done advertising art for Douglas Records. His work is text-heavy, but the art is original and some of his concepts are striking: one weapon in his strips has developed the disease of empathy. When used, it cries. Bodé, whose work has frequently appeared in certain "straight" media, was called "the apotheosis of industry and commitment in the comix field" by Bob Abel, in an article in *Cavalier* magazine. But according to Harvey Kurtzman, Bodé used to be one of the better underground cartoonists but "isn't really with it anymore." And some of Bodé's fellow underground cartoonists really get livid when his name is brought up. Bill Griffith says, "I bristle at the very mention of the terrible Vaughn Bodé [*author's note:* writing his name in tiny, tiny little letters]. I hate 'im!! It's not merely his dialogue, or lack of it, that ruins him, it's his humorlessness and the absence of 'human qualities.'"

There is **Art Spiegelman,** described by Justin Green as "a very productive guy," who has taught courses at Harpur College and the San Francisco Academy of Art; who has been published in Harvey Kurtzman's *Help!*, in *Cavalier* magazine, and elsewhere in the "straight" world; and who has an unusual way of balancing the comic with the grotesque.

There is **Meredith Kurtzman,** daughter of Harvey Kurtzman and thus a living link of the underground comics with the old E. C. line. Though she has done very little work on her own, she is an acute observer of the way underground comics reflect life (and a too-modest commentator on her own ability): "Everything in New York City is a Crumb comic, and he has already captured the things and people I see so well that I don't think I should bother and maybe I ain't capable. . . . I've kind of become a living cartoon character in the New York comic." Influenced simply by being around

Vaughn Bodé. *Gothic Blimp Works* No. 6.

comics all her life, Meredith drew *King Comics* at the age of eleven and then, several years later, was inspired by *Zap, Bijou,* and other underground comics to do more comic work: "I guess *Zap* affected me more than any other comic although I've been reading comics since I was very little."

There is **The Mad Peck,** a scholar of comic pornography and perpetrator of *Ghost Mother Comics, Extra! Commix,* and *The Mad Peck Catalogue of Good Stuff.*

There is **Willy Mendes,** another of the small number of women cartoonists and an especially forthright spokeswoman for the Women's Liberation movement (see Chapter 5). She is equally involved in comics and in rock music, and is married to rock musician Rick Rollings (whose real name is Kunstler: he is first cousin to radical lawyer William Kunstler). Willy Mendes is equally angry at sexism in both fields: "I could deliver torrents of hatred on the subject of sexism in rock music—I'd like to see all groupies exterminated en masse." She of-

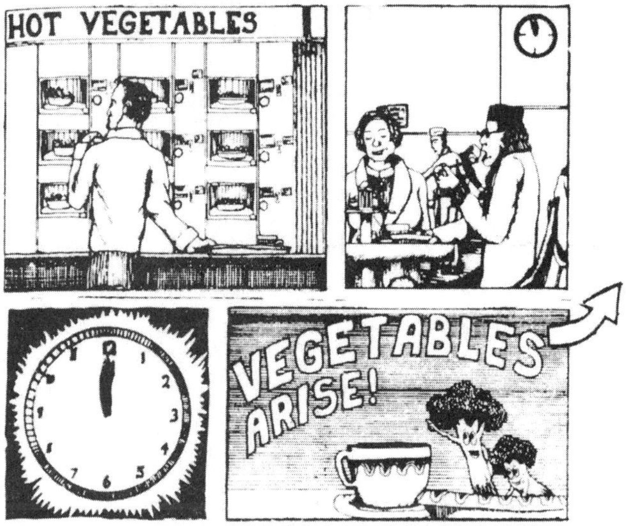

Far Left: Meredith Kurtzman. *It Ain't Me Babe Comix.* ©1970 Trina, Lisa Lyons, Carole, Michele, Willy Mendes, Meredith Kurtzman, Hurricane Nancy. By permission of Mss. Trina, Willy Mendes, and Meredith Kurtzman.

Left: The Mad Peck. *Ghost Mother Comics* No. 1.

Art Spiegelman. *Real Pulp Comics* No. 1. ©1971 Joel Beck, Roger Brand, Leslie Cabarga, Kim Deitch, Justin Green, Bill Griffith, Art Spiegelman, and Ron White. By permission of Messrs. Beck, Deitch, Green, Griffith, and Spiegelman.

ten combines comics and music by drawing comic-like posters advertising rock concerts.

There is **Spain** (real name: Manuel Rodriguez), creator of "Trashman, Agent of the Sixth International"—the most overtly revolutionary character in underground comics. Spain was once a motorcycle gang member and was never a hippie, which may account for the casual brutality of his strips. Spain has also developed a sort of underground answer to "Bullitt" in the person of Manning, a cop who hides behind his badge while using the law as an excuse for murder and sadism.

There is **Larry Welz,** creator of characters such as Garbageman and Captain Guts (a hippie-hating superhero who gets his

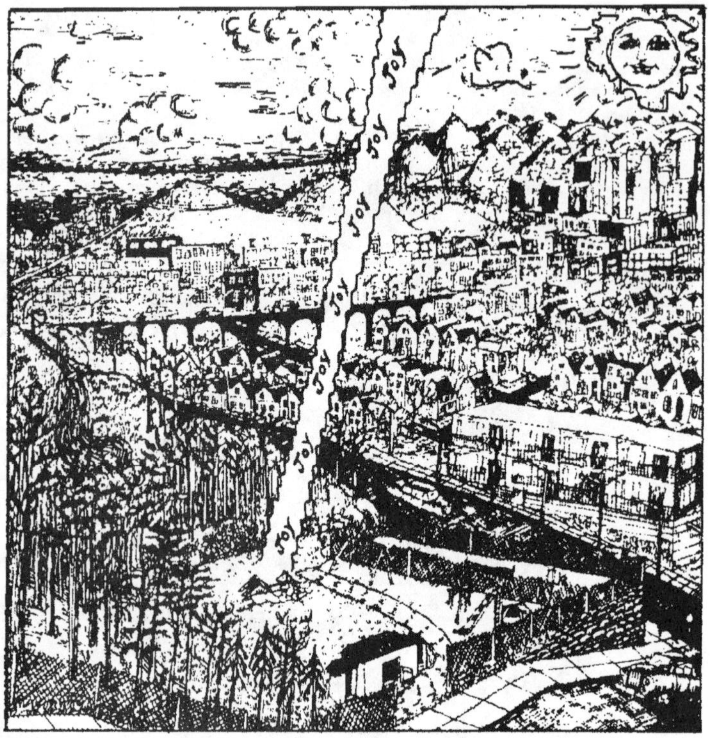

Far Right: Willy Mendes. *All Girl Thrills.*

Below Right: Larry Welz. *Yellow Dog Comix* No. 17.

Below: Spain. *Thrilling Murder Comics.* ©1971 B. Griffith, K. Deitch, S. Deitch, R. Crumb, Spain, Wilson, J. Osborne, Irons. By permission of Messrs. Griffith, K. Deitch, Crumb, and Spain.

A Few Hows, Whens and Wherefores

Andy Martin. *Yellow Dog Comix* No. 13-14. ©1969 The Print Mint. By permission of The Print Mint, by Bob Rita.

powers from beer).

There is **Ronald Lipking,** who uses a crude but original drawing style with some very odd characters: balls, eggs, and a pair of flying eyes.

There is **Andy Martin,** who developed the "Hop-Frogian Bible" for *Yellow Dog* and, in that strip, greatly extended the comic medium by having the character of the drawing reflect the character of that part of the story. Paul Buhle compares his style to that of George Grosz.

There is **Jim Osborne,** contributor to Crumb's sex comics and to a variety of horror books, whose characters are grotesque in every sense: they are so warped that it is horrifying to realize they have been drawn, much less to see them progress through stories. One of his milder characters is The Geek—a circus freak who tears the heads off live chickens and devours the birds raw, for the entertainment of a leering crowd.

Right: Ronald Lipking. *Yellow Dog Comix* No. 16.

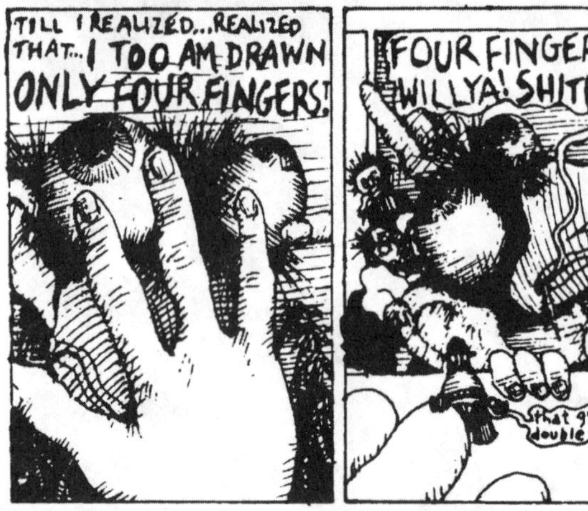

Far Right: Andy Martin. *Yellow Dog* No. 8. ©1968 The Print Mint. By permission of The Print Mint, by Bob Rita.

Jim Osborne. *Insect Fear* No. 2.

Next Page: From *Mom's Homemade Comics* No. 3. ©1971 Denis Kitchen. By permission of Denis Kitchen. *For a key to the answers, see page 104.*

IT'S FUN!

THE WHOLE FAMILY CAN PLAY!!

Just match the clean-cut All-American boy above with the sleazy underground artist below.

DON GLASSFORD

WENDEL PUGH

JAY LYNCH

JIM MITCHELL

BRUCE WALTHERS

DENIS KITCHEN

SKIP WILLIAMSON

ROBERT CRUMB

1

2

3

4

5

6

7

8

Answers on following page

Answers to photo-match on previous page: No. 1: Walthers; No. 2: Lynch; No. 3: Crumb; No. 4: Kitchen; No. 5: Mitchell; No. 6: Williamson; No. 7: Glassford; No. 8: Pugh.

Photographs by Clay Geerdes of (right) Gilbert Shelton; (far right) Spain. *Berkeley Comix Convention Programme.* ©1973 Clay Geerdes. By permission of Clay Geerdes.

These pages should by now have provided some idea of how wide, varied, personal, and intriguing the field of underground comics can be. It is worth pointing out that there are some cartoonists who do *not* exist, even though they sign drawings. A few underground cartoonists have developed aliases, for use when the mood strikes them. Thus, S. Clay Wilson is also Howard Arnherst, Crank Collingwood, and the Marquis von Crank. Wilson even signed one of his drawings "You Know" (his style is so distinctive that you did). Wilson occasionally predates his drawings by a hundred years, so you've found no rarity if you discover a Crank Collingwood masterpiece dated 1868.

Rory Hayes calls himself Hate and Hint; Jim Osborne uses the names Ozburn and Jackinov. But the grand master of names is undoubtedly Robert Crumb, who sometimes draws under these aliases: Cum, Crumbum, Crud, Krumb, Crustt, Grunge, Scum, Scrum, Crumbski, El Crummo, Crumarums, Krumwitz, Crum the Bum, Grubb, Crunk, Bob Scumb, and Little Bobby Scumbag. Crumb even drew one strip under the name "Steve Ditcum," a takeoff on the name of professional cartoonist Steve Ditko.

Let's close this chapter with a few comments by the artists on their fellow cartoonists. As might be expected, the underground cartoonists develop their own likes and dislikes among their compatriots' work, and their opinions show something about their own interests as well. Buckwheat Florida Jr., for example, says, "I think Crumb, Wilson, and Shelton are incredibly hilarious at times—they are really humorists. Ron Cobb is the best political satirist in America. John Thompson's strictly on his own trip." In Denis Kitchen's opinion, "Some of the underground comic books fail to communicate because the language is unintelligible (Florida's *Suds,* Thompson's *The Kingdom of Heaven Is Within You*). Others fail because of mediocre artwork (*Bogeyman,* for instance, and some of S. Clay Wilson's stuff). Robert Crumb, of the underground cartoonists, is most successful. Skip Williamson is also very good." For his part, John Thompson says, "Most hippies do not consider Denis Kitchen avant-garde, inventive, imaginative or of any quality. He, like Buckwheat Florida Jr., whom I have met, may be extremely nice people, but as artists they do not seem to have any following among the mass of connoisseur hippies who have been on the scene for years."

So there is a certain amount of dissension in the ranks—an important point, because all too

Below: Denis Kitchen self-portrait, especially drawn for this book. Right: Photograph by Dave Schreiner of (front) Robert Crumb and (back) Denis Kitchen. Far Right: Photograph by Clay Geerdes of (left to right) Jay Kinney, Roger Brand, and Bill Griffith. *Berkeley Comix Convention Programme.* ©1973 Clay Geerdes. By permission of Clay Geerdes.

Photograph by Bob Siederman of (left to right): Kelly, Moscoso, Griffin, Wes Wilson and Mouse, the original San Francisco poster artists. ©1971 Bob Siederman. By permission of Bob Siederman.

often the mass media portray underground culture as a vast morass of sameness and pounce on all differences of opinion as evidence that the Movement (whatever that may be) is crumbling. But the underground comics, if they represent some sort of "movement," are alive and well precisely because they remain experimental and self-critical.

Overviews of the field are almost impossible to come by. Harvey Kurtzman will only say of the cartoonists, "They're very talented—they're not God, but they're talented, and they have important insights." Mike Barrier, writing in *Funnyworld* No. 12, is willing to make more specific comments: "Crumb and Shelton are great storytellers. They work with the medium, not against it. After all, this is what a comic strip is—a narrative medium, a means of telling a story in a progression from panel to panel, through a combination of dialogue and drawings. You can embroider on that, but you can't get away from it . . . George Metzger . . . is not a synthesizer like Crumb and Shelton; he's always poking at and stretching the limitations that are built into the comic strip . . . [but] he doesn't—can't—disguise his experiments well enough. Although Metzger's story-telling *techniques* are more complex than those of Crumb and Shelton, their *stories* are more complex than Metzger's, because their mastery of their tools is more nearly complete . . . [In Spain Rodriguez' work] the brutality is heightened by his extremely crude and stiff drawing style. Like S. Clay Wilson, Rodriguez uses his crudity; he isn't restricted by it. But like Wilson's world, Rodriguez' is narrow and depressing, consisting of nothing but force, applied in various ways but always without pity."

Photographs by Clay Geerdes of (left) Dave Sheridan and (below) Simon (on left) and his brother Kim Deitch. 1973 Berkeley Comix Convention program. ©1973 Clay Geerdes. By permission of Clay Geerdes.

Far Left: Photograph from *It Ain't Me Babe Comix* of (sitting, left to right) Trina, Lisa Lyons, and (standing, left to right) Carole, Peggy, Michele, Willy Mendes.

Take any of these comments you like, for as much as you wish to take them. Beware of only one thing. Because the underground cartoonists draw without restrictions, some people assume that their drawings necessarily reflect their own personalities. *The Phantom Psychiatrist* cautions against such generalizations: "All you know is the product. From the product I feel it is unfair to try to make up a life history or a character history of the individual. I think it's fair

Below: Photograph of Hurricane Nancy. ©1970 Trina, Lisa Lyons, Michele, Willy Mendes, Meredith Kurtzman, Hurricane Nancy. By permission of Mss. Trina, Willy Mendes, and Meredith Kurtzman.

enough to say that what they draw must draw on their own personalities in some way. But something like this possibly—possibly—could be drawn by a guy with six kids and a dog and a house in the country, drawing on something inside of himself where the externals are all straight. Or these things could be drawn by somebody where the guy is strange as all hell outside and is *still* drawing on something inside. In order to do this, you've got to be drawing on something inside your guts. But whether the rest of you is like that—you can't make any inferences about the rest of the person."

A final note: most of the underground cartoonists are in their late twenties or early thirties. The range of ages extends, more or less, from Rory Hayes at the younger end to John Adkins Richardson and Hak Vogrin (who finds it humorous to consider himself "the word's oldest underground cartoonist") at the older end. So the underground comics, contrary to what might be expected, are *not* the product of a single age group—nor even, as we shall now proceed to see, of a single set of interests and concerns.

Guy Colwell. *The Inner City Romance Comic:* "Choices." ©1972 Guy Colwell. By permission of Guy Colwell.

Addenda:

Guy Colwell, one cartoonist whose work draws on reality rather than fantasy, writes that his comics "are semi-autobiographical. I was in prison for refusing to be drafted and my experiences during the years that followed my release are incorporated into *Inner City Romances #1.* My surrounding, the neighborhood of my small one-room ghetto studio, was populated by junkies, dealers, politicos, prostitutes, and ex-convicts. It was in fact a close friend who I had met in prison who suggested and urged that I do a comic book."

It's hard to tell just what sort of reality will make a person determined to draw underground comics. **Rand Holmes** became more rather than less intrigued by the field as a result of opposition to his interest: "I sketched in my notebooks at school while the others took notes—I got detentions—I got the strap—'get an

Below: Ed Badajos. *Filipino Food.* ©1972 David Dawdy. By permission of David Dawdy.

Far Left and Left: Rand Holmes. *Harold Hedd* No. 2. ©1973 Rand Holmes. By permission of Rand Holmes.

"education" first! then learn how to draw if you wish,' they said, reinforcing the message with a variety of punishments (God knows how many young minds irreparably mutilated by these misguided sadists with the unmitigated gall to refer to themselves as *teachers*!) . . . as for myself I persevered. I spent 13 years in school and managed not to learn anything except how to draw."

Holmes, whose style is so versatile that he had no trouble imitating the approach of a variety of other cartoonists when he drew the cover for this very book, tried to go the standard middle-class route, getting married and taking a job as a sign painter after school. Five years later, he was turned on to drugs and off to middle-class values: "In 1968 my brother turned me on to psychedelics—I woke up—left wife and job and split for the west coast, grew my hair down to my ass, moved into a communal house and vowed to never again do anything I didn't want to do, especially for money—after I made that simple decision I was suddenly free." Holmes' work appeared in underground papers such as *Georgia Straight* and the *Berkeley Barb* before being collected in comic-book form.

Despite Holmes' comments, not every underground cartoonist finds middle-class values and underground comics incompatible. **John Adkins Richardson,** a full professor ("of what full we shall not concern ourselves") of art and design at Southern Illinois University, says that he suspects he is "the most repulsively 'respectable' character associated with underground comix." Published in such scholarly magazines as *The Art Journal* and *The British Journal of Aesthetics,* author of a book called *Modern Art and Scientific Thought* and co-author of one

Left and Below: John Adkins Richardson. *Fever Dreams* No. 1. ©1972 Richard Corben, John Richardson, and Jan Strnad. By permission of Richard Corben and John Adkins Richardson.

called *Art: The Way It Is,* Richardson paints and does copperplate engraving as well as underground comics. He has done commercial and technical illustration, is in the midst of his second marriage, and says, "I consider myself very conventional and 'straight' but my students seem to think I'm odd in some way. . . . The Class President said that I was the only 'Radical middle-of-the-roader' anyone had ever heard. Strange. Anyhow, I guess I'm weird to them because of my somewhat Faustian past: a little dope when I was their ages and living with a black entertainer in the early '50's, for instance. (Don't much care for the effects; highs without hangovers are for sissies. American youth is soft!)"

Richardson is particularly interested in "the class-crossing popularity of 'funnies.' Westerns, tors, etc."—a sort of popularity which, he says, "suggests a far greater cohesiveness of the different 'levels' of culture than we normally presume."

The underground comics, in case you haven't yet realized it, have room in them for people having the widest possible variety of interests, backgrounds, turn, is one reason for their appeal to so many different kinds of people.

Richard Corben. *Up from the Deep* No. 1. ©1971 Jaxon, Corben, Deitch, and Irons. By permission of Messrs. Jaxon, Corben, and Deitch.

Guy Colwell. *Inner City Romance Comix* No. 2: "Radical Rock." ©1972 Guy Colwell. By permission of Guy Colwell.

Below: Richard Corben. *Slow Death Funnies* No. 2. ©1970 Jaxon, Sheridan, Osborne, and Gore. By permission of Messrs. Jaxon, Sheridan, and Gore.

Content: An Overview

4

Some of the most basic things that make underground comics "underground" are the great differences between the contents of these books and the contents of what are generally called "comics." Francis E. Barcus's study, "The World of Sunday Comics," took an overview of the "straight" comic field and discovered that the most important topics in that world were domestic relations, crime, nature and animals, the armed forces and war, love and romance, business and industry, and government and public affairs (in that order). The least important topics, almost completely absent in "straight" strips, were religion, literature and the fine arts, science and scientists, education and schools, race and nationality, historical events, the supernatural, and the entertainment world.

It would be nice to say that simply inverting this list gives a good picture of the contents of the underground comics, but the statement would unfortunately be inaccurate. It is true, however, that the underground cartoonists are almost never concerned with any of the most important topics of the "straight" strips, and that several of the "straight" strips' smallest concerns—religion, race relations, education, and the supernatural—are part of the underground cartoonists' stock in trade. In addition to these, the underground cartoonists are most interested in sex (all sorts), violence and horror, and social and political satire (including commentary on a variety of uniquely American diseases: Madison Avenue, televisionitis, etc.). The underground comics also contain healthy doses of chauvinism (mostly male) and attacks thereon, mysticism, drug consciousness, and other aspects of life which most "straight" comics are content to deal with peripherally and superficially, if at all.

As Bill Pearson, co-editor of *witzend* magazine, points out, part of the underground comics' charm is their extreme and unpredictable variety: "The fun thing about underground comics is that all manner of rascals—painters, designers, philosophers—are attracted to the medium because it is one of the very few (and probably the only *cheap*) communication form that can be created totally by one person, without mutilation of the result by editors, distributors, or *modifiers* of any sort before it reaches the audience for which it was intended. They don't always succeed—many are naively self-indulgent—but even these have the impetus and the vigor of originality."

Underground comics are not produced after lengthy story conferences and editorial meetings—in fact, this is one important area where they part company with their major historical predecessors. According to Jaxon: "I'm under the impression that E. C. Comics had meetings, or the artists were given scripts and a rough layout, etc.—in short, that the product was planned and/or dictated much more than ours is." And Jaxon goes on to emphasize that any "meeting of the minds" in underground comics occurs because people operate on the same wavelength, not because they have to do things in a certain format or a specified style: "I recognize the fact that there *are* better ways to get a particular idea across than the first one that pops into one's head. This internal 'censorship' is the only form of control that an artist should tolerate on his work. Strangely enough, I've found that a book put together by, say, four or five artists, need not go thru editorial sessions that hammer out 'directions,' plot lines, etc. Usually all that has to happen is to suggest the theme, i.e. horror comics, and wait for everybody to finish their strips."

There is room in the underground comics for all sorts of subjects, drawn for all sorts of reasons. Wendel Alan Pugh finds the medium an excuse for fantasizing: "When bombs go off and people get shot, it's like in cartoons, like with Roadrunner and the Coyote's chasing Roadrunner and all these terrible things happen to him but he never gets hurt. It's that kind of artificial world." Jay Kinney thinks he can do more than entertain: "Most comics just amuse. Underground comics have helped to expand the scope of comics. Comics are a genuine art form and have as much a right (and obligation) to explore sex, politics (particularly revolutionary politics), psychology, and drugs as do other art forms." In the same vein, Dave Sheridan writes, "The comix in general have opened up new ways of mirroring the present culture. This, along with other

George Metzger and Rick Shubb. *Yellow Dog Comix* No. 17.

Robert Crumb. *Big Ass Comics* No. 1. ©1969 R. Crumb. By permission of Robert Crumb. A unique handling of page layout, not only for Crumb but for any cartoonist to date—one example of the cartoonists' constant pushing at the boundaries of their medium.

assorted themes such as the releasing of certain hangups, American and otherwise, are the major reasons for the aesthetic validity given to the medium. When I realized that the opportunity for total freedom was lying in my lap, in a constructive and contributive form, I decided that the comix were 'where it's at.' I plan to continue doing comix until I either drop from exhaustion or the No-Knock Squad bursts in, in which case I shall 'continue to grow someplace else,' if possible." But then, to swing back to the other extreme, consider Buckwheat Florida Jr.: "I never really wanted to do strips in the normal sense. I just enjoyed sitting down and doodling with as few preconceived notions about the art as possible—hence mixed up, confused drawings, scattered all over the page. . . ."

You can take the underground comics pretty much as you wish. Seek social and political relevance and ye shall find. Seek pure escapism and ye shall find. Even seek enlightenment, and ye shall surely find. Some reasons for this are considered by one of the few philosophers in the field, Paul Buhle of *Radical America:* "The good comics are most definitely *NOT MEANT TO AMUSE READERS*, or minimally to amuse them on one level while other things are going on in other levels . . . No underground cartoonists are mainly attempting to titillate you in the same way that the daily comic strips in the bourgeois papers do . . . The actual drawing of the strips is like the actual writing of poetry: it is a side-product, an after-effect, of living and thinking a certain way. If that were not so, the comix artists would have watered down their stuff to get syndicated, and amuse as many people as possible."

So as a general rule, these are

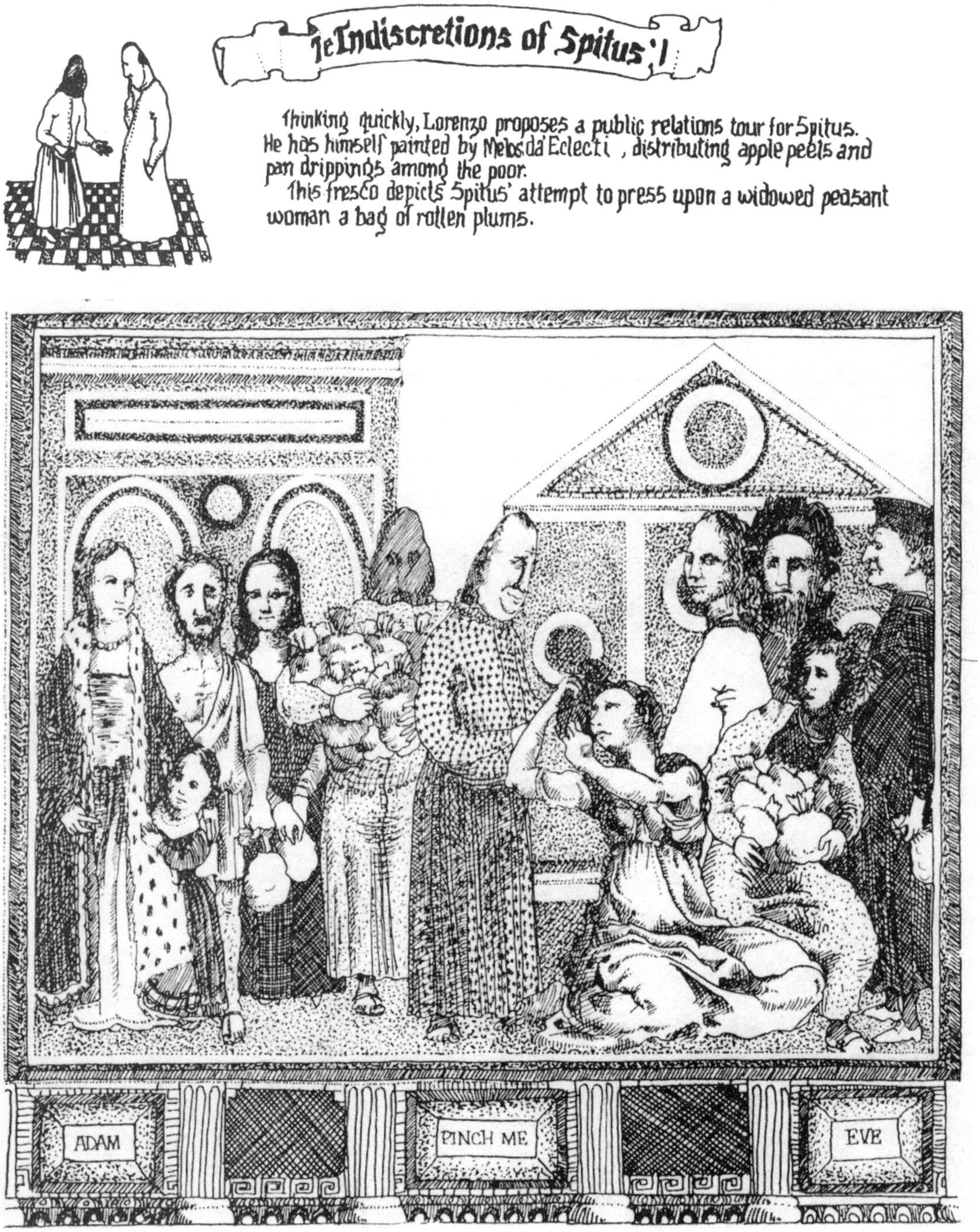

George DiCaprio and Laurie Anderson. *Baloney Moccasins* No. 1. ©1969 George DiCaprio. By permission of George DiCaprio.

not ordinary "funny comic books," nor are they entertaining little magazines designed to transport you to a fantasy world for a little while—at least not the sort of fantasy world to which you would willingly go. According to *The Phantom Psychiatrist,* these comics communicate one basic idea beyond fantasy: "That everything is shit and hopeless. I think that idea comes out *very* well—shit and hopeless and violent, but mostly shit and hopeless."

But stay, dear reader. While the most important part of the underground comics is this sort of heavy sociopolitical stuff, there is much lighter fare to be had as well. Indeed, the very best underground comics will educate you (or even enrage you) so gently that you'll scarcely know what's happened until it's over. And the freewheeling approach of the cartoonists practically guarantees that anyone willing to try just a little of the underground comics will rapidly become an addict.

It must be emphasized that the "freewheeling approach" of the underground comics is quite different from that of the best "straight" comics, such as "Pogo" and "Krazy Kat." In the latter strip, George Herriman constantly played on the English language as if it were a slightly out-of-tune violin (specific musical reference: Krazy saying, "Sounds like the Envil Choritz by Rigid Vogna, in beer flet"). The underground cartoonists, on the other hand, would rather print things in Persian or Hebrew than work out elaborate puns in English.

Robert Crumb. *Big Ass Comics* No. 1. ©1969 R. Crumb. By permission of Robert Crumb.

They are true cartoonists, and the words and pictures add up to a whole greater than the sum of its parts.

The general perspective of the underground cartoonists is quite different from that of the "straight" ones. Robert Warshow, writing of "Krazy Kat" in *Partisan Review* (Vol. XIII, No. 5, 1946), explains the general nature of the "straight" comic strip: " . . . the comic strip has no beginning and no end, only an eternal middle. It is an additional reality, running parallel with the *real* reality: for every day of one's own life, there is a day in the comic strip's life." Warshow's emphasis shows the difference between even the best "straight" work—such as Herriman's—and that of the underground cartoonists. The underground strips *are* a part of "real reality," both for their artists and for their readers. Furthermore, though some underground cartoonists (notably S. Clay Wilson) invariably present strips with "an eternal middle," this is an eternal middle only in the sense of a chunk from the time continuum. No underground strip is a continuing story for more than a very few episodes; that would be false to the whole approach of the artists. These strips are true slices of the very things which cause so much tear-drenched anguish to Mary Worth and company, such as sex and death. The difference is that the underground cartoonists are not preoccupied, as a general rule, with sex, death, and the like; rather, these things are facts of the artists' lives, and therefore facts of their characters.

Left: Robert Crumb. *Snatch Comics* No. 3.

One other point. In his book *The Comics* (1947), Coulton Waugh wrote that, "Quite possibly, comic books may emerge as the most influential form of teaching known to man." This potential, never realized in the "straight" strips—beyond some crude jingoistic wartime propaganda, some plugs for the Air Force's humanitarianism in "Terry and the Pirates," and some flag-waving cries to "support the Vietnam war effort" in a strip called "The Green Berets"—is today being explored by the underground cartoonists to an extraordinary degree. Though many of the cartoonists are on their own trips, most are sincerely trying to reach others with political or social messages. The underground cartoonists have made the important discovery that one can only teach what one understands (imagine Mary Worth teaching sex!), and indeed, that one *must* try to teach things that one has learned. Says Denis Kitchen, "We refuse to compromise our creativity, our gripes, our statements. The beauty of it is unrestricted expression. . . . All this stuff is *funny*. And you just don't read it in the Milwaukee *Journal* or New York *Daily News*."

Below: Hak Vogrin. *A Moon Book.* ©1963 Hak Vogrin. By permission of Hak Vogrin.

The next few chapters deal with what I, as one person, consider to be the major themes of the underground comics. The *major* themes—*not* all of them. If I knew all the themes of the comics, I'd find them predictable and therefore less fun to read. I hope you, as a comic-book reader, will come to share that feeling.

Robert Crumb. *Snatch Comics* No. 2. ©1968 R. Scrum. By permission of Robert Crumb.

Sex & Sexism

5

If you looked up this chapter first, you won't be disappointed. And if you've been reading this work sequentially, you won't be surprised.

Since American society has always placed particular emphasis on the nature of sex as something personal, private, eminently concealable, and of course not to be suggested or shown to children; since the most strictly enforced taboos of the Comics Code Authority of America, and of the Motion Picture Censorship Board, are against sex; since whatever illicit presentations of sex have existed in this country have appeared in plain wrappers, often (as in the case of sexploitation movies) with heavily moralizing narration to compensate, in some perverse way, for the clinical depiction of sex inside those wrappers—for all these reasons, the underground cartoonists absolutely revel in sex and sexuality.

In some cases, the cartoonists' satire focuses on the typically American, puritanical view of sex. Joel Beck's parodies of this attitude are particularly telling. In fact, all the best underground sex strips treat the whole sexual thing on a satirical or frankly humorous level. Their reduction of sex to just another animal activity is the breaking of a greater taboo than the portrayal of human genitals in clinical detail.

In his superb study of *Love and Death* (Breaking Point, 1949), G. Legman writes: "The censor's unequivocal 'You must not!' is seldom answered with an equally uncompromising 'I will!' Ashamed to oppose the censor's morality, and afraid to contravene his authority, the writer's first reaction is to evade the censorship, to see what can be sneaked through, what can be gotten away with, what can be disguised just enough to pass the censor but not so much as to escape the audience." Legman's statement has applied from time immemorial, or at least from time Shakespearean. In Act II, Scene 5 of *Twelfth Night,* Malvolio has this speech: "By my life, this is my lady's hand: these be her very C's, her U's and her T's; and thus she makes her great P's" (lines 96-99). Anyone needing assistance in reading this speech, which critics pass over in puzzled or outraged silence, should read the line as it would be spoken: "her C's, her U's, 'n' her T's." If Shakespeare had to spell out his sexual terms, what are we to expect from lesser men?

Whatever we might expect, we have gotten much from the underground cartoonists. They have found it unnecessary to meet the censor uncompromisingly; instead, they have merely ignored him. This has led to occasional obscenity busts of some dealers in underground comics (see Chapter 10); but in general, legal hassles have been avoided

Robert Crumb. *Snatch Comics* No. 2. ©1968 R. Scrum. By permission of Robert Crumb.

Robert Crumb. *Snatch Comics* No. 1. ©1968 R. Cum. By permission of Robert Crumb.

by the production of overtly sexual comics in very small numbers and for very limited (and rapid) distribution.

Sex in the underground comics is best approached by looking first at Robert Crumb's sex comics. A number of these were produced: three issues of *Snatch*, one issue each of *Jiz* and *Cunt* ("the only comic you can eat"), and several other titles. The sex comics came into being soon after Crumb began his association with S. Clay Wilson in 1968. Mike Barrier reports, in *Funnyworld* No. 10, that "the focus of Crumb's work shifted to the Forbidden, to all the words and things and activities that have been off limits to everyone but hard-core pornographers in the past. Sex and elimination, in other words." And for readers who haven't yet guessed, Barrier adds that *Snatch* "is at least as raunchy as you think it is." This first *Snatch*, which was unlike anything in comic-book form since the days of the old *Eight-Pagers* (see Chapter 2), caused more furor than any other underground sex comic. Crumb printed the comic in an addition of eight hundred copies, all of which quickly sold out in San Francisco, where they originated. *Snatch* No. 1 quickly became a collector's item, and copies were commanding prices of twenty-five dollars apiece and more less than two years after they were published.

In fact, though, Crumb's work in *Snatch* No. 1 does not match his later efforts in *Snatch* No. 2 and *Jiz*. *Snatch* No. 2, for one thing, contains the center spread, "The Family that Lays Together Stays Together" (see Chapter 7), a drawing which is both funnier and more sarcastic than "The Great Intercontinental Fuck-In and Orgy-Riot" which is the center of *Snatch* No. 1. And *Jiz* contains a truly classic sex strip, by far the funniest of its type to appear in any underground comic: "The Adventures of Dicknose." The "Dicknose" strip lasts a full eight pages, making it also the longest continuous strip in any of Crumb's sex comics.

All the Crumb sex comics contain drawings by artists other than Crumb himself: S. Clay Wilson (usually under the pseudonym "Crank Collingwood," or

Joel Beck. *The Profit*.©1966 Joel Beck. By permission of Joel Beck.

Right: Robert Crumb. *Jiz Comics*. ©1969 R. Crumb. By permission of Robert Crumb. From "The Adventures of Dicknose."

under another alias), Rory Hayes, Jim Osborne, Victor Moscoso, and others. The comics amount to a working out of personal hangups on paper, being more of a free-for-all for the artists involved than trenchant attempts at social satire—with the few exceptions (such as the "Dicknose" strip) invariably done by Crumb himself. Crumb has been quoted as saying, "If taboos were broken by *Snatch*—groovy! Then we can move on to something else." And Crumb *has* moved on (though how far and to where is a debatable point—see pages 127-138), though not all his collaborators have.

Since the sex comics, Crumb has been particularly successful in perfecting the character of Angelfood McSpade, who represents all white men's repressed sexual desires. An extensive piece on Angelfood in *Zap Comix* No. 2 explains: "For one thing, she's illegal. And she has been confined to the wilds of darkest Africa, the official excuse being that civilization would be threatened if she were allowed to do whatever she pleased. . . . Men would quit their jobs if they got a chance to see ol' Angelfood shake that thing! The overwhelming smell of her . . . er . . . ah . . . THINGIE tends to disrupt clear thinking. The stockmarket would take a nose-dive!"

Clearly, Crumb has moved beyond the overt, enjoyable, but finally pointless sexuality of his sex comics. This is not to say that readers invariably found these comics enjoyable in any sense. Writing in *Funnyworld* No. 10, Mike Barrier comments, "A detailed physical description of a sex act doesn't convey what's really going on, any more than a detailed physical description of eating conveys how it feels to consume a fine meal, and a detailed physical description is all that smut provides . . . [Crumb's sex comics are] relaxed and funny, but still . . . a dead end for a talent as great as his." Crumb seems to have proved Barrier wrong by finding new ways to use the overt sexual expressions of his sex comics; but not all the artists in those comics have been able (or willing) to go on to new things. S. Clay Wilson, for one, is still doing comics similar to those in the sex books.

Even in his criticism of Crumb's sex comics, Mike Barrier reserved the really harsh words for Wilson: "Wilson's work has far more to do with real

Robert Crumb's infamous center spread from *Snatch Comics* No. 1. ©1968 R. Cum. By permission of Robert Crumb.

Left: Robert Crumb. *Jiz Comics*. ©1969 R.Crumb. By permission of Robert Crumb. From "The Adventures of Dicknose."

Right: Jay Kinney and Ned Sonntag. *Young Lust* No. 2. ©1971 Jay Kinney and Ned Sonntag. By permission of Jay Kinney.

Far right: Bill Griffith. *Young Lust* No. 1. ©1970 Bill Griffith and Jay Kinney. By permission of Bill Griffith and Jay Kinney.

Right: Justin Green. *Young Lust* No. 2. ©1971 Justin Green. By permission of Justin Green.

Second from top, R: Robert Crumb. *Mr. Natural* No. 1. ©1970 R. Crumb. By permission of Robert Crumb.

Right: Robert Crumb. *Big Ass Comics* No. 2.

Third from top, R: Bill Griffith. *Young Lust* No. 2. ©1971 Bill Griffith. By permission of Bill Griffith.

Below: Denis Kitchen. *Smile* No. 2. ©1971 Krupp Comic Works, Inc. By permission of Krupp Comic Works, Inc., by Denis Kitchen.

S. Clay Wilson. *Jiz Comics.* ©1969 R. Crumb. By permission of Robert Crumb.

S. Clay Wilson. *Jiz Comics.* ©1969 R. Crumb. By permission of Robert Crumb.

John Thompson. *Love Poems.*

pornography than does Crumb's, since it reflects the fear and disgust felt by pornography's readers." This is a fairly typical reaction when comparing Crumb's sex with Wilson's; but the fact is that Crumb finds sex an object for enjoyment and satire, while Wilson sees it as just another symbol of decay. In Barrier's analysis, "There can be no valid 'moral' objection to Wilson's work, even though every imaginable sexual practice takes place in his strips. No girl is ever going to be seduced by an underground comic book. My basic complaint about Wilson's work is that it *is* moral, in the narrowest, nastiest sense. I have said that S. Clay Wilson impressed me as an uptight little old lady in disguise. By that I meant that he seemed to share an attitude common to many little old ladies, that sex—and, by implication, life itself—is dirty and disgusting. It is in his strips, certainly. His people are all warts, moles, sweat, flab, and body hair (he can make any part of the human anatomy unappealing), and all freaks in one way or another. However, there's no indication that 'normal' people would come out looking any better."

Barrier has touched on Wilson's basic point and then missed it altogether. Wilson is the complete nihilist—he *does* find life "dirty and disgusting." There are no "normal" people at all in Wilson's comics, because there are none in his world. What Wilson does is to celebrate the interrelationship between sex and violence. Writing of the comics and censors of an earlier day, G. Legman said, "The really surprising thing is the hypocrisy that can examine all these thousands of pictures in comic books showing half-naked women being tortured to death, and complain only that they're half naked. If they were being tortured to death with all their clothes on, that would be perfect for children."

Wilson's cartoons are not directed at children, of course; but they are so vivid that even adults react viscerally—including adults with the supposed professional objectivity of *The Phantom Psychiatrist:* "All the people are so degraded—it's a very one-sided story. Nothing really happens to show that any of these things is a little more fleshed out. What I mean, I guess, is that sex is more

Below: Robert Crumb. Logo from *Jiz Comics.* ©1969 R. Crumb. By permission of Robert Crumb.

Right: Jay Kinney. *Young Lust* No. 2. ©1971 Jay Kinney. By permission of Jay Kinney.

Below: Robert Crumb. *Uneeda Comix.* ©1970 R. Crumb. By permission of Robert Crumb.

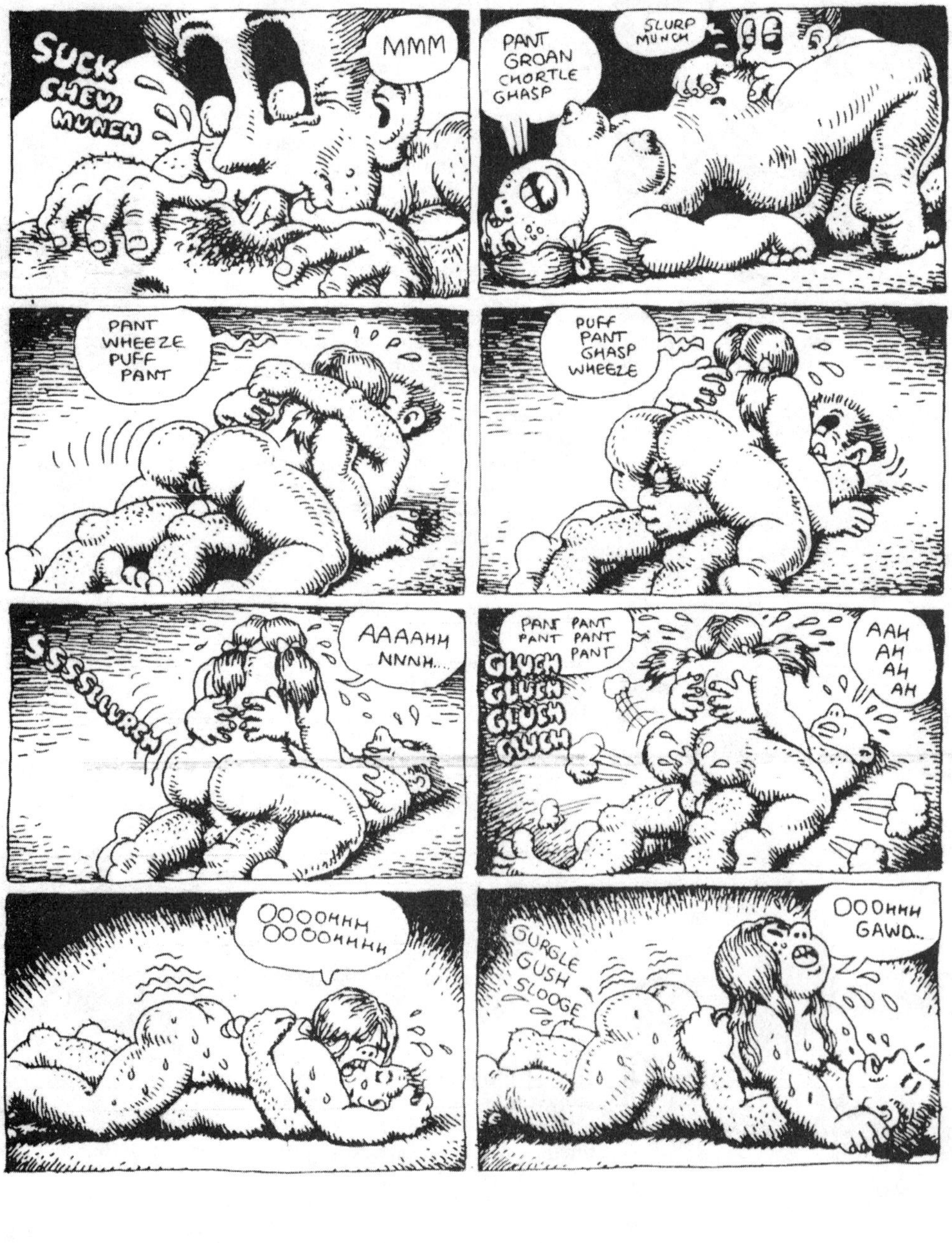

than just screwing. It can involve feelings of love, sharing, tenderness. And you can say, well, that's for movie magazines, not for underground comics, not for comics with political consciousness. Well, political consciousness does not necessarily mean that all these other things are thrown out. Violence is such a one-dimensional thing: someone gets ripped up, someone gets his entrails taken out. I mean, violence can be all kinds of violence; but there's no subtlety to it. You can say that the guy who's drawing it doesn't want any subtlety. Yet his medium is one of drawing, which can be subtle. It doesn't have to be hammered."

That sort of reaction to Wilson's work shows that Wilson *is* accomplishing something unusual. Getting that kind of gut reaction to violence, and the sex-violence interrelationship, is what Wilson's work is all about. Wilson happens to be a very good cartoonist, and a fine storyteller; but he has set himself into a totally one-dimensional world, and is concerned with exploring every aspect of that world, doing just the sort of "hammering" which *The Phantom Psychiatrist* finds so hard to take.

As it happens, even Wilson's sex cartoons are not quite so vicious, bludgeoning, and, by implication, unsubtle—to put it mildly—as they might appear at first glance. It depends on where you look. Wilson occasionally has forays into a very black humor in his drawings: in one, a pirate captain slaps a pirate dyke across the face ("the yap," as Wilson writes it) "with a big, stinking, dead, cross-eyed fish." That's not funny ho-ho, but it's clever—and the accompanying drawing, like everything by Wilson, illuminates the scene in neon Rapidograph, as it were. Even more significantly, Wilson has produced what this author considers one of the best cartoons in the entire underground comic field. What is remarkable in this strip is Wilson's simultaneous use of two time continuums—a static one for the masturbating demon and a standard, panel-to-panel moving one for the human couple.

Even with these accomplishments, however, we must recognize that Wilson's view of sex as a symbol of decay sets him apart from the other underground cartoonists, most of whom follow Crumb and either rejoice in sex for its own sake or regard it as a fit subject for

S. Clay Wilson. *Zap Comix* No. 3. Note the simultaneous use of two different time continuums.

satire. This view is itself a development. Back in the days of fanzines, when *Wild* was the publication point for cartoonists Jay Lynch and Skip Williamson, it was not these budding underground cartoonists who led the way into ribaldry, but rather *Wild*'s producers, Don Dohler and Mark Tarka. Dohler and Tarka ran a two-issue series of what Dohler calls "abstract and unappealing unclad women on the back covers of *Wild*s 4 and 5. Everybody, including Jay and Skip, disapproved of *that*." And it was Tarka who came up with articles on cleaning a stuffed toilet and similar "vulgar" stuff. According to Dohler, "Our art was rough, but in today's scene, our stories would work better. Lynch and Williamson had the good art, but they did more 'acceptable' stories, with an exceptional 'ribald' cartoon or two by Williamson here and there."

How things have changed! Today, there is scarcely an underground cartoonist who does not deal with sex, and the few who do *not* make sex one of their subjects (such as John Thompson) simply assume the existence of sexual organs and feel free to draw them whenever a panel warrants it (no carefully draped folds of clothing here!).

Justin Green. *Bijou Funnies* No. 3. ©1969 Bijou Publishing Empire, Inc. By permission of Bijou Publishing Empire, Inc., by Jay Lynch.

Robert Crumb. *Bijou Funnies* No. 3. ©1969 Bijou Publishing Empire, Inc. By permission of Bijou Publishing Empire, Inc., by Jay Lynch.

The satire of sex in the underground comics is generally directed at puritanical attitudes toward the subject, and is especially telling when aimed at the catch-phrases and platitudes about sex which so many people hold so dear. In this sort of satire, the portrait of the platitudes may be fairly realistic, as it is in Justin Green's work; or it may be totally distorted, as is more usually the case. In this too, Crumb leads the way, with strips like "O-So-Kleen Comics, Comics for the Clean at Heart." The whole point of this strip is to satirize the word "clean" as it is used by sexual puritans: Bob Kleen is in fact called "every mother's ideal" and shown to have nothing but sunshine in his head. (Incidentally, this strip gives special insight into the way Robert Crumb works. It was originally drawn on a ditto master for a fanzine called *Nope,* and its title came from the fact that the ditto master brand name was "O-So-Kleen." Crumb did the twelve-panel strip in ten minutes.)

One special feature of the underground cartoonists' sexual satire shows up in Gilbert Shelton's "Wonder Wart-Hog" strips. The satire here is many-sided, since the Hog of Steel is himself a parody of the traditional superheroes, and those superheroes (think, of course, of Superman) were totally asexual virility symbols—perfect examples of the sublimation of sex to satisfy the censors. Paul Buhle has written, in *Leviathan* (July-August 1969, pp. 13-17), about these heroes: "Even more than Tarzan or Prince Valiant, Superman was sexually starved: his infantile toying with lampposts is the only act of possible sexual significance I ever discovered (which is not to say more subtle actions were not understood: I have it on good faith that some pre-adolescents had sexual fantasies on Mighty Mouse). As a grownup, neither Clark nor Superman gets Lois Lane; Wonder Woman never marries Col. Steve Trevor; Batman (this is banal by now) has only one very obvious implied relationship."

Buhle need not have been surprised by pre-adolescent sexual

Below: Bobby London. *Rat,* March 7, 1970.

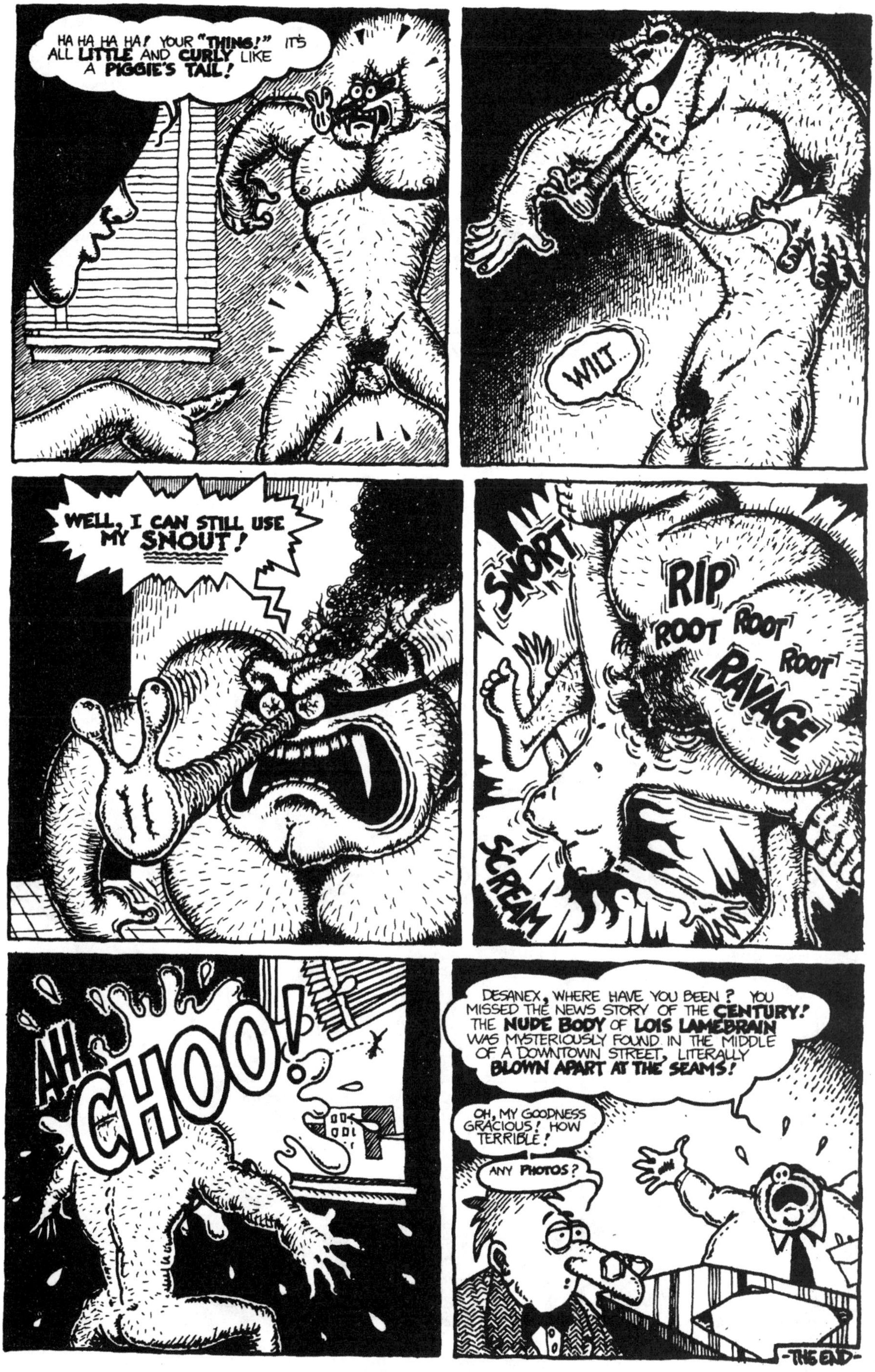

Gilbert Shelton. *Zap Comix* No. 4.

Gilbert Shelton. *Zap Comix* No. 4.

fantasies. In his classic study of sexual excitement in children (*American Journal of Psychology,* 1943; revised in Kinsey's *Sexual Behavior in the Human Male,* 1948), Dr. Glenn Ramsey discovered, among many other things, the following sexual stimulants for children: being scared, being near accidents, watching exciting games or war motion pictures, being afraid of punishment, being alone at night, looking over the edge of a building, finding money, entering an empty house, seeing wild animals, and being chased or frightened. So Mighty Mouse might well be a sexual stimulant. But Buhle's basic comments about superheroes are quite valid, and it is against such typical superhero traits that Wonder Wart-Hog's creator rebels. Thus, if Superman is a sexless symbol of ideal manhood, the Hog of Steel is the ugliest superhero going, but is sex-starved (he is especially stimulated by gory photos) and completely animalistic in his lechery. The twist is that the Hog is impotent (a problem he solves in one case by using his snout).

The effects of the exposure of sex in the underground comics (no pun intended) are debatable. Don Dohler, former editor of the fanzine *Wild,* says, "I don't consider the comics obscene or 'dirty'—just plain hilarious and fun. I look at them and all those little hangups in the back of my brain go flying out the window." Crumb himself, when interviewed by *Rolling Stone* magazine, said that even *Snatch* "isn't regular pornography. It comes at it from another angle. It's a satire on itself; it makes fun of pornography." There is even a question whether the underground comics make sex sexy. Mike Barrier writes in *Funnyworld* No. 11: "There's nothing

Peter Loft. *Snarf* No. 4. ©1973 Denis Kitchen. By permission of Denis Kitchen.

Opposite: Barney Steel. *Armageddon* No. 2. ©1973 Barney Steel and Last Gasp Eco-Funnies, Inc. By permission of Barney Steel and Last Gasp Eco-Funnies, Inc., by Ron Turner.

21

at all stimulating about *Snatch*. The kind of person who feels a stirring in the groin from reading it might just as well be turned on by a crate of avocados." But when I asked *The Phantom Psychiatrist* whether the underground sex comics were anti-erotic, he replied, "You know, you can get turned on by perverse kinds of things. I think they *can* be stimulating, sure—I think there's enough there, sure. If eroticism and being turned on are equal—if something is erotic if it turns you on—you know, guys get turned on by leather straps and all kinds of stuff. Some guys get turned on by violence. It depends on the person. I think if I was a middle-aged woman, I'm not sure that I would find these very erotic. If I was a fairly young man, I think I probably would."

All you crate-of-avocado freaks out there, rejoice. The

Larry Welz. *Bakersfield Kountry Komics.* ©1973 Larry Welz and Larry Sutherland. By permission of Last Gasp Eco-Funnies, Inc., by Ron Turner.

underground comics are your salvation.

Unfortunately, there's one area in which the underground comics have been largely unable to break from the society in which they were created. The comics remain, by and large, bastions of male chauvinism—no longer quite on the level of *Playboy* or *My Secret Life,* to be

Far Left: Zero Easter. *Ghost Mother Comics* No. 1.

sure, but generally not at a much higher level either. The role of women in the underground comics is particularly unfortunate; this is one area in which underground and straight media are

Far Left: Robert Crumb. *Motor City Comics* No. 2. ©1970 R. Crumb. By permission of Robert Crumb.

almost equally inept. In his analysis of "The World of Sunday Comics," Francis E. Barcus made the following observation, almost as an aside: "Men were twice as prone to be employed as women, who were usually portrayed as dependent housewives." Well, housewives may not be a major topic of interest to the underground cartoonists, but their common portrayal of women either as total sexual objects or as quintessential castrating bitches leaves much to be desired.

The problem is that male chauvinism pervades the entire medium, and keeps getting in the way of almost everything the (male) underground cartoonists do. And even when the female underground cartoonists are not actually trying to respond to this sort of sexism, it preoccupies their minds and interferes, to a greater or lesser degree, with

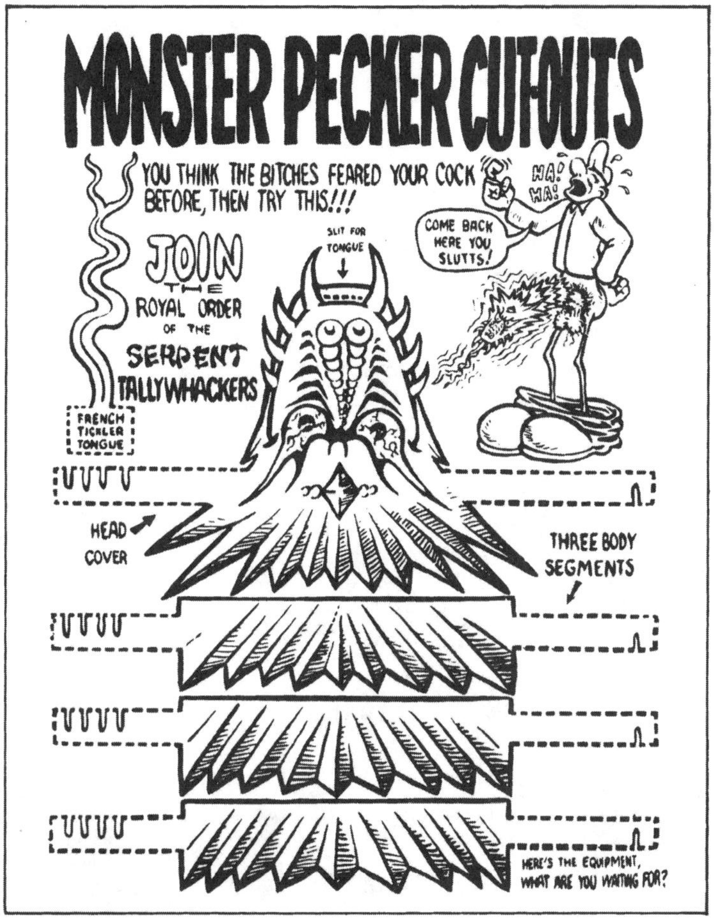

Left: Robert Crumb. *Snatch Comics* No. 3.

whatever message they may be trying to put across.

One of the few female cartoonists, Trina, when asked why there are so few women doing underground comics, says, "Maybe it's 'cause they think, like so many others, that underground comics consist solely of porn. Maybe they're frightened of a field that's mostly men. Women are brought up to be not very aggressive. Fact is, I really don't know. As for me, I love drawing—and I consider it a challenge." Trina's friend and sometime collaborator, Willy Mendes, is more forceful: "That's *the* answer to your 'why not more women' question: TIME!! Their unliberated men don't lift their lousy fingers and the incredible amount of bullshit work in life allows women *no time.*"

It's not surprising that few women are as willing as Willy Mendes and Trina to rise to the "challenge" of underground comics. According to Skip Williamson, there is no possible way to escape the male chauvinism of the medium: "To deny sexism is to deny the cultural heritage of the comics. That's one reason comics are basically counterrevolutionary." But it's not so easy for a woman—or any reasonably sensitive reader—to react so calmly to the constant parade of women-who-are-not-people-but-things that the underground cartoonists produce.

The jumping-off point for any discussion of sexism in these comics must be the sex books of Robert Crumb. Granted, these never pretended to be more than the working out of personal hangups on paper; but the fact that the books were produced at all, and the fact that some artists have never changed the attitudes they held while doing the sex comics, makes the Crumb sex books an exaggeration of typical cartoonists' attitudes, but not an exception to them.

Of course, one can hardly be surprised at sexism in the overt

Below: Robert Crumb. *Snatch Comics* No. 1. ©1968 R. Cum. By permission of Robert Crumb.

AND NOW, A WORD TO YOU FEMINIST WOMEN
LEMME AT 'EM!
From that ol' Male-Chauvinist Pig, R. CRUMB Himself!!
HI GIRLS! R. CRUMB HERE! I'D LIKE TO TALK FOR A FEW MINUTES TO ALL YOU CHICKS... ER, I MEAN WOMEN (HEH HEH) IN THE WOMEN'S LIB MOVEMENT!
I THINK IT'S TIME I ADDRESSED YOU DIRECTLY, BECAUSE THERE'S A FEW THINGS I'D LIKE TO GET OFF MY CHEST!!
FIRST, LET ME JUST SAY RIGHT NOW THAT I'M ALL FOR WOMEN'S LIB, BELIEVE IT OR NOT! HEH HEH.. AND I WOULD LIKE TO BE YOUR FRIEND... R. CRUMB IS FRIEND OF ALL PEOPLE!
BUT, TH' THING IS, I'VE BEEN RECIEVING A HECK OF A LOT OF NEGATIVE FEEDBACK FROM SOME OF YOU WOMEN ABOUT MY COMICBOOK FEATURES, AND THIS IS A SOURCE OF ANXIETY TO ME... IT REALLY IS!!
NOW PLEASE UNDERSTAND ME!! I DONT DENY THAT MY CARTOONS CONTAIN A GREAT DEAL OF HOSTILE AND OFTTIMES BRUTAL ACTS AGAINST WOMEN! I'M WELL AWARE OF THIS DARK SIDE OF MY EGO!
CALL ME A "SEXUAL CRIMINAL" IF YOU LIKE... A "PIMP", A "SEXIST PERVERT" IF IT PLEASE YOU... CALL ME ANYTHING YOU WANT! YOU'RE PROBABLY RIGHT!!
BUT DONT GET ME WRONG, LADIES! I'M NOT ADVOCATING THAT MEN SHOULD DO THESE BAD THINGS TO WOMEN! I'M NOT PORTRAYING THIS ANTAGONISM AS SOMETHING TO BE ADMIRED! SOMETHING HEROIC!!
FAR FROM IT!
I THINK IT'S AN OVERSIMPLIFICATION TO SAY THAT A PICTURE OR DRAWING IS PROMOTING SOMETHING JUST BECAUSE IT PORTRAYS IT! LIKE A FEMALE BEING BEATEN UP, LET'S SAY...
AND, BY THE SAME TOKEN, TO INSIST THAT AN ARTIST STIFLE HIS (OR HER) OWN INSTINCTS AND DRAW ONLY THAT WHICH IS PRESCRIBED BY SOME MOVEMENT OR CAUSE... WHY, THAT'S PURE TOTALITARIANISM! DICTATORSHIP! AND SHEER STUPIDITY TO BOOT!!
I MEAN, LOOK... LET'S GET IT STRAIGHT! I'M NOT A PROPAGANDIST FOR ANYBODY'S GOD-DAMN MOVEMENT AND I NEVER INTEND TO BE! I'M NOT A POLITICIAN! I'M AN ARTIST!
I'M NOT TRYING TO DEFEND MYSELF AS A PERSON... GOD KNOWS I'M AS FUCKED UP AS THE NEXT GUY... ALL I'M DEFENDING IS FREEDOM OF EXPRESSION... WOULD YOU DEPRIVE ME OF THIS GOD-GIVEN RIGHT?
IF I WAS TO TRY TO GEAR MY COMICS TO YOUR CAUSE OR ANYBODY'S CAUSE, I WOULD NO LONGER BE TRUE TO MYSELF... I WOULD BECOME A LIAR! IS THAT WHAT YOU WANT?
WOULD YOU LIKE ME TO STOP VENTING MY RAGE ON PAPER? IS THAT WHAT YOU'D LIKE ME TO DO, ALL YOU SELF-RIGHTEOUS, INDIGNANT FEMALES? ALL YOU POOR PERSECUTED DOWN-TRODDEN BOOSHWAH CUNTS? WOULD YOU RATHER I WENT OUT AND RAPED TWELVE-YEAR-OLD GIRLS? WOULD THAT BE AN IMPROVEMENT?
WELL, LISTEN, YOU DUMB-ASSED BROADS, I'M GONNA DRAW WHAT I FUCKING-WELL PLEASE TO DRAW, AND IF YOU DON'T LIKE IT FUCK YOU!!
THAT'S TELLIN' 'EM BOB! TEE HEE
RIGHT ON!

sex comics—that's their main reason for being, after all. Crumb's Dicknose complains, "Those broads are always on th' make fer my NOSE! Some of them never show the least bit of decorum about th' whole thing!!" This is so obviously a wish fulfillment that it's hard (though scarcely impossible) for even a militant feminist to get really angry about it.

But the treatment of women by some of the cartoonists in these books is so one-sided that it's hard not to react with a shudder. Mike Barrier writes, in *Funnyworld* No. 12, "There's Rory Hayes, for example, whose strips bespeak a hatred and fear of women appalling in its intensity, and expressed in a drawing style that is unrelieved in its crudity. This crudity is valued by some underground cartoonists, I understand, and Hayes is regarded by them as a sort of Grandma Moses of the underground. They obviously know very little about Grandma Moses."

Hayes is one of the very youngest cartoonists, so perhaps one can understand that he has more things to come to terms with than do the older artists. Likewise, one can perhaps find some understanding for S. Clay Wilson, whose drawings are equally debasing to everyone and everything and who is therefore less a chauvinist than an out-and-out misanthrope. But who wants to spend so much time forgiving people? These things are downright ugly, and if "straight" cartoonists produced things with so little understanding of the underground movement, it's likely that a few firebombs would wind up in someone's window.

(On the other hand, even the women cartoonists will forgive, or at least overlook, some of the male cartoonists' attitudes, since they see those attitudes as simply reflecting the values of society as a whole. Willy Mendes: "The world if it's smart will learn that S. Clay Wilson is a beautiful beautiful beautiful artist [and my favorite] and that Crumb is a genius, so let the world weep that its geniuses' heads are where they are! I would not have anyone as brilliant as Wilson, Spain, Crumb, Green, Deitch, or Bill Griffith do anything other than what their souls tell them, make them do. I know I have no choice of subject matter myself—my whole being just does what it must. But poor fucking America! Listen to your Artists! Look where they're at!")

The fact is that sex in the underground comics does not have to be degrading to women, and in some cases it isn't. *Young Lust,* by Bill Griffith and Jay Kinney, is a case in point. Griffith writes, "Women's Lib, in the person of Trina and a friend of mine who's involved in it, seems to have a favorable reaction to *Young Lust,* which doesn't surprise me too much since my sympathies showed through in my stories, I thought. I like lesbians, anyway."

It's fortunate that Griffith has shown how to put out a sexually oriented comic (albeit, in *Young Lust*'s case, with a heavy dose of satire) without treating women as mere objects. But even Griffith's comments reveal a problem, for they perpetuate (even though in an offhand, humorous way) the same sort of stereotypes about Women's Lib that his comic avoids. You can't win unless you really try.

Much controversy about sexism in the underground comics centers around Robert Crumb. Crumb perpetrated the porn books and was the major contributor to them, but he also said later that he hoped those books had broken some taboos and that the cartoonists could now move on to other things. At other times, Crumb has actually created a female protagonist and portrayed her at some length (this is Lenore Goldberg, on whom more below); while at still other times, he has treated his female characters with a sort of fond indulgence (Honeybunch Kaminsky is the best case in point). Then there's Crumb's treatment of Angelfood McSpade, who is doubly handicapped by being both female and black and who, with the "abom-

Opposite: Robert Crumb. *Big Ass Comics* No. 2.

Robert Crumb. *Snatch Comics* No. 1. ©1968 R. Cum. By permission of Robert Crumb.

Below: Robert Crumb. *Snatch Comics* No. 1. ©1968 R. Cum. By permission of Robert Crumb.

Robert Crumb. *Big Ass Comics* No. 1. ©1969 R. Crumb. By permission of Robert Crumb.

inable snow-woman" named Yetti, is the most overtly sexual female among all Crumb's characters (as if to perpetuate the myth about the special sexual prowess of the darker or "more

Robert Crumb. *Motor City Comics* No. 1. ©1969 R. Crumb Productions. By permission of R. Crumb Productions, by Robert Crumb.

Opposite: Robert Crumb. *Motor City Comics* No. 2. ©1970 R. Crumb. By permission of Robert Crumb.

primitive" races). Finally, there is an interview Crumb gave to an underground newspaper, the *East Village Other*, about *Big Ass Comics* No. 1 ("weird sex fantasies with the behind in mind"—this is supposed to be *after* "moving on to something else" from the porn books). Crumb said that the comic had been attacked for being very hostile to women, and this exchange ensued:

Dean Latimer (interviewer): Yeah? . . . I mean, what seven-year-old boy *isn't* hostile toward women?

Crumb: Yeah, but when you're twenty-five you should know better.

Latimer: Yeah, but when you're twenty-five and you can recreate the sensibilities of a seven-year-old, that's really something. Art . . .

Crumb: Who's recreating?

Latimer: You mean that's the way you *feel* toward women?

Crumb: Well, sometimes.

There is no real way to pin down and fix the attitudes of so complex a person as Robert Crumb. One reason his strips show so many different attitudes toward women is that he himself has not yet made up his mind about them (Jay Lynch says Crumb makes it a practice to run away from his wife once a year). Crumb is still working out his hangups through his art—the same thing he was doing in the sex comics, though he's now operating on a much larger scale and with considerably more skill.

What *is* upsetting about Crumb's attitude toward women is that he seems unable to escape chauvinism even when he really wants to. Crumb has actually created an important female protagonist, Lenore Goldberg, who is quite eloquent for, and committed to, Women's Liberation. But the lead stories in *Motor City Comics* Nos. 1 and 2, in which "Lenore Goldberg and Her Girl Commandos" are featured, both end with copouts: in one, Lenore talks revolution while blowing her boyfriend, and in the other she has had a child and decided that "life goes on an' things change." Furthermore, both these comics perpetrate some common myths about the "proper" role of women in society—the girls show quite a concern for their figures, Lenore calms down after having and nursing her baby, and so on. And there are some scenes straight out of the porn books, like one in which Lenore interrupts her lovemaking and runs out, vagina quite visibly dripping, to greet her friend Janet. Crumb apparently really *likes* women (a statement that's hard to make about S. Clay Wilson, for instance), but he doesn't really feel confident enough to treat them as people rather than as objects. This becomes strikingly clear if we see that Crumb never really tries to satirize the general characteristics of American society through women—it's not possible to conceive of him creating a female Flakey Foont or Potatoes Browning. He is still at the stage of assigning women to roles—and even the Lenore Goldberg stories confirm this, for the Women's Liberation movement is rapidly becoming just another role to which certain types of females are relegated.

Far Right: Robert Crumb. *Motor City Comics* No. 2. ©1970 R. Crumb. By permission of Robert Crumb.

Below: Robert Crumb. *Big Ass Comics* No. 2.

HEY LENORE! SOME ONE NAME OF JANET HERE SAYS SHE KNOWS YOU!
JANET! OH WOW!
JANET YOU CRAZY BITCH!! I KNEW WE'D BE TOGETHER AGAIN SOME DAY!
HEY HOW Y' DOIN' LENORE?!
HOW TH' HELL DID YA FIND THIS PLACE?
IT WASN'T EAZY! YOU COVERED YER TRACKS PRETTY WELL! I HAD TA PROVE I WUZ YER BLOOD SISTER 'FORE ANYBODY'D TELL ME ANYTHING!
YEAH... I GOT VERY PARANOID AFTER THAT BIG INCIDENT IN MICHIGAN... HOW'S TH' MOVEMENT DOIN'??
IT'S INCREDIBLE, LENORE! THOUSANDS OF NEW MEMBERS! SO MUCH HAS HAPPENED! IT SURE WOULD BE GROOVEY IF YOU COULD COME BACK... NOBODY CAN GRAB A CROWD TH' WAY YOU USED TO...
HEH... YOU KNOW I KIN NEVER GO BACK TO TH' FUCKIN' STATES... NOT THAT I'D EVER WANT TO!
THIS IS MY HOME AN' MY FAMILY NOW... I LOVE IT HERE... COM'ERE, JANET! I WANTCHA TA MEET SOMEBODY!
O.K.
HIS NAME IS CRANBERRY SUNRISE VISHNU MEADOW KING...
LENORE!! WELL, I'LL BE FUCKED!! I NEVER THOUGHT I'D SEE TH' DAY WHEN YOU'D—
WELL, Y' KNOW... LIFE GOES ON AN' THINGS CHANGE...
THE END
WILL LENORE GOLDBERG TURN OUT TO BE A "JEWISH MOTHER"? ONLY TIME WILL TELL!

It seems that even when Crumb tries, he can't escape himself or his culture. No one can, of course, but when someone as talented as Crumb comes along it's natural to expect a lot from him.

In addition to Lenore Goldberg, Crumb has developed another important female character, "Yetti," who is featured in a book-length story called "Whiteman Meets Bigfoot." This is a back-to-nature story, in which the standardized middle-class city dweller eventually finds that modern conveniences are really traps, and leaves the city and his middle-class family forever. The catalyst in the story is Yetti, a huge, semi-human

Right: Robert Crumb. *Big Ass Comics* No. 1. ©1969 R. Crumb. By permission of Robert Crumb.

Above: Bobby London's chief characters, drawn especially for this book. Left to right: Dirty Duck, Weevil, Annie Rat, the Mojo Mutant. ©1974 Bobby London. By permission of Bobby London.

creature who is as different from Whiteman as Crumb can make her. It is certainly and solely because of her that Whiteman eventually learns there's more to life than an overpriced chicken in every Teflon-coated pot.

But even here, Crumb's basic inability to give a female character true, unstereotyped characteristics comes through. Yetti is inarticulate, communicating through sign language and a series of grunts; she is sexually insatiable, just like the women chasing Dicknose; and, in fact, her very lack of civilized qualities (the same lack which eventually brings Whiteman to her permanently) makes her more of a prodigy (as in Ben Jonson's play, "The Silent Woman") than a protagonist.

Incidentally, Whiteman's wife, who appears briefly in the story, is every bit the shrieking harridan that a satirist of middle-class values would want to make her. She is just as one-dimensionally bad as Yetti is one-dimensionally good. And there's nothing liberated about being one-dimensional.

Excerpts from Correspondence between the Author and Cartoonist Trina

Trina: Glad you referred to the "obvious vein of male sexism in the comics"—glad you even *saw* it!!! Would you believe that there are a whole lot of men who don't even *see* it?

. . . I have a whole lot to say on the subject, but I'm a lousy writer (which is why I draw). I keep thinking of quotes, tho. Willy Mendes said to me today on the telephone, "Why are all male cartoonists on such bummers?" Referring to the fact that they're all hung up on something *gross:* shit, snot, cutting people's dicks off, rape, necrophilia, always *gross* sex, always *ugly* sex.

Women cartoonists that I know (and there are very few) aren't concerned with *gross*—rather, they're into *decorative.* I have been told that decorative isn't *heavy.* Well, it can be, and then again, sometimes it isn't. But neither is gross.

I'm not an amateur shrink; I don't know the answer. But I'd sure love to read a shrink's report. [*Author's note:* see page 137] What *does* concern me is the hostility towards women I see in this work, especially by Crumb. It's hard to relate to him

Right: Trina. *Illuminations.*

Opposite: Robert Williams. *Coochy Cooty Men's Comics* No. 1. ©1970 Robert Williams. By permission of Robert Williams.

Below: Robert Crumb. *Home Grown Funnies.* ©1971 R. Crumb. By permission of Robert Crumb. Here Yetti rescues Whiteman from middle-class life.

FREE
GLASSWARE
WITH EACH
FILL UP
WHAT THE...

QUICK BISMARCK, TO DER OLD CARNIVAL GROUNDS!
GOSH, YOU FELLOWS PICKED ME UP IN THE NIC OF TIME!
FRAU HILDAGRAD IS INTERESTED IN MEETING POTENT INDIVIDUALS WITH SUCH HIGH SPIRITED CHARACTER, LIKE YOURSELF!

as a person when you see what he does to women in his strips.

. . . Crumb's porn upsets me, as does the work of a whole lot of other guys who think underground comix means porn. Rape is NOT FUNNY!!!

M.J.E.: Sexism in the comics is a major problem for anyone in the underground—we have to face the fact that we share many of the attitudes and problems we spend so much time attacking in others. Why be ashamed of that, I wonder? So many of us (including me) are products of the middle-class values and morality we want changed so desperately; and the fact is that, your personality is being formed by the time you're around five, we've all been formed by those values we've now come to reject.

. . . I don't think the best underground cartoonists are totally hung up on gross things—rather, they're overreacting to the absence of those things in the sterile comic books we all read when we were kids. It's sickening for me to see young kids read things like *Archie,* with the girls' swelling bosoms and ample hips and with the obvious pandering to budding sexuality—*Archie* being a comic with the Comics Code Seal of Approval, of course, because it never suggests that there's anything real and fleshy under the skin-tight sweaters. Frankly, I prefer Crumb's porn.

Trina: You write about the Underground wanting desperately to change things in a political way: middle-class values and morality, liberating oppressed people, etc. Alas, I feel I must tell you that in my opinion, those underground cartoonists most guilty of sexism are politically *oblivious* and have the social conscience of an oyster. . . . If they have perchance drawn in the past for a cause such as the Chicago Conspiracy trial it's because all their buddies were doing it. Spain, who really considered himself political until I recently corrected him, thought that sexism had something to do with fucking.

If I sometimes sound like I despair of these fellows, it's because I *do*—they're mostly all nice guys but they're political and social cretins.

Sure, *Archie* is a drag, but that doesn't make underground porn any groovier. That's the old "What-about-the-lynchings-down-South" bit. Whenever I try to talk to these guys about porn they bring up the old commercials-on-TV-are-fucking-your-head-and-that's-worse line. And yes, sex in Crumb's work (even *besides Snatch* and *Jiz,* and why do you make exceptions of them anyway?) *is* ugly. It is ugly to

Above: Jim Osborne. *Snatch Comics* No. 3.

Right: Trina. *Tales of Sex and Death* No. 1. ©1971 The Print Mint. By permission of The Print Mint, by Bob Rita.

Opposite: Shary Flenniken. 1973 Berkeley Comix Convention program. ©1973 Shary Flenniken. By permission of Shary Flenniken.

YOU COULD HARDLY CALL WHAT YOU DRAW FEMINIST LITERATURE!
...AND BIRTH CONTROL, ABORTION, YEAST INFECTIONS AND...
CRUMB REFUSED TO BE IN IT SO THERE'S A SPACE FOR YOU!
REMEMBER NOW. WE WANT SEX, SEX, SEX!!
THINK WITH YOUR BRAIN NOT YOUR CUNT!
YOUR TREES LOOK PLASTIC!
DO A STORY ABOUT MY DIVORCE!
YOUR WORK IS WELL, UH, GENTLE.
SHARY! COME TO BED!
© 73 FLENNIKEN

see cum coming out of Honeybunch Kaminsky's nose in *Uneeda Comix*, for a start [*Author's note:* see page 120]. I have a 5-month-old daughter [*Author's note:* as of November 1970] and I already am worried about keeping that shit around where she can get at it later. What kind of fucked-up, ugly, distorted view of sex is this gonna give her? suburban housewife putting down porn, but I can't help that. It sickens me and it frightens me. . . . I don't think some of these guys *do* like women—I mean besides liking to fuck them.

M.J.E.: As a matter of fact, the influence of sexism in underground comics is probably worse than that of sexism in *Archie* and its relatives, because most letter—it's as ugly as anything in the pornographic comics, and the final-page stab at Women's Lib is as perceptive as all the things written by *Time* and *Newsweek* and other bastions of perceptive and enlightened cultural criticism.

Trina: Actually, I think Crumb made a very good point in *Uneeda Comix*—I just think his

Robert Crumb. *Uneeda Comix.* ©1970 R. Crumb. By permission of Robert Crumb.

Below: Evert Geradts. *Snarf* No. 1. ©1972 Denis Kitchen. By permission of Denis Kitchen.

I'm sure I sound like a classic people who go for *Archie* pap have such a low consciousness that the philosophy of underground comics could never reach them anyway. But these comics are usually read by somewhat more sophisticated, hopefully more politicized people—the kind of people who *might* be able to change sexism and other hangups in themselves, if they knew they were there. But the comics perpetuate the hangups rather than countering them—so the people most likely to change themselves only have their problems reinforced.

You're right about the sex in *Uneeda,* which I didn't get until two days after I wrote my last sex scenes were gross and unnecessary. However, he *does* understand the whole Women's Lib schtick. Honeybunch Kaminsky made her own trap by deciding to cook Projunior's favorite dinner, clean up his house, slavishly serve him beer and slippers, and then spring the baby bit on him. He, poor guy, just fell easily into the "master" role she had set out for him (that's natural—who wouldn't?) and reacted with shock and horror at the implications that the responsibilities of a wife and baby would have to go with the benefits he had received. Of course, poor Honeybunch was only doing what she had been culturally programmed to do—slaves are brought up to dig their slavery—so her final fury at Projunior was a bit unkind. Men *and* women are guilty of sexism.

It is unfortunate that sexism in the underground comics does cut both ways. There is a tendency on the part of some people in the field—such as Bobby Lon-

don, whose strips often appeared in *Rat*, a Women's Liberation paper from New York City—simply to reverse typical male chauvinism into the female variety. G. Legman, in *Love and Death* (and a different context) could well have been writing to some of today's militant feminists when he said, "Women have made and continue to make the tactical error of *accepting the enemy's values.* Consciously or unconsciously they allow themselves to be convinced that being a man is *per se* good, and that only those things are worth doing, that, by the rather obvious subterfuge of keeping women out, men have been able to do better. The reaction is either to try to be a man—pants, penis, and all the rest of it—and do what men do; or, failing that, to claw down the nearest male by whatever means one can, and so be faced with no invidious comparison."

An effective voice for female equality has yet to be properly heard by the underground cartoonists; but hopefully, sooner or later, the cartoonists will awaken to this area of social concern as they have awakened to others. Until that time, it's at least worth considering *The Phantom Psychiatrist*'s opinion that the treatment of women in the underground comics, while not praiseworthy, is at least not unusual: "Are women degraded? My assumption after reading the comics was that the whole *world* is shit, *everybody's* degraded. Women, dogs, demons—

Far Left: Robert Crumb. *Motor City Comics* No. 1. ©1969 R. Crumb Productions. By permission of R. Crumb Productions, by Robert Crumb.

Left: Larry Welz. *Captain Guts Comics* No. 2.

Left: Shelby. *Manhunt.* ©1973 Shelby. By permission of Shelby.

Below: Bobby London. *Rat*, March 7, 1970.

nobody really comes off well. There's a cataclysmic way of looking at things, a one-sided cataclysmic way: over there is Armageddon, and we're on a straight line over there, and that's the way it's going to be, and everything on the way gets thrown into that kind of a hopper."

Small wonder, then, that the underground cartoonists pay so little attention to their treatment of women. Small wonder—but no excuse at all.

Having dwelt so long on matters sexual, I feel it only fair to point out that not every underground comic contains overt sex material. Some exceptions are the works of John Thompson, who operates in a field where genitals may appear, but sex does not, and that of Denis Kitchen, whose *Mom's Homemade* is billed as "America's Most Wholesome Underground Comic." Kitchen *does* use sexual satire, but it is of a different order from that of Crumb's "Dicknose" (which Kitchen nevertheless calls "a classic"). Kitchen explains his attitude simply: "Rather than having my characters running around chopping each other's cocks off, I prefer to show them falling in love with manikins, or suggest screwing outer-space squids, or have a cowboy complain he has been shot in his 'doo dah.'" Kitchen feels that this restraint gains him a wider audience, and thus gives him a better chance of putting messages across than is given to artists whose clear depiction of genitals and sexual activity automatically precludes their being read by the very people who are most in need of new ways to look at life.

As a rule, though, sex *is* a preoccupation of the underground cartoonists. They are probably no more enthralled by the subject than are most of us; but they

Carole. *It Ain't Me Babe Comix.* ©1970 Trina, Lisa Lyons, Carole, Michele, Willy Mendes, Meredith Kurtzman, Hurricane Nancy. By permission of Mss. Trina, Willy Mendes and Meredith Kurtzman.

Larry Welz. *San Francisco Comic Book* No. 2. ©1970 Rick Griffin, Willy Murphy, Greg Irons, Robert Williams, Kim Deitch, Jim Osborne, Spain Rodriguez, Trina, Robert Crumb, Dan O'Neill, Larry Welz, Mervinius, and S. Clay Wilson. By permission of Messrs. Williams, Deitch, and Crumb, and Ms. Trina.

Below: Denis Kitchen. Madison-Milwaukee *Bugle-American,* Vol. 1, No. 12. ©1970 Krupp Comic Works, Inc. By permission of Krupp Comic Works, Inc., by Denis Kitchen.

have the skill and the willingness to put their fantasies down on paper. And many of the cartoonists are at least looking at sex and laughing, rather than placing it in a cabinet, like a special piece of china to be eaten from only on special occasions. Ultimately, it is likely to be their irreverence and not their willingness occasionally to stimulate their readers that will prove to be their most important contribution where sex is concerned.

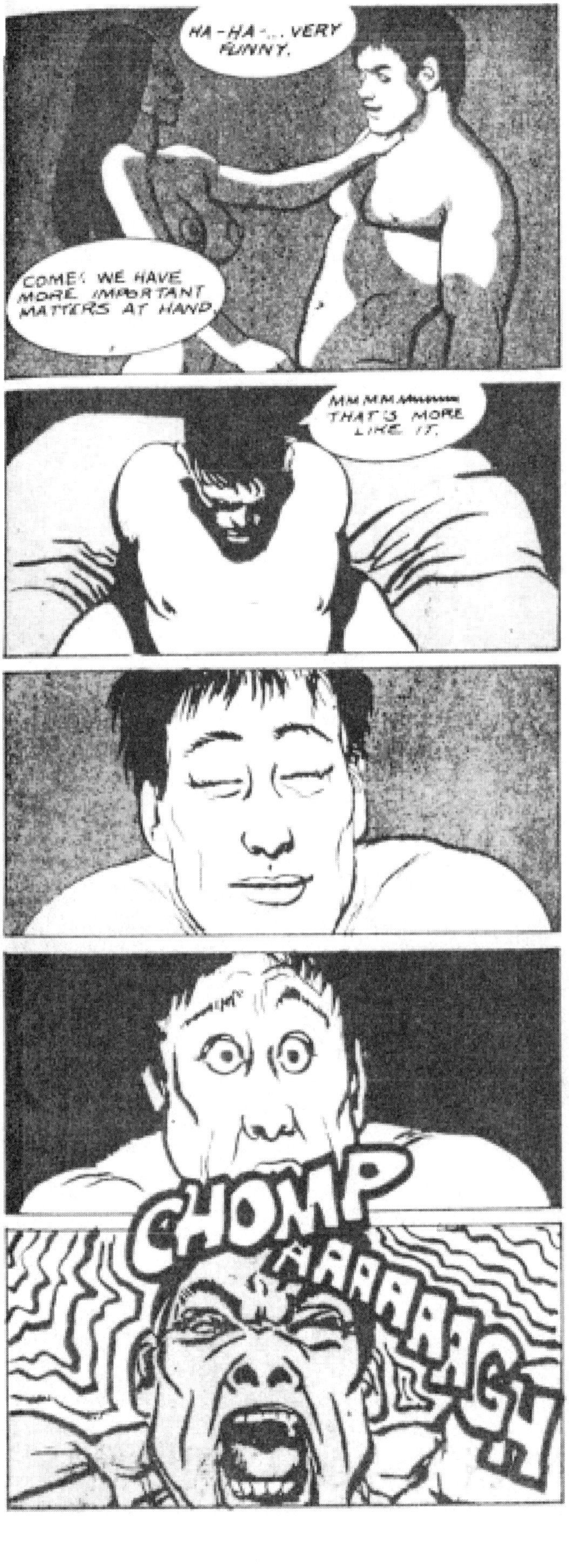

Richard Corben. *Death Rattle* No. 1. ©1972 Krupp Comic Works, Inc. By permission of Krupp Comic Works, Inc., by Denis Kitchen. Corben, a filmmaker as well as a cartoonist, has emerged quietly from Kansas City, Missouri to become perhaps the most consistently powerful creator of horror stories in underground comics. He is, as shown here, a master of the unexpected.

6 Violence

Opposite: Jim Osborne. *Bogeyman Comix* No. 2. ©1969 R.B. Hayes and G.E. Arlington. By permission of Rory Hayes and Gary Arlington.

Traditionally, sex in comic books has been sublimated into violence—often of an extreme kind. As G. Legman wrote in *Love and Death* (Breaking Point, 1949): "There is *no* mundane substitute for sex except sadism . . . But sadism does substitute. It is complete in itself. It can dispense with all earthly relation to sex—can even dispense with orgasm—thus allowing its adherents publicly to preen themselves on the 'purity' of their ruthless delights."

You might expect there to be less violence in the underground comics than in the sexually repressed "straight" ones, due to the underground cartoonists' free expression of matters sexual (see Chapter 5). You'd be wrong. Horror and violence do exist in the underground comics, often to a frightening degree. But this is not violence of the repressed-sexuality type—it is, rather, a symptom of the cartoonists' new freedom in the medium, an accurate if exaggerated portrait of the society they live in, and (perhaps most important of all) a violence coupled with sexuality rather than substituting for it.

It is a basic principle of the Comics Code Authority of America's censorship rules that comic-book violence be "clean." That is, there can be as much death and destruction as the artists wish (well, almost as much), but there shall be no dwelling on the gory scenes themselves, no spattering of blood about the page. This provision of the code is basically a reaction to the clinical depictions of violence in the old E. C. Comics, particularly in the horror books. Thus one would expect *Bogeyman*, an avowed E. C. imitation put out by Gary Arlington of the San Francisco Comic Book Company, to have gore galore. One would not be disappointed, however much the horror might be vitiated by the unrealistic art of Rory Hayes.

Yet *Bogeyman* is not the only repository of extreme violence in the underground comics, nor indeed the most notable. It is, in fact, one of the poorer imitations of the E. C. horror books. Another, *Skull Comics* (also originally from the San Francisco Comic Book Company), comes much closer to the flavor of the old E. C. line than does *Bogeyman* (*Skull* even calls itself E. C.—"An Exorpsychic Comic"). And *Death Rattle* too is with the E. C. line in spirit.

Actually, there is violence throughout the underground comics, and not specifically in the horror stories. The underground cartoonists live in a violent world (as do you, dear reader), and they reflect that world in their drawings. And when the cartoonists *do* depict violence, they generally do so extremely graphically. This is not done so much in a con-

S. Clay Wilson. ***Yellow Dog Comix*** **No. 13-14. © 1969 The Print Mint. By permission of The Print Mint, by Bob Rita.**

Below: S. Clay Wilson *Gothic Blimp Works* No. 6.

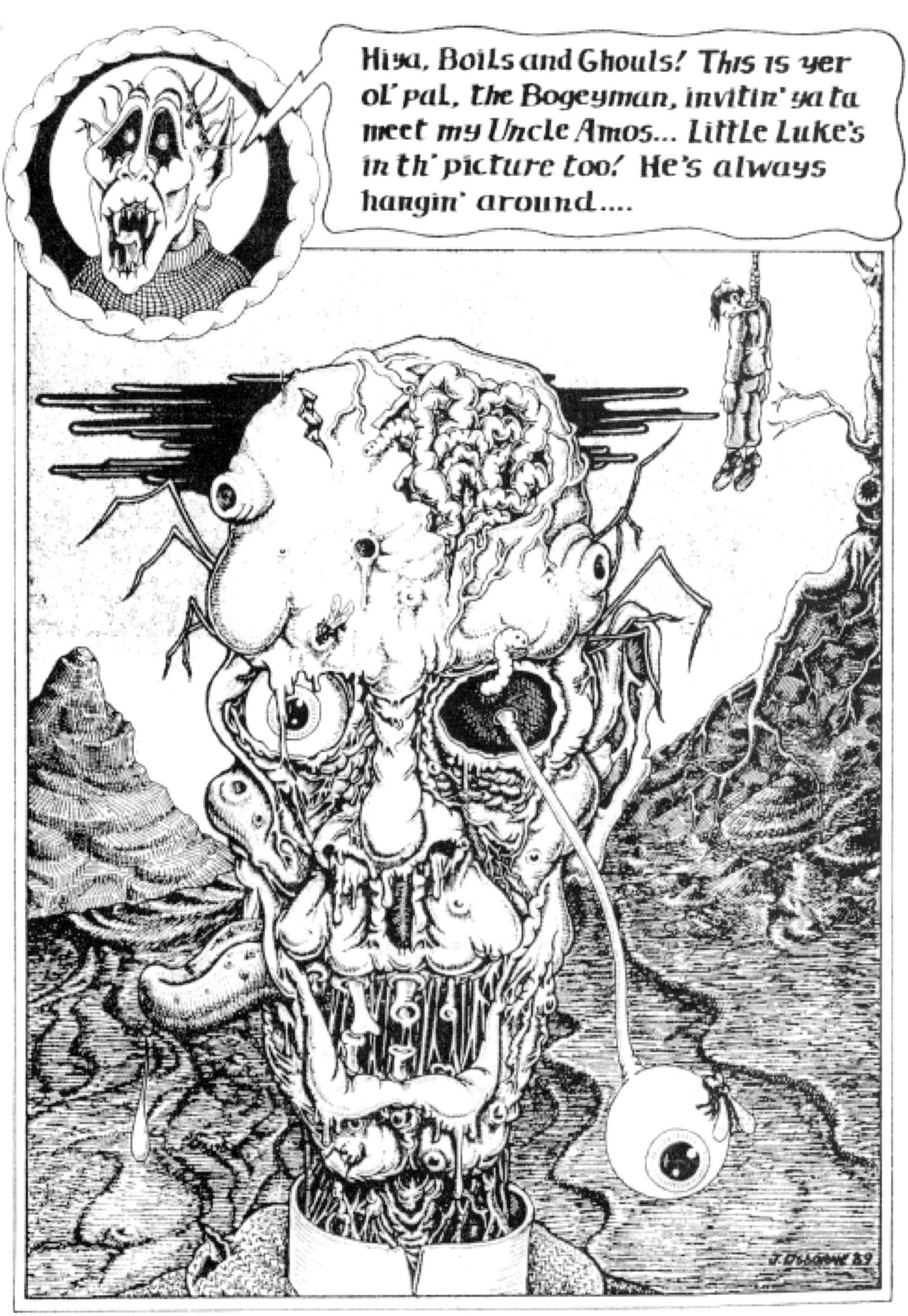
Hiya, Boils and Ghouls! This is yer ol' pal, the Bogeyman, invitin' ya ta meet my Uncle Amos... Little Luke's in th' picture too! He's always hangin' around....

scious attempt to break taboos, but as the result of a clear and logical approach to comic-book art: if you are going to show violence, why in heaven's name not show violence? It is odd that the same Comics Code which emasculates sex should emasculate violence as well.

Of all the underground cartoonists' work, it is S. Clay Wilson's that is the most consistently and viciously violent. Wilson sees total decay around him, and violence is but a symptom of that decay. Wilson's are the clearest depictions of violence: In single-panel drawings and stories alike, his work is obsessed with people and things performing very inventive acts of mayhem upon each other.

Opposite: S. Clay Wilson. *Zap Comix* No. 3.

Yet Wilson's violence of decay is less typical of underground cartoonists' approaches to the subject than is a series by Gilbert Shelton entitled "Scenes from the Revolution." In this series, Shelton is more realistic in his depictions of the violence that would accompany a second American Revolution than most young radicals would like to believe.

Shelton's "Scenes from the Revolution" brings us to another point about violence in the underground comics: the cartoonists often feel they are simply reflecting the society in which they live. As a general rule, the results of violence are portrayed without exaggeration, though the situation in which the violence occurs may be beyond present reality. Thus, there may not yet be a second American Revolution, but if there ever is, Shelton will show you what a beer bottle can do to a man's face.

One could argue that spelling out the mayhem with such care makes the whole idea of violence less attractive—just as a clinical depiction of male and female genitals makes one wonder why the opposite sex's organs should be so attractive. If this is so, then the violence in the underground comics may be providing an outlet for readers' hostility rather than channeling that hostility into the practical action that many underground cartoonists claim to be seeking (see Chapter 7).

There are, to be sure, times when the underground cartoonists do not show violence realistically. In one Daniel Clyne strip, for example, two men are not killed when they are run over by a steamroller, but are turned into pancakes—a typical "old-style" sort of comic device. The use of this device allows Clyne to pull out all stops a few panels later, depicting cannibalism and, for the first time, the drops of blood which mean death. Holding back on such panels sometimes makes especially effective points. A reaction of sheer horror to Clyne's panels is unlikely, due to the black humor of the woman's lines in the first few panels; yet a reaction of complete amusement is equally unlikely. It is thus that the underground cartoonists may distort violence in order to evoke

Below: Gilbert Shelton. *Feds 'n' Heads Comix.* ©1968 Gilbert Shelton. By permission of Gilbert Shelton.

CAPTAIN EDWARD ST. MIGUEL TILDEN BRADSHAW AND HIS CREW COME TO GRIPS WITH BLOOD THIRSTY FOX PIRATES.
HISSSSS... M GONNA USE SOMEBODYS UTS FOR A NECK-TIE.
KEEP KNOCKIN' 'EM DOWN AND PUTTIN' 'EM OUT MISTER OWENS... YOU'LL LOSE MORE THAN THAT SMELLER IF YOU DON'T STAY ON YOUR TOES
YAARRRGGH THESE YOUNG MATES ARE FIRED UP LIKE THE DEVIL-- THEY'RE MEAN, MEN!
CLOP
SKRK
TAKE THAT YOU BILGE RAT!!
YAAAAAAA
BLUM
GET HIS ASS FELIX HE'S AIMIN' HIS ARN THIS WAY... HE'S GONNA URK
GRUNNKK
YOU ROTTEN FISH-HEAD EATIN' JACK A' NAPES OOOF
CRUNCH
BAP
ALL THIS CONFUSION! MY EYES HURT FROM ALL THIS SMOKE...
FUCKIN' KNIFE'S STUCK IN THIS LUBBER'S FOOT... UMPFF

different reactions from those the reader would have if the violence were both detailed *and* realistic.

Another use of violence in the underground comics, which overlaps the previous ones, couples it with explicit sexual activity. I asked *The Phantom Psychiatrist* whether young people might find the comics erotic *because* of that sex-violence coupling, and was told, "I . . . I don't know. I'm kind of tempted to say yes, but I'm really not that sure that it's because of these two things that the eroticism comes through. You know, eroticism technically is not based necessarily on violence; it doesn't have to be. Over here it is. Reading these comics, you don't know where one stops and the other one begins. As a matter of fact, I don't think I can pull them apart. Sex is violent over here, sexuality is violent—by definition in these comics, sex is violence. Not necessarily the other way around—violence is not neces-

Daniel Clyne. *Yellow Dog Comix* No. 16.

Spain. *Mean Bitch Thrills.*

Opposite: S. Clay Wilson. *Insect Fear* No. 2.

SPIDER JOY
AND I'M WANDERIN' HOW MY SPIDERS ARE TODAY...
TELL ME IT CAN'T BE! MOTHER OF CHRIST... MY SPIDERS ARE GONE!
GLUK
THE SPIDERS ARE GONE
YOUR SPIDER'S ARE GONE
HIS SPIDERS ARE GONE
WHO TOOK MY SPIDERS, DID YOU, YA ROTTEN CREEP HUH?
BLOM
I'M THAT ROTTEN CREEP'S SOUL, AND FOR YOUR INFORMATION... NONE OF US TOOK YOUR FUCKING SPIDERS
YOU TELL 'IM SOUL...
YEAH, WISE ASS, TASTE RAZOR AND SAY GOODBYE!!
SOUL WAS WRONG, BECAUSE I'VE GOT THEM SPIDERS... (GIGGLE)
OH WELL

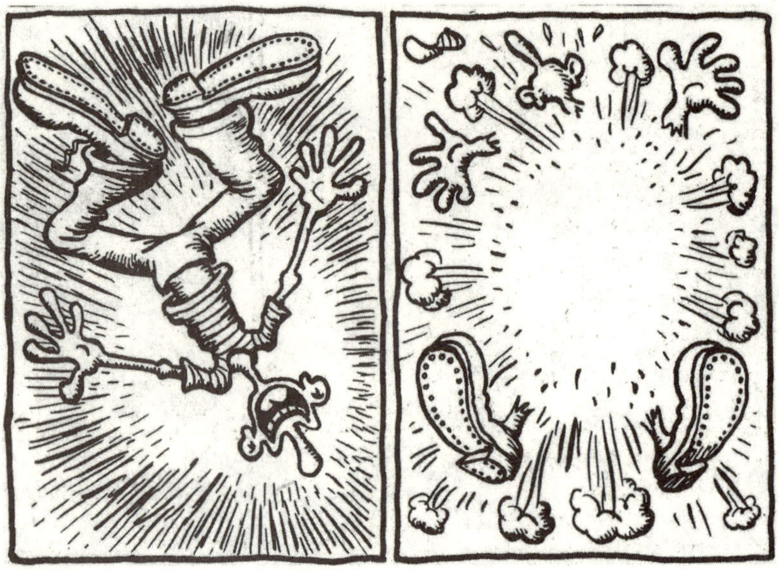

Robert Crumb. *Zap Comix* No. 1.©1967 R. Crumb. By permission of Robert Crumb.

Robert Crumb. *Bogeyman Comix* No. 2. ©1969 R.B. Hayes and G.E. Arlington. By permission of Rory Hayes and Gary Arlington.

Opposite: Gilbert Shelton. *Insect Fear* No. 1.

sarily sex—but sex always is violence."

The underground comics actually do not revel in violence in quite the way that the comics of the forties did. At that time, the emphasis was on extreme verbal as well as physical violence, as G. Legman writes: "Full capitals throughout, bold-face accents liberally besprinkled, and exclamation points galore; with illiterate little cartouches, where no conversation is thought necessary, saying Pow, Zow, and Whammo! to indicate the administration of violence, while the victims respond with Awrrk, Aagh, Aieee, Ooof, and Uggh." This is not the way of the underground comics, where violence of action is likely to be just that, unaccompanied by "illiterate little cartouches." Furthermore, the comics of the forties and early fifties were very often cast in a cops-and-robbers format, while the violence in the underground comics is more likely to cut across all strata of society and to be completely pointless—an accurate reflection of present-day America.

There was a special kind of hypocrisy in the violent comics of the forties and fifties which showed itself in the publishers' guilt feelings (or simple fear of public outcry) if the "good guys" did not always win in the end. (When the Comics Code Authority was established, it insisted that evil not be seen triumphant within its jurisdiction.) This led to the titles' big-and-small letters combinations, a few of which were: "GANGSTERS—can't win"; "CRIME—and punishment"; "CRIMINALS—on the run"; "Justice traps the GUILTY"; and, the *pièce de résistance,* "Hard-hitting agents of the law strike at the UNDERWORLD."

(The underground comics have even adapted *this* tradition, picking it up in the spirit of the old E. C. line, which was named with typical E. C. contempt for the guilt complexes that originally created the form: "Here are tales that will usher you into THE HAUNT OF FEAR"; "This isn't a magazine! This is a PANIC"; and, of course, "Tales calculated to drive you MAD." In the hands of the underground cartoonists, titles such as the following emerge: "Plunge into the depths of DESPAIR"; "Teen-age horizons of SHANGRILA"; "Thrill to stories of YOUNG LUST"; and, in direct imitation of the E. C. line, "Tales contrived to flip you out of your SKULL.")

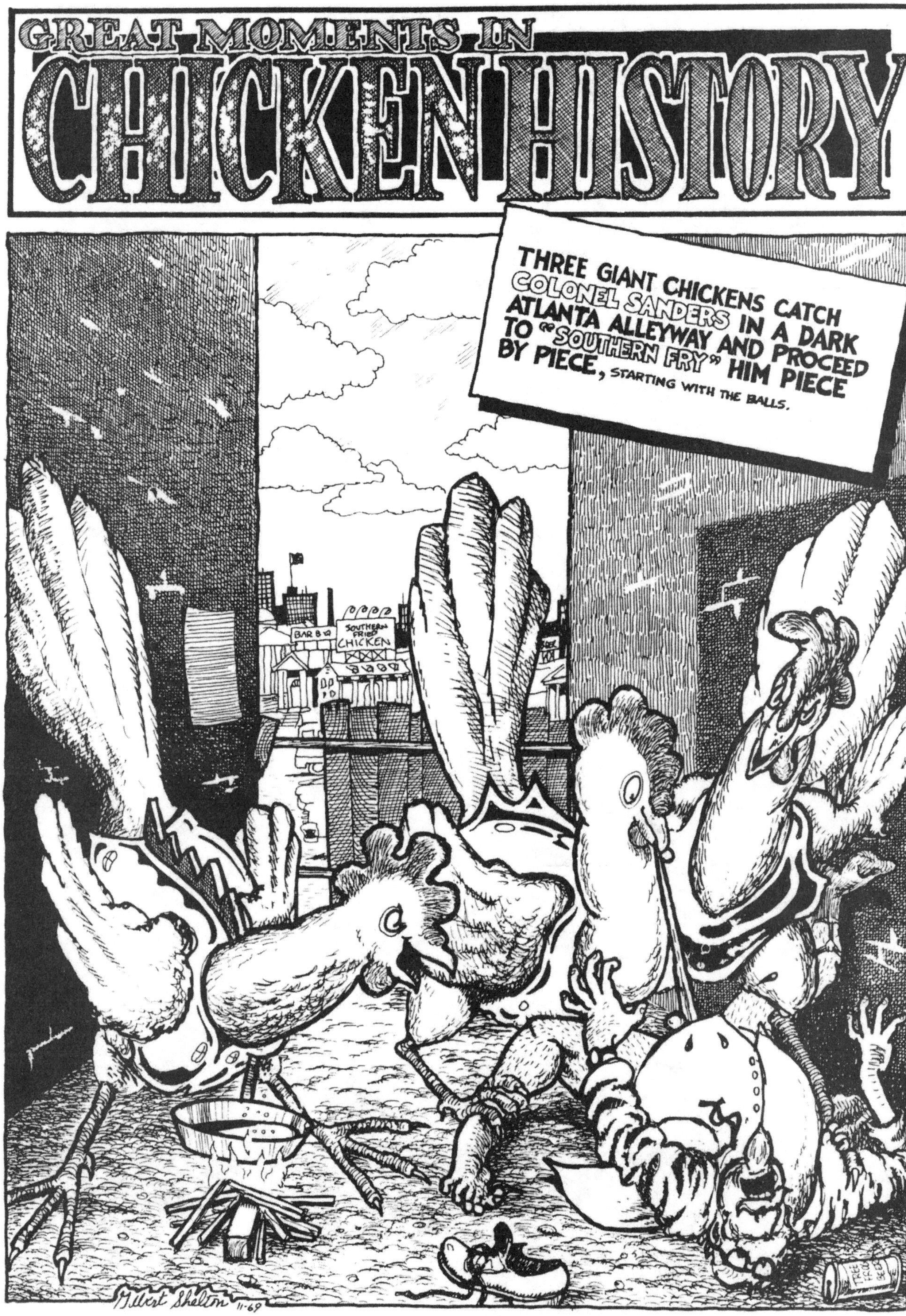
GREAT MOMENTS IN
CHICKEN HISTORY
THREE GIANT CHICKENS CATCH COLONEL SANDERS IN A DARK ATLANTA ALLEYWAY AND PROCEED TO "SOUTHERN FRY" HIM PIECE BY PIECE, STARTING WITH THE BALLS.
BAR B Q
SOUTHERN FRIED CHICKEN
Gilbert Shelton 11-69

KTAK
KTAK
WHO...?

Marshall McLuhan feels that the special form of comics justifies virtually everything put into them. In *Understanding Media,* he criticizes the censors thus: "Having noticed nothing about the *form,* they could discern nothing of the *contents,* either. The mayhem and violence were all they noted. Therefore, with naive literary logic, they waited for violence to flood the world. Or, alternatively, they attributed existing crime to the comics. The dimmest-witted convict learned to moan, 'It wuz comic books done this to me.'"

Top: Jaxon. *Skull Comics* No. 3. ©1971 Irons, Sheridan, Gore, Spain, and Jaxon. By permission of Messrs. Sheridan, Gore, and Jaxon.

Left: Spain. *The Collected Trashman.*

Opposite and Below Left: Rich Veitch. *Two-Fisted Zombies* No. 1. ©1973 Veitch Brothers Enterprises. By permission of Veitch Brothers Enterprises, by Rick Veitch.

The underground comics, unlike the violent books of the forties and fifties, are notably free of hypocrisy (for which the authors simply see no reason). This freedom gives the artists a chance to take an ironic, if not necessarily humorous, perspective on the violence they depict, as in Robert Crumb's portrayal of an unthinking and pointless murder, shown in exaggerated but realistic terms, followed immediately by the character reminding the readers that the whole thing is only a drawing.

A special application of violence in the underground comics occurs with Gilbert Shelton's Wonder Wart-Hog. Paul Buhle has written of the relationship between the "straight" superheroes' asexuality and their violence: "The outlet for such sexual starvation was, of course, violence. In the early superhero series vengeance-murder by the hero himself was not unknown, but whatever the justification for retribution, it was always di-

Below: Art Spiegelman. *Funny Aminals* [*sic*] No. 1. ©1972 Art Spiegelman. By permission of Art Spiegelman.

rected against the indispensable, perennial outsiders—spies during wartime, later mostly crooks—who seek to disrupt the community or nation-state. The 1960's run of new comic heroes . . . are [*sic*] generally better drawn and more ironic than their predecessors. But in the fight against the

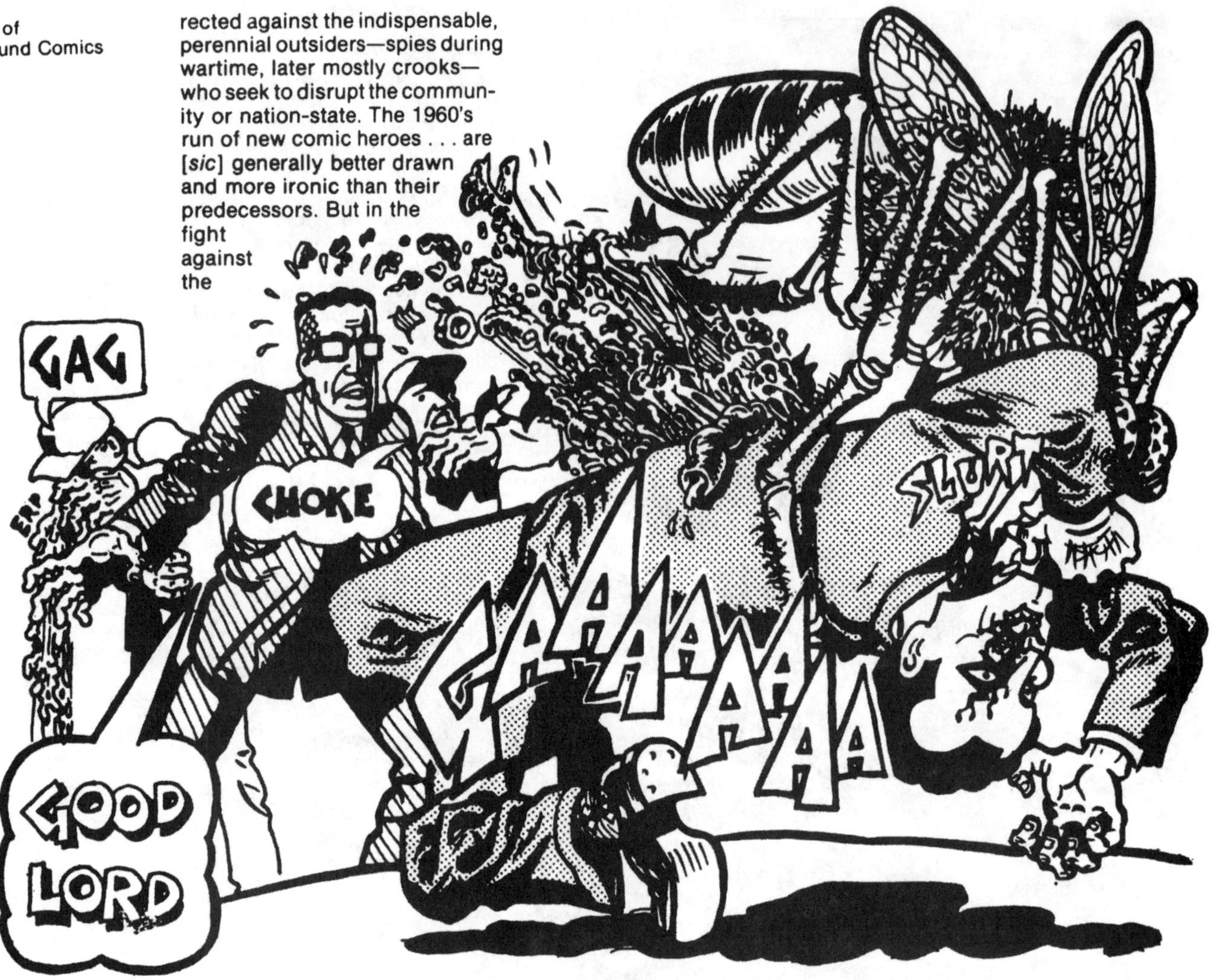

Above: Spain. *Insect Fear* No. 2.

Gooks there is no question which side they join, and equally no question about their consternation with a return from their superidentities to everyday life, which they transcend simply to cheerfully defend."

Wonder Wart-Hog carries these principles to an extreme of absurdity. Aside from being superpowerful, he weighs in at six hundred and thirty-nine pounds. Yet he persists in being human enough to get extremely angry at anyone who crosses him, the result generally being dismemberment for the unfortunate individual. In fact, Wonder's temper prevents him from being the good law enforcement official he should be: he has a tendency to tear crooks apart before they can give him information about their crimes.

Wonder Wart-Hog is also, of course, a satire on superheroic sexuality (see Chapter 5). His sexual desires have a way of erupting into violence and murder. And Wonder, like the

Right: Gilbert Shelton. *Zap Comix* No. 3.

Opposite: Jay Kinney and Ned Sonntag. *Young Lust* No. 2. ©1971 Roger Brand, Justin Green, Bill Griffith, Jay Kinney, "Pap" Shmeer, and James Osborne. By permission of Messrs. Green, Griffith, and Kinney.

THIS CALLS FOR DISCIPLINARY ACTION... SUCH AS A GANG BANG... RIGHT, BOYS??
MAN, I BEEN DYIN' FER SOME O' THAT HIPPIE CUNT! HOW 'BOUT YOU, FRED?
DAMN RIGHT LARRY! I LOVE TO FUCK!!
WANT
BERNAD DOHR
GROOT
YEEEE!
POW BUDDA POW BUDDA POW BUDDA POW
INSTANT KARMA TIME
WHRAM!
WHRAM!
JIM!
BARAM!
NG!
LATER
I CAN SEE THAT SELF-DEFENSE IS IMPORTANT... BUT...
WELL, SHEILA, LOVE AND VIOLENCE ARE TWO SIDES OF THE SAME COIN...
Detroit Free Press
20 COPS FOUND DEAD IN UNDERWEAR
Suspect Ritual Murder
US TROOPS DRIVEN OUT OF N. VIET-N
AS CHAIRMAN MAO SAYS: "LOVE COMES OUT OF THE BARREL OF A GUN!"
The End

OOPS!
...SORRY...
BOK
SORRY!!?...
LOOKIT THIS MESS!!! ...TAKE OFF THOSE GLASSES I'M GONNA REARRANGE YOUR FACE!
MMMM.... YESSS... WELL ...FRAID NOT OLD MAN
...GIVEN UP PHYSICAL VIOLENCE, Y'SEE...
FRIGHTFUL WASTE OF ENERGY....
...BLOODY INFANTILE TOO!!
FLICK
DON'T FIGHT EH??
WELL THIS IS YOUR UNLUCKY DAY, FELLA!.. ...CAUSE I DO!
UHHH... COULDN'T WE JUST.... ...FUCK INSTEAD?

"straight" superheroes, has no difficulty in returning to everyday life. Therein lies Gilbert Shelton's satire, which is double-edged because the Hog always seems so damned lovable.

(Parlous words from *The Phantom Psychiatrist:* "There may be a part in a lot of people who kind of, as the guy is pulling people apart, can say, hey, you know, that's pretty good—I like that. And a part of the person may resonate to this—saying hey, that's pretty good. Then there may be another part of the same person which may say, Jesus Christ, that's a horrible way to be, a horrible way to act. This may be in the same person—in the guy who draws this character—both the emphasizing of violence and the guilt feelings about the emphasis.")

As Coulton Waugh has noted in his study of *The Comics* (The Macmillan Company, 1947), the masking and hooding of the "straight" superheroes, despite the fact that these characters are always on the side of goodness and the democratic way, suggests the Ku Klux Klan far more than the democratic process, since it is the pictures in comic books which speak most directly to the readers, not the words. Wonder Wart-Hog is the logical extension of the kind of above-the-law, lynch-mob justice espoused by Superman and his ilk and favored by the same elements in American society which are always the first to cry "law and order" and "use the democratic process" when those phrases suit them.

In violence as in sex, the underground cartoonists are extreme, unhypocritical, wry, and sarcastic. The freedom with which these artists depict violence has the inherent value of any uncensored form. But it is when the violence is incorporated into a form of social satire that the underground cartoonists are at their best.

Opposite: Rand Holmes. *Harold Hedd* No. 2. ©1973 Rand Holmes. By permission of Rand Holmes.

Left: Bill Griffith. *Tales of Toad* No. 2. ©1971 Bill Griffith. By permission of Bill Griffith.

Left: Kim Deitch. *Insect Fear* No. 2.

Left: S. Clay Wilson. *Real Pulp Comics* No. 1. ©1971 Joel Beck, Roger Brand, Leslie Cabarga, Kim Deitch, Justin Green, Bill Griffith, Art Spiegelman and Ron White. By permission of Messrs. Beck, Deitch, Green and Griffith.

Below: Jay Kinney. *Young Lust* No. 2. ©1971 Roger Brand, Justin Green, Bill Griffith, Jay Kinney, "Pap" Shmeer, and James Osborne. By permission of Messrs. Green, Griffith, and Kinney.

7 The World Around Us

"Like any potentially subversive cultural mechanism, komix serve at best to destroy an old view of the world and to replace it with a new one."—Paul Buhle, editor of *Radical America.*

Far Right: Robert Crumb. *Zap Comix* No. 0.

Opposite: Gilbert Shelton. *Hydrogen Bomb and Biochemical Warfare Funnies.* ©1970 Rip Off Press. By permission of Rip Off Press, by Gilbert Shelton.

Right: Bill Crawford. *High-Flyin' Funnies Comix and Stories.* ©1970 Bill Crawford. By permission of Bill Crawford.

Below Right: Skip Williamson. *Bijou Funnies* No. 3. ©1969 Bijou Publishing Empire, Inc. By permission of Bijou Publishing Empire, Inc., by Jay Lynch.

Below: Pete Poplaski. *Snarf* No. 4. ©1973 Denis Kitchen. By permission of Denis Kitchen.

"Picasso has long been a fan of American comics. The highbrow from Joyce to Picasso, has long been devoted to American popular art because he finds in it an authentic imaginative reaction to official action. Genteel art, on the other hand, tends merely to evade and disapprove of the blatant modes of action in a powerful high definition, or 'square,' society. Genteel art is a kind of repeat of the specialized acrobatic feats of an industrialized world. Popular art is the clown reminding us of all the life and faculty that we have omitted from our daily routines." —Marshall McLuhan, *Understanding Media.*

Let there be no mistake: many underground cartoonists have tried to reach people through more "socially accepted" means of artistic expression than comic books and found they were not able to get through. Writes Foolbert Sturgeon, "It seems to me that fine art is becoming cheap and sleazy—responding to the knowledge that images (because of tv, magazines, etc.) are so plentiful it is almost impossible to get anyone to really *look* at a piece of art, the artist simplifies, cheapens, uses shock tactics to get attention. The end result is that when he looks at the image, the viewer finds it is not worth considering. Given a choice between cheap sleazy boring art (Ernest Trova or Frank Stella) and cheap sleazy fascinating art ("Little Orphan Annie," S. Clay Wilson's demons), it seems a natural human response to prefer the comics. There at least you retain the sense of humanity."

Sturgeon's frustration at "highbrow" art is echoed by other cartoonists who have tried that route and found it at best ineffective. Wendel Alan Pugh: "I feel the gallery and museum art being done today is decadent and more talent should be directed toward mass media, i.e., television, newspapers, comics, magazines, radio, 'cause lotsa' kids are lookin' and listenin' to this stuff and more good stuff ought to be done for 'em to look at. . . . Paintings are very insular. You're playing to a set audience, an elite. It's like paying homage to money or something." Justin Green: "I made the 'grand tour' of Italy and was led through heavily guarded corridors plastered with smoky canvasses of the Old Masters. . . . I was always thinking about my own roots while I was confronted with the carcass of this dead culture, and I realized that the most powerful visual experiences I had had were Donald Duck (Fox and Crow taught me how to read and write), Howdy Doody, Popeye. . . ."

Given such background, it is not surprising that the underground comics have their finest hours in the field of social satire. In the past, social criticism has been more likely to come from critics of comics than from the comics themselves. Thus, G. Legman, in *Love and Death,* was inspired by the violence of the comics of the forties to write: "Murder is a crime. Describing murder is not. Sex is not a crime. Describing sex *is.*

Why? The penalty for murder is death, or lifelong imprisonment—the penalty for writing about it: fortune and lifelong fame. The penalty for fornication is . . . there is no actual penalty—the penalty for describing it in print: jail and lifelong disgrace. Why this absurd contradiction? Is the creation of life really more reprehensive than its destruction? . . . Is our future to be more and more policemen restraining the incubated murderers of more and more tabloids, of more and more murder-mysteries, comic-books, picture-mags, movies, radio and television horror; protecting us from the breast-fed whelps of more and more bitch-heroines?"

Now that a time has come in which the police do feel constrained to protect us from ourselves, especially if the "ourselves" are young and unenchanted by those police, the underground cartoonists have begun to explore, in the medium of comics, the concerns which Legman was prompted to discuss by observing the medium in a much earlier stage of development.

The underground cartoonists often express the view that they are satirists working for social change. Bill Griffith does it lightheartedly: "Don't you know it's all part of the plot to break down the bourgeois family?" Buckwheat Florida Jr. does it modestly: "I guess I express thoughts already held by many people, because I'm just one more person that feels that way—a propagandist, but not a very good one." Denis Kitchen backs into

Little Orphan Amphetamine
DON'T YOU GET BORED JUST SITTING AROUND THE MANSION ALL DAY, ANNIE? WHY DON'T YOU GO OUT AND GET A JOB?
AW, GET FUCKED, "DADDY." I'VE HAD ENOUGH BULLSHIT OFF YOU.
"GENUINE EQUALITY BETWEEN THE SEXES CAN ONLY BE REALIZED IN THE PROCESS OF THE SOCIALIST TRANSFORMATION OF SOCIETY AS A WHOLE." —MAO TSE-TUNG
COME ON, GRUNTCAKES. WE'RE GOING TO GO AND LIVE OFF THE LAND!
FIRST, I GOTTA GET MY STASH...
ARF! WHIMP!
GOING TO - CALIFORNIA?
SURE, LITTLE GIRL! HOP IN!
DROOL?
FIVE MINUTES LATER...
IT WON'T DO YOU ANY GOOD TO CRY, LITTLE GIRL! NO ONE EVER COMES ALONG THIS BACK ROAD!
WOW, MAN, WHAT KIND OF FUCKEDUP TRIP ARE YOU ON? OH WELL, GO ON AND DO YOUR THING!
AFTER A NUMBER OF RIDES...
WELL, GRUNTCAKES, HERE WE ARE IN SAN FRANCISCO. THERE'S A GROOVY LOOKING GUY...
HEY, YOU KNOW ANY PLACE WHERE I CAN CRASH?
?
HEY, LOOKY WHAT I FOUND!
ALWAYS ROOM FOR ONE MORE... (HEH HEH)
HERE, DO SOME SMACK 'N ACID...
HI! YOU CAN COME SIT ON MY FACE!
WHATCHA GOT IN THAT BAG?
BORN TO LOSE
WOW! YAY! DEXAMILS! (GULP)
HEY, DO YOU HAVE FORTY-FIVE DOLLARS SO WE CAN GO AND SCORE SOME SKAG
HEY, I KNOW A GUY WHO MIGHT PAY TWENTY BILLS TO FUCK YOU, SWEETHEART.
WOW, A PHONE CREDIT CARD!
QUIT CLEANING YOUR FINGERNAILS WITH MY WORKS, MAN!
HAW! HAW! HAW! I LAUGHED SO HARD I SHIT IN MY PANTS!
YOU EVER SHOT UP BIRTH CONTROL PILLS, BEAUTIFUL???
LETS COOK UP THAT BIG FAT DOG AND EAT IT!
ME NEXT.
AAH!
ARG!
URP.
"DADDY," GRUNTCAKES AND I NEED $400 SO WE CAN FLY HOME AND SEE MY DOCTOR AND MY SHRINK!
LOOK AT ALL THOSE BIG BLACK SPIDERS ON THE CEILING!
I'M DY-ING!
I THINK I HEAR THE POLICE COMING UP!
THIS IS THE END!
EEE!
LIVE SNAKES EVERYWHERE!
I MUSTA O.D.'D AN' GONE TO HELL!
MY HEART HAS STOPPED!
ONE AND ONE HALF WEEKS LATER...
THE TROUBLE WITH YOU, "DADDY," IS YOU'RE A CAPITALIST PIG! WHY DON'T YOU DROP ACID AND GET OFF YOUR INCREDIBLE POWER TRIP?
?
AND SO ON.

the role, saying that he considers himself an entertainer and then adding, "But there are political and social messages . . . which make the label 'entertainer' inadequate. Perhaps 'satirist' is the most apt, if not presumptuous."

The underground cartoonists do *not* want to be presumptuous in their presentation of social messages and do not want to talk down to their readers. When they feel themselves starting to sound like preachers, their reaction is immediate, as in the following exact excerpt from a letter to me by Justin Green: "I have a social conscience and I would like to use my work as a vehicle for social change. That may be an indirect (though welcomed) side effect but by changing consciousness I mean that reality is so much richer utilitarian notions of man sorry this is just so much bullshit."

Jay Kinney. *Bijou Funnies* No 2. ©1969 Jay Lynch. By permission of Jay Lynch.

It is only the most arrogant preacher or critic who has the nerve to tell other people how to run their lives. The social reformer, to avoid that arrogance and show respect for the intelligence of his audience, must concentrate on exposing the problems of society rather than on proposing solutions to those problems. This is a point often misunderstood by critics of the young radicals of today (and indeed of earlier times): it is not nihilism or anarchy to spend all one's time pounding away at the rot and decadence of society, because it is only when the consciousness of that decadence becomes universal that there is real potential for changing society for the better.

From this point of view, every underground cartoonist who addresses himself to social issues (as almost all of them do) is a social radical. The satire often cuts at the radical establishment as well as at the "overground" one (which led one SDS member

Denis Kitchen. *Mom's Homemade Comics* No. 3. ©1971 Denis Kitchen. By permission of Denis Kitchen.

Below: Skip Williamson. *Bijou Funnies* No. 1. ©1968 Jay Lynch. By permission of Jay Lynch.

to tell Paul Buhle that his *Radical America Komiks* was "counterrevolutionary"), but there is no doubt that the conservative and liberal thinkers are more subject to satire than the radical ones.

In one especially important case, an underground cartoonist has addressed himself exclusively and vividly to social issues, particularly the issue of ecology, and has even designed what is now a well-known symbol being used by groups seeking to slow down man's rapid destruction of his natural environment. This cartoonist is Ron Cobb, who designed the simple-looking ecology symbol from the letters "e" and "o" in the word "ecology"—but only after passing the letters through an extensive set of logical and philosophical meanings. The letter "e," for instance, was at one point referred to as "the ellipse: a symbolic demonstration of the transcendent unity that pervades all dualities"; and the letter "o," first transformed into a circle, next appeared to Cobb as "the square: same as circle but more as concept or idea than actual experience (C. G. Jung)."

Cobb's symbol was quickly

The ecology symbol created by Ron Cobb in the opening panel of ***Raw Sewage.***

John Pound. ***Death Rattle*** No. 1. ©1972 Krupp Comic Works, Inc. By permission of Krupp Comic Works, Inc., by Denis Kitchen.

Opposite: Robert Crumb. *Home Grown Funnies.* ©1971 R. Crumb. By permission of Robert Crumb.

Below: Ron Cobb. *Raw Sewage.* ©1968 R. Cobb. By permission of Sawyer Press, by Eric Matlen.

adopted by various ecologically oriented groups and publications. More important, Cobb continues to produce acute, superbly drawn cartoons about man and his environment. For Cobb, this social consciousness in the cartoons is the natural by-product of his own concerns: he realizes, as few people do, that "ecology, in a very sinister and sneaky way, is anti-capital and anti-civilization as we know it. I don't think a lot of people realize this. They're just out there starting to clean up the environment because it obviously is unpleasant—even deadly to some. But fully accomplished, their goal spells out the end of the *idea* of production which is the traditional idea of progress! Progress was always a measure of just how far we had overwhelmed the environment; progress represented our conquest of nature. But we *are* nature, nature is in our bodies, it's in our bones. And sure enough, as we destroy nature, we are destroying our bodies."

Cobb is aware of the difficulties posed by ecological planning, and equally aware of the problems ecological concerns can create. In his Sawyer Press book *Raw Sewage,* which opens with the creation of the ecology symbol, Cobb obviously came face-to-face with an ecological reality: Eric Matlen's introduction to the book ends with the words, "When this book no longer has any meaning for you as a book, rip the pages out and use the paper in some other manner. Remember, a lot of trees had to die to put it in your hands."

HE SHEDS BITTER TEARS FOR THE STATE OF THE HUMAN RACE!!
THE DUM SHITS!
THE STUPID FUCKING SONS OF BITCHES!! THOSE FUCK-ING ASSHOLES!!
SOB SOB
THEY'RE RUINING IT FOR ALL OF US!! THEY'RE DESTROYING OUR PLANET!! THOSE BLIND ARROGANT BUNGLING FOOLS!!
THOSE VISCIOUS POWER-HUNGRY INSANE MANIACS!
THEY SHOULD ALL BE KILLED! EVEN NOW THEY CONTINUE TO CREATE EVEN MORE AND GREATER METHODS OF DESTRUCTION!!
WHY? WHY?
HOW CAN WE STOP THEM? OR IS IT... IS IT...
IS IT TOO LATE?
ALREADY THE BOTTOM OF THE OCEAN IS LITTERED WITH DEADLY NERVE GASSES AND OTHER POISONS THAT ARE DAY-BY-DAY EATING THEIR WAY THROUGH THEIR LEAD CONTAINERS!!!
STUPID LANDOPOIDS!
TO THINK OF IT FOR EVEN ONE MINUTE I BECOME ENRAGED!!
THESE EVIL MEN MUST BE STOPPED!! AND SOON!! WE HAVE TO MOVE AGAINST THEM AS SOON AS POSSIBLE, FOR THEY WILL NOT CEASE TO DESTROY LIFE ON EARTH OF THEIR OWN FREE WILL...
BUT HOW?
HOW DO YOU GET AT THEM?
WHAT ARE THE MEANS ??
THEY ARE WELL-ARMED AND THEIR POWER STRUCTURE IS VAST, BUT HOW MUCH CONTROL DO THEY REALLY HAVE!? HOW SMART ARE THEY?
SHOULD WE TAKE THE OFFENSIVE? OR WOULD THAT BE TOO DANGEROUS? WOULD IT BE A MISTAKE TO BECOME AGGRESSIVE?? WOULD IT MAKE THINGS WORSE? WOULD WE BE-COME LIKE THEM??
I DONT KNOW... I JUST DON'T KNOW...
FUCK IT!

Cobb's situation shows, in microcosm, the problems faced by underground cartoonists seeking social change. Cobb knows that ecological balances can only be restored after people realize that nature is not compatible with *any* system of government which measures progress in material terms. But trying to put that idea across would lead to his instant labeling as a "radical freak" who is out of touch with reality. Consequently Cobb must continue to do cartoons showing

Jim Osborne. *Slow Death Funnies* No. 1. ©1970 The Visual Yoyo Tribe. By permission of The Visual Yoyo Tribe, by Ronald E. Quinn

Patrick Cosgrove. *Yellow Dog Comix* No. 16.

what's wrong with our present situation—thus leaving himself open to charges of seeking to tear down a system without planning to replace it with anything new.

Caught in the middle of such problems as this, the underground cartoonists often direct their social satire at the approaches of other social reformers, particularly self-styled

Richard Corben. *Slow Death Funnies* No. 2. © 1970 Jaxon, Sheridan, Osborne, and Gore. By permission of Messrs. Jaxon, Sheridan, and Gore.

liberals. Consider Robert Crumb's interpretation of a speech at "a gathering of America's intelligentsia for the purpose of defining the goals and image of the United States in the world": "Looking at it from the socio-humanist point of view you get a whoosis on America that contradicts the very whatsis of the something-or-other and therefore you must come up with a whole schtick on the thingie gingie ramadama ding dong consarned dagnabbed floop doop problem of existential time-space muthafuggin' continuum howsomever contradictory to the theory put forth here early today that I've been talking thru my hat when I expressed the belief that the present crisis in American civilization was due chiefly to the snark-farkin' ape-shit asshole syndrome being promoted by the mugwump faction of America's pork 'n' bean-fartin' fishface wing and not only that . . ."

Needless to say, this speech is done in lettering so small that it takes up only part of a single panel, the rest of which is given over to a scene of total boredom on the part of everyone present at the meeting. Anyone who has attended such a "solve the world's problems in twenty-four hours or less and win a Kewpie doll" session will recognize the speech at once, and perhaps plug in some words of his own where Crumb writes nonsense syllables. It is Crumb's hope, and the hope of the other underground cartoonists, that enough exposure to material like this, which shows the absurdity of present approaches to society's problems,

Larry Welz. *Slow Death Comix* No. 3. ©1971 Corben, Irons, Osborne, Jaxon, Welz, Sheridan, and Last Gasp Eco-Funnies, Inc. By permission of Messrs. Jaxon, Sheridan, and Last Gasp Eco-Funnies, Inc., by Ron Turner.

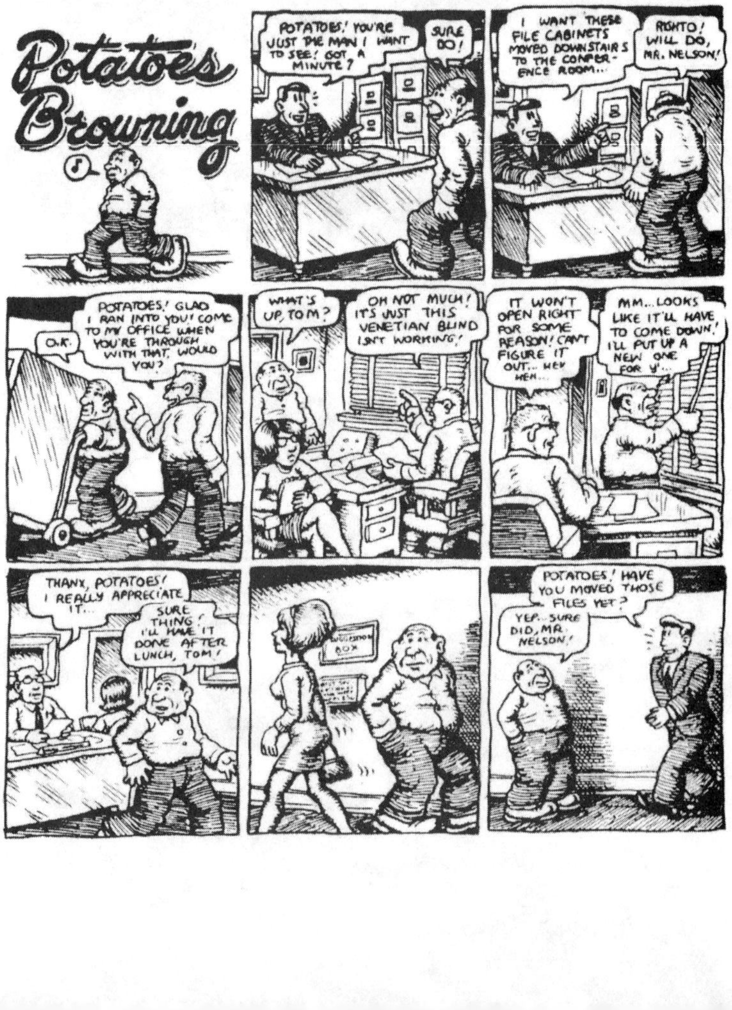

Far Right: Robert Crumb. *Motor City Comics* No. 2. ©1970 R. Crumb. By permission of Robert Crumb.

Right: Gary Grimshaw. *Slow Death Funnies* No. 1. ©1970 The Visual Yoyo Tribe. By permission of Visual Yoyo Tribe, by Ronald E. Quinn.

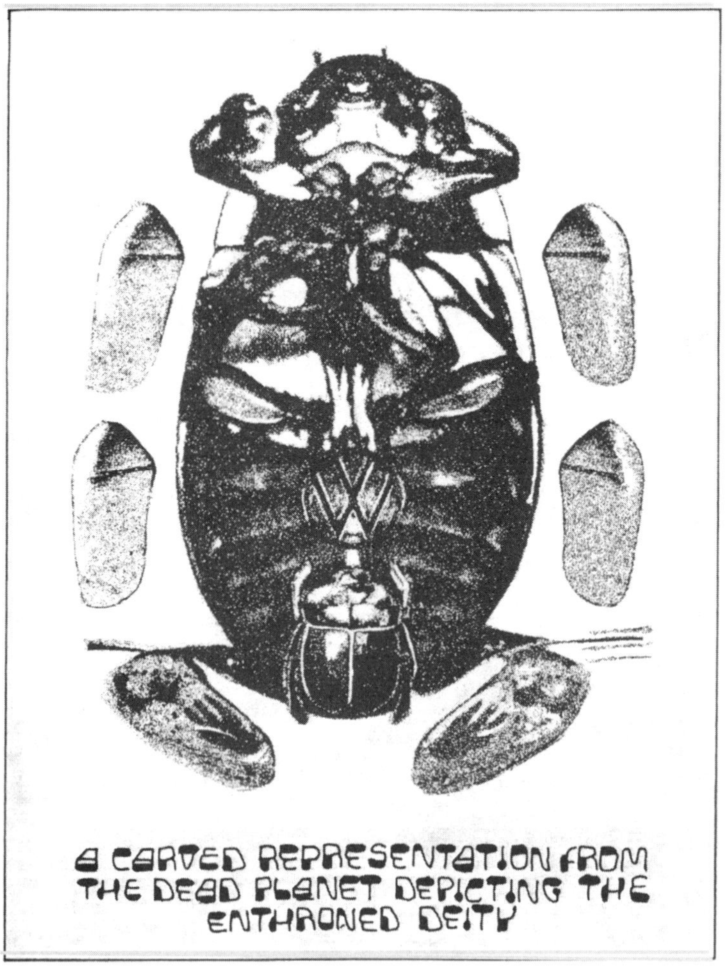

Jaxon. *Happy Ending Comics.* ©1969 Jaxon. By permission of Jaxon.

Dan O'Neill. *Dan O'Neill's Comics and Stories.*

will eventually make the reader feel the necessity for radical action and be willing to take such action. The idea is that even a reader who is unwilling to take radical action himself will have his consciousness sufficiently altered by these comics so that, when others do take radical action to change society, the reader will support that action—or at the *very* least will not oppose it.

Social satire in the underground comics usually takes the form of humorous (sometimes bitter) exaggerations of various aspects of American society, from money hunger to art and music. At times, the satire is found mostly in the words, as in the Crumb example already cited and in several stories—actual, unillustrated short stories—in books like *Happy Ending Comics.* The stories in this book (which also contains cartoon strips) reduce all of society to absurdity by simple vocabularies and a childlike approach to the material: "Some of the toys could be used for different games—like the 'bow and arrow.' The men who played with these toys in certain ways got special names—'rulers'—because it took so much work to figure this all out. To make it a 'fair deal' the rulers gave the men who didn't play their game so well a name too—'slaves.'"

This quintessential history book in comic form was a unique product of the mind of Jaxon, and even the cartoonist himself says he tried to stretch the medium a little too far with the experiment and will not do a similar book again. But the all-written comic-book story, while it could never be as effective as the picture-plus-words stories which have always given comics their special power of communication, is important evidence of the lengths to which the underground cartoonists will go in their attempts to bring readers their views on social questions.

In attempting to put across social messages, other underground cartoonists have stretched the bounds of the traditional comic strip quite a bit. The more usual underground social satire, which is sarcastic toward American values and institutions, could easily be dismissed by a "straight" reader, who might ask, "What's so funny about that? Where do those kids come off mocking the Marines (or baseball, hot dogs, or apple pie)?" But Robert Crumb has developed a new type of strip (of which "Potatoes Browning" on page 162 is an example) which short-circuits a "straight" reader's intuitive hostility. Crumb's social realism (for it is more that than social satire) causes the reader to ask, "What's wrong with that?" rather than "What's funny about that?" The question of what's wrong does not permit an easy retreat behind defense mechanisms on the reader's part, while the question of what's funny does. In this type of strip, Crumb plays on people's intuitive "feel" for comic-strip content—perhaps you too could not understand why "Potatoes Browning" should be a comic strip in the first place.

In his "social realism" strips, Crumb does not mock American society; rather, he presents it for what it is and trusts the reader eventually to realize that the strips are funny because the society itself is absurd. It is noteworthy that a strip like "Potatoes Browning" completely avoids profanity, while ones featuring "The Old Pooperoo, the Cosmic Shit Shoveler"—a more sarcastic version of Potatoes—overflow with it. This is a matter of aiming the strips at different audiences.

Crumb has not been the only underground cartoonist to attempt the special brand of social realism exemplified by "Potatoes Browning." On occasion, Jay Kinney has also worked in this manner. Kinney describes his approach as follows: "With strips like 'Chicaga Tribune Wholesome Comics' I try to put down on paper relatively true visions of middle-class life as I see it. . . . Hopefully by capturing all this on paper, I can help people to see themselves more objectively and insightfully. Heheheheheh."

Robert Crumb. *Zap Comix* No. 3.

Robert Crumb. *Despair.*

The general philosophy of the underground cartoonists may be summed up by Paul Buhle's comments on Crumb: "The suggestion is, of course, that *only* mythological figures can be free in capitalist America; the rest of us just squeeze by." It is not necessary to have Buhle's political consciousness to accept this statement, since even apolitical underground cartoonists (there are some) *do* believe that most of us "just squeeze by" in American life.

Some special aspects of American life come up for special treatment by the cartoonists. One of these is religion. Here the harsh satire is likely to be directed against people who pervert religion for their own personal gain, or who have forgotten the basic precepts of brotherhood and loving your neighbor in their urge to wave American flags and Bibles at anyone wearing a beard.

Several underground cartoonists have independently created stories in which Jesus Christ returns to the modern world and interacts with modern man. There are churchmen who have lately been expounding "the radical nature of Christ as man," but it is the underground cartoonists who are truly interpreting Jesus in a radical context. One

Below: Jay Kinney. *Bijou Funnies* No. 3. ©1969 Bijou Publishing Empire, Inc. By permission of Bijou Publishing Empire, Inc., by Jay Lynch.

plot which has appeared in several stories has Christ returning to earth and attempting to preach the same sentiments which may be found in the Gospels. A typical reaction of bystanders to this bearded man who preaches peace and love is the following: "Fuckin' queer!" "Goddamn weirdo beatnik commie!" "Beat th' shit out of 'im!" In one story, Jesus does in fact get the shit beaten out of him by two policemen whom he then turns into pigs. The political implications of that are obvious; but in general, religious satire in the underground comics is not so overtly political. In many stories, Jesus is simply given a sense of humor and a sense of anger (both of which are attributed to him by the Gospels anyway). Bringing these characteristics to the fore changes the course of many events.

The most important underground religious critic is Foolbert Sturgeon, whose own religious background was very conservative. Sturgeon is responsible for *The New Adventures of Jesus* ("If you liked the New Testament, you'll LOVE this NEW IMPROVED Testament"). Sturgeon is fond of retelling various parables, such as the one in which Jesus warns, "Let he who is without sin cast the first stone." Naturally enough, *Jesus* is offered the first stone, which leads to a remark the Gospels somehow missed: "The problem isn't sin. It's stupidity."

Sturgeon says he has no trouble remembering how he got started drawing the *New Jesus* adventures: "I had a lot of fury pent up at being in the Army, and was feeling very anarchistic at the time. Looking back on the con-

Richard Corben. *Up from the Deep* No. 1. ©1971 Jaxon, Corben, Deitch, and Irons. By permissions of Messrs. Jaxon, Corben, and Deitch.

Robert Crumb. *Despair.*

Denis Kitchen. *Mom's Homemade Comics* No. 2. ©1969 Denis Kitchen. By permission of Denis Kitchen.

Right: Victor Moscoso. *The New Comix* (Phoenix Gallery poster).

Far Right: Foolbert Sturgeon. *The New Adventures of Jesus.* ©1969 Foolbert Sturgeon. By permission of Foolbert Sturgeon.

stant rage I was in I think I must have been about half nuts. Jesus's behavior represented a perverse, but very personal rationale for me, and I used to chuckle to myself as I did the stories."

An occasional underground strip will appear which takes place in Heaven. Notable among these is "The Spiritual Stag Film," which John Thompson

drew for early issues of *Yellow Dog* (before he became entirely involved in more obscure mysticism). Sam R. God, whose profile reveals him to be half devil and whose dirty bath water, when drained, goes straight into Man's mind, discovers such things as the fact that "All prayers have two goddamn parts: One—Butter Him up; Two—Ask for something."

Another character of this type is Jaxon's God Nose, who first appeared to the general public in a comic called *God Nose* (*Snot Reel*)—"God knows 's not real," see? God Nose roams the world doing wonders with his magic Sinus Wand and gets involved in every question from The Se-

Left and Far Left: Joel Beck. *The Profit.* ©1966 Joel Beck. By permission of Joel Beck.

John Thompson. *Cyclops* (title originally spelled out in Greek letters). ©1969 John Thompson. By permission of John Thompson.

Far Left: Jaxon. *God Nose.* ©1964 Jaxon. By permission of Jaxon.

cret of the Universe to the best available method of contraception.

Religion has produced quite a few extreme, even violent people and groups, and lack of religion has sometimes produced people equally worthy of satire. The underground cartoonists are there. Whether Robert Crumb is portraying his version of the sex-and-violence cult, led by Charles Manson, that committed multiple grisly murders in California in 1969, or Jay Lynch is having a go at outspoken atheist Madalyn Murray O'Hare (who engineered the United States Supreme Court decision banning prayer sessions in public schools), the underground cartoonists' social satire is always directed at one topic: people and their human frailties.

All in all, the underground cartoonists' satire of religion is surprisingly easygoing—perhaps because there is a vein of mystical religious feeling in the comics themselves. When Marshall McLuhan wrote that the earliest comic books to appear were ". . . as difficult to decipher as the *Book of Kells*," he was presumably referring to the quality of the printing rather than the sublimity of "Mutt 'n' Jeff." But in any case, it's obvious that, at the time of *Understanding Media*, McLuhan knew little or nothing about underground comics. If he had known about the mystical comics, he would have realized that *they* are as difficult to decipher as the *Book of Kells*—and that the difficulty isn't caused by poor printing.

Actually, mysticism is not one of the major concerns of the underground cartoonists. John Thompson, the best known and most prolific producer on this topic, says, "I am but a small part of this movement, but I am a part, with my mystical things. A sizable segment of the hip community is interested in mysticism, poetry, and the occult." Thompson and the other artists of the mystical comics do not expect to come through to all readers and do not see why they

Richard Corben. *Up from the Deep* No. 1. ©1971 Jaxon, Corben, Deitch, and Irons. By permission of Messrs. Jaxon, Corben, and Deitch.

Above: Jay Lynch. *Bijou Funnies* No. 1. ©1968 Jay Lynch. By permission of Jay Lynch.

Right: Jim Gardner. *Yellow Dog Comix* No. 18. ©1970 The Print Mint. By permission of The Print Mint, by Bob Rita.

Above: Robert Crumb. The center spread from *Snatch Comics* No. 2. ©1968 R. Scrum. By permission of Robert Crumb. Compare with the center spread of *Snatch Comics* No. 1, page 117.

Left: Pete Poplaski. *Quagmire No. 1.* ©1970 Pete Poplaski. By permission of Pete Poplaski.

HE'S HERE! HE'S HERE! AFTER NINETEEN HUNDRED AND SEVENTY YEARS OF BLASPHEMY AGAINST CHRIST...ALL THE SHAME...ALL THE GUILT...THEY CAN'T HIDE IT ANY LONGER! IT'S THE SECOND COMING! IT'S...
JUMPIN' JACK FLASH!
I AM JACK AND JACK IS ME ...ALL ARE ONE.. YOU ARE ME.. YOU ARE JACK... CEASE TO EXIST.. KILL THE EGO.. BECOME NOTHING... BECOME ME...
JACK FLASH IS GOD!
HE'S THE ONLY REAL MAN I EVER MET!
JACK FLASH IS LOVE!
HE'S THE ONE WHO CAN SAVE HUMANITY!
HE'S A GAS GAS GAS!

Art Spiegelman. *Funny Aminals* [*sic*] No. 1. ©1972 Art Spiegelman. By permission of Art Spiegelman.

Shary Flenniken. *Dopin' Dan* No. 1. ©1972 Shary Flenniken. By permission of Shary Flenniken.

Opposite: Robert Crumb. *Thrilling Murder Comics.* ©1971 B. Griffith, K. Deitch, S. Deitch, R. Crumb, Spain, Wilson, J. Osborne, Irons. By permission of Messrs. Griffith, K. Deitch, and Crumb.

should do so. The mystical comics generally reproduce scenes from within their creators' minds; they do not try to put across any special message. In some cases, mystic symbols are used by the artists only as tools, the net result being a posterlike effect which may have no message outside its own being. For these cartoonists that is enough.

Commenting on John Thompson's work, cartoonist Buckwheat Florida Jr., whose own production bears some superficial resemblances to Thompson's, has said that Thompson is "strictly on his own trip." Indeed he is—but it is a very sensitive, peculiarly warm sort of trip and is expressed in panels of great beauty. Writing of his earliest general-distribution comic book, Thompson says, "In *kingdom of heaven is within you comix,* I played with trying to avoid the usual cartesian rational linear sequential mode of cognition. New more spontaneous modes of cognition flow in eye pattern rhythms. The marriage of word to symbol is relative in terms of widest conscious dynamics. Western mystical systems are invoked in juxtaposing patterns which resolve the polarity between SET & RANDOM. The usual structure of cartesian systematics is transcended for an attempt towards infinite statement. I am conscious of the fact that these works can serve as a mirror to the self-principle. The viewer as relative evaluator puts the value into these things. Thus they are mirrors of consciousness. Some folks think they stink. Some folks think they hold great cosmic truth. Some think them obscene. Some are bored. Some are scared. Your reaction to them is relative to your frame of mind. This is obvious."

There is virtually nothing which can be added to Thompson's comments, which apply to such other works of his as *Cyclops* (a comic titled in Greek), *The Book of Raziel*, and to the work of such other mystics as

Right: Greg Irons. *Yellow Dog Comix* No. 17.

Opposite: John Thompson. *The Book of Raziel.* ©1969 John Thompson. By John Thompson.

Far Right: Jay Kinney. *Conspiracy Capers* No. 1. ©1969 The Conspiracy. By permission of The Conspiracy, by Skip Williamson.

Robert Williams. *Zap Comix* No. 4.

THE VOID
ANTICHRIST
FREEDOM
OF ASSEMBLY
FREE
SPEECH
RELIGION
FREE
PRESS
INVOLUNTA
SERVIT
CALIFORNIA
BERKELEY
PROPER
RIGHTS
POWER
VIOLENCE
PREJUDICE
WAR
RACISM
DRAFT
KRISHNA KRISHNA KRISHNA HARE
HARE KRISHNA HARE
HARE HARE RAMA HARE RAMA RAMA
SELF ACTUALIZATION
ABRAXAS
AIR
ESTEEM
WATER
LOVE & BELONGING
FOOD
SAFETY
SEX
SLEEP
THE HERMAPHRODITIC ANDROGYN
CHRIST
CALCINATION
DISTILLATION
SUBLIMATION
CONGELATION
SEPARATION
FIXATION
SOLUTION
MULTIPLICATION
FERMENTATION
CERATION
VENUS
COPPER
IRON
MARS
TIN
SUN
GOLD
MOON
SILVER
SATURN
LEAD
JUPITER

AIR
WATER
ALPHA
ALPHA
ALPHA
ALPHA
ALPHA
OMEGA
OMEGA
OMEGA
OMEGA
EARTH
FIRE
SEPHER YETZIRAH!
SEPHERHA ZOHAR!
APOCALYPSE!
SPIRIT
HORIZON of ETERNITY
MATTER
ROAD OF LIFE
GOD
DOG
RICK GRIFFIN
FOR BABY BLUE

Jim Evans *(The Dying Dolphin)* and Rick Griffin.

A few underground cartoonists bring their irony even into mystical drawings—something which people who are deeply into mystical experience find rather offensive, but an attitude which is very much in keeping with the underground cartoonists' habit of looking rather wryly at everything around them. Jay Kinney explains why he created one such ironic panel: "'Mysticism For You And Me' is sort of an ironic comment on psychedelic induced mysticism—ironic because I do think that psychedelics can be genuinely used in this regard." Kinney adds that the full significance of his panel is available "only to people familiar with LSD or Eastern thought."

Left: Jim Evans. *The Dying Dolphin.*

Opposite: Rick Griffin. *Zap Comix* No. 3.

Even Rick Griffin, most of whose mystical drawings are quite serious, occasionally shows a touch of humor in his drawings—as in his "Oxo" panel, which on closer inspection proves to be pure penises and vaginas. And probably the most irreverent comment yet on the mystical experience was one of the very earliest, drawn by Jim Gardner for the very first issue of *Yellow Dog*.

Of course, to be truly irreverent one has to be somewhat distanced from one's subject. John Thompson could not easily kid around about the mystical experience, and Willy Mendes could not easily find humor in society's role assignation to women. Even more generally, the underground

Jim Gardner. *Yellow Dog* No. 1. ©1968 The Print Mint. By permission of The Print Mint, by Bob Rita.

Rick Griffin. *Snatch Comics* No. 2. ©1968 R. Scrum. By permission of Robert Crumb.

cartoonists often find it difficult—or impossible—to be irreverent about politics. This is not because they feel close to the American political system, but because the abuses of that system make them so damned angry. Indeed, some cartoonists talk and write on this subject with a vehemence quite unlike their reasoned statements on artistic and social issues. Foolbert Sturgeon: "I don't trust movements, or societies, or trends or authorities or institutions or gangs. I think Richard Nixon is the biggest turd that ever lived."

Robert Crumb. *Bijou Funnies* No. 6. ©1971 Bijou Publishing Empire, Inc. By permission of Bijou Publishing Empire, Inc., by Jay Lynch.

In its most constructive form, this sort of anger is channeled into a cartooning philosophy, as in the case of Justin Green: "There is a statement of Jung's that at puberty the initiate male must adopt the adult value system to displace the blissful childhood world; and when there is aberration or incomplete assimilation, neurosis strikes and the conflict between freedom and responsibility is never resolved. Cartoons, particularly the animal variety, afford an ideal vehicle for mimicking the goals of society in a simplistic childhood way." But even in its most constructive form, the political consciousness of the underground cartoonists invariably comes from a sense of how wrong things are more than a sense of how to make them right—a fact which has led Harvey Kurtzman to remark, "The whole underground movement is so fucking anarchistic. Anarchy may be a lot of fun, but it carries within itself the seeds of its own destruction."

The use of comic characters, with their stock appearance and the clear images they call up in many minds to achieve political ends, is well understood by a few overtly revolutionary Americans. In his book *Seize The Time,* Bobby Seale writes, "Many people have heard me talk about the Superman notions. I try to make this relevant to an everyday situation by talking about the concepts of the comic books; the Donald Duck comic books, Mickey Mouse, Archie and Jughead, etc. These put forth puritanical notions and symbols that are directly related to racism. I began see that Superman was a punk, that Superman didn't relate to replenishing the earth, like Huey Newton [Minister of Defense of the Black Panther Party] and other real people do. Superman is really a superficial fantasy that relates to a steel man. Steel men can't relate to any reality because steel doesn't produce real human life and real human flesh. I talked about how Superman never related to Lois Lane, and that Tricky Dick Nixon and Lynchin' Baines Johnson and those types were the ones that were trying to play Superman, the almighty gods with their anti-tank weapons, and anti-anti-missiles, and hydrogen bombs and missiles that really destroy life. In essence, Superman is a phony and a fake. He never saves any black people in this country in any comic-book stories. And this thirty-year-old figure and the other figures of Donald Duck, all should have beards on. They are older than the hills. They are phony and absurd.

"The *fact* is that a man and a woman relate to each other, that through sexual relations they produce another real human being. Mickey Mouse and Donald Duck never tried to have sexual relations in the comic books with Daisy and Minnie Mouse. Archie

Justin Green. *Illuminations.*

Below: Gary Hallgren. 1973 Berkeley Comix Convention program. ©1973 Gary Hallgren. By permission of Gary Hallgren.

and Jughead never tried to relate sexually to Betty and Veronica in the comic books. These things are very important in terms of how people are brainwashed in society—two-and-a-half billion people on the face of this earth came here through the process of a man and a woman having sexual relations. The omnipotent administrators taboo these things. It's this kind of brainwashing that produced the kind of people who believe that sex is nasty, and talk about 'illegitimate' children. A child, a human being, cannot be illegitimate."

At times, the underground comics can be as overtly propagandistic—and every bit as powerful—as Seale's oratory. At other times, the cartoonists are aware that it's much easier to get a message across, especially a critical one, if you use a bit of humor—preferably about both the other person and yourself. Dr. Jean Rosenbaum, president of the New Mexico Psychoanalytic Association, makes just this point in a panel discussion in the *National Enquirer* (September 13, 1970), and then goes on: "But it's hard to envision Agnew joking about himself. Like most of the rest of us, he takes himself very, very seriously. And if you can imagine President Nixon telling a funny story, I'd really like to hear it."

The underground cartoonists share and extend this attitude. It is usually a basic assumption of the comics that the reader shares the artist's feelings and needs no convincing, but only reinforcement of his present attitudes. This fact alone makes Harvey Kurtzman (who feels that "the New Left takes itself too seriously, anyway") impatient with the politics of the underground cartoonists. Even someone like Robert Crumb, Kurtzman says, begins to sound like "such a hackneyed, clichéd, run-down, old man *bore*" when he turns from "reality, humor and satire" to overt political themes. Besides,

Robert Crumb. *Bijou Funnies* No. 6. ©1971 Bijou Publishing Empire, Inc. By permission of Bijou Publishing Empire, Inc., by Jay Lynch.

Kurtzman says, the underground cartoonists really have nothing new to offer in the way of political comment and have to fall back on spouting quotations from Chairman Mao and other "dummy dum-dum stuff."

There are some underground cartoonists who share Kurtzman's views, such as George Metzger: "I'm not much interested in politics, as it appears to

Ed Badajos. *Filipino Food.* ©1972 David Dawdy. By permission of David Dawdy.

be a loser system. Militancy and revolution (violent revolution) do not appeal to me. Terrorism much abhorred. Violence begets violence, so on like. No 'them or us,' it's all us, all brothers, all on the same planet, race, nationality, all not reality but conceptualizations that hinder our seeing ourselves and our objective reality. I suppose a spiritual Revolution is about the only revolution I'd back . . . Now trying to put stuff like that across in a comic book is mucho difficult." Likewise, John Thompson's philosophy makes him uninterested in politics: "All men are brothers and no one is more or less intelligent than anyone else. No one is more or less creative than anyone else. It's just that some brothers' energies are so scattered out that they at times feel confused and believe themselves uncreative. Each man is God. Each man is an artist in what he does. Each man is a cartoon. We are all cartoons in this spiritual stag film of life. The light in the projector is God."

Yet Metzger's and Thompson's rejections of political orientation in their comics are not the rule. More usually, even those cartoonists who are not politically oriented have at least experimented with that involvement. Says Bill Griffith, "When I was at art school, I was told art and politics require too much energy and time to be anything but mutually exclusive. I was a pacifist (those were the days) and tried hard to prove the exception to the 'rule.' I only ended up proving that the rule was all too real, and my Student Peace Union days came to a close. I still think, perhaps cynically, that politics per se have no value in comics. Things have gotten too serious for that luxury."

But most underground cartoonists are not convinced, at least not yet, that their comics should not contain political messages and cannot, in any case, be politically effective. At the very least, the cartoonists use their work as a way to let out the frustration and anger they feel toward an American political system that claims to bring "liberty and justice for all" but is in reality at the mercy of all sorts of influence peddlers. It is not surprising, therefore, that underground comics are less likely to be oriented toward "positive" political action plans than toward nihilistic, dadaistic, anarchistic satire of existing political figures and institutions.

In the "straight" world, Walt Kelly's "Pogo" strips dealt with political themes, and at times were very harsh on specific political figures. But the satire there differed from that of underground comics because Kelly always disguised his characters somewhat and because, crucially, he retained his basic respect for the American political system which brought those characters into being. This type of respect, which amounts to self-censorship (call the President a murderer, perhaps, but a pervert, never), is diametrically opposed to the attitude of the underground artists. In the underground comics, political figures appear without disguises and without redeeming features, and the political system itself is more often assumed to be evil than to be good.

A peculiar irony in the underground comics is that the most effective political satire does not necessarily come from the most politically oriented cartoonists. Paul Buhle, editor of *Radical America* ("An SDS Journal of American Radicalism"), has written that the underground comics "are subversive thrusts at capitalism coming right out of a popular cultural tradition." But *Radical America Komiks,* which Buhle published as Vol. III, No. 1 of his magazine, was not well received. At the SDS Convention (just before the organization fragmented), reactions to the comic ranged from backhanded compliments ("It's counterrevolutionary but, you know, I like it") to overt,

Far Right: Tom Christopher. *Snarf* No. 3. ©1972 Denis Kitchen. By permission of Denis Kitchen.

Below Right: Pete Poplaski. *Snarf* No. 3. ©1972 Denis Kitchen. By permission of Denis Kitchen.

Below: Ted Richards. *Dopin' Dan* No.1. ©1973 Ted Richards. By permission of Ted Richards.

Skip Williamson. *Bijou Funnies* No. 5. ©1970 Bijou Publishing Empire, Inc. By permission of Bijou Publishing Empire, Inc., by Jay Lynch.

Left: Gilbert Shelton. *Zap Comix* No. 5.

bitter disapproval ("petty bourgeois radicalism"). Buhle has since said that the only really favorable feedback he received came in the form of "Early New Left innocence—use of the comix in organizing, for their own sake to enjoy, etc.—the kind of thing one could have gotten in far greater portions in, I suspect, 1966 or 1967, when people's minds were more fluid." Buhle now believes that "the American scene does not at the present time allow the development of a Revolutionary Esthetic such as illuminated Breton and the other surrealists: here, to become self-conscious to this point means to become stale."

Another cartoonist with strong political leanings, Skip Williamson, is unsure whether comics can be politically effective at all: "It may be a paradox to mix comics with revolutionary culture, because comics deal with the cliché situations created by a decadent society." However, Williamson is still drawing highly political comics. But the feelings of Harvey Kurtzman on the underground cartoonists as political satirists are instructive: "I think Gilbert Shelton is really the most political. I don't think anybody can touch him. I guess I'm thinking in terms of effective politics—I forget a lot of stuff I see, but I always remember Shelton's. When Shelton makes a statement about something it sticks.

"I'm completely intrigued by the effect of art on history and on politics. Art can have an enormous effect. For instance, I think the thing that made the 'youth movement' is music and rock groups, beginning with the Beatles. [*Author's note:* George Metzger says the Beatles were "not a rock band but a great blessed event and phenomenon."] These rock groups aren't people who are into politics—I mean, they're into it, but

Gilbert Shelton. *Hydrogen Bomb and Biochemical Warfare Funnies.* ©1970 Rip Off Press. By permission of Rip Off Press, by Gilbert Shelton.

Below: Skip Williamson. *Bijou Funnies* No. 1. ©1968 Jay Lynch. By permission of Jay Lynch.

Excerpts from two stories in *Conspiracy Capers*. Top by Daniel Clyne; bottom by Jim Osborne. Both ©1969 The Conspiracy. By permission of The Conspiracy, by Skip Williamson.

they're really interested in music. They're artists. And this happens right through history, that an art movement generates a mood and the mood brings people together and then pretty soon they're marching. All of a sudden, you have a 'movement'; and then the political guys come in verbalizing. They're the guys with the vipers' tongues—God, *beware*! Williamson as opposed to Shelton—the fact that he draws Nixon—I couldn't care less, and I suspect that the public is the same way."

Whether or not Kurtzman's reaction is typical (it's worth remembering that he comes from an earlier generation than almost all the underground cartoonists), it points to an interesting bit of irony: Gilbert Shelton, whom Kurtzman praises for his political effectiveness, specifically denies that he is interested in political satire (all he'll say about politics is, "Just like George Wallace, I believe that the least government is the best government"). Furthermore, Shelton actually thinks his political material isn't very successful—and he finds it harder to do than more general social satire, because it goes against his grain to put overt political sentiments into his cartoons. Maybe it's because of such feelings that Shelton *is* so telling and successful: self-proclaimed revolutionaries are usually too hung up on slogans to spend their time radicalizing other people. Shelton provides the classic case in which underground comics must be read on several levels—even his most politically oriented material is, on the surface, funny as hell.

The political involvement of most underground cartoonists goes far beyond that of any "straight" cartoonist. In fact, underground cartoonists sometimes put their art directly at the service of revolutionary politics. One comic, *Conspiracy Capers,* was created for the express purpose of taking in money for the defense fund of the Chicago Eight (later the Chicago Seven) in the conspiracy trial that arose from the riots at the 1968 Democratic National Convention.

The story of *Conspiracy Capers* gives some idea of the problems underground cartoonists can be made to face when their orientation becomes too heavily political to suit the masters of the present system. Abbie Hoffman gave cartoonist Skip Williamson the check he had received as an advance for the book *Woodstock Nation*; this was the money used to produce and print *Conspiracy Capers*. The troubles started immediately: Williamson couldn't find any place in Chicago that would cash a check bearing Hoffman's signature. Finally, through another cartoonist—Howard Friedman of *Tasty Comix*—Williamson found a Washington, D.C. printer who would produce the comic. Williamson says it took three weeks for the comic stories, which were mailed first class, to get from Chicago to Washington, and that the package, when it finally arrived, had been opened in transit and not even resealed. A day after the printer received the comic, Williamson says, two FBI agents came to the print shop and threatened it with loss of future government business if it produced *Conspiracy Capers*. The printer was advised by his lawyer that there was no legal reason not to print the comic, but that it would be better not to do so; the printer took his lawyer's advice, and the comic was finally put out by another printer in the Washington area. All proceeds from the comic, after it finally got published, went toward the legal defense of the Chicago Eight.

Robert Crumb. *Zap Comix* No. 1. ©1967 R. Crumb. By permission of Robert Crumb.

Small wonder that the underground cartoonists who *are* heavily into political areas keep hammering away at their subject! Even someone like Buckwheat Florida Jr., who is *not* a politically oriented cartoonist, traces his development in underground comics partially to "being hassled for long hair, crazy clothes, political ideas, etc. . . . (USA, Georgia, etc. under stupid, fascist politicians, cops, businessmen, etc.)."

In the past, "straight" comics have occasionally expressed political ideas similar to those of the underground cartoonists. The best example is a famous series of "Krazy Kat" strips in which Offissa Pupp tells Ignatz that the mouse is entitled to a hearing before a judge—and then climbs to the bench himself. In a later strip, Offissa Pupp sounds strikingly like Chicago Conspiracy Judge Julius Hoffman when he says, "If you'd rather be found guilty by twelve men instead of one, there is always a 'jury.' "

Yet this kind of political involvement in "straight" strips is extremely rare. The underground cartoonists live in a set of political realities different from those of previous years, and these realities are reflected in the comics themselves. Like many young radicals, most underground cartoonists see the ideal society as a sort of "creative anarchy"—but they are always more concerned with exposing the rot of present society than with developing a new system of government. This is partially because the cartoonists are careful never to degenerate into mere polemicists—but also, as Harvey Kurtzman suggests, because they themselves are not sure how they would cope with success: "I think that they're more interested in the battle than in what the battle is for. What would revolution get any of these guys? In any one of the revolutions we

Below: Robert Crumb. *Despair*.

Spain. *Subvert Comics* No. 2. ©1972 Spain. By permission of Spain.

Below: Robert Crumb. *Despair*.

Spain. *The Collected Trashman.*

know about—Russia, China, Cuba—Shelton and Crumb would be the first ones they'd have to get rid of. Revolution has no end for these guys, but the *fight* is what they're good at, because they're angry men. But without battlefields, they've got no more reason to exist."

Despite Kurtzman's words of warning, one underground comic seems openly to advocate violent revolution, or at least think it inevitable. This comic is Spain Rodriguez' "Trashman, Agent of the Sixth International"—the only out-and-out, continuing "adventure" strip to emerge so far from the world of underground comics. Trashman ("able to decipher meanings from random objects or alter his molecular structure to last week's copy of the *East Village Other*") is an active revolutionary of the most idealized type—a fulfillment of young revolutionaries' Che Guevaran ideals as much as Superman is of other people's Doris Day ones. But his situation is not so simple to define. Trashman operates in a cold, brutal environment, where extreme violence by both sides—operating on opposite ends of a never-quite-defined political and social system in a futuristic world—is the norm. And Trashman isn't out for change, but for revenge—not the healthiest political attitude. The unremitting violence of the strip (influenced, perhaps, by Rodriguez' former membership in a motorcycle gang) eventually seems to occur more for its own sake (as in S. Clay Wilson cartoons) than toward any political end.

It is ultimately violence and not politics around which all Rodriguez' work centers. Next to Trashman, for example, his best-developed character is a vicious

Spain. *Subvert Comics* No. 2. ©1972 Spain. By permission of Spain.

cop named Manning, who uses the law simultaneously as a club and as a shield for murder. But Rodriguez' violence in "Trashman" does operate in a political context—and, incidentally, is made eminently readable because Trashman has so many very human characteristics: he rolls joints, makes love, and even catches a venereal disease. On occasion, Trashman talks to the readers—at which times he keeps a wry enough perspective on his own revolutionary activities to keep those readers interested.

It remains to be seen what kind of political impact the underground comics will have. *The Phantom Psychiatrist* doubts that the comics' effects will be positive: "I think the obvious effect that anything like this will have is the time involved. If you spend your time reading comics, you don't have time for doing a lot of other things, because there's just so much time you've got. Reading comics by itself is kind of passive—it's a non-action kind of thing. So I question it in terms of revolutionary ferment. I don't have the feeling that you're going to be able to get a group moving by everybody sitting down, passing out the comics, and then expecting them to go to the barricades."

Harvey Kurtzman feels that politics distracts the cartoonists from more original work: "In a sense, I resent the people who

Gilbert Shelton. *Zap Comix* No. 5.

Spain. *Zap Comix* No. 4.

Below: Robert Crumb. *Despair.*

Foolbert Sturgeon. *Jesus Meets the Armed Services.* ©1970 The Rip Off Press. By permission of The Rip Off Press, by Gilbert Shelton.

Jay Kinney. *Bijou Funnies* No. 2. ©1969 Jay Lynch. By permission of Jay Lynch.

Skip Williamson. *Conspiracy Capers* No. 1. ©1969 The Conspiracy. By permission of The Conspiracy, by Skip Williamson.

would make these things political, not because I don't believe in being political—we should all have a political point of view—but they're usually so hackneyed, so corny. When these guys get into politics, they don't come up with anything new. They point to the Left, to China and Cuba—but those philosophies are so tired, so old-fashioned. The only thing they have in common with these guys is that they're on the side of change. Of course, they're on the side of *revolutionary* change, but that isn't enough for me. I don't want to change just for the sake of change—I want the world to be better. And what's exciting is the guys who are making new changes. What Crumb and Wilson and Shelton do naturally, *artistically*—it's all creative and it's all new."

Of course, both Kurtzman and *The Phantom Psychiatrist* are older and less radical than most underground cartoonists. (The latter admits, "I guess I come from a generation where revolution needed a little more organization and getting together and planning.")

No underground cartoonist actually expects his work to send readers to the barricades (though some wouldn't mind if theirs did). At least, the politics in the underground comics prevent the comics from degenerating into mere escapism, keep certain issues and attitudes in front of the readers—and perhaps make the atmosphere a little more charged, encouraging radical thought if not yet radical action. The underground cartoonists are contributing to a revolution of the mind. If and only if a more physical revolution comes will we know how deeply they have affected their readers. And let us not forget one other point: no society can long stand before ridicule, and the ridicule of American society (both stated and implicit) which pervades the underground comics is therefore likely to prove a far stronger subversive force, if a far less obvious one, than the specific political messages which the comics carry.

Of course, the underground cartoonists don't only attack targets as difficult as ecology and the American political system. In fact, Madison Avenue is almost too *easy* a target. By this time, we all know that Marlboro Country was created in the midst of smog-choked New York City. If *Mad Magazine* can do ad satires, why should the underground comics bother? Yet advertising is such a basic part of American society that it is impossible to ignore, and the underground cartoonists have found an approach to the field which only they can use: translation of the implied sexuality of so many Madison Avenue ads into out-and-out appeals to sexual inadequacy and frustration.

Paul Krassner, in his introduction to the Viking Press edition of *R. Crumb's Head Comix,* remembers selling *Mad Magazine* an article about what would happen if comic-strip characters answered those little ads in the backs of mid-fifties magazines: "But Olive Oyl was not permitted to buy falsies, Linus was not permitted to purchase Power over Others, and Steve Canyon was not permitted to view his own sex life in one of those little comic books that men like—wow!"

Being derived from "those little comic books that men like," the *Eight-Pagers* (see Chapter 2), the underground comics obviously can, and do, print the very sort of satire which *Mad* and other "straight" publications shun. It is true that at times this satire seems a bit juvenile beside the deeper social and

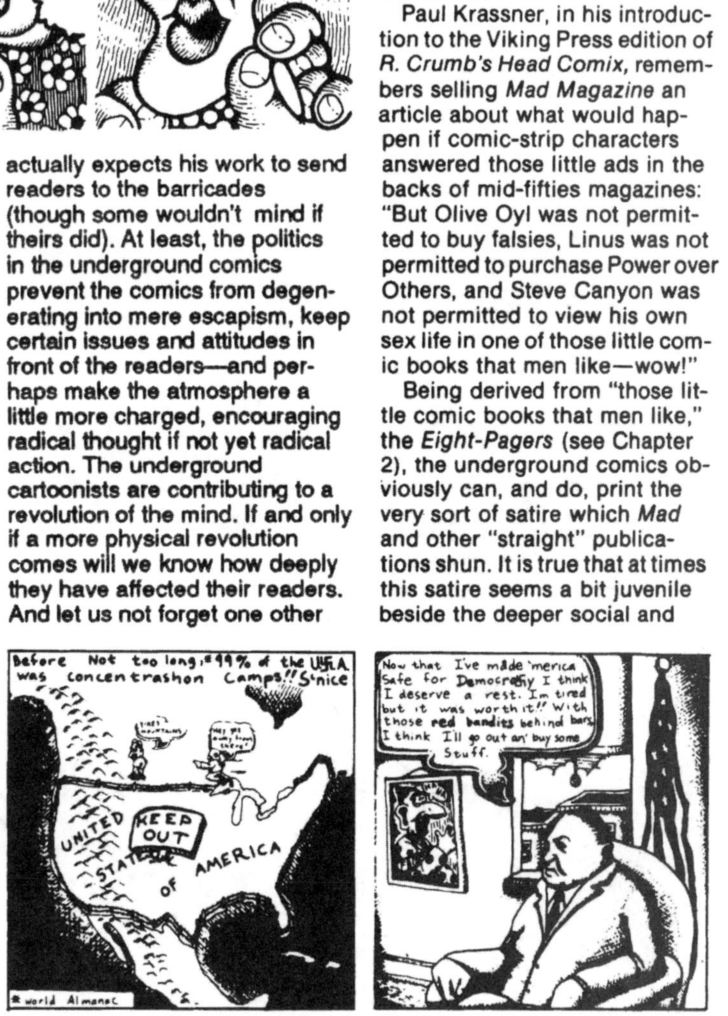

Below Left: Daniel Clyne. *Conspiracy Capers* No. 1. ©1969 The Conspiracy. By permission of The Conspiracy, by Skip Williamson.

Below: Robert Crumb. *Despair.*

Right: Gary Grimshaw. *Slow Death Funnies* No. 1. ©1970 The Visual Yoyo Tribe. By permission of The Visual Yoyo Tribe, by Ronald E. Quinn.

Far Right: Jim Mitchell. *Mom's Homemade Comics* No. 3. ©1971 Denis Kitchen. By permission of Denis Kitchen.

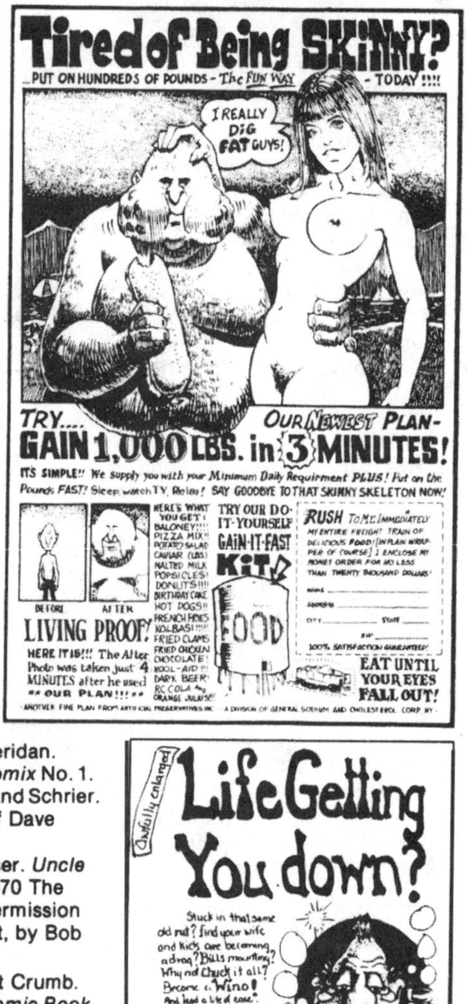

Above: Dave Sheridan. *Mother's Oats Comix* No. 1. ©1969 Sheridan and Schrier. By permission of Dave Sheridan.

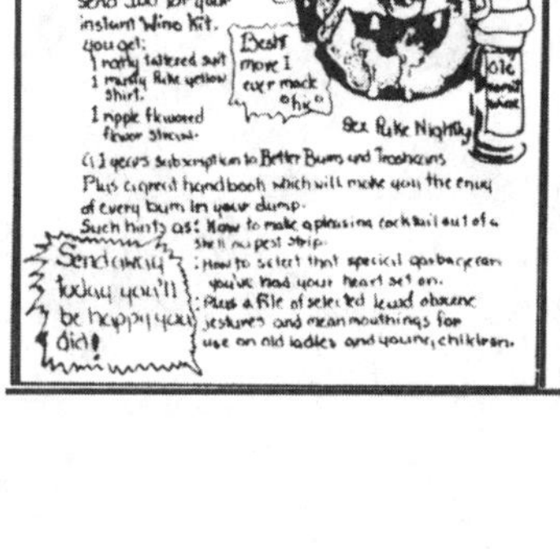

Right: Dave Geiser. *Uncle Sham* No. 1. ©1970 The Print Mint. By permission of The Print Mint, by Bob Rita.

Far Right: Robert Crumb. *San Francisco Comic Book* No. 1. ©1970 Rory Hayes, Ric Sloan, Willy Murphy, Larry Welz, S. Clay Wilson, Dan O'Neill, Rifas, Jim Osborne, Spain, Mervinius, R. Crumb, Rick Griffin, Jaxon, Robert Dougherty, and Dave Sheridan. By permission of Messrs. Hayes, Crumb, Jaxon, and Sheridan.

Left: Robert Crumb. *Zap Comix* No. 0.

Far Left: Don Glassford. *Snarf* No. 1. ©1972 Denis Kitchen. By permission of Denis Kitchen.

Far Left: Jim Osborne. *Jiz Comics*. ©1969 R. Crumb. By permission of Robert Crumb.

Left: Lee Marrs. *The Further Fattening Adventures of Pudge, Girl Blimp.* ©1973 Lee Marrs. By permission of Lee Marrs.

political messages of these comics; but at least when it takes the form of overstating the sexuality that Madison Avenue usually barely implies, the comics' ad satire stands well beside their concern with more pressing social problems. And in any case, it is just as well to be reminded of Madison Avenue's selling techniques as frequently as possible, since even many reasonably well-informed people are not aware just how deep subliminal sexual advertising goes. For example, Vance Packard reports in his book *The Waste Makers* that the American hardtop au-

Mike Vosburg. *Bizarre Sex* No. 3. ©1973 Krupp Comic Works, Inc. By permission of Krupp Comic Works, Inc., by Denis Kitchen.

tomobile is sexual in origin. This came about because dealers found that men tended to come into showrooms which emphasized the display of convertibles, even though the men usually bought sedans. The Motivational Research boys decided that this happened because the convertible represented a flashy mistress and the sedan a more ordinary but useful wife. And lo, the hardtop was born—a car costing more than a sedan, having more body noise because it lacks center supporting pillars, usually having less leg room in the rear seat, and being harder for rear-seat passengers to get into and out of. And the hardtop is not only an enormous success—it is also virtually the *only* automobile used in American car advertising. Check your local papers.

So your Dart Swinger is a wife with flair. And where better to learn that than in comics? In *Understanding Media*, Marshall McLuhan says, "The comic strip and the ad, then, both belong to the world of games, to the world of models and extensions of situations elsewhere." It may be only in the underground comics—which, incidentally, never carry advertising except promotional notices for other underground publications—that the world of advertising and the world of comic-book art can be brought together so effectively. Some of the cartoonists, in fact, may be working overtly toward that kind of McLuhanesque effectiveness. Gilbert Shelton writes, "Marshall McLuhan sez comix are the literature of the future, and that's good enough for me."

Of course, McLuhan's main concern is with mass media, not with comics *per se*; but here, too, the underground cartoonists have made their mark—not necessarily ahead of McLuhan, but in a somewhat different way. Since Madison Avenue brings its messages to the public via mass communications, it shouldn't be surprising to find the underground cartoonists turning their eyes, minds, and Rapidographs upon mass communications. "Robert Crumb's work is a stoned throw-up to the paranoia communicated by mass media," says Paul Krassner. And what Krassner says applies as well to the work of numerous other underground cartoonists. Why, you ask? As Walt Kelly once said, "Our newspapers have made 'love' into a four-letter word."

Joel Beck. *The Profit.* ©1966 Joel Beck. By permission of Joel Beck.

R. Scott Pflug. *Funnybook* No. 1. ©1971 The Almighty Publishing Company. By permission of The Almighty Publishing Company, by R. Scott Pflug.

Right and Below: Three aspects of the mood of a nation, as seen through the eyes of Robert Crumb in *Despair*.

Kelly's experience with his "Pogo" strip during 1968 was instructive. As he describes the events in *Equal Time for Pogo*, one newspaper "thought it detected a Familiar Resemblance" in the strip for March 21. "Quivering with courage, it dropped all future uses of the caricature," declaring that such use was "beneath its dignity." Kelly had used the caricature—which was (horror of horrors!) of then-President Lyndon Johnson—in two earlier strips, on March 11 and 12, but apparently no one at the paper noticed it at those times. Nevertheless, said Kelly, after the complaint was made, "There was not much to do except offer alternate strips for such days as people left their feelings lying around loose."

At the time Kelly drew his caricature, Johnson was being subjected to much editorial criticism (though apparently not by the complaining newspaper) as the political battles of the spring wore on; LBJ finally withdrew from the race for President on March 31, April Fool's Day eve (which may show that he too had a previously untapped sense of humor). But the point is that the mass media will not allow more than a certain amount of political commentary in the "straight" comic strips—unless the point of view agrees with their own, as in the New York *Daily News'* use of the jingoistic strip "The Green Berets" a couple of years ago. This is a sort of backhanded compliment to the power of communication through the comics; but beyond that, there is little that is encouraging about this arbitrary censorship.

But if the newspapers are bad, the radio and television stations are worse. Attempting to explain why the humor seems to have gone out of American life today, Dr. Robert Michels, Assistant Professor of Clinical Psychiatry at the College of Physicians and Surgeons of Columbia University, told the *National Enquirer* on September 13, 1970 that "the origins of humor were social. It was a vital part of communicating with others. But it's easy today to picture a man in front of his TV set, laughing uproariously at what he sees with absolutely no contact with any other real person. When things like this happen, the whole definition of humor begins to change."

While this author finds it rather hard to conceive of anybody laughing uproariously at most things on television, there is no doubt that Dr. Michels' basic point is valid. Television has encouraged people to be more and more alone, to communicate less and less with each other—to retreat into a private world which, in its extreme form, is called insanity.

Why were the TV networks so susceptible to the 1969 speech in which Vice President Spiro Agnew accused them of being run by a bunch of "effete snobs"? Because it happened to hit home. The TV stations in America *are* the property of small numbers of wealthy businessmen, and those men often *do* know each other and discuss things together. That's not a crime, as Agnew seemed to think—except to the underground cartoonists, who see, as Agnew did not, that much of what is wrong with television stems from the fact that all top TV executives have similar, completely businesslike and profit-oriented attitudes toward their industry. It is this pervasive prejudice caused by similarity of attitudes which is the real enemy of people who want to use the airwaves as a true medium of teaching and *two-way* communication. The TV executives could not cope with the underground cartoonists as they coped with Agnew—should it ever come to a confrontation between the groups. The cartoonists would not think much of a series of "holier and better than thou" speeches (which, when the TV newsmen offered them, only proved that Agnew was less intelligent than many television executives, for whatever that's worth). Those very speeches are the type of thing at which the underground cartoonists aim their satire. Ultimately, the cartoonists have less respect for television (and for all American institutions) than Spiro Agnew does.

Underground comics satirize TV in a way that the medium could not stand on a large scale. Laughter is a powerful weapon, and a medium which puts it in cans is a poor match for one which genuinely provokes it (all things being equal, which at present they are not). In *Yellow Dog* No. 5, for instance, an announcer proclaims "a roundup of late local, state and national news," and the television set promptly shits all over the viewer. How much of that can the medium which brought you "The Bevery Hillbillies" take? After all, the people laughing are the ones who'll be expected to buy the sponsors' products (how ludicrous to put a car commercial with rock and roll music, even very diluted rock and roll music, on in the middle of "Petticoat Junction"!).

In the underground comics, newspapers appear most frequently as objects being read by various characters, and they usually sprout exaggerated or absurd headlines. In addition, some direct satire comes from *Extra! Commix*, which is printed in newspaper format but, by its very title (the same as one used by an unsuccessful E. C. comic in the fifties), makes a complete mockery of the tradition of the newspaper "extra" being used only for what the media managers consider the most important news of the decade.

It is interesting to note that the underground comics come off about as well in the "straight" media as the "straight" media do in the comics (see Chapter 11). It figures. This is despite the fact that the underground comics are even willing to satirize the comics medium itself—a kind of self-examination which is rare in any form, and completely nonexistent in any *strong* form in the "straight" media. Since comics themselves are an indigenous American form of communication and a part of present society, the underground cartoonists reason that they too are fit subjects for satire. And many of the cartoonists have a superb sense of comics history to go with their wit. After all, how many people know that Fontaine Fox, the character drawn in old, thirties style by Jay Lynch, gets his name directly from Fontaine Fox, the "straight" cartoonist who created the Toonerville Trolley?

When the underground cartoonists pick a specific type of comic to satirize, they usually settle on the Marvel Comics Group. Marvel scored a big hit with high school and college students in the early sixties by presenting "superheroes with super problems." Yet these characters finally proved disappointing to underground cartoonists, for reasons like those of Justin Green: "Caricature in cartoons is much more important than the Marvel brand of academic realism, for more believable satire . . . Little Lulu is more real to me than any Marvel Super Hero because she speaks in terms of line, which is the medium of drawing." The Marvel heroes, and more lately some of the better-known DC Comics characters (Superman, Green Lantern, etc.), have occasionally mused about their

Jay Lynch. *Bijou Funnies* No. 1. ©1968 Jay Lynch. By permission of Jay Lynch.

Below: Bill Crawford. *High-Flyin' Funnies Comix and Stories*. ©1970 Bill Crawford. By permission of Bill Crawford.

TRUE BATTLE STORY!
SMILING SERGEANT DEATH
AND HIS MERCILESS MAYHEM PATROL
USMC
MEET THE MEN!
ZEB TURNIPSEED — SEVEN FOOT FOUR OF FIGHTIN' HILLBILLY FROM TENNESSEE...
IGGY SCHWARTZ — AT AGE TEN, HE WAS THE TOUGHEST KID IN BROOKLYN, AND NOW...!
MANUEL LOPEZ — HE LEFT A GOOD JOB IN TIJUANA TO JOIN THE CORPS...
WATERMELON JONES — THINGS WEREN'T HOT ENOUGH FOR HIM IN WATTS...
ALGERNON TRUFFLE — A PH.D. FROM HARVARD AT 16, BUT HE GOT BORED...
MICHAEL O'RAFFERTY — A MIDGET, HE HAD TO FORGE HIS MEDICAL PAPERS TO GET IN...
AND
TH' SARGE — FROM ANYTOWN, U.S.A. — HIS MOTTO: DEATH TO COMMUNISM!

Richard "Grass" Green's Wildman. *Snarf* No. 2. ©1972 Denis Kitchen. By permission of Denis Kitchen.

own ultimate inability to solve all the world's problems through superpowered heroism. But this is scarcely enough for the underground cartoonists, for reasons pinpointed by Mike Barrier in *Funnyworld* No. 10: "Traditional comic books—and their fans—are tied to the tired old superhero concept, and technical trickery can't make a superhero story the vehicle for an artistic statement." The underground cartoonists, by presenting characters having many of the attributes of the "straight" superheroes, have succeeded in making the sort of artistic statements which the "straight" comics have been unable to come up with.

Much satire of superheroes is done simply by creating new superheroes, of course. Gilbert Shelton's Wonder Wart-Hog is the best-known such creation by an underground cartoonist, and in one exceptional strip the whole first half of the story is given over to a satire of Marvel Comics, with the Hog of Steel himself not appearing until the tale is almost over—and then only as a porcine *deus ex machina.* Even the Marvel format is parodied by Shelton: this story, called "Smiling Sergeant Death and His Merciless Mayhem Patrol," is laid out just like a story of Marvel's "Sergeant Fury and His Howling Commandos." The plot is similar, too—except that everything in Death's plan fails, while similarly far-fetched plans by Fury invariably succeed.

This kind of careful parody makes Wonder Wart-Hog the most important superhero satire in the underground comics. But the brutal, lecherous, woefully incompetent superpig is not the only underground comment on the traditional "straight" superheroes. There is also Captain Guts, an ultra-right-wing American hero (his emblem is a human intestine) whose powers come from drinking beer and whose sole aim in life is to kill all the hippies. Captain Guts is the creation of Larry Welz, who in one story has the Captain battle and defeat the forces of Black Power. This story, one of the few in which an underground cartoonist uses black characters (see page 200), makes a few funny and telling points—particularly in the final scenes, when Captain Guts bests his nemesis, Ambrosia Sweetmeat, in a grand orgy contest. Ambrosia turns white-skinned, blue-eyed, and blonde-haired, and every Wednesday night thereafter receives "a visit from her friendly local superpatriot."

Since Welz's artwork comes nowhere near matching Shelton's, since his treatment of black characters (or, in another story, of a group of white radicals who are trying to foment revolution) is quite lacking in depth, and since Captain Guts

Opposite: Gilbert Shelton, *Radical America Komiks.* ©1969 Radical America. By permission of Radical America, by Paul Buhle.

Larry Welz's Captain Guts. *Yellow Dog Comix* No. 13-14. ©1969 The Print Mint. By permission of The Print Mint, by Bob Rita.

himself lacks the profundity and sly humor of Wonder Wart-Hog, Welz's satire of the superheroes is never as compelling as Shelton's . But on the other hand, its very directness makes it easier to follow than Wonder Wart-Hog's adventures, if not as funny.

A third hippie-style superhero parody is Freon P. Sandoz, who is really a meek fraternity member (Troy Honeydew III) who becomes a protector of drug freaks when he drinks LSD-spiked punch and, during his trip, sees God ("ye can call me Zappa"). Patrick Burk has made Sandoz less a true superhero than a sort of superhippie, who accomplishes with aplomb many things his readers wish they could do (like facing down the armed forces, singlehandedly). Burk, like Welz, cannot match Shelton's wit or technical skill, but he has managed to give Freon P. Sandoz a rather unique personality, and some very strange experiences. At one point, Freon advertises in the newspapers for a "faithful Indian companion" and is visited by V.K. Savarahna Mightyfine, who knows one hundred and eighty-eight sexual positions and can cook curry forty-three ways. (Turns out that's just what Freon wants.)

Though the underground superhero parodies operate on a fantasy base which is different from that of their "straight" counterparts, they retain the "straight" heroes' basic characteristics. Discussing the best-known superhero of all in *Love and Death*, G. Legman writes: "Instead of teaching obedience to the law, Superman glorifies the 'right' of the individual to take that law into his own hands. . . . Most significant of all, instead of being brave and fearless, Superman lives really in a continuous guilty terror, projecting outward in every direction his readers' paranoid hostility." Small wonder that the underground cartoonists have looked within Superman and discovered the likes of Wonder Wart-Hog. Yet the underground superheroes, like the "straight" ones, are personified fantasies of power, daydreams of a world in which problems can be solved by might alone. They are saved from Superman's mediocrity by the touches of wit and irony in their adventures, but they are not, ultimately, all that different from him.

Furthermore, according to *The Phantom Psychiatrist*, it's simplistic to assume that the superheroes are pure parody, just because that's the way they appear on the surface: "This Wart-

Gilbert Shelton. *Zap Comix* No. 4.

The Mad Peck satirizes Wonder Wart-Hog in *The Mad Peck Catalogue of Good Stuff* No. 2.

Hog really got to me, because he reminded me so much of the storm-trooper tactics that I lived through. You know, this guy is closer to what a storm trooper walking through a German town was like than a lot of other things I know. But put that aside. Shelton, the guy who's producing this work, may feel that the Wart-Hog is—a part of me feels this way, this is the way I want to deal with things. Well, you can say, wait a minute, isn't this a parody, isn't he making fun of a system? Yeah, right—part of him is saying, 'Hey, look at this system, I think it's a horrible way of being.' But can't you equally say that a part of him resonates or swings with this kind of thing, while he's parodying it at the same time? You can be at both ends of this thing, you see."

Actually, the Wonder Wart-Hog situation is even more complicated than I have already indicated, for the Hog of Steel has shown definite growth in the years since Shelton created him. Originally a rather juvenile, scratchily drawn figure, Wonder Wart-Hog began to flesh out (figuratively and literally) when he appeared in Harvey Kurtzman's *Help!* From there the Hog moved to *Drag Cartoons,* a West Coast hot-rod comic magazine (no kidding) which Shelton edited for a while. The change was an odd one for the Hog, who on the one hand began thinking badly of the police in his new setting, but on the other hand moved from his pro-civil rights position in *Help!* to active battles with the Viet Cong in *Drag*.

At this point, another underground cartoonist—The Mad Peck—got into the act, doing a sloppy version of the Hog and confronting him with Elliot Ness in issue No. 2 of *The Mad Peck Catalogue of Good Stuff.* Writes The Mad Peck, "I just couldn't stand to see a bad character go good . . . By confronting Wonder Wart with Elliot Ness, world's most repressive fascist, I hoped that he would realize that if he wasn't part of the solution he would be part of the problem. Happily, Wonder Wart-Hog

Carole. *It Aint Me Babe Comix.* ©1970 Trina, Lisa Lyons, Carole, Michele, Willy Mendes, Meredith Kurtzman, and Hurricane Nancy. By permission of Mss. Trina, Willy Mendes, and Meredith Kurtzman.

Pete Poplaski. *Snarf* No. 3. ©1972 Denis Kitchen. By permission of Denis Kitchen.

NATIONAL LAW & ORDER COMMITTEE
WE HAVE GREAT NEWS FOR YOU... GENTLEMEN WE JOIN YOU WITH OUR SOLUTION TO THE GREAT PROBLEM THAT PLAGUES OUR SOCIETY TODAY!
OH MY GAWD!
OH NO!
GAD!
BANG!
BANG
WE HAD TO DO IT SPIRIT... IT WAS THEM OR US!
THIS IS THE LAST TIME I TRY TO WORK WITHIN THE SYSTEM!
LEGALIZE CRIME COMMITTEE

chose to join the age of asparagus and was later seen hanging around with Janis Joplin and smoking dope." As Dick Tracy, in an earlier time, had been parodied by Al Capp through Fearless Fosdick, and as Fosdick became so established that Bill Elder eventually parodied *him* in an early *Mad* comic, so Superman had been parodied by Wonder Wart-Hog, who himself wound up in the hands of another cartoonist once he became somewhat "established." Makes one wonder what there *is* that's new under the sun.

Not all satire of other comics done by the underground cartoonists deals with superheroes. Many science-fiction stories—the ones by Nicola Cuti and Ronald Lipking, for instance—are satires not only of science-fiction characters, but of plots and drawings in the Wally Wood "extremely complex and realistic but unnecessarily hard to decipher" school. And once in a while, the underground cartoonists mention "straight" strips quite directly. This type of parody is nothing new: one of George Herriman's "Krazy Kat" strips is about nothing less than the ruinous consequences, for both Ignatz and Offissa Pupp, of attempting to gorge themselves on spinach and thus become as strong as Popeye. More recently, the E. C. Comics—both *Mad* and *Panic*—absolutely gorged themselves (and glutted their readers) on just such satire; Walt Kelly did a parody of "Little Orphan Annie" in his 1953 book *The Pogo Papers;* and so on. But here, too, the underground cartoonists give a special flavor to this sort of satire.

For example, in *Yellow Dog* No. 11-12, the Dog is seen standing next to a group of Peanuts characters who are looking at a globe. Lucy says, "Behold ...... OUR WORLD!!" As might be expected, the Yellow Dog promptly pisses all over the thing. As the Dog runs away, we see Snoopy's thoughts: "My sentiments exactly." It's not every parody of a comic strip that can make a comment on how restricted the whole "straight" comic world really is.

Other strips of this type include John Thompson's "Clock" (*Bijou Funnies* No. 2), in which one character wonders if the strip is "a manic depressive Annie Fanny" or "a psychotic Batman"; and finally, a Joel Beck series called "Mickey Mouse Today!" which once again proves, to the outraged and envious alike, that to the underground cartoonists not even Walt Disney is sacred.

It would be nice to end this chapter with a ringing pronouncement to the effect that the underground cartoonists are producing the most trenchant satire in the history of America,

Opposite: Will Eisner takes an updated look at his most famous character. *The Spirit* No. 1. ©1969 Will Eisner. By permission of

Left: Will Eisner's Spirit in his original form. *The Spirit* No. 1. ©1969 Will Eisner. By permission of Will Eisner.

Below: Joel Beck. *Yellow Dog* No. 1. ©1968 The Print Mint. By permission of The Print Mint, by Bob Rita.

and within a few years will undoubtedly have saved us from ourselves. Unfortunately, that is by no means the case—the cartoonists still have a fair amount of their own housecleaning to do, and, in fact, are often more involved with problems within the comics movement than with concerns of the outside world. More to the point, the cartoonists—as products of American society—are still having understandable trouble in distancing themselves and their work from some of the society's problems. The vein of male chauvinism in the comics has already been indicated (see pages 127-138), and there is another real absence of social awareness in the cartoonists'

Jim Mitchell. *Projunior Comix* ©1971 Denis Kitchen. By permission of Denis Kitchen.

general lack of sensitivity to the problems of blacks and other minority groups in the United States. This blind spot may be simply due to the fact that underground comics are by and large a lily-white medium—not through discrimination, but through the absence of black cartoonists working in this particular field.

On the other hand, the black characters who *do* appear in the underground comics are not given the sort of treatment one might expect from socially concerned young artists, though at least the underground cartoonists are not as hung up on racial questions as the "straight" syndicates. Writing in the *Columbia Journalism Review* (Vol. 8, No. 4, Winter 1969-1970, pp. 58-59), Jack E. White synthesizes the attitudes of "straight" comic art directors this way: "'We'd like to have some black characters because the times have changed. But we can't make them major characters in our existing strips because our readers might think it manipulative. We can't feature them in story segments because they'd eventually disappear and that would be tokenism. So, we'll create a new strip that's integrated from the beginning. It can't be a humor strip, because jokes directed at the black character might be interpreted as racist. So it will be an adventure strip. But we can't have the character do anything that might offend Southerners, because then we couldn't sell the strip in the South.'"

Underground cartoonists are not supposed to worry about problems like that. But the best treatment blacks get is a double-edged one, as in strips like the 'social realism" one drawn by Robert Crumb for *Motor City Comics* No. 1. In this strip, two black men surround a white man and then beat him up, calling him "muv fuckin' honky bastid." The man protests, "Wait! Stop! I'm on your side . . . I . . ." The blacks take the man's wallet and go off to "git us some chitlins," leaving the man to mumble, "I understand why they beat me up."

In this strip, both white and black characters are presented in a completely one-dimensional form—as if the blacks had drawn the white man and the white man the blacks. This is the point of the strip—to make the reader think about the situation, rather than to tell him or her either that it's not nice to beat people up or that it's necessary to commit violence when you are "culturally deprived."

The strip is sensitive to a certain kind of urban situation, but it shows little sensitivity to the blacks themselves—no hostility, but no sympathy either. Here the blacks are treated just as the whites are, and this is about the best treatment that the underground cartoonists ever accord them. Crumb usually treats blacks like objects. His characterization of Angelfood McSpade is a prime example: she is always having things done to her and is condemned to be a central character but never a protagonist. It's hard to believe that Crumb's stereotypes of blacks are supposed to make some general point about American racial attitudes. He treats the characters simply as objects of manipulative amusement, without the understanding he lavishes on, for example, Mr. Natural and Flakey Foont.

It is odd to see how infre-

Above: Robert Crumb. *Zap Comix* No. 1. ©1967 R. Crumb. By permission of Robert Crumb.

Left: Larry Welz. *Captain Guts Comics* No. 2.

Below: Jay Kinney. *Bijou Funnies* No. 4. ©1970 Bijou Publishing Empire, Inc. By permission of Bijou Publishing Empire, Inc., by Jay Lynch.

quently black characters turn up in the underground comics. Both Jaxon (in *God Nose*) and Paul David Simon (in *Conspiracy Capers*) retell an old joke punning on the words "Negro" and "knee grow"; and elsewhere in *Conspiracy Capers*, there is a story in which young Ambrose Adams eats a "Bit 'o' Honkey" candy bar and is transformed into Afro Boy. There's a Don Glassford strip, inoffensive but certainly not socially or politically aware, about "Studley." And there's an occasional use of a black character as a major part of a story—as in one Captain Guts story by Larry Welz (see page 193). But Welz's use of Ambrosia Sweetmeat (even his naming of her) is instructive—not just because Captain Guts eventually turns her white, blonde, and blue-eyed by beating her in a grand orgy (since that scene does have satirical purpose and power), but because she is pictured throughout as a great repository of female sexuality. That's the same sort of myth which Robert Crumb perpetuates, however innocently, with Angelfood Mc-

Robert Crumb. *Despair.*

Spade—and it is not the sort of thing we have a right to expect from artists who are so sensitive to problems confronting the environment, the political system, and other aspects of American life.

Yet for all their lacks, the underground comics have probably engaged in more overt social commentary in the few years of their existence than all the "straight" comics have since *Famous Funnies* first hit the stands in 1934. There is no real way to assess what effect this plethora of concern may eventually have on American society. Harvey Kurtzman, spiritual granddaddy of the underground comics, is at least willing to try to think ahead: "What these guys draw affects everybody. How it affects them is mysterious, you can't really put your finger on it, but the fact that it draws people into an orbit *is* significant—because people don't get smarter. People are what they are, and you know, youth hasn't gotten suddenly brilliant. I mean, old peo-

Robert Crumb. *Despair.*

Guy Colwell. *Inner City Romance Comix* No. 2: "Radical Rock." ©1972 Guy Colwell. By permission of Guy Colwell.

Guy Colwell. Wrap-around cover of *Inner City Romance Comix* No. 2: "Radical Rock." ©1972 Guy Colwell. By permission of Guy Colwell.

RADICAL ROCK
50¢
ADULTS ONLY
LAST GASP
BY
GUY
COLWELL

Jim Mitchell. *Teen-Age Horizons of Shangrila* No. 1. ©1970 Denis Kitchen. By permission of Denis Kitchen.

ple are dumb and youths are dumb too. The world has never gotten smarter as far as I'm concerned—it's the same dumb old place.

"But people suddenly choose to collect at a certain moment and march off in a body, and that's when things start happening. It's fascinating how somebody creates a point of focus and the like spirits suddenly come out of the cracks and from under the rocks. I mean it might be Mahatma Gandhi, or it might be Adolph Hitler that makes the point of focus, but all of a sudden you've got a million people in the streets. But why people are galvanized into action—that takes a mysterious quality which you can't quite put your finger on. But it happened with the Beatles, with rock music. I'm sure it happened during the Crusades, when these inspired idiots marched off to do battle in Jerusalem. The Children's Crusade, where they all marched off into slavery. Julius Caesar, the French Revolution—why do these things happen? They don't happen because a guy says, 'All right, I'm going to solve all the riddles of politics.' It usually happens because somebody has the artistic profundity to really stir people deep down inside. Like Jesus Christ—my God, what that one man did! And I'm sure he wasn't working on a consciously political level. It was a very emotional appeal that he had, a very human appeal that had nothing to do with parties or emblems, which general to follow or which country is right.

"And look what happened to him. Crucified!"

Addenda:

Some cartoonists find they *cannot* avoid social relevance in their comics, simply because their own experiences prevent them from doing so. Guy Colwell, whose awareness of both social issues and comic books increased markedly after he was imprisoned for draft evasion, reflects his own life in the comics he draws. In one case, he says, "The starting point of *Inner City Romances #2* was my coverage of a massive and destructive bust of the Good Times Commune in Haight-Ashbury, but all the energies of the radical movement around which the commune focused were included until it became an historical play." In another story, Colwell found that a science-fiction theme was a chance to discuss contemporary reality—not to minimize or escape from it. In the story, Colwell creates "a future young hippy wanderer type, who is searching the surface of the earth for some natural country, which he only knows about as a kind of mythology since in his age the planet is covered practically from pole to pole with concrete and steel. It no longer orbits the sun but wanders alone outside the galaxy, guided by the artificial intelligence created by humans and now replacing them." Summing up the attitude he takes in his work, Colwell says simply, "My comics are based upon what I see happening in my own environment and my society."

John Adkins Richardson, like Colwell, is influenced by present society when he creates his work—but unlike Colwell, he does not try to provide direct reflections of society in all his work. Richardson, a writer as well as a cartoonist, gives vent to his opinions in words at least as strongly as he does in drawings: "Generally speaking, I think that the situation in America is very dire and that social reorganization is essential. But I also have the feeling that there's virtually no difference among the fundamental premises of the variously prominent proponents of what appear to be antagonistic positions. With very rare exceptions all of them are obsessed with freedom. That's true of the rightest wing no less than of the left. And the left seems not to understand that some of the radical solutions which give them freedom of a sort take away the kinds they pretend to want. . . . My conviction is that the problems are not those of freedom or equality—neither of which is attainable in any normal sense in a society—but justice. To have social order in which no segment (e.g., the military-industrial bloc) can behave anarchistically and in which one can take a stroll without being 'ripped off' by some mechanized savage (black or white, cop or hood) and yet be reasonably sure of just distribution of goods, services, and law is the problem with which I am always involved."

Certain cartoonists would quarrel with Richardson's statements—not necessarily because they disagree with the sentiments, but because they feel the comics have to speak for themselves, without benefit of interpretations by their creators. Says Rand Holmes, "In my opinion

Rand Holmes. *Harold Hedd* No. 2. ©1973 Rand Holmes. By permission of Rand Holmes.

if an artist (any artist) were to discuss or explain the message content of his work it would actually be damaging to the art itself. What an artist means is important only to himself—the *message received* varies with the individual viewer. I feel that the real value of art is in its *ability to evoke* insights from *within* the observer—insights which, again, are meaningful only to him or herself. Obviously then if a person were to view a work, forearmed with a knowledge of 'what the artist means,' there is the danger that this is all he'll see. For this reason I never explain my work. I'm always fascinated when others explain my work though, because it gives me insights into *them*."

The one thing which unites the attitudes of all underground cartoonists toward the messages their works carry is that all of them feel a need to communicate—not necessarily specific ideas or philosophies, but at least an overall impression that they are there, that they care about what they are doing, and that they care about the people viewing their work. Whatever the message the cartoonists finally put across, and whatever the ultimate effect of their work on their readers, this factor of caring about the audience is in many ways the most important difference between the underground comics and the slick commercial products produced for the "straight" comic-book market.

John Adkins Richardson and Jan Strnad. *Fever Dreams* No. 1. ©1972 Richard Corben, John Adkins Richardson, and Jan Strnad. By permission of Richard Corben and John Richardson.

8 Drugs

Joel Beck. *The Profit.* ©1966 Joel Beck. By permission of Joel Beck.

Opposite: Lee Marrs. *El Perfecto Comics.* ©1973 Lee Marrs. By permission of Lee Marrs.

Wouldst be surprised to learn that the artists of underground comics are not complete strangers to the worlds opened up in the mind by drugs? Of course thou wouldstn't. The use of drugs is, in fact, an assumption lying behind many of the stories in the underground comics.

But let one thing be made clear at the outset: it is not usually necessary to be high on anything in order to enjoy the cartoonists' work. Paul Krassner, in his preface to the Viking Press edition of *R. Crumb's Head Comix,* said much when he told the following anecdote: "Someone who starred in Andy Warhol's *The Chelsea Girls* once told me that I should get thoroughly zonked to truly dig the film, but if any art has to *depend* on drugs in order to be appreciated, then I don't exactly consider it the pinnacle of creativity." (The emphasis is Krassner's.)

Being high may make the underground comics more fun to read, as it makes many activities more pleasurable; but, with a few exceptions, most comics do not *require* a reader to be turned on in order to enjoy the cartoonists' work.

It's unfortunate that antidrug feeling runs so deep in many otherwise perceptive, even brilliant people, that they cannot see the underground comics' message for all the marijuana smoke. G. Legman, whose quotes from *Love and Death* besprinkle the present work, is so vehement in his reactions to "hippieism, drugs, and the rest of that tragedy" that he misjudges the underground comics quite completely: "Robert Crumb and *Zap Comix e tutti quanti* are *not* where it is at. Just a by-product of the LSD optical disorganization school." It's hard to expect understanding from lesser people when so perceptive a social critic is so obtuse whenever the word "drugs" is mentioned. But then, Legman has always been a study in contrasts (see the Bibliography).

Below: Robert Crumb. *Hytone Comix.* ©1971 R. Crumb. By permission of Robert Crumb.

For the cartoonists themselves, drugs are generally a fact of life. George Metzger was already into them in the early sixties: "Discovered dope, lived with a weird chick in the middle of early S.F. dope and hipster-folk musicians scene—got caught for army in '63 and went in and was in Oklahoma. A trip to California kept me and friends supplied in dope, the first I ever bought and it *was* gold, nowadays I can't tell and anyway stoned is stoned."

Some artists trace their development at least partially to drugs. Before he seriously began to do comics, writes Buckwheat Florida Jr., "I began to use drugs—marijuana and LSD and occasionally others—I soon

Gilbert Shelton. *Further Adventures of Those Fabulous Furry Freak Brothers.* ©1972 Gilbert Shelton. By permission of Gilbert Shelton.

UNDER THE UNSUSPECTING ROOFTOPS ACROSS AMERICA DWELLS A...
NATION of ADDICTS!
NORMAL AND EVERYDAY AS THIS HOUSEWIFE MAY SEEM...
SHE AND ALL THESE CITIZENS ARE VICTIMS..
OF A TERROR THAT CAUSES DESPERATE, SLEEPLESS NIGHTS..
AND NERVE-SHATTERED DAYS!
POURING GOOD MONEY AFTER BAD, TIED TO A FORCE STRONGER THAN WILL, SHE'S A...
CAFFEINE FIEND
..OH NO!
MILLIONS OF SOULS GRIPPED BY THE KILLER COFFEE! BRAIN-WASHED BY SICK SOCIETY WHICH AUTOMATICALLY LINKS "HELLO" WITH "YA WANNA CUPA COFFEE?"
QUICK! QUICK
THERE ARE THE FETISHISTS....
THE SELF-DECEIVERS...
AND THE MAINLINERS!!!
BRAZ
TEHRA
EAST MONGRO
WELL, IF I JUST ADD 3 TEASP
PUMP
15 CUPS A DAY
FONDLE
FONDLE
SAFE FROM PROSECUTION, A NETWORK MORE DECEITFUL THAN THE MAFIA PUSHES THIS ADDICTIVE TOXIN!
OUR OLE COFFEE X
PERK
SUN
CUP
SOUTH
BOING
BOP
DRUGGED BY THE BILLIONS OF $ SPENT ON ADVERTISING, OUR VERY LANGUAGE HAS BEEN ALTERED.
COFFEEHOUSE
Coffee KLATSH
COFFEE CAKE
Coffee Shop
COFFEE BREAK
Coffee table
KICK THE HABIT
WAKE UP!
AND TURN ON
OR DRINK TEA, AND SOMETIMES CHOCOLATE, OR APPLE JUICE, OR O.J.. OR BEER, OR COKE OR RUM OR BANANA SPLIT..
©1973 LEE MARRS—

left Florida—too uptite and racist, etc.—I only worked when I had to—I decided I wanted to be an artist of some sort." And Kim Deitch, after beginning his cartooning, created one character (in 1967) specifically because of drugs: "Under the influence of marijuana and the then current East Village vibes I created Sunshine Girl, a nice clean psychedelic strip for the whole family."

On the other hand, at least one cartoonist found that drugs had a very negative effect on his work. Jay Lynch says, "Time drifted by, and then came the 1966 summer of love. A guy named Crazy Louie gave me some LSD-25, as it was called then, and I started doing surrealistic comix. Then Skip Williamson moved to Chicago and convinced me that LSD was leading to my downfall, so I quit takin' the stuff 'cause all I was drawing was paisleys and flowers. When I was taking drugs, I could only draw organic looking things, and my work from that era was really awful. Today I am vehemently anti-drug, and Skip is th' biggest acid head in town." And there are at least a few artists for whom drugs are totally irrelevant—for example, Foolbert Sturgeon: "I don't use drugs. I live sort of a quiet life. If I sometimes find myself moving with some sort of tide, I'd just as soon not."

In most cases, the underground cartoonists have at least

Right: Gilbert Shelton. *Feds 'n' Heads Comix.* ©1968 Gilbert Shelton. By permission of Gilbert Shelton.

Below: Robert Crumb. *Hytone Comix.* ©1971 R. Crumb. By permission of Robert Crumb.

Withdrawal with a difference. Gilbert Shelton. *Radical America Komiks.* ©1969 Radical America. By permission of Radical America, by Paul Buhle.

Left and Below: Gilbert Shelton. *The Collected Adventures of the Fabulous Furry Freak Brothers.* ©1971 Gilbert Shelton. By permission of Gilbert Shelton.

Gary Hallgren. *Left-Field Funnies* No. 1. ©1972 Gary Hallgren. By permission of Gary Hallgren.

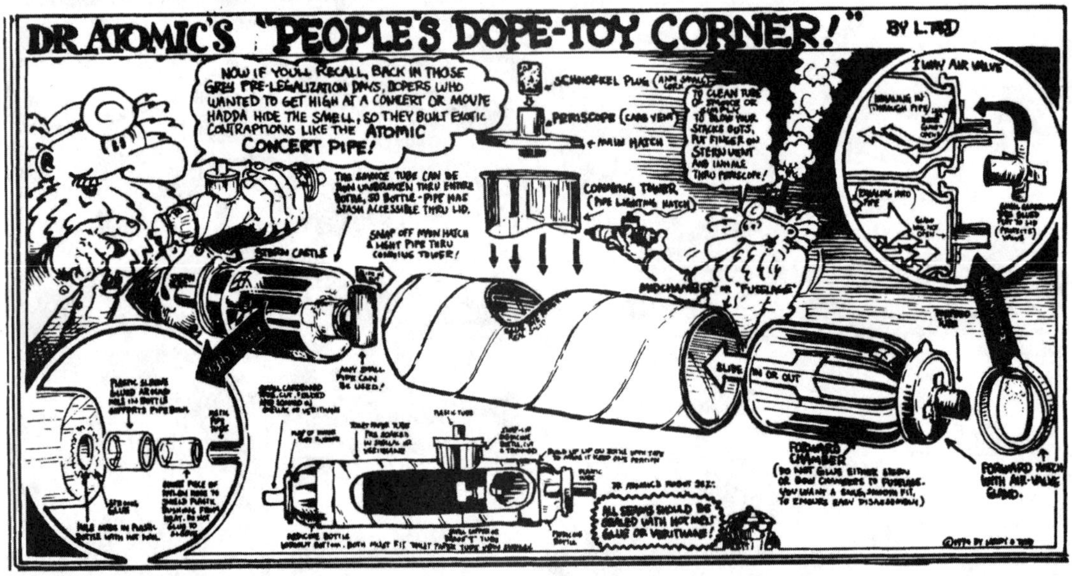

Larry Todd. A previously unpublished drawing from the cartoonist's portfolio. ©1974 Larry S. Todd. By permission of Larry Todd.

Below: Sharon Rudahl. A strip drawn for Amorphia (the California Marijuana Initiative). ©1974 Sharon Kahn Rudahl. By permission of Sharon Rudahl.

experimented with the milder drugs, such as marijuana and hashish, and have absorbed their experiences and made them topics for their comics. As might be expected, the most common drug referred to in the underground comics is marijuana, since more people have used that drug than any other and it is therefore most likely to give the cartoonists an audience with shared experience. The assumption that the reader knows about and uses grass allows the cartoonists to play around a good deal with what might be called the marijuana ethos. Gilbert Shelton's Fabulous Furry Freak Brothers are constantly having hilarious adventures in which drugs play a

Larry Welz. *American Flyer Funnies* No. 2. ©1972 Larry Welz, Larry Todd, and Larry Sutherland. By permission of Larry Welz.

Below: Robert Crumb. *Hytone Comix.* ©1971 R. Crumb. By permission of Robert Crumb.

My new job allows me to get lots of fresh air and I meet all sorts of interesting people.
A Letter Home
Dear Mom, It sure was nice to hear from you. Dont worry about me.
and dont worry about me not getting enough sleep. I spend loads of time in bed.
You wouldnt recognize your fat daughter — I've lost weight and look quite fashionable!
You'd like my friends — they're nice quiet people. Sometimes we just sit around and listen to music.
And thanks for the beautiful pearl necklace you sent for my birthday — I just loved it!
By the way, could you send me $50.00? Some unexpected ex-penses came up. If you dont have that much I'll take $20.00 or even $10.00.
Your loving daughter
Trina 5-71

part—though occasionally, Shelton is guilty of perpetrating such myths about grass as the one which says that only the female plant produces a drug which can get humans high. (The same myth says that the male plant's leaves go to make catnip.)

The marijuana ethos contains cops and dealers as well as users, and once again the cartoonists assume their readers to be familiar with the procedures of obtaining the drug in frightened America, and with the attendant paranoia. The reader is also assumed to know a bit about the practices of police who are trying to stop the criminal upsurge in the country by busting marijuana users and letting heroin pushers (to say nothing of murderers) go free. (Marijuana use is often a felony, while murder is not. The assassins of John and Robert Kennedy and Martin Luther King could only be brought under federal jurisdiction for "violating their victims' civil rights." Smoke a joint and see what happens—especially under the sort of repressive drug laws enacted, for example, in New York State in September 1973.)

Larry Welz. *San Francisco Comic Book* No. 2. ©1970 Rick Griffin, Willy Murphy, Greg Irons, Robert Williams, Kim Deitch, Jim Osborne, Spain Rodriguez, Trina, Robert Crumb, Dan O'Neill, Larry Welz, Mervinius, S. Clay Wilson. By permission of Messrs. Williams, Deitch, and Crumb, and Ms. Trina.

Incidentally, though the underground cartoonists assume their readers know *about* marijuana, they do not necessarily assume that their readers use even that very mild drug. Krupp Comic Works, in fact, put out a special comic (for only ten cents) called *The Great Marijuana Debate*—sarcastic, to be sure, but quite accurate in putting forth the different attitudes of the people who believe in using the drug and the people who don't. It helps to know about drugs when you read many underground comics, but that knowledge doesn't have to come from personal experience.

As frequently as marijuana use is a topic, or merely an assumption, of the underground cartoonists, grass itself has had little effect on the comic art *per se*. The reason is obvious: the effects of marijuana are mild and quite transitory. But the effects of hallucinogens, particularly LSD, are vivid and long-lasting; so these drugs have often had specific influences on cartoonists' work (not necessarily good ones—see Jay Lynch's comments, page 208).

When the readers of underground comics have taken hallucinogens, the results may be exotic, as Denis Kitchen relates: "One guy in California was high for three days, during which he read and reread *Mom's Homemade Comics* No. 1 and wrote rambling discussions about it in flowery script (in various colors yet)." But as intriguing as such reactions are, the effects of drug trips on the cartoonists themselves are even more interesting.

Artistically, the major characteristic of drug-influenced underground comics is their incredible wealth of detail. Since the insides of underground comics are almost always printed in black and white, the artists very rarely have any opportunity to dupli-

Far Left: Larry Welz. *Bakersfield Kountry Komics*. ©1973 Larry Welz and Larry Sutherland. By permission of Last Gasp Eco-Funnies, Inc., by Ron Turner.

Opposite: Trina. *Tuff Shit*. ©1972 The Print Mint. By permission of the Print Mint, by Bob Rita; and Trina.

Below: Jay Lynch. *The Great Marijuana Debate*. ©1972 Krupp Comic Works, Inc. By permission of Krupp Comic Works, Inc., by Denis Kitchen.

WHAM!
NOW HOP UP HERE ON THIS TABLE LIKE A GOOD GIRL!
WHY?
"WHY" YER ASS!! YOU JUST DO LIKE I TELL YA!
C'MON! C'MON!
NOW HOLD STILL... THIS IS A DRUG INSPECTION!
NO!
YOU AINT GONNA PUT THAT IN ME!!
I SAID HOLD STILL!!
GRIP!
OWW! YOWW!
QUIT SQUAWKIN'! NOBODY'S IMPRESSED! GODDAMN BRATS ALLA BUNCHA CRYBABIES!
WHIMPER WHINE YELP WHINE
OW OW OW
SHIT... I CANT SEE MUCH WITH THIS FLASHLIGHT
BETTER DOUBLE-CHECK WITH TH' OL' SURE-FIRE FINGER METHOD!
OUCH!
JAM
HMM... DOESN'T SEEM TO BE ANYTHING IN THERE!
SQUISH SKOOCH
OKAY! ALL DONE, SWEET-HEART... YER CLEAN... WAIT! I ALMOST FORGOT T' SPRAY YOU FOR LICE...
FSHHHH
UGH! THIS STUFF IS REALLY STRONG!

cate the color effects which generally accompany LSD trips. But effects of perspective and detail can be put across extremely effectively, and often are.

One of the cartoonists most into the acid experience is John Thompson, whose exquisite mystical artwork (see Chapter 7) shows distinct LSD influence. Thompson tries to put into words some of his intense feelings after early acid use: "In 1966 start doing political cartoons for *berkeley barb.* take acid qualitatively heavy intro-extrospective spiritual context fast sugarless die on acid am reborn continue drawing

Assid Mic. *Yellow Dog Comix* No. 17. Assid Mic was one of the Telegraph Avenue "street people" in Berkeley rather than a regular cartoonist.

full page detailed drawings for underground papers do posters for poetry magazines rock dances stuff to hang on the wall political posters. draw and write prolifically have friends mess around hang out daydream cry giggle all in beautiful nature orchestrational flux." But even Thompson's words cannot capture his inward feelings the way his drawings can—and those drawings, influenced by Eastern culture as well as by drug use, show the value of Thompson's LSD experiences in a way that verbal communication can never match. The intensely felt drug experience which illuminates Thompson's work also helps explain why readers of his material react so powerfully and immediately, one way or the other: there's either an instant feeling of oneness with Thompson, or there's no communication at all.

Bobby London. *El Perfecto Comics.* ©1973 Bobby London. By permission of Bobby London.

Opposite: Robert Crumb. *Uneeda Comix.* ©1970 R. Crumb. By permission of Robert Crumb.

Luis Medina. *Yellow Dog Comix* No. 19. ©1971 The Print Mint. By permission of The Print Mint, by Bob Rita.

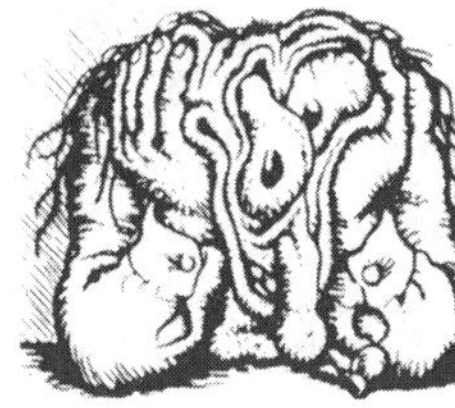

Below: Robert Crumb. *Hytone Comix.* ©1971 R. Crumb. By permission of Robert Crumb.

GODZILLA MUTHAFUCKERS! I MUSTA O.D.'d ON THAT SHIT!!!
WITH
WITHOUT
TODAY
AND NOW...
CRYPTO
THE WONDER MOOSE
$19.95

Another artist whose work shows drug influence is S. Clay Wilson, who once used drugs but later switched almost completely to beer. Nevertheless, the extreme complexity and detail of Wilson's drawings—the things which give them their peculiar power and vehemence—show early drug influence. The realism with which he portrays his degenerate characters, shaping individual hairs and warts with what one could call tender loving care (if the final results weren't so vicious), indicates that Wilson's drug experiences did influence his style. And Wilson's peculiar sense of time, in which his stories never begin or end but are always chunks from somewhere in the middle of an infinite time continuum, also shows an effect fairly common among LSD users.

Other cartoonists have assimilated their drug experiences more completely or have rejected those experiences and incorporated only a few feelings from them into their work. Crumb, Shelton, and indeed a majority of the underground cartoonists fit this category. So do Dave Sheridan and Fred Schrier, but they fit it differently, for their *Mother's Oats Comix* No. 1 is uniquely clever in the presentation (and deliberate distortion) of drug effects. Writing of this book in *Funnyworld* No. 12, Mike Barrier says: "The fantasies are dreamlike, combining insanity and perfect clarity. Sheridan and Schrier know comic-strip techniques, and apply them with skill to the most unlikely material. The results are exhilarating."

At times, the underground cartoonists deliberately work

Far Left: Larry Welz. *Tuff Shit.* ©1972 The Print Mint. By permission of The Print Mint, by Bob Rita.

Left: S. Clay Wilson. *Jiz Comics.* ©1969 R. Crumb. By permission of Robert Crumb.

Opposite: Dave Sheridan. *Mother's Oats Comix* No. 1. ©1969 Sheridan and Schrier. By permission of Dave Sheridan.

Jay Kinney. *Young Lust* No. 1. ©1970 Bill Griffith and Jay Kinney. By permission of Bill Griffith and Jay Kinney.

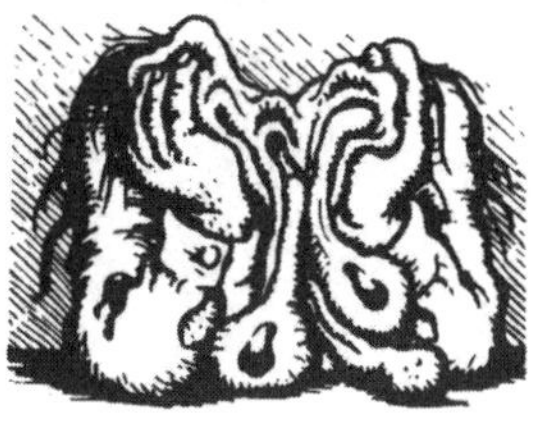

Below: Robert Crumb. *Hytone Comix.* ©1971 R. Crumb. By permission of Robert Crumb.

BUT ENOUGH TALK.... KOTH COMES!! CRINGE BEFORE THE ANCIENT ONE!!
BY CROM'S GREAT BRONZED BALLS! HOW'N FUCK'M I GONNA GET OUTTA DIS?
MY DOPE BAG!... ...OF COURSE!!
AS THE LOATHESOME, SLIME ENCRUSTED, MONSTROSITY INCHES CLOSER BALDRIC HURRIEDLY SPRINKLES A GENEROUS DOSE OF PURE CRYSTAL ON THE BACK OF HIS HAND AND SNORTS IT UP!!
SZNURRK
AND AS THE POWERFUL STIMULANT TAKES HOLD... BALDRIC GOES "APESHIT"
SNAP
TWANG
PING

Robert Crumb. *Zap Comix* No. 3.

against the use of certain drugs, particularly speed (the evils of heroin being assumed). The most famous such case is a two-page spread by Robert Crumb attacking the use of speed. Crumb kids around about drugs as much as anyone, and unfortunately the power of his strip is somewhat limited because there are other stories in which the use of speed —even, in one story, by a 13-year-old girl—is accepted and joked about. Nevertheless, Crumb's powerful attack on

Gilbert Shelton. *Gothic Blimp Works* No. 6.

Opposite: Rand Holmes. *White Lunch Comix* No. 1. ©1972 Rand Holmes and Jim Jones. By permission of Rand Holmes.

Below: Robert Crumb. *Zap Comix* No. 3.

Above: Spain. *The Collected Trashman.*

Top: Denis Kitchen. *Smile* No. 2. ©1971 Krupp Comic Works, Inc. By permission of Krupp Comic Works, Inc., by Denis Kitchen.

Right: Trina. *Tales of the Armorkins.* ©1971 Larry Todd. By permission of Larry Todd and Trina.

Below: Robert Crumb. *Hytone Comix.* ©1971 R. Crumb. By permission of Robert Crumb.

speed—which has found its way into museum art shows (see Chapter 11)—stands as one of the real "public service" cartoons in the underground comics. And it goes without saying that this sort of thing is likely to keep more people from the drug than are parental regulations and the laws of a country they do not respect.

In general, the underground comics are much more likely to be defending drugs against Establishment propaganda than warning people not to use them. The ridiculous statement that every drug is addictive and invariably leads to the use of other, stronger drugs, is often joked about. Gilbert Shelton, for instance, has suggested you might as well say the same thing about food (see page 209).

The importance of drugs to the underground comics is not, all in all, as great as might be imagined. As Paul Buhle has written, "Even at the most head-oriented, drugs are viewed by these artists simply as *one* way of seeing a new world." And drugs themselves have lost much of their significance in the radical subculture as a whole. Buckwheat Florida Jr., whose work appears more drug-influenced than that of most underground cartoonists, sums up the growing feelings of many of the artists (and many of their readers): "Things have started to quiet down among the so-called hip scene—People are spreading out, getting into their trip—I think drugs are losing a lot of their importance—I still use them—but not compulsively—You can takem or leave em—I think I would be in pretty much the same place—drugs or no drugs—artistically—(so much for drugs)."

Far Left: Larry Todd. *Laughing Gas.* ©1973 Larry Todd. By permission of Larry Todd.

Left: Gilbert Shelton. *Gothic Blimp Works* No. 7.

Far Left: Simon Deitch. *Bogeyman Comics* No. 3. ©1970 R. Hayes, Jaxon, S. Clay Wilson, Simon Deitch, Greg Irons, Jeff Hayes, Jayzey Lynch, Spain, Rick Griffin, and The Company and Sons. By permission of Messrs. R. Hayes and Jaxon.

Below: Robert Crumb. *Zap Comix* No. 4.

9 A Few Oddities

The title of this chapter refers not to the cartoonists, but to some unusual aspects of the comics they produce—some things which just can't be neatly pigeonholed under the earlier discussions of the comics' contents. Some of the most interesting of these oddities come about because the number of cartoonists, though growing, is still fairly small, and the number of underground comic-book publishers even smaller. Hence, several cartoonists often turn up at the same place at the same time—and since many of the cartoonists are friends anyway, there are meetings at places other than the publishers'.

What occurs at these get-togethers isn't necessarily the usual round of conversation and social amenities. What sometimes happens is the production of "jam sessions"—multi-person comic strips in which each artist draws something, taking off from what the previous artist has done. The results can be a little weird, as you can see; and the strips put together this way almost never have a story line or any sort of cohesiveness at all. Indeed, most of the jam sessions are held purely for fun, and the work produced at them usually doesn't get published. But when it does appear, it's easy to see that the artists tend to fantasize in these jam sessions even more strongly than usual, letting purely visual considerations determine what they draw. And the jam sessions make for guessing games on the parts of readers: no one signs his part of the work, and you can only tell who did what if you really know the cartoonists' styles.

Actually, jam sessions *per se* are nothing new—the old *Mad* artists, among others, used to get together and draw things *en masse*. But "straight" jam sessions had a tendency toward becoming simple collaborations—like Harvey Kurtzman's collaboration with Bill Elder in "Little Annie Fanny." What results from a collaboration is a mixing of styles, so you really can't tell just who did what most of the time. But what comes from a jam session is a total hodgepodge, together with a sense of sheer vitality and fun.

Of course, there's a spaniard in the works, as John Lennon would have it. Since the underground cartoonists are almost all satirists, and most of them are more-than-competent draftsmen, they often use the jam sessions to put together their interpretations or satires of the characters of other cartoonists—who may or may not be at that particular meeting. So what may appear to be an obvious Robert Crumb drawing might have been put out by someone else imitating his style. No one but the artists can tell for sure—and they're the first to admit that they don't always remember themselves.

With their penchant for carrying everything to its logical extreme, or even a bit beyond, a group of underground cartoonists got together in 1973 and decided to do a comic book entirely of underground satires of other

Jam session from *Occult Laff-Parade* No. 1. ©1973 Jay Kinney, Kim Deitch, Ned Sonntag, Justin Green, Larry Todd, Rory Hayes, and Rick Griffin. By permission of Messrs. Kinney, Deitch, Green, and Hayes. A somewhat atypical jam session, with a more coherent theme than most and with the artists involved having signed their names.

Opposite: A more typical jam session from *Zap Comix* No. 4.

SPLAT
SPIN
ZIP
RIP
SPLAT
YIPE!
SPIN
RIP ZIP
HOLY HOLY
GREAT ZOTH!
THAT ROBOT IS A MOTHER
I'M GOIN' TA THE LOWER EAST SIDE
YOU DIRTY ASSED ME YOU CUNT LAPPER I AWTA PISS YOUR PIG!!
GRIND
YOW
BUZZZ
THE WATER RISING
YES... I KNOW.
HRRMF! SKZKX ZRRZLSH! SLVRR!!
THIS MY BROTHERS I SAY UNTO YOU... KILL
KILL FOR THE LOVE OF KILLING
KILL FOR THE LOVE OF KALI
DID YOU HEAR THAT J.B.?
WE'LL GET THIS BASTARD!!

FIRE'S OUT ONCE AGAIN
SSSSSS POIT
MEANWHILE...OUT IN THE MOONLIGHT!
ZZZ ZZZ ZZZ
!?
The Deputy's Hat!
!
CLUK
..BUT DON'T WORRY KIDS !!!!
SAFE OUTSIDE!
GUESS SO!
OOPS!
FOR THE LOVE OF KALI!
I JUST SQUASHED ONE OF 'EM IN THE TRAP,
HEY!
IS IT SAFE?
RUB THE CLOWN
NO CLOWNS ALLOWED IN THE MACHINES
RUB HIM?
JUST KEEP ME HAPPY, THAT'S ALL...
CLOWN CUM IS A YUM!

Jay Lynch. *Bijou Funnies* No. 8. ©1973 Bijou Publishing Empire, Inc. By permission of Bijou Publishing Empire, Inc., by Jay Lynch. From Lynch's satire of Gilbert Shelton's Fabulous Furry Freak Brothers.

Opposite: Continuation of jam session from *Zap Comix* No. 4.

underground comics. Rather than a jam session, this was the first cohesive attempt by the cartoonists to do self-satire of the type that used to appear in *Mad* comics in the early fifties. In fact, *Bijou Funnies* No. 8, which contained this set of parodies, looked more like an old E.C. comic than anything before produced by the underground—even to a Harvey Kurtzman cover and a serious editorial about censorship of the comic-book market (see Chapter 12).

It's not only in jam sessions and books like *Bijou* No. 8 that one cartoonist may draw another's characters. Once in a while, a cartoonist will dedicate one or more of his works to another artist—and may choose to include one of that artist's creations in the strip dedicated to him. This sort of "good wishes" use of the comics—now less common than in the earlier days of underground comics, when the field was smaller—reached a special sort of height when cartoonists Kim Deitch and Trina Robbins had a child, and several other cartoonists congratulated them via little notes in their own strips.

A cartoonist will sometimes

Below: Bill Stout. *Bijou Funnies* No. 8. ©1973 Bijou Publishing Empire, Inc. By permission of Bijou Publishing Empire, Inc., by Jay Lynch; and William G. Stout. From Stout's satire of Skip Williamson's . Snappy Sammy Smoot.

use another cartoonist's drawings to make a specific point—as The Mad Peck did with Gilbert Shelton's Wonder Wart-Hog (see page 195). The Mad Peck is fond of making points through the work of others as well as through his own. In *Ghost Mother Comics* No. 1, for instance, The Mad Peck satirized "straight" attitudes toward sexuality by reproducing the S. Clay Wilson drawing seen on page 119, top—adding a heavily moralizing narration about the goodness of pinup girls and the evils of underground comics, and also adding a sloppy "X" over the girl's genital area (while making sure that the "X" didn't actually block anything out).

Sexual satire often descends on Robert Crumb, particularly because of his overt sex comics (some of which were reprinted and widely distributed in 1973, after many people heard about them by word of mouth and started asking for copies). Gilbert Shelton, for instance, brings Crumb into a Wonder Wart-Hog story, using an accurate drawing of Crumb to satirize some people's belief in the potentially corrupting influence of underground comics. The little girl, of course, is good old Wonder Wart-Hog in disguise, and Wonder soon reveals himself and

Pat Daley. *Bijou Funnies* No. 8. ©1973 Bijou Publishing Empire, Inc. By permission of Bijou Publishing Empire, Inc., by Jay Lynch; and Pat Daley. From Ms. Daley's satire of Vaughn Bodé's Cheech Wizard.

beats the comic-book "pusher" to a pulp, as children stand around happily screaming for blood (see page 124). Thus do we hear of a society that so thoroughly approves of violence and so thoroughly condemns sexuality.

Much of the time, infighting among the cartoonists is rather gentle (and should perhaps be called "inloving"). This is game-playing, not intended to make specific satirical points. For instance, when the underground comics were a little younger, Joel Beck, Denis Kitchen, Robert Crumb, and others all toyed with the idea of being the best in the field. In one case, Kitchen printed a drawing by Crumb with a fake letter (in *Mom's Homemade Comics* No. 1), then had another joking reference to Crumb in *Mom's* No. 2. Lest there by any doubt, Kitchen emphasizes that he never meant seriously to compare his work to Crumb's, which he deeply admires.

In another case, Gilbert Shelton was "victimized" by a page which pointed out that he was cursed with the same last name as Robert Shelton, Imperial Wizard of the Ku Klux Klan.

These little comments on the field from within the field don't necessarily deal with personalities at all, but with general characteristics of the underground comics. One strip, for instance, opens with comments on the famed underground penchant for lousy spelling—and note that, when the story actually begins, the word "phenomenal" is *again* misspelled, which makes one wonder if the cartoonists really can't spell or just don't want to bother. John Adkins Richardson offers a serious comment on this sort of poor spelling: "Most misspellings are deliberate, but it's awfully easy to make mistakes when you're lettering because you tend to focus on a letter as a design form independent of other conventions." If oddities sometimes result from the cartoonists' ignoring the conventions of writing and drawing, they'd just as soon have it that way.

A Few Oddities

S. Clay Wilson. *Gothic Blimp Works* No. 6. Wilson's rendition of Gilbert Shelton's Wonder Wart-Hog is subtly different from Shelton's own.

Below Left: Gilbert Shelton. *Zap Comix* No. 4.

Below: Denis Kitchen (including drawings by Robert Crumb). *Mom's Homemade Comics* No. 1.

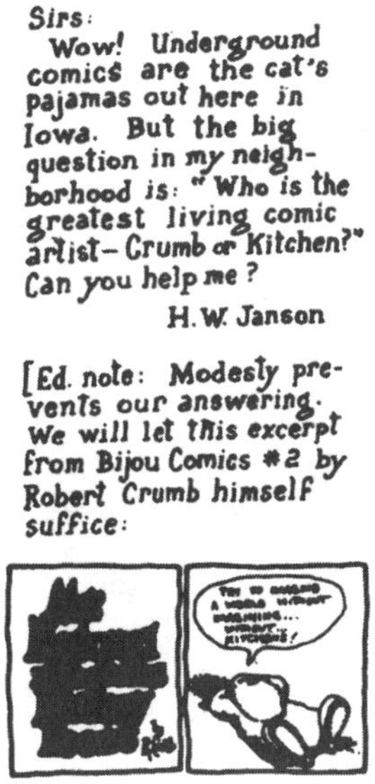

Spain. *Zap Comix* No. 4.

The victimization of Gilbert Shelton. *Conspiracy Capers* No. 1. ©1969 The Conspiracy. By permission of The Conspiracy, by Skip Williamson.

Opposite: Thaddeus. *New Earth Catalogue.* ©1972 Intergalactic Government Printing Office. By permission of Intergalactic Government Printing Office, by Phoenix and Arabeth.

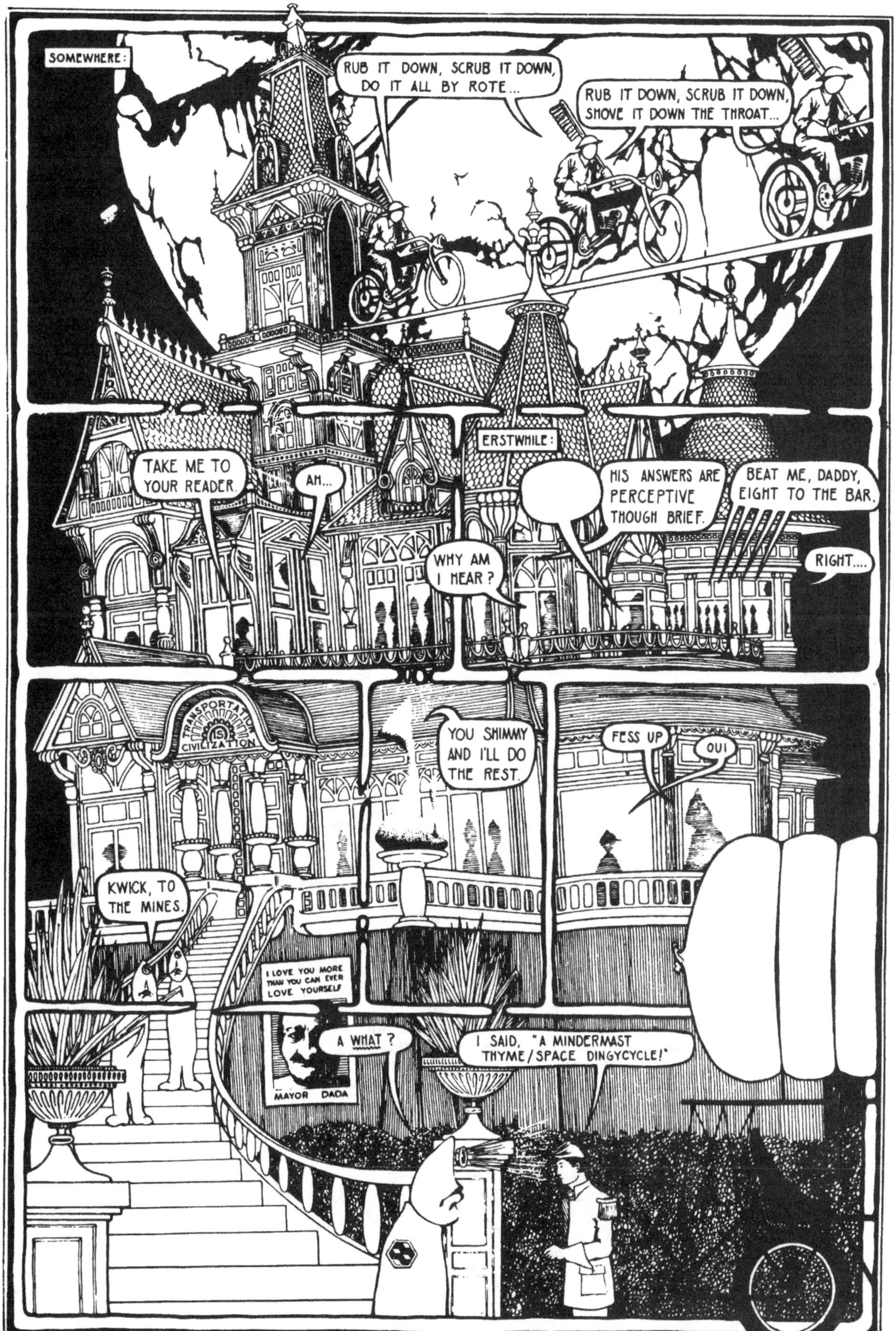
SOMEWHERE:
RUB IT DOWN, SCRUB IT DOWN, DO IT ALL BY ROTE...
RUB IT DOWN, SCRUB IT DOWN, SHOVE IT DOWN THE THROAT...
ERSTWHILE:
TAKE ME TO YOUR READER.
AH...
WHY AM I HEAR?
HIS ANSWERS ARE PERCEPTIVE THOUGH BRIEF.
BEAT ME, DADDY, EIGHT TO THE BAR.
RIGHT....
TRANSPORTATION IS CIVILIZATION
YOU SHIMMY AND I'LL DO THE REST.
FESS UP
OUI
KWICK, TO THE MINES.
I LOVE YOU MORE THAN YOU CAN EVER LOVE YOURSELF
MAYOR DADA
A WHAT?
I SAID, "A MINDERMAST THYME/SPACE DINGYCYCLE!"

10 Suppression

A 1969 notice from The Print Mint. Actually, *Zap* No. 4 truly went underground during the court cases, but was always available through the right channels. It emerged into open printing again in 1973 and was not legally attacked at that time—even in New York City.

> DUE TO PRESSURE BY LOCAL AND FEDERAL AUTHORITIES, AND PENDING A JUDGMENT ON OUR RECENT ARREST, ZAP NO. 4 WILL NO LONGER BE AVAILABLE FOR SALE.
>
> THE PRINT MINT WILL CONTINUE TO PUBLISH AND DISTRIBUTE ALL OTHER BOOKS CURRENTLY ON OUR ORDER FORM AND NEW BOOKS AS THEY APPEAR.

There are some things you may do if you wish to satirize American society. You may draw cartoons depicting the country's leaders as fools and madmen, the communications media as inanities run by robber barons, and the social system as a degrading, materialistic cycle leading to nowhere and back again.

But you may get in trouble if you couple this social satire with depictions of people doing things with their own and others' private parts.

Welcome to the American legal system.

Some local authorities have decided that the underground comics are indeed the threat to puritanical American values which the cartoonists want them to be. Instead of causing them to look inward (Crusader, heal thyself!), this decision has led some of them to attempt obscenity busts involving the underground comics. Like the under-the-counter pressure used against the E. C. Comics in the Joe McCarthy era of the early fifties, these arrests have hit at the distributors and dealers of the comics, this being the most efficient way of preventing the material from reaching the public. Moe's Bookstore in Berkeley was busted for selling *Snatch Comics* and *Zap Comix.* The Phoenix Gallery (also in Berkeley), after developing an art show featuring the work of numerous underground cartoonists (see Chapter 11), was busted for displaying obscene material. In Encino, California, an employee of the Third Eye bookstore was arrested for selling *Zap Comix* No. 2. And so on, and on, and on and on.

In almost every case, the obscenity busts have come to nothing. In the Third Eye bookstore case, a judge in Division 21 of the county court ruled that the strip which allegedly made *Zap* No. 2 obscene—an S. Clay Wilson story in which one pirate cuts off another's huge penis—was not obscene because it did not arouse one's prurient interests. But in one case, the Establishment pressed really hard, and in that case—since the Establishment has one arm which prosecutes, another which judges—a conviction of the dealer was obtained.

This happened in the best-known underground comics bust of all, which involved *Zap Comix* No. 4. Almost as soon as this issue was published, in August 1969, it was removed from circulation by a series of busts on both the East and West Coasts. Charges on the West Coast were soon dropped, though informal pressure continued—particularly against The Print Mint, which published *Zap* No. 4. But in New York City, the charges were pressed with vigor—and the result was a classic demonstration that the Establishment can use its laws as a club against underground culture, if it so chooses.

In June 1973—nearly four years after the busts involving *Zap* No. 4—the United States Supreme Court gave each local community new leeway to determine what is or is not obscene for that particular community. What the Court essentially did was take an earlier Supreme Court decision determining standards for obscenity and declare that each community could decide what the terms of that decision meant. In the New York City case involving *Zap* No. 4, the forces of "Law 'n' Order" had apparently already decided to bring to the fore a highly personal interpretation of the Supreme Court's guidelines on obscenity: 1) the material must appeal predominantly to a "prurient interest" in sex; 2) it must be "substantially beyond contemporary community standards"; and 3) it must be "utterly without redeeming social value." The New York State obscenity statute contains these three provisions, then adds what seems like a protection but can actually be used as a bludgeon: a provision that a person cannot be convicted of selling obscene material unless he "knows" that the material is obscene. This seems to protect the person whose opinions on obscenity differ from those of the police and censors, but there is another provision which turns the "protection" *against* the alleged "smut peddler." To prevent everyone busted on obscenity charges from claiming he didn't know the character of the material, and therefore should be set free, the New York statute contains a presumption: "A person who promotes obscene material, or possesses the same with intent to promote it in the course of his business, is presumed to do so with knowledge of its content and character." This is a legal masterpiece, because it shifts the burden of proof to the defendant—he must show he did not know the material was obscene, which is a little like being guilty until you're proven innocent. Furthermore, since the legal concept of promotion takes in the act of selling, this means that anyone who sells something which is *later* judged obscene, and who is unable to prove to a judge that he did not know that the material *was* obscene, can be fined, jailed, or both, for violating the obscenity statute.

This is exactly what happened in the *Zap* trial in the Criminal Court of the City of New York. The prosecution, conducted by Manhattan Assistant District Attorney Richard Beckler, made no arguments and presented no witnesses. Beckler simply gave Judge Joel Tyler (a morality crusader who several years later viewed and then suppressed the film "Deep Throat") a copy of *Zap* No. 4 and asked that it be found obscene "as a matter of law"—that is, it would be "obvious" that the comic met the three Supreme Court obscenity tests. To prove that the defendants "knew" the material was obscene, Beckler relied entirely upon the New York provision which, in effect, makes them prove they did *not* know it was obscene.

The defendants were sales clerks at two of New York's "head" bookshops: Peter Dargis, manager of the East Side Book Store, and Charles Kirkpatrick, co-manager of the New Yorker Bookshop. The defense introduced evidence that neither of these stores was a "smut shop," and that in each store underground comics accounted for less than one percent of the yearly income.

However, the main part of the defense—which was run by Robert Levine with the assistance of Stephen Rohde—consisted of the testimony of four so-called "expert witnesses": Gil Kane, a "straight" cartoonist whose characters have included Superman, Batman, and Captain Marvel; Robert M. Doty, curator of New York's Whitney Museum of American Art; Steven Marks, a nursery school teacher and freelance writer who has also taught at Columbia University; and Sidney Jacobson, an editor at Harvey Publications, publisher of such children's comics as *Casper, the Friendly Ghost* and *Playful Little Audrey*. The idea was to show that *Zap* No. 4 had "redeeming social value" and was therefore not legally obscene.

All four witnesses said they admired the work of the cartoonists in *Zap* No. 4, particularly Robert Crumb, S. Clay Wilson, and Gilbert Shelton. Kane attributed to the cartoons "the vitality of expressionistic paintings." Doty told of displaying Crumb's and Wilson's work at the Whitney Museum's exhibit, "Human Concern and Personal Torment: The Grotesque in American Art," and contrasted the "positive art form" of the underground cartoonists with such things as advertising and billboard art. Marks said he had used earlier Crumb strips in his Humanities course at Columbia University, and would have used some of S. Clay Wilson's visions of Hell if he had been teaching Dante when *Zap* No. 4 came out. Jacobson defended the underground comics for "using the medium to enter into all sorts of adult stories and adult situations," and got into a discussion of *Archie Comics* which revealed how set in his ways and attitudes Judge Tyler really was:

Jacobson: I certainly think that *Archie* is certainly a little sexy comic book.

Q (by Mr. Levine): *Archie* is supposed to be a child's comic?

A: Yes.

Q: You think that is sexual?

A: I know.

Judge Tyler: You know? Is there more than one *Archie*?

A: *Archie Comics,* which would be Archie and who—the teenage character.

Judge Tyler: But there is just one *Archie* that you mentioned, is that so?

A: I'm sorry—

Judge Tyler: You mean a magazine? Is there any other comic book called *Archie*?

A: No, there is the famous one that's about twenty years old that has been successfully going.

Judge Tyler: You are talking about that, Mr. Jacobson, only one?

A: As far as I know.

Judge Tyler: You say that deals in sexuality?

A: Absolutely.

Judge Tyler: Tell me in what way.

A: What way?

Judge Tyler: Yes.

A: Purposely written and drawn to arouse sexualities in teenagers. I think this is done without question.

Q (by Mr. Beckler): What do you mean by "sexuality" in *Archie*?

A: I mean by that the publishers, the editors and writers are putting in—the people involved in drawing and creating *Archie* are trying within it to appeal to the sexual desires of their public, which is a little different.

Q: Would you say arousing the prurient interest?

A: No, I wouldn't say that. I would say arousing the sexual interest.

Q: Would you say that *Zap* No. 4 arouses sexual interest?

A: No, not really.

Q: So, it would seem to me, on the sliding scale of yours, that *Archie* would arouse more interest of the sex appeal than *Zap* No. 4, is that correct?

A: Yes, to its reader.

Judge Tyler: How about *Archie*? Is that obscene?

A: No, I don't think it's obscene, I think it's sexual.

Judge Tyler: Do they intend in *Archie* to appeal to the sexuality of the teenager?

A: Yes, they do.

Judge Tyler: Do you deem that to be an obscene purpose?

A: No, I don't.

Robert Crumb. *Zap Comix* No. 4. Opening panel of the controversial "Joe Blow" story.

Throughout the trial, Judge Tyler's comments made it clear that he couldn't (or wouldn't) understand the witnesses' testimony that *Zap* No. 4 had social and artistic value. At one point, he said to Kane, "I am having a little difficulty because I can't think in the abstract. My training requires me to think in the particular." When Marks testified that strips like Crumb's "Joe Blow" would not appeal to people's prurient interest, Tyler asked, "A word was used the other day, the area of superior sophistication, I think that's your area of acquaintance, but isn't it so that others would not get the same story as—the same concept as those with whom you are acquainted or yourself?"

Later, when Marks said that he had brought some prints with him to show that sexual images were an important part of portraying the world of the grotesque, Judge Tyler said, "Can't get away from the fact that you're a professor, can you?" And still later, when Jacobson began a discussion of the "straight" comics market by saying that his firm, Harvey Publications, put out books for the lowest age group on the age ladder, Judge Tyler said, "I beg your pardon, I read these regularly."

When all testimony had been given, Judge Tyler deliberated for several months, and then turned in an opinion rejecting all the expert testimony and accepting the prosecution's contention that *Zap* No. 4 was legally obscene. He also accepted Beckler's contention that New York law gave sufficient support to the idea that the defendants, in strictly legal terms, "knew" the material they were selling was obscene (though it only became legally obscene after the judge ruled it so).

Judge Tyler's approach to his decision is worth noting: "In the final analysis, the Court must be the expert in assessing what is the dominant theme, prurient interest, community standards, any redeeming social value, and the like . . . . Merely because the magazine in question does not appeal to the prurient interest of the sophisticated or other small group of intellectuals does not remove it from the prohibition [against obscenity]. To do so would permit the substitution of the opinions of defendants' sophisticated and intellectual experts for those of the average person in the contemporary community . . . . The cartoon is ugly, cheap and degrading. Its purpose—to stimulate erotic responses, and does not, as claimed, deal with basic realities of life. It is grossly shocking, demeaning the sexual experience by perverting it. . . . It is a part of the underworld [*sic*] press—the growing world of deceit in sex, and it is not reality or honesty, as they often claim it to be. It represents an emotional incapacity to view sex as a basis for establishing genuine human relationships, or as a normal part of human condition."

Spain. *Zap Comix* No. 4. The first page of "Mara, Mistress of the Void." Note the words "Spa Fon" which were used originally in some of the E.C. Comics of the fifties (see page 32).

Thus the Establishment closes ranks. In strictly legal terms, Judge Tyler wrought a subtle change upon the Supreme Court's three guidelines for obscenity as they stood in 1969-1970. The second standard ("substantially beyond contemporary community standards") had been held to refer to the standards of the community at large; but "redeeming social value" could be shown, the courts had held, if *any* group in society found such value in the work.

Thus, *Fanny Hill* was found not obscene by the United States Supreme Court because, while it did go beyond the standards of the community at large, it had "redeeming social value" as an example of eighteenth-century literature. The community at large is not interested in such literature; nor is it interested in *Zap* No. 4, with its nihilistic sociopolitical view of man and its graphic attack on "hot dog and apple pie" attitudes toward sex and the family. But Judge Tyler found that *Zap* No. 4, though it might have value to the "sophisticated and intellectual," was utterly without such value when judged by members of the community at large—such as himself.

Robert Crumb. *Zap Comix* No. 4. The final page of the "Joe Blow" story, intending to make the satirical purpose very clear.

He essentially stated that the underground comics can, indeed *must* be judged by the standards of the very society-at-large which they satirize and reject.

It's worth noting that all is jaundiced to the jaundiced eye, including the judicial one. Prosecutor Beckler spent most of his time with the expert witnesses discussing Robert Crumb's strip "Joe Blow" and alleging that the incest in that strip was of such a type as to put it past the point of "redeeming social value." Yet the Crumb strip neither opens nor ends with incest, as can be seen from the examples in this chapter. It begins with an obvious satire on the classic suburban-couple-with-television-set scene that the underground cartoonists attack so often, and ends with six panels (a full comic-book page) which make it clear that Crumb is satirizing the whole rosy concept of "get together with your family and do things" that Middle America holds so dear. Could anything be clearer than the satire of the final panel? But Beckler constantly directed Judge Tyler's attention only to the sex acts, and that was all the judge wound up seeing: "I cannot discern any genuine idea."

Judge Tyler's lack of discernment extended to every single story in *Zap* No. 4. Bristling with moral indignation, he roundly condemned each individual strip for its sexual content, and in every case stated that he—supposedly representing the average man in the community—could see nothing *beyond* the sex in the

Above: Robert Crumb. *Zap Comix* No. 4. The entire "Horny Harriet" vignette.

Victor Moscoso. *The New Comix* (Phoenix Gallery poster). Moscoso's personal, jam-session-like commentary on "Joe Blow."

POLICE SHOULD BE OBSCENE AND NOT ABSURD
HEY HAROLD!.... WHAT'S "OBSCENE" MEAN?
PORK PRESS
GEORGIA STRAIGHT BUSTED FOR DISTRIBUTION OF OBSCENE COMICS
PILES
WHY STAY
IT PROBABLY MEANS "ANYTHING THE MORALITY SQUAD DISAGREES WITH AT ANY GIVEN TIME"
LIKE THIS SIMULATED "HARD-ON" HERE
KITCHY KOO...
NOW IF THIS WAS A FOR REAL "HARD-ON" THIS CARTOON WOULD BE JUDGED OBSCENE... GOOD THING IT'S ONLY A FAKE RUBBER DILDO!
HAVE I GOT IT RIGHT SIDE UP?... I FORGET HOW THEY WORK
AIN'T CAPITALISM GRAND?! ...IT TAKES YOUR PRICK AWAY VIA SEXUAL REPRESSION... TO MAKE YOU MORE WORK ORIENTED... THEN SELLS YOU AN IMPROVED PLASTIC MODEL THAT'S BIGGER! HARDER! AND GUARANTEED TO STAY UP!!
SQUISH
ROOKIES TAKE NOTE! THIS IS NOT A DRAWING OF A REAL PENIS... IT'S A DRAWING OF AN IMITATION! YOU KNOW ...LIKE THEM ONES SOLD LEGALLY UP ON GRANVILLE ST.
..MAKES A GREAT PARTY HAT!
FOOP
GEE...I DUNNO HAROLD... DOESN'T LOOK VERY OBSCENE T'ME...
LOOKS KINDA CUTE
WE REPEAT ....NOT A GAZEBO NOT A PLACEBO BUT A DILDO!*
BY GOBS-ELMO!...Y'KNOW, MAYBE THAT'S IT!..MAYBE OBSCENITY-LIKE BEAUTY-IS IN THE EYE OF THE BEHOLDER... KINDA DEPENDS ON WHAT YER LOOKIN FOR...
AN WE ALL KNOW WHAT THE MORALITY SQUAD IS LOOKING FOR
YEH!..AN MAYBE AN INDIVIDUAL WHO EXPECTS A CIVIL SERVANT TO DECIDE FOR HIM IS GUILTY OF A MORAL COP-OUT!
ARRGH! CHARGING RHINOSAWURST
FSSST
WELL "I" THINK IT'S SICK-SICK-SICK!
AND ANYONE WHO DISAGREES WITH "ME" IS UNDER ARREST!
* FOR ALL YOU NOSTALGIA FREAKS

stories. In the strongest possible language, he denied the expert witnesses' testimony concerning the underlying social criticism of the comic. He said that *Zap* No. 4 existed merely to exploit the fact that some people lack proper moral and ethical values. He added that the potential moral harmfulness of the comic was great—because, he said, material like *Zap* No. 4 "contains its own antidote and eventually becomes a repetitious bore—but, unfortunately, by that time it has rendered its victims shock-proof, jaded and permissive to the point of indifference toward moral values and tolerable behavior."

Judge Tyler thus suggested that an average person could be irreparably corrupted, in a moral sense, by *Zap* No. 4 and similar material. Since he had set himself up as just such an average person (in contrast to the "sophisticated" defense witnesses), it would have been interesting if he had commented on the effect of the comic on *his* personal life. But Judge Tyler did not see fit to say whether *Zap* No. 4 had corrupted his own moral behavior—any more than he chose to comment on the effects upon his moral life of the film "Deep Throat," which he also had the right to view and then prevented the people in his jurisdiction from seeing.

Unfortunately, the quality of a judge's morality and the peculiarly narrow standards under which he lives his own life do not provide grounds for the appeal of any decision in the American legal system. Robert Levine needed other grounds for appealing the decision—and he chose to appeal on the grounds that the "presumption" statute in New York State law was unconstitutional, violating guarantees of due process and freedom of speech. Levine admitted that the New York State Court of Appeals would avoid deciding a constitutional issue if it possibly could, but still hoped for a reversal of Judge Tyler's decision—since there was no way the defendants could afford to appeal the decision to the United States Supreme Court.

The Association of American Publishers and the New York Civil Liberties Union both filed *amicus curiae* briefs in support of Levine's appeal. But the Court of Appeals rejected those briefs and the appeal itself, affirming the original obscenity conviction by a vote of 4 to 3 in March, 1973. Judge Charles Breitel (now Chief Judge of the Court of Appeals—the highest judicial position in New York State) spoke for the majority when he said (as reported in the *New York Law Journal* of March 29, 1973), "Needless to say, the inference of knowledge rests on the probabilities of human transactions. It is rare that one does not know what one possesses. Since the inference of knowledge is but that, the burden of going forward and negativing [*sic*] the inference is a slight one and, by the nature of things, rarely is there occasion to invoke it. It must be an extraordinary circumstance which prevents one from knowing what one possesses." Thus, Judge Breitel ignored the fact that this case *was* extra-

Opposite: Rand Holmes. *Harold Hedd* No. 2. ©1973 Rand Holmes. By permission of Rand Holmes. A typical underground attitude toward obscenity busts.

Various cartoonists comment on law enforcement, obscenity, etc. Below Left: Howard Cruse. Bottom Left: Bill Crawford. Both from *Commies from Mars* No. 1. ©1973 Krupp Comic Works, Inc. By permission of Krupp Comic Works, Inc., by Denis Kitchen. Below: R. Scott Pflug. *Funnybook No. 1*. ©1971 The Almighty Publishing Company, Inc. By permission of The Almighty Publishing Company, Inc., by R. Scott Pflug. Both the "poster" and the "desecration" are shown just as they originally appeared on the comic's back cover.

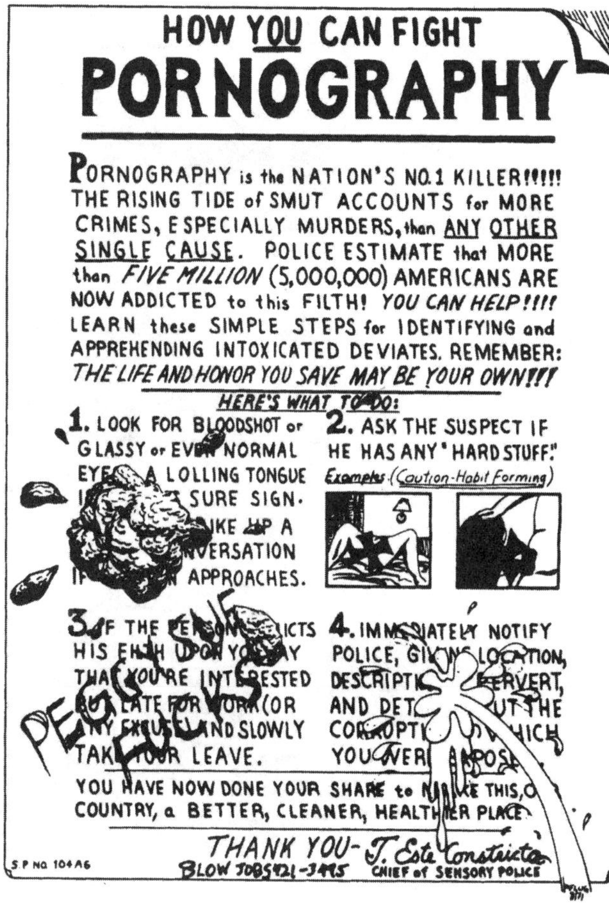

ordinary, because there had been no previous trials involving similar comics and the booksellers had no way of knowing that a certain Judge Tyler would personally deem *Zap* No. 4 obscene. One bookseller said he had glanced through the comic and did *not* consider it obscene—but the American legal system, in cases like this one, doesn't care about differences of opinion. The attitude was that if Judge Tyler thought the comic obscene, that obscenity should have been obvious to any bookseller—even if his personal attitudes were less repressive than Judge Tyler's.

Judge Breitel's comments undoubtedly made prosecutor Beckler happy: after the original trial, Beckler had said, "It's no undue burden on the owners to glance through these things. They sit around and B.S. so much in those stores, anyway." But Peter Martin, owner of the New Yorker Bookshop, and Jim Rose, owner of the East Side Book Store, insisted that the decision, in Martin's words, "will tend to make us chicken. They want us to do their censorship for them: I'm supposed to look at something and say, 'Oh my God, maybe they're going to act on it!'" After the decision of the Appeals Court, Roysce Smith, executive director of the American Booksellers Association, termed the ruling "frightening" and added (as reported in *Publishers Weekly*, March 21, 1973), "No one can possibly know in advance what a court will consider obscene. The effect of the decision is to make every bookseller in the state a censor."

What the long-range effect of this decision may be is, of course, impossible to guess. No other major cases like the one involving *Zap* No. 4 arose, even after the Supreme Court returned some extra power to determine obscenity to local communities. Indeed, the lack of parallel cases—despite the continued and undiminished sexiness of many underground comics—has led many cartoonists to declare that the *Zap* trial in New York was a political bust of the counterculture, not an obscenity trial at all. These cartoonists feel the bust was deliberately planned to

Bill Griffith. *Tales of Toad* No. 2. ©1971 Bill Griffith. By permission of Bill Griffith.

come at a time when the underground comics were beginning to reach a wider audience—to reach beyond a certain "hard-core" readership into the larger community. At that point, the cartoonists suggest, the comics became a potential threat and were attacked through the legal system.

To be sure, there *was* a change in the readership of the underground comics at around the time of the *Zap* trial. This was part of a development in the comics themselves, as Will Eisner of *The Spirit* pointed out: "Now today, the underground is emerging from giggling graffiti toilet-wall jokes, to professional-experimental art and thoughtful stories. New styles, new ideas, new directions are emerging like wild flowers in an unplowed meadow." Many underground cartoonists, smarting under legal pressure from the *Zap* trial, concluded that society saw them as weeds in a carefully cultivated garden—and attacked their work through the courts.

Yet defense lawyer Stephen Rohde denies the allegation that the *Zap* bust was politically motivated—for the interesting reason that "the D.A. was honestly astonished to hear about the sociopolitical content. To the police, comics are for children, no matter what the covers say. They just don't see anything but 'dirty pictures' in comic-book form."

Rohde also realizes the special problems posed for the American legal system by the underground comics: "How can we talk about 'contemporary community standards' in this case? We're dealing with a counterculture, a culture which works by standards quite different from those of the established culture. But in this case, the product of that subculture must be judged by the laws of the established culture." Or, as *The Phantom Psychiatrist* asks, "What the hell is a social redeeming value? Is a social redeeming value that you walk around with a flag and believe in mother and country?"

Mike Barrier, in *Funnyworld* No. 12, suggests that *Zap* No. 4 was hit so hard specifically because, in "Joe Blow," "Crumb made the mistake of refusing to feign shock. That was his true sin. The portrayal of incest is forgivable, even profitable, so long as you provide a frosting of morality. The authors of those thick novels that middle-aged women read are well aware of that; they're experts at titillation without guilt. Crumb, who remains an 'underground' artist in all the important ways, has the unfortunate habit of taking things as they come, without blinking, and many people find that hard to take."

In light of Barrier's comments on Crumb, it's interesting to see how the underground cartoonists themselves react to the common charge that all they produce is pornography. A typical comment is the one Robert Williams inserted on the inside front cover of his *Coochy Cooty Men's Comics:* "Any persons found in the act of masturbation with this material in their possession must be considered subject to fetish as this

Victor Moscoso. The wrap-around cover of *Zap Comix* No. 4. The transformation of "Mr. Peanut" on the front cover to "Mr. Penis" on the back is typical of the attacks on "normal" American values in this comic, and lends fuel to some cartoonists' belief that the trial in New York City was a politically motivated bust of the counterculture.

FAR OFF IN A CLEAN VACUUM VOID, FREE OF GENITALIA, COCKS, PUSSYS, TURDS, AND THINGS THAT RELATE TO CRUDE, BASIC, ARCHAIC MAMMAL EXISTENCE, PRESIDED A NEBULISTIC DEITY. THIS GREAT CLOUD FORMATION SHAPED A GIANT SOUL, MADE OF A TRILLION GALAXIES COMPOSED INTO ONE MASTER LIFE FORM...
THE SUPREME CONSTELLATION OF
-HARMONY-

Robert Crumb. *Mr. Natural* No. 1. ©1970 R. Crumb Productions. By permission of R. Crumb Productions, by Robert Crumb. From a story which originally appeared in a paper called *Organ*.

Opposite: Robert Williams. *Zap Comix* No. 4. First page of "The Supreme Constellation of Dormasintoria."

Below Left: S. Clay Wilson. *Zap Comix* No. 4. The center spread.

Below: S. Clay Wilson. *Zap Comix* No. 4. A complete story.

material is hardly prurient."

True pornography actually serves a socially useful function by providing an outlet for repressed sexual energy—energy which must be held in check to permit society to operate at all. For that reason, out-and-out pornographic literature is at least tolerated, and often eagerly sought, by many self-appointed guardians of public morality. Also, not unexpectedly, this sort of literature finds its greatest market among middle-aged businessmen and similar cornerstones of society, who in New York City may often be seen in out-and-out porn shops every lunch hour.

The underground comics are quite different from this sort of "release" pornography, and this difference perhaps explains why they were hit so hard by New York's guardians of public morality. For the underground comics, far from providing a release for repressed sexuality and thus helping society function more efficiently, couple their sexual freedom with overt, often vicious *attacks* on society. Thus, should there be any sort of sexual "charge" transmitted to readers of the underground comics, that stimulation would not be a release—it would be directed, so far as sexual energy can be directed, toward society's destruction rather than its support. In this philosophical sense, then, the underground comics really *do* lack "redeeming social value"—but *only* in this sense, and this was scarcely the legal basis for the harassment in New York.

Many people find the *Zap* busts as hard to take as Judge Tyler found *Zap* No. 4. In fact, Don Schenker, founder of The Print Mint, ended his association with the organization because of them. "Yes, the charges out here were dropped, but it bent my head. I put my time in, and I got this thing off the ground and I was —it really got to me."

Other people, less personally affected by the legal harassment, decided that the busts might actually serve a useful purpose for the underground comics—at least in the long run. Will Eisner commented, "The Porno laws will not stop honest statements about sex and life; maybe discourage phonies. But in a sort of cathartic way it will force the Comic Book comic artist to produce material of more substance, material not totally dependent on coitus, cunnilingus, and cunts." Eisner's optimism, however, is dismissed by many cartoonists, who respect his work but do find him, when all is said and done, a representative of an earlier generation—and a cartoonist who has not, himself,

dealt explicitly with sexual matters and thus become subject to legal pressure. And whatever their opinion of statements like Eisner's, the underground cartoonists can point out that there *have* been problems with sales and distribution of their work because of obscenity busts like the *Zap* trial.

Of course, the underground isn't that easy to keep down, as the spirit of the underground comics produced since the New York *Zap* trial makes clear. The underground culture in America, and the comic books it has produced, cannot be wiped out by people who use American law the way Spain Rodriguez' brutal cop, Manning, uses it—as a shield for their prejudices and a bludgeon for those who disagree with them. The cartoonists would not stop producing and distributing their work under these circumstances, even if

S. Clay Wilson. *Zap Comix* No. 4. First page of "A Ball in the Bung Hole."

they had to go back to the hand-drawn, hand-distributed copies that many used to make. "There is nothing so powerful as an idea whose time has come"—and the time for the underground comics is now, even if the cartoonists have to look at Judges Tyler and Breitel and say, with Bob Dylan, "Something is happening here, but you don't know what it is. Do you, Mr. Jones?"

Suppression

Larry Todd. *Paranoia.* ©1972 Larry Todd. By permission of Larry Todd.

11 Into the Overground

The scene is an office somewhere in mid-Manhattan. A sign on the wall reads "Guns Unlimited, A Gun in Every Home." Two men are reading a newspaper called *The Underground.* Says the first, "Look at this shocking stuff! Did you ever see such shocking stuff!" The second replies, "This sure is shocking stuff! Turn the page for more shocking stuff!" The first opines, "Shut the window so's I can turn the page for more shocking stuff." Admonishes the second, "More! More shocking stuff! Keep it steady so's I can see the shocking stuff!"

The scene may be found on page twenty-three of *Gothic Blimp Works* No. 8; but it might well be occurring several times a day in the real world, considering the way the "straight" media and publishing business have so far treated the underground comics.

When the "overground" media first deigned to bestow recognition on the underground comics, the editing might just as well have been done by the people at "Guns Unlimited." For instance, the *National Insider* (one of those "leer-at-the-grossness-and-evil-and-then-tsk-tsk-loudly-and-go-to-church-on-Sunday" things that somehow deserve currency on newsstands, while the underground comics do not), on December 15, 1968, ran an article called "Latest 'Art' trend—Hippie Sex Comics." The article, as heavy in its moralizing as the most degrading skin flicks, explained just how evil and depraved these comics are. Of course, examples of the nasty, perverted strips were given, including drawings by S. Clay Wilson and Spain Rodriguez, but—get this punchline—there were *big black blotches* placed over words and pictures that the editors thought would just be *too* offensive to the delicate sensibilities of their readers. Oh yes—and the *Insider* didn't bother about such niceties as crediting the material or including copyright notices.

This sort of rip-off (which is a nicer-sounding word for thievery, but also carries the connotation of deliberate exploitation of the stolen material) is all too common in the "straight" world—extraordinarily common, considering that the underground comics are quite a new medium.

Every "straight" medium you can imagine has picked up, and picked on, the underground comics and cartoonists—occasionally with the heavily moralistic hatchet of the *Insider,* but more often with a sense of the comics' importance but a total lack of understanding. The December 1970 issue of *Playboy,* for example, carried an article by Jacob Brackman entitled "The International Comix Conspiracy." The article was one-third author's reminiscences, one-third corny philosophizing about the sort of society that has produced the comics, and one-third a discussion of the comics themselves. The emphasis was heavily on Robert Crumb (not surprising, since he is by far the best-known underground cartoonist, but a little upsetting because it made the article lopsided). The cartoonists were not generally happy with the piece (to put it mildly). George Metzger shrugged it off: "Read *Playboy* article on comics. About what I'd expect from them. (If my name'd been mentioned I'd have bought two copies.)" John Thompson said there were "misrepresentations in article I think—not complete information data and history, influenced by prejudicial sources (as we all are)." And Jay Lynch, who lives in Chicago and can therefore appear in person at *Playboy*'s offices there, was disgusted with the magazine's attitudes: "I had to sit in an outer office at *Playboy* for five fucking hours before I could get them to pay me for reprinting that thing of mine in their comix article. They were three weeks late when I started to demand payment. I bet they aren't late in paying F. Lee Bailey and Mort Sahl and those other guys who write stuff for that magazine."

Gary Hallgren. A one-dollar gift coupon issued for the opening of The People's Comic Gallery in San Francisco.

That's precisely the kind of treatment which keeps the underground cartoonists totally turned off by the "straight" media.

Of course, *Playboy* does want to exploit the underground comics commercially. Skip Williamson was on the *Playboy* staff for a while, and the magazine signed Gilbert Shelton to a contract for a three-page "Feds 'n' Heads Board Game" which was published as an article, then marketed nationally. At least *Playboy* took the trouble to sign Shelton to a contract, did not censor him, and did pay him (and, ultimately, Lynch as well).

Some other overground acknowledgments of the underground comics have been far less admirable. The first serious attempt to look at the comics was an article by Bob Abel in the April 1969 issue of *Cavalier* magazine. The author, then a senior editor at Dell Publishing Company and collaborator on an earlier book on "straight" comics (see the Bibliography), was intelligent enough to let the cartoonists he interviewed do most of the talking, and at least he had had some previous contact with underground humor: Abel worked with Paul Krassner on *The Realist* magazine for seven years, during which time he held the title of "Featherbedder." But Abel never defined or limited his subject (he called the underground books "comix" and seemed to think that sufficed as a definition); he ended his piece with a puerile philosophizing postscript ("Often they are out to outrage the already outrageous, but of course we must judge them on accomplishment, not on intent"); he was guilty of extremely hasty judgment and overstatement (Vaughn Bodé "impresses this writer as probably the one true genius in the field"); and he had a tendency to trivialize the comics and their cartoonists (for example, by describing Trina as "a long-haired, pretty lady, whose drawing style is a lot more elongated than she is").

Furthermore, the ten samples of underground comics which *Cavalier* chose to print (an admittedly generous sampling) were one and all of the innocent-but-sarcastic type which would surely make *Cavalier*'s readers won-

Bill Griffith. *Tales of Toad* No. 1. ©1970 Bill Griffith. By permission of Bill Griffith.

Below Left: George Metzger. *Truckin'*. ©1972 George Metzger. By permission of George Metzger.

Below: Spain. *Thrilling Murder Comics*. ©1971 B. Griffith, K. Deitch, S. Deitch, R. Crumb, Spain, Wilson, J. Osborne, Irons. By permission of Messrs. Griffith, K. Deitch, Crumb, and Spain.

der what the reason was for bothering with the article in the first place (or, at any rate, *should* have made them wonder). And the magazine opened the article with a picture of a bare-topped woman reading a tabloid-size underground comic—scarcely the sort of image one associates with an honest study of the field.

Some other cases in which the "straight" printed media have acknowledged the underground comics have not even *pretended* to be serious or honest analyses. *Art and Artists* magazine for December 1969 carried an article on some of the comics and cartoonists, written in a fairly straight descriptive style. It was uninteresting and unpretentious—*but* it was illustrated with *only* the first four panels of the S. Clay Wilson "Tit Tales" strip—the attitude apparently being that it's all right to show a girl's tits but not a guy's prick. That's exactly the sort of arbitrary censorship which the underground cartoonists went un-

The Mad Peck. *Extra! Commix.*

derground to avoid, and it's frustrating to find "straight" publications which are willing to acknowledge the existence of the underground but unwilling, really, to show their readers what it's all about.

Many other early "straight" references to the underground comics were brief and without insight. Peter Plangens mentioned them once in a long piece on "The Possibilities of Drawing," in *Artforum* magazine, October 1969: "Gilbert Shelton, Robert Crumb, and Ron Cobb, messengers from the 'underground' could be called Pop from the safety of the fact that their art is intended for popular consumption, rather than for galleries, museums and connoisseurs." That sort of nice, safe, meaningless statement is typical. The same sort of statement showed up in a "Media" column called "Californian Scenes," written by Richard Gilbert for *The Listener* of November 6, 1969. The column also dealt with California radio stations, NBC-Television's "Laugh-In," the Dick Cavett late-night talk show, and the ABC network's programming problems. The piece did not pretend to be more than a quick survey of some media scenes in California, but "quick" and "superficial" need not be synonymous—as in this case they were.

At least the piece in *The Listener* showed that American underground comics were starting to get some *inter*national attention: the paper is published by the British Broadcasting Corporation. But that international recognition wasn't necessarily for the good: a book called *Gung-Ho,* published in Holland in 1970, is an overt rip-off of the underground cartoonists' work. This book, which often sold (according to Jay Lynch) for the equivalent of fifteen American dollars ("it actually cost only $2.50, but some evil European newsdealers charged $15.00"), contained over two hundred pages of comic strips by Lynch, Skip Williamson, Gilbert Shelton, and other cartoonists, and supposedly sold quite well. The text was in Dutch. None of the cartoonists was asked for the use of his material, and none received a penny of the Dutch publisher's profits. Despite this, Jay Lynch's attitude toward the situation is a typical one for the underground cartoonists, and helps explain why their work has been so frequently exploited: "I ain't upset about the Dutch using my stuff in *Gung-Ho,* since its publisher isn't making very much money off it anyway—and he's really spreading the word all over Europe and getting arrested and stuff." But of course, this statement ignores the fact that there are plenty of European underground comics, and that European publishers are more careful not to exploit those than they

S. Clay Wilson. *Snatch Comics* No. 2. ©1968 R. Scrum. By permission of Robert Crumb.

Opposite: Rick Griffin. *Zap Comix* No. 3.

O.K.
OLD FAITHFULL
gung ho!
GO AHEAD ON!
ITS GETTING BETTER ALL THE TIME...
all AMERICAN comicks
get a good education!!..
—step up to big pay!!!..
UH OH—WE'VE REACHED A CUL-DU-SAC

are about the American variety. Rip-offs, like political scandals, unite the world.

Once in a while, art galleries and other viewing places for "established" art take notice of the underground cartoonists. Art galleries in Washington, D.C., New York City (the Whitney Museum —see Chapter 10), and Berkeley, California, have displayed interest in the underground cartoonists' work. Berkeley's Phoenix Gallery, in fact, had a two-month showing of the work of some forty underground cartoonists in October and November 1969 (and had some hassles with the police as a result).

But it's mostly the print media of the "straight" world which have paid attention to the underground comics. One such publication has been interested in the field for quite a number of years —since all the way back in 1964. In September of that year, *Esquire* magazine ran one of Gilbert Shelton's early Wonder Wart-Hog strips. The strip was accompanied by a rather cute, patronizing paragraph about Shelton himself—but to notice this sort of work at all in 1964 was quite an achievement. It's worth noting that the mention of Shelton was called "Superman Goes to College" and was included in the annual *Esquire* back-to-school issue. There was as yet no sense that the underground comics were a medium (which, come to think of it, they really weren't in September 1964).

Once the underground comics began to appear regularly, *Esquire* noticed them again. Robert Crumb's work was mentioned twice in a long article called "The New Humor" in the December 1969 issue. Then, in April 1970, Crumb was referred to again, and this time his strip condemning the use of speed (see page 219) was reproduced in full. The article itself was not about underground comics, however, or even about Crumb—it concerned New York City's Whitney Museum, where an art show had been showing Crumb's work, among many others'.

Esquire continued to acknowledge the underground comics, for instance in the issue for December 1970. In a *Saturday Evening Post* parody called "The Great Speckled Post," *Esquire* united Robert Crumb with the spiritual founder of underground comics, Harvey Kurtzman. Crumb did almost all the artwork, and Kurtzman all the writing for the parody. But unfortunately, "The Great Speckled Post" contained one of the typical rip-offs which destroy whatever small faith the underground cartoonists retain in the "straight" media. For their parody on the "Post Scripts" cartoon page from the old *Saturday Evening Post,* Kurtzman and Crumb solicited contributions from other underground cartoonists. S. Clay Wilson, Victor Moscoso, Gilbert Shelton, and Spain Rodriguez sent things in. But the plan to put out what Kurtzman called "a potpourri of underground gag cartoons" was stymied, with Kurtzman's cooperation, because the S. Clay Wilson cartoon was considered too much for *Esquire* to print. According to Kurtzman, "His thing was just too pornographic. It has this motorcycle guy and his girl, and the girl had sticky jizz all over her, and the caption was something like 'Come on, Bernice.' Come, on Bernice. They just wouldn't reproduce it, so they changed the caption, and they asked me, should we go ahead? And I said well, what the heck. And Wilson called me up to complain when the drawing was reproduced. He swore a blue streak. It was just awful. Called me at six in the morning, collect, and I had to take like a half hour—just a stream of abuse poured out of the phone. But he sent me a Christmas card later."

Whatever the value of Kurtzman's and *Esquire*'s judgment (not everyone involved in underground culture thinks Kurtzman knows where it's at anymore—see Appendix A), the change of caption completely ruined Wilson's point and provided another example of the "straight" media using the underground comics unfairly. When printed, the Wilson cartoon bore the caption, "I don't know what's wrong with this machine, Bernice. The timing is off and it seems to be missing." Wilson must have stopped writing that way when he was about ten years old.

S. Clay Wilson. *The Rip Off Review of Western Culture.* ©1972 Rip Off Press. By permission of Rip Off Press, by Gilbert Shelton. This is the original panel, with the original caption, which Wilson intended for use in *Esquire.*

Kurtzman and *Esquire* do at least remain committed to articles on the underground comics, and Kurtzman himself is well aware of the way the comics reflect the larger society. Only six months after "The Great Speckled Post," in *Esquire* for June 1971, Kurtzman and the underground comics were again in the magazine's pages, this time in a piece called "®&%$#!! or Takin' the Lid Off the Id." The article had nine pages of good reproductions of comic strips that reflected certain aspects of American society at the time they were produced: everything from "Pogo," "Bringing Up Father," "Blondie," "Prince Valiant," "Popeye," and "The Katzenjammer Kids" to an early *Mad* parody and one of the old *Eight-Pagers.* The underground comics got their due, with reproductions of the cover of Crumb's *Despair* and of a number of panels from Gilbert Shelton's story of "Smiling Sergeant Death and His Merciless Mayhem Patrol." But even in this piece there was exploitation of a sort: since Shelton's story, like almost everything in the underground comics, was in black and white, and the other story illustrations were in color, a color wash of the Shelton panels was done by Kurtzman. That's scarcely a major rip-off, but it's typical of the cavalier treatment the underground cartoonists receive at the hands of even the best-meaning "straight" media.

To a certain extent, the underground cartoonists brought this

Below: Photo by Clay Geerdes of the doorway of The People's Comic Gallery in San Francisco, showing the store's full-size plywood figure of Robert Crumb's Lenore Goldberg. ©1973 Clay Geerdes. By permission of Clay Geerdes.

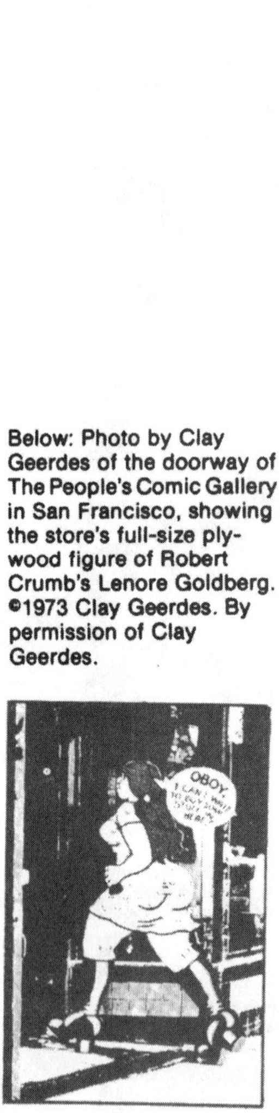

sort of exploitation on themselves by the very freedom of their field. Many early underground comics—and even a few published quite recently—bore no copyright notices, so the material in them was available for anyone who cared to use it. Some comics actually showed a willingness (now increasingly rare) to let anyone who was interested use their material, because many cartoonists felt the comics were a medium of the people and for the people—not realizing that some of those people would distort the whole purpose of the comics and the cartoonists. The inside front cover of *Snatch* No. 3 reads, "Reproduction of all material in this magazine is up for grabs and is o.k. with us . . . feel free to reprint . . . spread it around . . . strew yo' mess . . . but pay us." That last phrase, even if a lawyer contended it was serious, would be unlikely to stand up in court, since the book bears no copyright and the earlier part of the statement invites everyone who feels like it to use the material. A particularly careful sort of rip-off artist could theoretically send one penny to Robert Crumb, who was in charge of the *Snatch* books, and have perfect legal grounds for saying he complied with *every* provision of that statement before he made eight million dollars selling tee shirts bearing Crumb's art work.

Joel Beck. *The Profit.* ©1966 Joel Beck. By permission of Joel Beck.

As a matter of fact, tee shirts and other products bearing underground cartoonists' art *have* appeared all over the country and *have* made huge profits for at least some manufacturers—but the cartoonists are no longer so naive or trusting as they once were, and many have retained lawyers and fought this sort of exploitation. Not all cartoonists are happy that they have been forced to change their former liberal attitudes about allowing re-use of their material. In *Tasty Comix* No. 2, a notice specifically warned against using the material without permission, and the comic was copyrighted. But Howard Friedman, one of the artists and producers of *Tasty*, considered necessary legal protection to be in conflict with his own ideals: "It is impossible to rip off something which belongs to the people. We foolishly added 'no more commercial exploitation' to *Tasty* 2. It takes more than words to stop that. Anyway, how can you trust people who kill trees?"

Indeed, as Robert Crumb discovered when his copyrighted cartoons started sprouting on tee shirts, and as other cartoonists found in other situations, it *does* take more than words to prevent commercial rip-offs of underground material. But the "straight" world is beginning to learn that the cartoonists, whatever their personal philosophies, will fight back if they have to—even if that means working through a legal system which many of them reject and disown on a philosophical level. Words are indeed part of the battle—though the cartoonists often make it clear that they don't really enjoy having to copyright material to keep it out of unscrupulous hands.

In some cases, a cartoonist will try to allow free use of his material by underground publications, though not in the "straight" world. An example comes from *Coochy Cooty Men's Comics:* "Copyright 1970 . . . the exclusive property of its creator, Robert ('Bobby' to his friends) Williams, and any commercial application of this material for any reason is prohibited! Exception being subcultural publications that may lend the proper association by the use of words 'shit, hell, fuck' or their graphic equivalent." If someone used parts of that book, without specific permission, in a way that Williams didn't like, and he took the case to court, a judge would have an awfully hard time deciding just who had the right to use the material, and under what circumstances!

Below: Robert Crumb. *XYZ Comics.* ©1972 R. Crumb. By permission of Robert Crumb.

Similar legal problems are created by language like the following, from *Funnybook* No. 1: "Copyright 1971 by the Almighty Publishing Co., with the exception of 'Hero of the Beach' by Gilbert Shelton. Anyone reproducing without permission will hopefully suffer from a guilty conscience, along with more corporeal pains." Aside from the problems created by the final sentence (is it a threat of violence, or a promise that no actual legal action will be taken if

Robert Crumb. *XYZ Comics.* ©1972 R. Crumb. By permission of Robert Crumb. Note that the original "Keep on Truckin'" panel, which caused the copyright problems, now bears four separate copyright notices plus the phrase "all rights reserved."

someone exploits the book?), this statement sets up another problem in the Gilbert Shelton strip it mentions by name. On the page where it appears, that strip is *not* listed as copyrighted—so does the copyright notice mean Shelton holds the rights to his strip, or does it simply mean the strip is in the public domain? This may sound like legal hair-splitting, as indeed it is; but the underground comics have run into problems with legal issues before (see Chapter 10), and may be creating more of the same for themselves.

And what might a legal mind make of the copyright notice inside *The Dirty Duck Book?* It reads, "Copyright 1971 . . . Reproduction of contents in whole or in part without written permission from either artist or publisher is B-A-A-D Karma (like in 'Karma Desappio'!). We will gladly grant permission to the underground press if we're notified beforehand."

Statements like the ones already cited are very, very common in the underground comics, despite the numerous rip-offs which the cartoonists have already suffered. One more example should suffice to show the problems these statements can create. In *Comix and Stories from the Balloon-Vendor,* there is a notice which announces that the book is copyrighted 1971, and then adds, "With a written request and our consent you can probably rip off this material." There aren't likely to be major legal arguments in this particular case, since there is a pretty specific statement there that the copyright holder wants a written request for permission to use the material. But what about the words "rip off"? They usually mean material is used *without* permission. Lawyers being what they are, and the legal system being what it is, someone might come along and contend that the notice constitutes an invitation to rip off the material. Certainly, the *Balloon-Vendor* copyright notice lacks the forcefulness (and anger) of the one in *It Aint Me Babe Comix:* "All rights reserved. Any ripping off will be dealt with swiftly."

Many cartoonists who were once pretty cavalier about use of their material have become very careful about copyrights. Robert Crumb now copyrights everything. In what may be the funniest and most telling use ever made of the right to copyright original material, Crumb took off from the hassles he had when his "Keep on Truckin'" panel was reproduced on tee shirts without his permission: he put together an entire page of similar panels, reproducing the original and adding a number of others such as "Keep on Boppin'" and "Keep on Hoppin'," and then carefully put a separate copyright notice within every single panel!

Not all cartoonists can stay as good-natured about rip-offs as Crumb did in that instance. In some cases, a cartoonist simply lets his publisher handle all copyright notices, and people who want to use his material have to get the publisher's permission and pay a fee for the privilege. This is the case, for instance, with Ron Cobb (whose work is distributed by Sawyer Press) and with many of the artists whose work is published by Krupp Comic Works. In other cases, cartoonists have retreated behind walls of total hostility and have simply not let their work be reproduced except in a very few cases. The best example of this is S. Clay Wilson, who copyrighted very little of his early work and was badly stung by a series of rip-offs—and who then started copyrighting everything he drew in his own name, and reacting with total hostility to anyone who even suggested the possibility of re-using his later material.

Hak Vogrin, a cartoonist who has personally copyrighted his work for many years, says this sort of protection is absolutely necessary—despite the cartoonists' personal socialistic feelings: "The 'Dog Eat Dog' concept is a real one—and we are, like it or not, wrapped, knotted by it to the extent we are involved in it. When I throw my drawings into 'the barrel' I understand that game, and use its laws for myself and others whom my work may benefit."

Other cartoonists have banded together to form semi-official unions, which are designed to keep everyone looking out for exploitation of everyone else's work and to provide a united front for any legal action which may be necessary. Robert Crumb, Roger and Michele Brand, Justin Green, Bill and Nancy Griffith, Jay Kinney, Art Spiegelman, and Spain Rodriguez are among the artists listed in *Young Lust* No. 3 as members of "the famous United Cartoon Workers of America." The UCWA actually has its own imprint, which first appeared on Crumb's *Homegrown Funnies* in early 1971 and soon began to show up on such books as *Hytone Comix, Bijou Funnies* No. 6, and many others. The union was formed without specific aims, but the general idea of solidarity has indeed kept a large number of the cartoonists looking out for each others' best interests. There's even a second semi-formal organization of cartoonists: the Cartoon Workers of the World.

One unfortunate result of the very real exploitation of the underground comics by certain members of "straight" society has been the creation of a climate of suspicion, even paranoia, within the underground-comics movement itself. If S. Clay Wilson's case, already cited, is the most extreme one, it certainly

Below: Union seal from *The People's Comics.*

Denis Kitchen. A limited-edition union button. ©1973 D. Kitchen. By permission of Denis Kitchen.

Below: Union seal from *Hytone Comix.*

does not stand alone. Indeed, many producers of the comics have sometimes felt that even their *own* publishers are trying to make unfair use of their material.

The earliest producer of the comics, The Print Mint in Berkeley, has been putting out comics since 1966 (see Chapter 2). The Print Mint has built up a rather efficient national distribution system, especially by the standards of the world of underground comics—but, to do so, has used the same businesslike attitudes that many underground cartoonists condemn. Both in terms of how and why the comics are produced, and in terms of paying the artists, The Print Mint has developed the instincts of a publisher, according to its manager, Bob Rita: "The artists come in here because they know that we've done so much work, and because we have a reputation for putting out the best quality books. The decision on what we're going to produce is based on a lot of different things, such as how many books we have in stock, how much money we can afford to spend, and whether or not the book merits printing. It takes a lot of work before the book comes off. When we put it into production—when we give the artwork to our man who does the negatives—about that time, pretty formally (but if we don't have the money we don't give it to them), the deal is approximately the day the book goes into production we give the artists half the money, and then the day the book comes on the market, when it's produced, we give them the other half. Then we pay the same amount for all reprints—a certain amount per ten thousand books. We work in press runs of twenty to thirty thousand."

Photo by Clay Geerdes of Bob Rita, manager of The Print Mint. ©1973 Clay Geerdes. By permission of Clay Geerdes.

Rita says of The Print Mint, "We're groovily efficient—or efficiently groovy," but not all the underground cartoonists agree. When The Print Mint was first started by Don Schenker, cartoonists were so happy to have found a way to get into production that they came out with comments like Buckwheat Florida Jr.'s: "A lot of comic-book artists got a start or a chance to be published because of Don Schenker and The Print Mint. Considering the weird artists and the nature of their art, it took a broad-minded, radical-thinking person to put out the amount of comics he has. Don Schenker is an important person!" More recently, The Print Mint has shown its continued concern with the basic attitudes of the underground cartoonists by helping in the distribution of *Conspiracy Capers* (which was printed in Washington, D.C.—see Chapter 7), then turning all the money it took in over to the defense fund for the Chicago Eight, for whom the comic was produced as a benefit.

But many underground cartoonists have come to feel that The Print Mint is too business-oriented, too concerned with money, and unwilling to give the artists a fair share of the money which their books take in. In 1969, Gilbert Shelton and a group of other artists broke from The Print Mint and formed their own publishing house, The Rip Off Press (as Shelton says, "to rip off more of the profits for the artists"). Since then, The Print Mint and Rip Off Press have been somewhat in competition with each other, The Print Mint concentrating on developing new artists while Rip Off Press distributes much of the work of the better-known ones. And the Rip Off Press has itself been accused of Print Mint tactics: S. Clay Wilson says he asked for promised payment for some work and was told, "We're not called the Rip Off Press for nothing."

Another major distributor of underground comic books is The San Francisco Comic Book Company of Gary Arlington. Arlington, a real nut for old comics as well as new, started two major underground horror comics, *Bogeyman* and *Skull,* in an attempt to imitate and pay homage to the E. C. Comics of the fifties. But Arlington, like the people at The Print Mint, often comes under fire from the underground cartoonists, a typical comment being John Thompson's: "He seems to be on an ego trip of some kind."

The antithesis of the ego trip is the collective, and that is the way many underground publishers try to operate. These collectives spring up—and die—rapidly, and everyone who has tried one has his or her own ideas about

Below: S. Clay Wilson. A Rip Off Press emblem.

Right: Dave Sheridan. Rip Off Press *logo.*

Below: The usual logo on comics published by The Print Mint.

the good and bad elements. The theory of the collectives is to publish books by having the artists take equal shares of production costs and work, and then take equal shares of the income. There are many variations on the basic pattern, but all seem to share one problem: an apparent conflict between being a good cartoonist and being a good businessman.

Joel Beck. *The Profit.* ©1966 Joel Beck. By permission of Joel Beck.

For instance, The Company and Sons, a minor publishing outfit which tried to make it as a collective but collapsed during 1973, felt it was good to spread itself thin. Nick Cohn wrote, during the group's period of operation, "As to our existence and intent, your guess is as good as ours. We are currently [early 1973] operating with many hats and many roles. Our projects include publishing our own books, job printing, marketing of novelty items such as incense, hand-screened tee shirts, and essences, and cinema too, with two films in the can already and two more on paper. Whew." But The Company and Sons ultimately failed, despite an attempt to reorganize in a more businesslike way, using capitalist formalities but avoiding the exploitation its members associated with most businesses. Nick Cohn said, "The intent of the company is to provide funds and services for any and all worthwhile projects in alternate media. We'll incorporate into a profit-sharing corporation, with emphasis on non-leadership and anarchy in business. We're trying like hell to get away from the role-playing greed oriented hip businessman mystique that is so evident in San Francisco these days. Our success depends on each individual's willingness to de-emphasize his importance for the collective goal."

Those words are ones to which most underground cartoonists would subscribe. But for The Company and Sons, as for many cooperatives, things just didn't gel, and philosophy was unable to save the business end of the enterprise.

What's interesting about the failures of the cooperatives, though, is that the underground cartoonists remain true to their anarchistic/socialistic business outlook despite those failures, and new cooperative efforts keep springing up to replace the ones which fall apart. Around the time The Company and Sons disappeared, in fact, another group of cartoonists in the San Francisco area was starting another cooperative venture. Bill Griffith described that effort as "a new move

Below Left: Photo by Clay Geerdes of the weighing-in of inventory for *Zap Comix* No. 2 at The Print Mint. ©1972 Clay Geerdes. By permission of Clay Geerdes.

Below: Photo by Clay Geerdes of David Moriaty checking the printing of the "guts" of a comic at the Rip Off Press. ©1972 Clay Geerdes. By permission of Clay Geerdes.

Willy Murphy. Advertising circular for the Cartoonists Co-Op Press.

by underground cartoonists out here to save our necks and our commitment to comics by forming a publishing co-op. It's called the Cartoonists Co-Op Press.... As long as distribution holds up—or can be revived—and as long as backers can be found, it's a pretty profitable, if energy-draining, arrangement for the cartoonist. The cut on a book can be anywhere from two to six times that which a publisher would give us."

The ultimate fate of the Cartoonists Co-Op Press is, of course, in doubt; but it's significant that its members are established artists, who already have loyal followings and whose books can be expected to sell reasonably well, and that Griffith's description of the enterprise emphasizes practical financial matters in a way that Nick Cohn's comments on The Company and Sons do not. This is more than a difference of philosophy; it's a difference of attitude. Indeed, cartoonist Trina says she thinks the Cartoonists Co-Op Press is not a true collective effort at all, but an excuse for ego trips by the few cartoonists who belong to the group. It may be that neither the outright ego trip nor the collective will satisfy the cartoonists' needs both to reach an appreciative audience and to survive on the proceeds from the sales of their works. The fact remains that the most successful publishers of underground comics are the ones who regard the field as a business—even though they are also the ones most frequently criticized by the cartoonists.

At one major publisher, Last Gasp Eco-Funnies, an attempt was made to take a businesslike attitude without alienating the cartoonists. Ron Turner—who definitely looks like the "role-playing greed oriented hip businessman" so strongly attacked by Nick Cohn, but whose honesty and real interest in comic-book art have brought him many artists who were highly antagonized by other publishers—says Last Gasp actually consulted the cartoonists before determining how much to pay them for their work, and then followed their suggestions. Nevertheless, Turner says, he gets complaints from some people that they are underpaid; maybe that problem comes with the territory.

Last Gasp grew out of an ecology project which began in late 1969 and led to the publication of *Slow Death Funnies* No. 1 in April 1970. Run as a business, the company thereafter began to publish a greater and greater variety of comics, and moved away from specific involvement with ecology. Ron Turner says the ecology movement became "a whole propaganda trip, not a straight ecology trip but an unstraight trip," once ecological awareness increased throughout American society. Turner is bitter about the way the ecology movement was, in his opinion, used: "It's easier to go out and save a tree than a black person." But he had no trouble expanding the Last Gasp line, taking over as distributor on other publishers' comics while also putting out books under the Last Gasp imprint. Last Gasp, like The Company and Sons, got into projects other than comics—a Kids' Liberation Coloring Book, for instance. But unlike the philosophical collectives, Last Gasp made decisions on a business basis. The company's Dealer McDope Board Game was so successful that it sold out in mid-1973, according to Turner. But it could only have been reprinted, he said, at the cost of failing to print a series of new underground comics. Turner decided to do the comics rather than reprint the board game—but never even considered attempting to spread Last Gasp as thin as a

Below: Larry Welz. *Kid's Liberation Coloring Book.* ©1971 Last Gasp Eco-Funnies, Inc. By permission of Last Gasp Eco-Funnies, Inc., by Ron Turner.

Left: Jim Himes. One cartoonist's sketch of Ron Turner at work—drawn especially for Turner and given him as a gift.

Below: Versions of the Last Gasp logo by Greg Irons and (bottom) Guy Colwell.

Above: Last Gasp logo by Dave Sheridan.

Photos by Clay Geerdes. Right: Ron Turner of Last Gasp (on left) and Gary Arlington of The San Francisco Comic Book Company. Far Right: Don Donahue of Apex Novelties. ©1972 Clay Geerdes. By permission of Clay Geerdes.

collective like The Company and Sons spread itself. The result was some antagonism from some underground cartoonists, but a more stable picture for Last Gasp—and a larger number of comics in circulation.

By late 1973, Last Gasp had become a clearinghouse for the publications of many other companies, particularly small, independent ones with only a few books to their credit and no hope of wide distribution without outside assistance. Last Gasp distributed books published by itself, by its San Francisco-area competitors (e.g., The Print Mint), and by independent companies in Laguna Beach, California (Nanny Goat Productions); Los Angeles (Myron Moose Comic Book Works); New Orleans (Big Muddy Comics Refinery); Aspen, Colorado (Head Press); New York City (Starflower Inc.); Kansas City, Missouri (Kosmic City Komix); Chicago, Illinois (Adam's Apple Distributing Company); and by various artists who have published their own work, such as Dave Geiser (San Francisco), John Aulenta (Seal Beach, California), Hale Han and Bob Sidebottom (San Jose, California), and Dave Faggioli (Salt Lake City, Utah).

A Rand Holmes illustration for a mail-order brochure from Last Gasp Eco-Funnies, Inc.

Below: Photo by Clay Geerdes of Dave Sheridan. ©1972 Clay Geerdes. By permission of Clay Geerdes.

In stark contrast to the far-flung enterprises of Last Gasp there stands Apex Novelties, a small publisher with only a few titles to its credit. But what titles! Don Donahue of Apex is responsible for many of the most important and influential underground comics ever produced: *Zap Comix* Nos. 1 and 0, for instance, and several of Robert Crumb's sex comics. Donahue's story of the publication of *Zap* No. 1 in February 1968 says a lot about the state of underground comics at a time which seems ages ago. Donahue had been working for the Berkeley *Barb* in late 1967, but, he says, "I always wanted to publish something myself." He saw a cartoon by Crumb in the underground paper *Yarrowstalks,* and was so interested he tried to reach the cartoonist—only to find out that no one at *Yarrowstalks* seemed to know who Crumb was or where he could be contacted. Shortly afterward, Donahue says he saw another Crumb cartoon in the *East Village Other,* but again discovered that no one at *that* paper seemed to know the artist. Donahue finally met Crumb at the house of a mutual friend, and was so turned on by the comic which Crumb had with him that he decided to publish the book. Having no money, Donahue traded his tape recorder to a friend with a printing press, receiving in return five thousand copies of *Zap* No. 1—which Donahue and Crumb then folded and stapled by hand, packed into an orange crate, and sold on the streets of Berkeley.

Donahue later published the Crumb sex comics, which he agreed to do only on the condition that no one be told who printed them, and has more recently published Crumb books featuring Mr. Natural. But he lost *Zap Comix* to The Print Mint because, he says, The Print Mint had money and knew its business, while he was still trying to learn to be a printer. Apex Novelties—where Donahue is now in partnership with Susan Goodrick—continues to publish occasional books, but is important more for its early contributions and its continued contact with Crumb than for the breadth or depth of its line.

The dissension in the underground comic ranks goes deep in the area of publication. Cartoonists often change publishers, or publish with more than one organization. Resentment emerges at every level, even at organizations which are designed to keep the artists firmly in control of their material, such as the Bijou Publishing Empire, Inc. and Krupp Comic Works, Inc. Bijou, which is Jay Lynch's creation, puts out *Bijou Funnies*, but has no distribution network at all, and has turned to Krupp for help in that area.

Krupp Comic Works, Inc., is the creation of Denis Kitchen and several other cartoonists, and is the center for the distribution of underground comics produced in the Midwest. In an article in *Funnyworld* No. 13, Kitchen explained that Krupp "is not as big as its gargantuan German namesake. Nor does it intend to be. Its intention is merely to publish as many top-quality underground comics as possible. To become successful doing so might be hypocritical. Already, many in the hip subculture consider us 'rip-off capitalists' or 'sexist pigs.' And, needless to say, most of 'straight' society considers us 'pornographers' or 'subversive bums.' But we struggle on."

So here, too, an underground comic producer is pressured by members of the field. Krupp gets accused of rip-off capitalism because it does things like publishing a catalogue listing its books and satirizing the old *Eight-Pagers* (see Chapter 2); because Denis Kitchen's background in journalism seems somehow suspect to certain cartoonists, especially when added to the fact that Kitchen has been profiled in as "straight" a publication as the Milwaukee *Journal* (in its *Insight* magazine section for April 29, 1973); because Kitchen doesn't mind working in the overground media as well as the underground ones, having, in fact, drawn for the *Journal* long before it profiled him, and worked elsewhere in the "straight" world as well; and, finally, because Kitchen—who was the Socialist Labor Party candidate for lieutenant governor of Wisconsin in 1970—says

You VILL enjoy our comix!
Krupp Comic Works, Inc.
PUBLISHERS OF UNDERGROUND COMIC BOOKS
DENIS KITCHEN DON GLASSFORD JIM MITCHELL MIKE HERMAN

Dear MARK,
What the FUCK is the Big MAGGEGGIE? and Howcum you HAVE SUCH UNRULY Pissants? & BAD KARMA? We believe, DOESN'T EVERYONE? YOU SHOULD Make WAR, NOT CHICKENS!

Walt Disney
Jayzeylynch
Jay Kinney
Denis Kitchen
R. Crumb
Darnold Glassford

2560-A N. FREDERICK AVE. MILWAUKEE, WIS. 53211 PHONE (414) 332-4605

Above: Apex Novelties logo by Robert Crumb.

Left: Letter to the author from the Krupp Comic Works gang.

Left: Pete Poplaski. *Death Rattle* No. 1. ©1972 Denis Kitchen. By permission of Denis Kitchen.

Below: Logo of Kitchen Sink Enterprises. Kitchen Sink was a predecessor of Krupp Comic Works, Inc.

Don Glassford. Cover of Krupp Comic Works catalogue, in size and shape of the old *Eight-Pagers.*

Above: Another version of the Kitchen Sink Enterprises logo.

directly that what he calls his "economic feelings" are very different from what he has to do to keep himself and Krupp in business. Kitchen admits he doesn't feel comfortable advocating socialism and practicing capitalism, but he points out that Krupp practices capitalism with a number of differences—such as the fact that the organization pays royalties to cartoonists, while "straight" publishers simply buy people's work for a one-time-only fee.

The conflict which keeps arising around the publishers of underground comics is enough to make one wonder whether the cartoonists would be interested in real distribution efficiency if it were handed to them on a silver platter. Kitchen admits that he doesn't want success in any standard sense of the word. He says his aim is to be successful enough to be able to keep doing what he and the other cartoonists want to do, while not being so successful that "it spoils us." And Harvey Kurtzman adds that Kitchen's attitude seems to pervade the medium: "There's a real freaky thing going on with these guys. Gil Shelton says to be successful in what these guys are doing, you've got to be unsuccessful. Because once you're successful, then you are unsuccessful. Everything you say thereafter is automatically suspect. Once you start making money and you hit it big, you're out of it. You've got this paradox—yes, you do your best work when you don't have conditions, but when you become part of the 'establishment' of success, you unavoidably inherit the conditions of that establishment, i.e., the easy life, formula work, material possessions. So the cartoonists have kind of a suicidal philosophy, and all of them are very frustrated guys. They're just busting inside, every single one of them, because in another, practical sense, they *don't* have the success they want."

Right: Denis Kitchen. *Snarf* No. 2. ©1972 Denis Kitchen. By permission of Denis Kitchen.

If there is one underground cartoonist who has had some of the material success which Kurtzman feels they all want (at least to some extent), it is Robert Crumb—and the story of his treatment by the "straight" media would practically fill a book by itself. Crumb seems to be seen by the Establishment as an independent entity, not one underground cartoonist but THE underground cartoonist, and he has been treated accordingly. Articles written about him are usually just that—much as one could once have written pieces about Albert Einstein while ignoring the fact that he was, after all, only *a* scientist.

Crumb has been seen in art shows at New York's Whitney Museum; he has been studied by Harvey Pekar in the Spring 1970 issue of Bowling Green University's *Journal of Popular Culture;* he's been talked about in *New York* magazine (June 22, 1970); and *The Village Voice* (October 30, 1969) even carried an article by Blair Sabol considering him as a fashion designer. He has also been the jumping-off point for such studies of the whole underground-comics field as Mike Barrier's in *Funnyworld* (an article about Crumb in No. 10, and comments from readers and Barrier in No. 11, led to a long article on the whole field by Barrier in No. 12—and to articles on Crumb by Pekar, and on the establishment of Krupp Comic Works, by Denis Kitchen, in No. 13). Crumb has received mention in *Parade* and *Eye* magazines, and even in *Newsweek* (which mentioned him favorably, if briefly, in its "Art" section). Indeed, he has become Mr. Underground Comics for the great majority of the overground media. In fact, Crumb himself has appeared in an enormous number of "straight" publications simply as the artist that he is. He was in several issues of Harvey Kurtzman's *Help!*, in *Yell* No. 2 (a poor imitation of *Mad*), and in *Cavalier.* This last magazine, which published Bob Abel's article on underground comics in April 1969, had earlier syndicated a "Fritz the Cat" story by Crumb, giving it two to three pages in each monthly issue from February to October 1968, inclusive.

Some of the "straight" publications carrying Crumb's work are rather unusual. He did several hundred greeting cards for the American Greetings Company, produced a series of comic strips ("Roberta Smith, Office Girl") for that company's in-house newsletter in 1964, and illustrated John Gibbons' *The Sad Book* for the same company in 1966. He drew the cover for the Columbia Records album *Cheap Thrills* by Big Brother and the Holding Company. And he even did a series of fifty bubblegum cards for the Topps Company in 1965.

Crumb also has the dubious distinction of having his drawing style, if not his exact material, ripped off for many television commercials, including one for something called "Fiddle Faddle" (a supposedly edible snack) and another for 7-Up soda. Jay Lynch explains what happened in the former case: "Originally the agency wanted Skip Williamson to do the story board for the commercial using Snappy Sammy Smoot, but they thought Sammy looked too faggy. They knew what they wanted, and they knew that they couldn't get Crumb, so they just had some studio copy Crumb's drawing style. It's the most flagrant bit of exploitative bullshit that anybody has pulled yet. Cycle Films in Chicago, a small animation studio run by some friends of mine, refused to do the animation on it. But the agency just brought it to a different animation studio . . . . The comix are the

Below Left: Robert Crumb. *Hytone Comix.* ©1971 R. Crumb. By permission of Robert Crumb. An ad for *Thrilling Murder Comics.*

Below: San Francisco Comic Book Company logo.

Left: A card drawn by Robert Crumb for the American Greetings Corporation. ©1968 American Greetings Corporation. By permission of American Greetings Corporation, by Paul H. Ozan.

Below: A version of the National Recovery Administration symbol by Trina. From the 1973 Berkeley Comix Convention program.

art of the people, and must not be corrupted by the prostitutes that stroll down that sinful boulevard known as Madison Avenue." (This is not to say that this is the first time television has used an underground cartoonist's ideas. Lynch himself once developed a strip called "Chicken Man" and sent the idea to Jay Ward, producer of television's "The Bullwinkle Show." Ward never responded, but later came out with a cartoon called "Super Chicken." Don Dohler, who used to publish Lynch's material in the fanzine *Wild*, says, "I had to assume that Ward copped the idea from whatever material Lynch sent him about it. Another one of life's little frustrations.")

Robert Crumb. *R. Crumb's Head Comix.* ©1967, 1968 Robert Crumb. By permission of The Viking Press, Inc., by Nancy Schafer.

Robert Crumb. *R. Crumb's Fritz the Cat.* ©1969 Robert Crumb. By permission of Ballantine Books, Inc., by Marlene Siminow.

Crumb's work was the first to be collected and published in book form by overground publishers, thus paving the way for the production of such mass-market paperbacks as Bantam's *Deadbone Erotica* (by Vaughn Bodē) and *Swift Premium Comics* (by Kim Deitch, Art Spiegelman, Allan Shenker, and Trina), plus other, similar works. The first Robert Crumb book to appear was published by Viking as *R. Crumb's Head Comix*, and contained a selection of strips Crumb did for early issues of *Zap* (especially No. 1), plus an original story, "Fritz the Cat." The strips were well reproduced, and the book had an interesting introduction by Paul Krassner, editor of *The Realist;* but there was a peculiar form of arbitrary censorship exercised by Viking over Crumb's work. In a strip called "Life Among the Constipated," Viking decided not to risk offending potential purchasers, so it removed the words "niggers" and "Schwartz" (!). (But Viking left the word "niggers" in the strip "Whiteman," which had originally appeared in *Zap Comix* No. 1!). Then, in "Abstract Expressionist Ultra Super Modernistic Comics," Viking decided that the picture of a gaping vagina was too much to take, so the publisher plastered it with band-aids!

Robert Crumb. Censored panel from *R. Crumb's Head Comix.* ©1967, 1968 Robert Crumb. By permission of The Viking Press, Inc., by Nancy Schafer.

Below: Robert Crumb. Original panel from *Zap Comix* No. 1. ©1971 R. Crumb. By permission of Robert Crumb.

Crumb was engaged by Viking for another book, this one featuring his character Fritz the Cat, but Viking became so uptight about some mild sex scenes in the book that they rejected it—after paying Crumb $2500 in advance. This may have been the first underground reverse rip-off. Anyway, the work was picked up and published by Ballantine Books—and when Viking Press got worried about continuing to publish *R. Crumb's Head Comix*, Ballantine picked up and reissued that as well.

Unfortunately, the Crumb stories for the Ballantine Book weren't up to his usual work. Indeed, *R. Crumb's Fritz the Cat* had poorer writing and much poorer art than almost anything else produced by Crumb. Why the work was poorer than Crumb's usual standards remains an uncertain question, but Paul Buhle, editor of *Radical America*, suggested the most cynical reason: "Crumb did a mediocre book, quite obviously for the bread."

Oddly, and perhaps ironically, the character of Fritz turned out to have unusual fascination for the "straight" world. The Viking book had contained an original Fritz story; the Ballantine one was all Fritz; and Warner Brothers, which used to make the Bugs Bunny and Road Runner cartoons which themselves influenced underground cartoonists so heavily (see Chapter 2), then bought the rights to make movies of the character.

Or rather, Warner thought it had the rights. The situation with the movie company became perhaps the biggest rip-off ever in the field of underground comics—or perhaps merely the most confusing situation yet. A movie of *Fritz the Cat* did indeed come out, and had the distinction (another first for the underground cartoonists!) of becoming the very first X-rated animated cartoon in motion picture history. The movie played at theatres throughout the country, made a decent amount of money, and generally pleased the people who put it together. But it didn't please Crumb, who wound up in long and complex legal battles with the film's producers and eventually, some three months after the movie came out, won an agreement to have his name removed from the credits.

The producers of *Fritz the Cat*, Ralph Bakshi and Steve Krantz, themselves wound up in a series of fights about the movie and about their own personal plans.

In fact, the team (which had previously made Spiderman cartoons for TV, among other things) split up after making *Fritz the Cat*, and Krantz alone was left to work on a second Fritz feature called *The Nine Lives of Fritz the Cat*. Indeed, it is remarkable that the second film could be made at all—but Albert Morse, a San Francisco attorney who handles copyright problems for Robert Crumb, says that Krantz has the right to make just about as many Fritz films as he wants. And, of course, films similar to *Fritz the Cat* but *not* using Crumb characters can also come out—hence features like *Heavy Traffic* and *Coonskin*.

For Crumb and Morse, the *Fritz* arguments were a very complicated situation, which showed clearly the legal hassles that underground cartoonists have been running into since the "straight" media have started to take more notice of their work. Crumb, who complained vehemently after the movie was finished, had not complained during the actual production process. Attorney Morse said the argument between Crumb and the movie's producers finally had to be settled by having them agree to stop using Crumb's name, and to pay Crumb for using certain characters (e.g. Angelfood McSpade) to whom they had no rights originally.

The situation of *Fritz the Cat* was even more complex than it would normally have been because Morse was handling a variety of other lawsuits for Crumb while the movie mess was going on. According to Morse, some of the materials which overground producers have brought out bearing Crumb characters are drinking glasses, balloons, beach mats, buttons, light bulbs, magnetic plastic stickers, plastic bags, posters, dope pipes, leather belts—and, of course, tee shirts. Morse said it was an unending stream of material, and that it was legally almost impossible to keep up with the copyright infringements. But he says he has learned a lot in a very short time, out of necessity, and has developed certain effective techniques for preventing future copyright infringements and handling ones which have already occurred. The most important of these, he says, is that he really is willing to sue, and has actually brought suit against many companies. Since the companies are used to threats but unused to lawyers who are willing to carry out those threats, Morse has become something of an *enfant terrible*—and has gotten a number of good financial settlements for his clients (who now include many cartoonists besides Crumb—see Chapter 12).

In line with the continuing underground penchant for breaking new ground, in early 1974, Albert Morse became the first person to develop a suit called a "multi-district panel litigation" in the field of copyright law. This type of litigation, designed to soften the burden on courts and private individuals by hearing large numbers of similar cases at the same time, is a new development in law, and was never applied to cases of copyright infringement until Morse brought his suit—a collection of several dozen actions on behalf of Robert Crumb. But the ultimate effectiveness of Morse's move cannot be predicted, because of the underground-comic history of cavalier copyright notices and because Crumb in par-

Robert Crumb. *R. Crumb's Head Comix*. ©1967, 1968 Robert Crumb. By permission of The Viking Press, Inc., by Nancy Schafer.

Advertisement for the Ralph Bakshi/Steve Krantz production of *Fritz the Cat*. From the Washington *Post*, April 11, 1972.

Opposite: Robert Crumb. *Tales from the Leather Nun* No. 1. ©1973 Robert Crumb. By permission of Robert Crumb.

ticular has proved so appealing an artist that his work is an effective selling point even among people who have never heard of underground comics and have no idea where Crumb's characters originated (or who Crumb himself is!).

Robert Crumb is definitely Big Time, and if he isn't alone in suffering from overground rip-offs, he is certainly more conspicuous in that suffering than any other underground cartoonist. What's interesting, though—if not likely to be personally satisfying to Crumb and the other cartoonists—is that the underground has now occasionally tried to turn the tables on the "straight" media by pulling some rip-offs of its own. Unfortunately, the overground media are old hands at legal battles involving copyright infringement—and, unlike the underground cartoonists, the "straight" people have no feelings about their work being for the public or even, necessarily, image of innocent delightfulness with these characters, known and loved by people all over the world, particularly, but not now only by children." The U.S. District Court in Chicago agreed with Disney Studios—thus proving that it's okay to wink at illegal uses of Mr. Natural but a deep offense to show the Seven Dwarfs sexually molesting Snow White, to show Mickey Mouse shooting heroin, or to portray Pluto the dog lifting a leg in his master's direction—in true *Yellow Dog* fashion.

Of course, the tee shirt controversy wasn't the end of the underground's interest in doing some ripping off of its own for a change. Indeed, the Disney Studios were taken on within certain underground comics themselves—specifically, a series with the overall title *Mickey Mouse Meets the Air Pirates.* These books used Disney-style characters in true underground-comic ways and didn't do much for the Pollyanna wholesomeness that Disney Studios feels the characters have to project. Uninterested in the obviously sarcastic and satirical intent of the stories, Disney Studios brought suit—and the underground cartoonists went down again. But this time, they insisted on a last Bronx cheer at the Disney people: they published a comic called *The Tortoise and the Hare,* with the following notice inside the front cover: "Episode #1, the Tortoise and the Hare, is reprinted from *Air Pirates* #2 which is now banned in Boston, Berkeley, and the rest of continental Disneyland. As of December 1971, *Air Pirates* #3 will not be allowed either . . . so here's the story." Whether the cartoonists involved really found that sort of notice soul-satisfying is, however, a moot point.

So the underground and overground media remain at each other's throats, the overground adapting and adopting whatever

Below: Gary Hallgren. Title of *Air Pirates Funnies* No. 1. ©1971 The Air Pirates. By permission of The Air Pirates, by Gary Hallgren.

Right: Will Eisner. *Snarf* No. 3. ©1972 Will Eisner. By permission of Will Eisner.

in the public interest. Private rights are private rights, and the watchword is "keep your hands off."

So it shouldn't be surprising to learn that a number of people were slapped down, and slapped down hard, for carrying satires of American society into the ultra-pure world of Walt Disney comic-book characters. Crumb has lost a lot of time and had a lot of trouble preventing illegal use of his copyrighted characters —but Walt Disney Productions quickly filed suit when, in June 1971, tee shirts portraying the too-too-wholesome Disney characters in less than wholesome poses were distributed through a number of outlets in Chicago and elsewhere. Disney Studios complained that, by depicting Jiminy Cricket, Donald Duck, and Peter Pan as drug addicts and dope fiends, the tee shirts and the stores which sold them were "destroying the plaintiff's work of many years to acquire an

Below: An advertisement by cartoonist Leslie Cabarga for a book he has written about animation (see page 272).

The Adventures of
R. CRUMB
Himself
by R. Crumb
REG. U.S. PAT. OFF.
I THINK I'LL GO FOR A WALK...

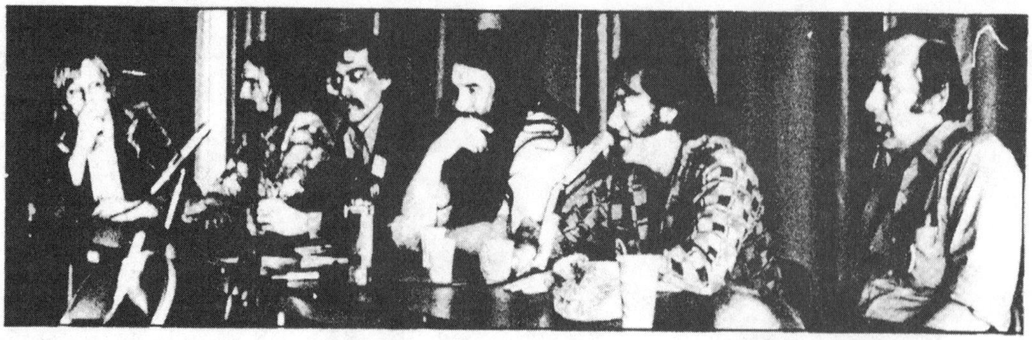

Photo by Clay Geerdes of the publishers' panel at the 1973 Berkeley Comix Convention. ©1973 Clay Geerdes. By permission of Clay Geerdes.
Left to right: McLeod (Georgia Straight), J. David Moriaty (Rip Off Press), Denis Kitchen (Krupp Comic Works, Inc.), Ron Turner (Last Gasp Eco-Funnies, Inc.), Don Donahue (Apex Novelties), Don Schanker (The Print Mint).

seems most saleable in the underground and the underground fighting for the right to see and do things in its own way and on its own terms. It's not a rosy picture for anyone but the Disneyites. Even Will Eisner, who is quite optimistic about the long-range possibilities of underground comics, sees the sorts of financial problems which the cartoonists may run into because of rip-offs and a one-way legal system—through he feels the interest of the comics' readership will prevail in the long run: "The underground is an establishment in itself, and the only thing that could kill it is economics. Not very likely as long as there are emerging talents hungry for an audience, and an audience hungry for emerging talent with new things to say and new ways to say it." But not everyone in the field thinks the sheer ability of the underground cartoonists will pull them unscathed through a period of severe rip-offs. Mike Barrier of *Funnyworld* comments, "The 'creative' and the 'commercial,' in underground comics as in other forms of mass communication, are inextricably intertwined, and the underground cartoonists are now suffering the consequences of trying to ignore that." Indeed, some of the cartoonists have themselves become disillusioned with the medium, even to the point of hiring other cartoonists to ghost some of their strips for them: for instance, Gilbert Shelton hired Tony Bell to draw Shelton's Fabulous Furry Freak Brothers.

Meanwhile, the "straight" media have gone their merry way, taking over more and more of the underground comics' spirit by taking over more of their ethos and *none* of their attitudes. The situation reached a low point of sorts with an unsuccessful pilot for a TV series called *Jarrett*, shown during the 1972-73 television season. The movie starred Glenn Ford as a private eye specializing in fine-arts cases . . . and Anthony Quayle as his nemesis Cosmo, who appears nastily and (temporarily) triumphantly in his evil lair to announce that he is a comic-book freak who owns everything in the field —even the latest *Zap* and *Freak Brothers* books. That sort of attention is precisely what the underground cartoonists do not want, do not need, and have never sought.

The straight media persist in recognizing that the underground cartoonists have got something to say, then turning around and distorting the message by ripping off underground material and misusing and abusing it. True, the cartoonists have left themselves open to exploitation by the cavalier attitudes they have often taken toward copyrights and other legal pro-

Photo by Clay Geerdes of a mural by Spain in San Francisco's Mission District. ©1973 Clay Geerdes. By permission of Clay Geerdes.

Below: Logo by Spain for the 1973 Berkeley Comix Convention.

Above and Below Left: Photos by Clay Geerdes from the 1973 Berkeley Comix Convention. ©1973 Clay Geerdes. By permission of Clay Geerdes. Above: The panel on women's comics, which consisted of (left to right) Patricia Moodian, Shelby, Lee Marrs, Trina, Sharon Rudahl, Chin Lively, Joyce Sutton. Below Left: Jim Pinkoski holds a strip he drew to advertise the convention.

tection; true, they were quite naive to think the overground media would fail to regard every omission of legal protection as a potential loophole. In fact, the cartoonists made the mistake of acting on their basic attitudes—the same attitudes toward people and society which they try to put across in their work. But as everyone knows, or should have learned by now, it's fine to believe intellectually in honesty and fair treatment and socialistic equality and freedom of expression; but if you want to have a semblance of those things in your own life, it helps to remain obscure and not even talk about your thoughts too loudly.

The underground cartoonists have made the mistake of becoming a little too big to ignore. Some of the best underground comics have sold hundreds of thousands of copies—not a lot by the standards of "straight" publishers, some of whom require sales of a quarter of a million books merely to break even, but a very respectable figure under the peculiar publication and distribution systems which exist in this particular field. The comics have carried anger and irreverence to a point at which society can no longer ignore them: they must be absorbed into movies and tee shirts, or slapped down in the courts. The only question is how long the disintegration process is going to take—and what will happen once it is complete.

Underground cartoonists of one type or another have been around a long, long time—whether they have been snappish, ribald rabblerousers like Benjamin Franklin, opponents of artistic convention like Gustave Verbeek, canny observers of the comic-book medium like Harvey Kurtzman, or acute, anarchistic social critics like Robert Crumb. Society found Franklin too big to ignore, so it remade him through its history books; it found Verbeek odd enough so that he could merely be forgotten; it successfully assimilated Kurtzman through the old lures of home, family, and financial comfort. What society will eventually do with the present-day underground cartoonists remains to be seen. But whatever may happen to these artists, rest assured that there will be others. The names will change, but the concerns and the vitality will remain the same.

And that, to understate the case, is a good thing. It's bad enough to be in a long, dark tunnel apparently leading nowhere. It would be a lot worse to go without some occasional flickers of light to show us where we are, where we have been, and maybe—just maybe—where we are going. Without the light, how would we know in time to turn aside?

Below: Richard Corben's characters bid a cheery hello to their fans. From the 1973 Berkeley Comix Convention program.

12 Cycling and Recycling

During the five-year period I have spent writing about underground comics, the comics and cartoonists have gone through the same changes which have afflicted American life in general in the late sixties and early seventies. Being especially attuned to social reality, many of them have felt those changes more intensely than the majority of people appear to have felt them—

Robert Crumb. *XYZ Comics.* ©1971 R. Crumb. By permission of Robert Crumb.

and have had accordingly strong reactions. In fact, with the comics' movement into the overground media (see Chapter 11), the line between underground and "straight" comics has been blurred more and more. Today, many people have decided that the very name "underground comics" no longer applies to the works described in this book, and some are suggesting the productions hereafter be called something like "counter-cultural comics." It remains to be seen whether that appellation, or some other one, will stick, or whether the name "underground comics" is here to stay. It also remains to be seen whether the comics themselves will survive—for a combination of legal problems and assorted other troubles has forced many of the cartoonists quoted in this book out of the comics medium altogether, or at least into marginally related fields such as that of satirical magazines (several underground cartoonists work or have worked for the *National Lampoon,* for instance).

By the time this book reaches your hands, dear reader, you will be unable to find comics by a number of artists quoted in these pages—and will find plenty of material by artists mentioned only occasionally, or not at all. Underground comics are an extremely fluid medium, and the "big names" in the field are changing all the time. But what's more interesting than the change itself is the stability of the *type* of people drawn into this exceptionally free and uncoercive medium of expression. Underground comics seem to fill a real need for a certain sort of creative person, and that fact seems to indicate that—practical problems or no practical problems—the field will continue to flourish, in some form or other.

The cyclical nature of the field becomes clear if we examine recent comments by several cartoonists not yet treated at any length in this book. Artists who stop doing underground comics are replaced by artists whose styles may be very different but whose backgrounds and attitudes are often quite similar. The influences on the cartoonists, their life styles, and their reactions to certain social and political trends in American society have a ring of familiarity every bit as striking as the diversity of their artistic styles and approaches.

For instance, **Willy Murphy** offers these comments: "It should be apparent to the most casual observer that I am almost totally unable to draw, so my strongest admiration is naturally reserved for the similarly afflicted—Jules Feiffer, Milt Gross, Harvey Kurtzman, Saul Steinberg among them. I also like a few who *can* draw, like Al Capp and Walt Kelly. Draw or not, you'll notice that all are fundamentally good writers, and specifically writers of comedy and satire. That says something about my point of view right there. To me, comics are what they *say* they are—comic. Marvel 'comics,' DC 'comics,' body fetish fantasies of somebody like, say, Frank Frazetta (a totem in certain quarters), the kind of hippie 'oh wow' acid fantasies that appear in a lot of undergrounds, all fill some need or other, but have very little to do with either the history or best possibilities of the medium. If there is any significance to comics, it is their significance as comedy. As for how I got into this mess: like everybody else, I suppose, I had an early inclination for it as a child. Later, being a realistic sort, I got a job as a copywriter in New York. Still later, being also an *un*realistic sort, I took a lot of acid, got an intense case of 'late sixties,' dropped out and kind of reverted to form. What are my goals? Just like everybody else's, of course: to rule the world and be omnipotent. How about you?"

Murphy's individuality shows clearly through his drawings, and the particular combination of experiences which he has gone through is of course unique (isn't everyone's?). But it's interesting that Murphy's capsule history of himself as underground cartoonist almost explains the whole field in microcosm. His basic background, his early interests, his artistic influences, his experiences with the "straight" world and with drugs, and his wry outlook on himself

Opposite: Michael J. *Rubber Duck* No. 1. ©1971 Rob Lawson and Michael J. By permission of Michael J. Becker.

CUT!
SNIP!
EDIT-IN POLITICALLY ACCEPTABLE ENDING #37--AND HURRY! ONLY 10 MINUTES UNTIL THE LIVE BROAD-CAST STARTS!
YESSIR!
...BUT WHAT'LL WE DO WITH HIM? NO BLACK HAS EVER WON BEFORE!
WE'LL HAVE TO FREE HIM...
...BESIDES, THE CROWD WILL LOVE IT!!
CLICK
I HEREBY DECLARE YOU A FREE MAN!
ARRGGH!
"AND REMEMBER, FOLKS: WHAT YOU SEE IS WHAT YOU GET!"
PORTIONS OF TODAY'S PROGRAM WERE PRE-RECORDED

Right and Below Right: Willy Murphy. *San Francisco Comic Book* No. 4. ©1973 Willy Murphy. By permission of Willy Murphy.

and his work all stand as rather typical for underground cartoonists. There seems to be a certain combination of attitudes and circumstances which produces the prototypical underground cartoonist, and that combination still provides a deep well from which the field will be able to draw.

A background similar to Murphy's is that of **Michael J.** (whose last name, which he doesn't use when cartooning, is Becker). Describing himself as "a comic-book freak from way back," Michael J. started reading comics when living with his parents on a Navy base in the Mojave Desert. The base, which he says was larger than the state of Rhode Island, turned out to be a primary target area during the Cuban Missile Crisis of 1962—and this had something to do with shaping his political feelings and outlook on life ("They kept telling us we were a tertiary target").

Michael J.'s adult life, he says, has been "mainly drugs and politics," the politics being "a convenient tie-in for strong emotions." Michael J. has become worried about the apparent predictive power of his comics: they keep coming true, he says, and he's a little scared to keep drawing them. He did *Rubber Duck* No. 2 just before the 1972 elections, and "the story wouldn't really make a point unless Nixon won, so I sort of had to root for him, which was very strange." Michael J. traces his style to a combination of his political attitudes, his readings of various underground comics, and his early interest in the Marvel Comics Group.

Each cartoonist has his or her personal axes to grind, Willy Murphy's emphasis on the comedic element in comics and Michael J.'s political outlook being examples. The vitality of the underground comics will remain as long as the field has room both for the sketchily drawn, humorous characters of Murphy, the politics of Michael J., and the artistic, super-Romantic characters of **Barney Steel**—who also got interested in comics early, but whose concerns are quite different from Murphy's: "I started drawing in the second grade. By the third grade I was in trouble for drawing instead of doing math assignments. By the tenth grade I got my head bashed into the lockers by a home room teacher: I had been caught with my work, fifteen pages of smooth, pencil roughs ready for ink, an erotic story of Eric the Warrior and Saundra the Princess. The work was confiscated and as far as I know, destroyed, but many of the scenes

Far Right: Barney Steel. *Armageddon* No. 2. ©1972 Barney Steel. By permission of Barney Steel.

Below: Barney Steel. *Armageddon* No. 1. ©1970 Barney Steel and Last Gasp Eco-Funnies, Inc. By permission of Barney Steel and Last Gasp Eco-Funnies, Inc., by Ron Turner.

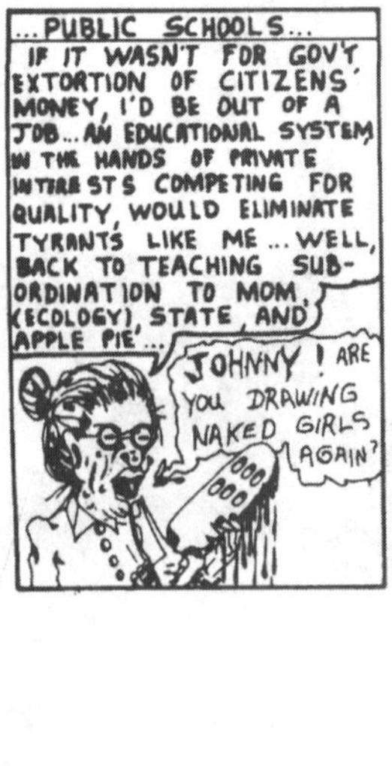

appeared fourteen years later in *Armageddon* No. 1. I've kept up my art work through various occupations—Merchant Marine, longshoreman, powder monkey, commercial deep-sea diving and four years in the Navy's Underwater Demolition Teams. The Navy UDT unit in San Diego and several diving companies that service the off-shore oil industry have large oil paintings of mine. The goal of my art is to depict humans, to the best of my ability, as being capable of heroism,

Michael J. *Rubber Duck* No. 2. ©1972 Michael J. and Robbie Landeros. By permission of Michael J. Becker.

bravery, and great success."

Another contrast in style, another contrast in art, and another similarity of background—and we have another of the newer underground cartoonists, **Bill Stout:** "Cartooning is just a part of my occupation, which is entertaining. I have found through trial and error and self-examination that the vocation that best suits my needs and talents is the one called entertainer. This includes acting, singing, illustrating, cartooning, song writing, and, well—entertaining!" Stout attended the California Institute of the Arts, but says he had to learn cartooning on his own because there were no courses in that subject offered. Inspired by seeing the work of Robert Crumb, Rick Griffin, and Robert Williams, Stout produced his first comic-book story in early 1970. He later did a series of stories for a magazine called *CYCLEtoons,* while beginning an occasional and sporadic job doing inking and coloring for the overground "Tarzan" comic strip.

Stout's burgeoning career brought him into contact with, of all people, Harvey Kurtzman, when he worked with Kurtzman and Bill Elder on "Little Annie Fanny" for *Playboy* magazine's issues of September and November 1972. A few months later, Stout was offered the job of assistant cartoon editor for *Playboy* and *Oui*—but, in testimony to the trend toward blurring of boundaries between "straight" and underground media, he was then also becoming involved in drawing several dozen covers for bootleg record albums. Stout says, "My interest in comics began with superhero stuff (about 1960-61). I became a heavy collector and also drew little characters and strips of my own. . . . My influences are broad and varied,

Bill Stout. *Let Sanity Die.* ©1972 William G. Stout. By permission of William G. Stout.

from comics illustrators like Foster, Frazetta, and Al Williamson, to conceptualists like Eisner and Kurtzman, to storytellers like Toth, to the great old illustrators of yesteryear like Leyendecker and Rockwell, to the classic art of Toulouse-Lautrec and Leonardo da Vinci. . . . In my work I try to put across a diverse array of personal messages —but only if they can be worked into the story *without* detracting from my *main interest:* to entertain."

Stout is by no means averse to working in "straight" media, and in fact says he looks forward to high-paying commercial jobs and would like to find some. Indeed, in the more cynical seventies, the cartoonist who retains an idealistic commitment to underground work and is unwilling to compromise that idealism for the sake of a livelihood is becoming increasingly rare.

Some cartoonists have found the tendency of certain "straight" publications to become more like underground ones a real blessing. For instance, **Jeff Jones,** whose work has appeared in the "straight" *National Lampoon,* is nevertheless basically hostile to the overground media: "After many hassles at trying to become a physicist or geologist, I surrendered to myself, and started for New York to become an illustrator. I was disillusioned quite soon. Those guys with the money wouldn't let you draw all those deepest thoughts. You had to draw something that would sell their product, and from sales reports they were quite sure what that something would be. I found during this time that by doing work for fanzines, I could draw again those deepest thoughts. It came harder than before, though. I found that my very brain had been washed. Somewhere along the line I had been tricked. I was Pavlov's dog being given a reward every time I was clever, and punishment every time I was sensitive or truthful. Rewards were given for gimmicks. This had to stop."

Jones, who says drawing has been a lifelong passion with him ("I could make my deepest thoughts come alive on paper"), did his first comic book when he was nine years old and "sold it at school for two cents a copy. Many of the kids didn't have pennies, only nickels for milk, and I didn't have change, so to them I sold two for a nickel (nobody was looking for a bargain in the fourth grade)." Years later, displeased with his work for fanzines, Jones again looked to comic books, but went underground because "there were too many restrictions in mass-market comic books. So I set out to sell myself, not my cleverness." Today, Jones says, "My work does not have any particular message. I am only writing and drawing generalized perceptions. It is very non-specific. I try not to tie my work to any particular time period (especially current). I'm not a satirist. I'm fascinated by human thought patterns. . . . I love logic, paradoxes, and abstraction. My writing is pretty abstract. I'm an idealist, a romanticist, and an artist."

Far Left and Below: Bill Stout. Far Left from *Let Sanity Die.* ©1972 William G. Stout. Below from *Dorrgsheett Digest* No. 1. ©1973 William G. Stout. By permission of William G. Stout.

Gilbert Shelton. *Zap Comix* No. 4.

Following Pages: Jeff Jones. *Spasm* No. 1. ©1973 Jeff Jones. By permission of Jeff Jones.

GODDAMN GHETTO CHEAP CRIMINAL RATS!
POLICE
GOTTA RUN...
LET'S TRY THAT 'INTERRUPTER,' NOW.
SHE SHOULD NEVER HAVE RUN. SHE SHOULD NEVER HAVE LIED. SHE SHOULD NEVER HAVE HAD THE OPERATION UNDER PREMEDITATED CRIMINAL PRETENSE.

OH UH...
AIIIEEE
UHHGNH
AAAHHHhhh...
AND ETHICALLY... THE ARTIFICIAL HEART ONLY HAD A LIFETIME GUARANTEE.

WIMMEN'S COMIX #1 COPYRIGHT 1972 BY (ABOVE, LEFT TO RIGHT): MICHELLE BRAND, LEE MARRS, LORA FOUNTAIN, PATRICIA MOODIAN (EDITOR), SHARON RUDALL, SHELBY, ALINE KOMINSKY, TRINA, KAREN MARIE HASKELL, & JANET WOLFE STANLEY

Cabarga, who made it well before page 357 this time, is irregular both in quality and quantity of output, but does not consider the creation of underground comics his entire life or even, necessarily, his major commitment.

For other cartoonists, though, underground comics *must* be top priority—for these are the women cartoonists, whose ranks have swelled substantially but most of whose work is still confined to collections including *only* cartoons drawn by women. Sexism in underground comics continues to draw the women cartoonists' anger, and many of them have banded together to resist what they see as discrimination. This group, which contains nearly fifty women cartoonists (but whose membership is in a constant state of flux), is called the Women's Cartoonist Collective.

The group was formed to put together *Wimmen's Comix*, which (according to super-articulate Collective member **Lee Marrs**) was intended from the start to be femin*ine* without necessarily being femin*ist*: "We would try for artistic quality, story coherence, although so many of us were beginners. There was to be no feminist line, no theme restrictions. The deal was for everyone to do what turned them on or pissed them off. We wanted to show women as they really are." *Wimmen's Comix* was also founded as a forum for beginners (and has remained one), and as a clearinghouse for the work of women cartoonists across the country. Lee Marrs, like other women cartoonists, had tried to get her work into comics which also contained male cartoonists' work, but found that "straight" and underground media sometimes share unpleasant pre-publication requirements—specifically, "the usual step-into-this-broom-closet, my dear, heh, heh, and my sex life was already taken care of at the time, thank you." But when the Women's Cartoonist Collective *did* succeed in producing several books, "At first, people in the undies seemed to fear that 'the women were banding together against us,' whoever the 'us' might be. All this organization was weird, a threat. Were we going to squeeze men out?"

Though the men were certainly not squeezed out, the problem of sexism in the underground comics obviously remains a very large issue. It won't for long, if people like Lee Marrs have anything to say about it. A *cum laude* graduate of American University (B.A. in Art), Lee Marrs has produced an animated film, assisted Phil Blaisdell on the "Li'l Orphan Annie" comic strip, worked as a graphic artist for Standard Oil of California, done freelance cartooning for the *Washington Post*, and worked as the news bureau artist for WTOP-TV, the CBS affiliate in Washington, D.C. Born in Alabama, she started drawing cartoons in kindergarten, and got interested in comics because

Above: Artists' self-portraits from *Wimmen's Comix* No. 1. ©1972 Michelle Brand, Lee Marrs, Lora Fountain, Patricia Moodian, Sharon Rudall [*sic*], Shelby, Aline Kominsky, Trina, Karen Marie Haskell, and Janet Wolfe Stanley. By permissions of Mss. Marrs, Moodian, Shelby and Trina.

Right: Leslie Cabarga. *Real Pulp Comics* No. 2. ©1973 Leslie Cabarga. By permission of Leslie Carbarga.

Of course, there remain artists who assess themselves and their place in the field briefly and modestly, and for whom cartooning is only one part of existence rather than a way of life. **Leslie Cabarga,** author of a book on animation, says, "I sort of consider myself on the second string of comers into the comics world, although my early stuff is nothing much to speak of . . . I always thought my career in comics would not be worth a plug nickel if I didn't make at least page 357 of some comics book someday."

Leslie Cabarga. *Modern Medical Romances.*

"until you got old enough to neck there was nothin' to do but read and go to movies." She did cartoons for her high-school newspaper "and learned the joy of social commentary. Allegories, thinly disguised critiques—ho boy! Poking fun at the faculty and getting away with it. Delicious!"

Lee Marrs cites many of the same influences that have intrigued other underground cartoonists: "I most admired Walt Kelly, Harold Foster, Carl Barks' early-fifties *Uncle Scrooge* (Huey, Dewey, Louey and that goddam Jr. Woodchuck Manual! Wow!) and Joe Kubert. I bought all those war books just to see Joe's work. My granny was alarmed at my violent tastes—never could convince her it was the drawing. Then Joe's *Viking Prince!* Yum yum! *Loved* that Jon! Had my first remembered sex fantasies off his adventuresome bearskin-bikinied self. Storywise I liked *Little Lulu* (Jesus! Those dream sequences about Witch Hazel were the weirdest fucking things I'd seen—until I discovered Jonathan Winters and Nichols and May—other strong influences), *Wonder Woman* and *Tomahawk* (drawing was good there too)."

Why does she draw? "Doing cartoons gives me a real charge. I enjoy doing a lot of different artwork, but cartooning is dessert, banana splits, Hershey bars, eskimo pie. I act out all the expressions, voices, live the whole scene as I draw. The nearest thing to making my own movies I can afford. . . . Primarily I want to make people laugh. To see what happens to them every day in a new light and laugh, even ruefully. Life *is* crazy, absurd. Cartoons now are neck and neck with real life. Few exaggerations are too extreme—next week you'll see it on the six o'clock news. . . . I have some of the downhome zen methodist in me too. The political cartoonist lives on in some brain recess. Commentary sneaks in here and

This Page: Impressions of self and the world by Lee Marrs. Top from *The Further Fattening Adventures of Pudge, Girl Blimp.* Below Left: From *Wimmen's Comic* No. 1. Both ©1973 Lee Marrs. Below: Drawn especially for this book. ©1974 Lee Marrs. By permission of Lee Marrs.

Robert Crumb. *Tales from the Leather Nun* No. 1. ©1973 Robert Crumb. By permission of Robert Crumb.

there. I guess my ideal reader would read a panel, laugh hysterically, and five minutes later see some insight they hadn't gotten to before. . . . Being a lifelong aggressive female, I dig stories centered on women. Having women be who they really are/could be in comix is one of the innovative potentials of underground comix. In the undies as well as everywhere else, we have had the bubble-headed busty babes with insatiable lusts *or* the malevolent busty babes with insatiable lusts. Not saying my insatiable lusts are less than any other babe's, still there are a few alternative characters. There's a whole world outside and many worlds inside—*anything* should be possible!"

Right and Below: Patricia Moodian. *Wimmen's Comix* No. 1. ©1973 Moodian. By permission of Patricia Moodian.

Though most women cartoonists still feel there's a long way to go before sexism is conquered —in the underground or anywhere else—they are at least pleased that more women are trying to make it in the field. The Women's Cartoonist Collective has drawn together a number of women whose work is starting to attract avid readers, and it's likely that the next cycle of interest in underground comics will bring people like **Patricia Moodian, Shelby** (last name Sampson—but she doesn't use it in her work), and the other Collective members into prominence.

Yet the Women's Cartoonist Collective, while it has helped women into underground comics, has not been the only way for interested women to get into the field. **Pat Daley,** for instance, just naturally grew into the role of cartoonist—or maybe, based on her own capsule biography, the growth wasn't completely natural: "Born in the middle of a German potato salad on New Year's Eve, 1947. Soon afterward informed (forcefully) that children should be seen (rarely) and not heard: learned to read. Howard Pyle's *Book of Pirates,* illustrated by N.C. Wyeth, who was *not,* however, a Significant Influence. The thirty-odd books by Walt Kelly *were.* Soon after I received *Pogo,* I switched from notebook paper to an honest-to-god sketchbook and began a monumentally forgettable tale of a counter-earth populated by balloon-headed stick figures most of whom wore white sox caps. (For crying out loud, I was only about *seven*—at

that time, stick figures were my *peak*.) The cast changed as I did, and I am still not certain who (it's still happening) is influencing *whom*. So far I have not mentioned what went on in realtime [*sic*] at all—my partners and I in the books were off somewhere in the galaxy fighting off some giant anchovie or other, and I seem to have missed the fifties and sixties. I am informed I went to school a lot. By 1966 (as good a year as any) the books numbered twenty, and my partners numbered ninety-plus (have since pruned the cast, too many internecine squabbles—and the overhead was in*cred*ible). Bought first underground comic *(God Nose*) in '67 or '68. Was hooked (had stopped reading comics some years earlier, when Superman collected such a crowd of refugees from Krypton that it became unbearable, and the Marvel Group developed too much muscle and not enough dialogue). Took out a subscription to *Blazing Combat*—parents finally admitted they had a *strange* daughter. . . . As my pile of comix grew, I was reassured by Gore, Lynch, S. Clay Wilson, etc. that I was not all *that* kinky, that there were others of my ilk around, but *they* were in *print*. Ergo: heard about a course in comix being taught by Jay Lynch himself!! at the Art Institute of Chicago. Took it." And so another underground cartoonist drifted into being: "Goals? Blessed with a lack (not total) of ambition. Only hope I keep filling books, and that the day never comes when I have nothing to put down on paper."

Cycling and recycling, the underground comics continue—new faces, new names, new artists, but continuing similarities of themes, backgrounds, and enthusiasms. *Plus ça change* . . . .

In some ways, the work of the underground cartoonists simply has not changed with the passing of time. Though there has been a decrease in overtly revolutionary cartooning, there remains among many cartoonists the belief in using comics for specific causes. Like *Conspiracy Capers* several years earlier (see Chapter 7), *El Perfecto Comics* was produced as a benefit—not for a group of people, but for Dr Timothy Leary, founder of the League for Spiritual Discovery and high priest of LSD. The book didn't free Leary from prison, but Lee Marrs thinks it did much to convince male cartoonists that women would work with them rather than against them: *El Perfecto's* woman editor "Aline Kominsky put together a book in only two months that artists had been brainstorming about for ages but never really attempted." More than two dozen cartoonists, both men and women, contributed to this book, which was billed as a "benefit comic book for the Timothy Leary Defense Fund." The book showed not only that the underground cartoonists could still put their work at the service of a cause, and that men and women cartoonists could do an anthology together, but that the cartoonists remain very much aware of earlier underground work: one Bill Griffith strip specifically in-

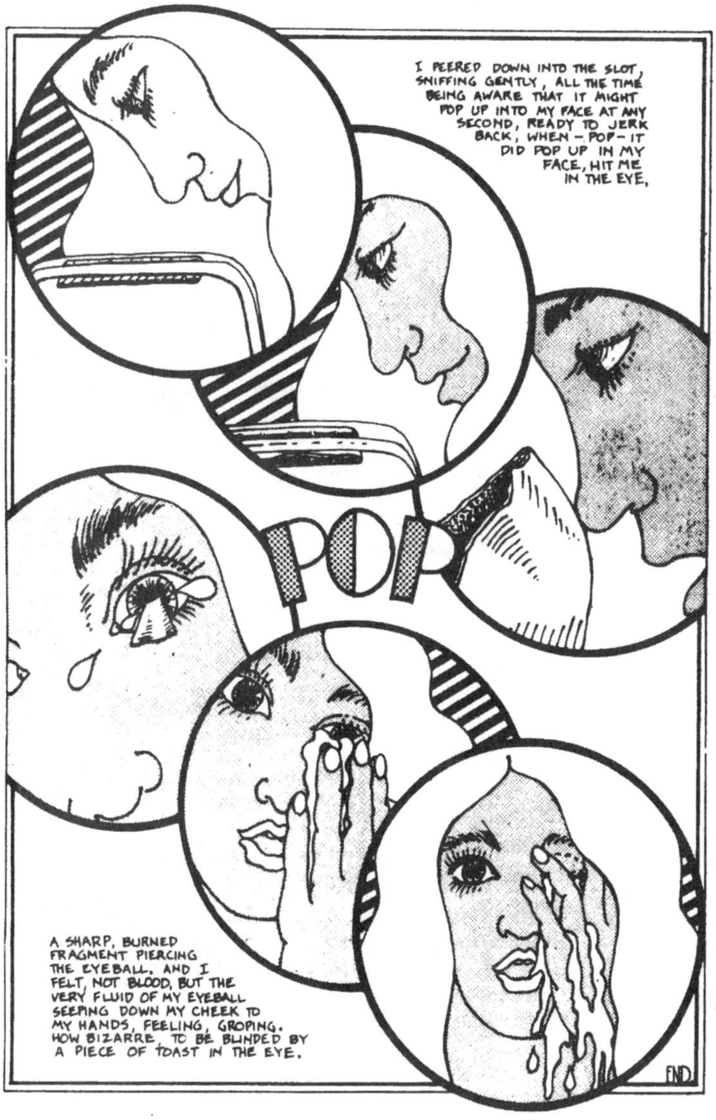

Left: Shelby. *Wimmen's Comix* No. 2. ©1973 Shelby. By permission of Shelby.

Below: Pat Daley. *First Empire Funnies*. ©1972 Kleine Reich Ego Funnies. By permission of Kleine Reich Ego Funnies, by Pat Daley.

volved Alfred Jarry, creator of the proto-dada play *Ubu Roi*.

The underground cartoonists showed their awareness of the past in other ways as well. As paper became scarce and prices went up, a series of several dozen seven-cent, black-and-white comic books appeared, each eight pages long (though differently shaped from the old *Eight-Pagers*, for which see Chapter 2). Pat Daley's longtime project (see page 274) has seen the light of day only once, in one of those short, inexpensive comics: *First*

Trina. *El Perfecto Comics.* ©1973 Trina. By permission of Trina.

Pat Daley. *Bijou Funnies* No. 8. ©1973 Bijou Publishing Empire, Inc. By permission of Bijou Publishing Empire, Inc., by Jay Lynch; and Pat Daley. From Ms. Daley's satire of Vaughn Bodé's Cheech Wizard.

Bill Griffith. *El Perfecto Comics.* ©1973 Bill Griffith. By permission of Bill Griffith. The "shitr" is one rendition of the French "merdre" ("merde," or "shit," with an added "r")—a most common word in Jarry's *Ubu Roi.*

Empire Funnies.

The underground cartoonists have paid homage to the old E. C. Comics of the fifties (see Chapter 2) in a number of ways. The art of E. C. artist Basil Wolverton (see page 38) was imitated by Gilbert Shelton for the cover of *Zap Comics* No. 6, and a book of Wolverton's own sketches was actually published as an underground comic. *Bijou Funnies* No. 8, in which underground cartoonists parodied the work of other underground cartoonists, looked more like an E. C. comic than anything produced since the E. C. days themselves (see also Chapter 9). As the E. C. horror and science-fiction comics had adapted Ray Bradbury short stories, the underground artists began a series of adaptations of H.P Lovecraft tales (in *Skull Comics* Nos. 4 and 5, for instance), and characters derived from Lovecraft even made their appearance in stories which were not themselves adaptations of his work—an example being Jaxon's interpretation of Alhazared [*sic*], based on Lovecraft's Mad Arab, Abdul Alhazred, fictitious author of the fictitious book of ultimate black magic, the *Necronomicon.*

As characters from Lovecraft came into non-Lovecraftian stories, stories not actually by Lovecraft were included in the books of Lovecraft adaptations because they seemed to fit the mood. In fact, one new underground cartoonist, **Charles Dallas,** had a long story in *Skull Comics* No. 4—the only story in that book which *wasn't* a Lovecraft adaptation. The use of Dallas' tale showed once more the flexibility of the underground comics, for

Above and Left: A sampling of covers from the seven-cent, eight-page underground comics. Above: Pat Daley. *First Empire Funnies.* ©1972 Kleine Reich Ego Funnies. By permission of Kleine Reich Ego Funnies, by Pat Daley. Far Left: Leslie Cabarga. *Modern Medical Romances.* Center Left: Leslie Cabarga. *A Plain Talk with Puerto Ricans.* Left: Art Spiegelman. *Self Destruct.* ©1973 Art Spiegelman and Bill Griffith. By permission of Art Spiegelman and Bill Griffith.

Jay Lynch. *Bijou Funnies* No. 8. ©1973 Bijou Publishing Empire, Inc. By permission of Bijou Publishing Empire, Inc., by Jay Lynch. Incorporating Wonder Wart-Hog, but from Lynch's satire of Gilbert Shelton's Fabulous Furry Freak Brothers.

Far Left: Gilbert Shelton. *Zap Comics* No. 6. ©1973 Apex Novelties. By permission of Apex Novelties, by Don Donahue.

Jaxon. *Skull Comics* No. 4. ©1972 Jaxon. By permission of Jaxon. This story is a close adaptation of a Lovecraft tale of the same name.

Cycling and Recycling

Left: Jaxon. *Tales from the Leather Nun* No. 1. ©1973 Jaxon. By permission of Jaxon. This story has Lovecraftian elements, among them the name Alhazared, but it is *not* an adaptation of Lovecraft.

Below: Richard Corben. *Skull Comics* No. 5. ©1972 Gore, Spain, Todd, Sheridan, Jaxon, Deitch, and Dallas. By permission of Messrs. Gore, Sheridan, Jaxon, Deitch, and Dallas. Carefully adapted from Lovecraft's "The Rats in the Walls" by Corben, who draws under the name "Gore."

this relatively unknown artist was included in the same book as Dave Sheridan, Jaxon, and other "big names" in the field. Dallas himself credits Jaxon with bringing him into underground comics—significant help in a field where vehicles for new artists (with the exception of *Wimmen's Comix*—see page 272) are rare (that's why so many new artists publish their own books). Dallas studied art for a year at Syracuse University, but dropped out and moved to the West Coast. Less committed to West Coast life styles than many other cartoonists, he continues to return East fairly often, and feels he lives on both sides of the country. Dallas describes himself as "just generally turned on to comics."

Though the full books of Lovecraft adaptations were a new field for underground comics, the use of certain Lovecraft material had been tried before. The *Necronomicon* was mentioned occasionally even in the days of *Gothic Blimp Works*—just half a decade ago chronologically, but centuries in the past as far as the minds of many cartoonists are concerned. Since the underground comics have always been somewhat aware of their roots, none of their Lovecraft adaptations and E. C. Comics formats could strictly be considered a part of the nationwide American "nostalgia trip" which became more widespread as the seventies progressed.

Charles Dallas. *Skull Comics* No. 5. ©1972 Gore, Spain, Todd, Sheridan, Jaxon, Deitch, and Dallas. By permission of Messrs. Gore, Spain, Todd, Sheridan, Jaxon, Deitch, and Dallas. From Dallas' graphic interpretation of an H.P. Lovecraft poem.

Charles Dallas. *Psychotic Adventures* No. 2. ©1973 Charles Dallas. By permission of Charles Dallas. From a story written by Dallas himself.

But the underground comics *did* show some nostalgia, and existed in a field where reprints of "straight" comics flourished and the nostalgia was stronger still. As underground imitations and reinterpretations of E. C. Comics increased, an East Coast publisher began releasing actual reprints of some of the famous E. C. Comics of the fifties! Within the underground comics themselves, the early work of Robert Crumb suddenly became a subject of interest during 1973, as

Far Left and Below: Sketches by Robert Crumb. *Artistic Comics.* ©1973 R. Crumb. By permission of Robert Crumb.

Left: Robert Crumb. *The People's Comics.* ©1972 R. Crumb. By permission of Robert Crumb. This is the mock script conference involving Ralph Bakshi and Steve Krantz, producers of the movie *Fritz the Cat* (not to mention Fritz himself).

Jim Janes. *Greaser Comics* No. 2. ©1972 G. DiCaprio and Jim Janes. By permission of George DiCaprio.

YOUR ALL FUCK'N NUTS!
PERAGENE, DO YOU REALIZE THAT THIS IS ALL OUR DOIN!
YEP!
DOC'S
GOTTA GET DIS STUFF STASHED!
AC
FINIS

Artistic Comics offered a special, extra-long sampling of works from Crumb's sketchbooks. And a whole series of rip-offs of Crumb's characters and styles was put into print by a Midwest outfit called Adam's Apple Publishing Company.

Robert Crumb's bad experiences with the overground media (see Chapter 11) led him to create *The People's Comics*, in which he satirized his own popularity and success and also killed off his character Fritz the Cat (having first satirized a Ralph Bakshi-Steve Krantz script conference for one of an apparently endless series of movies starring Fritz).

Crumb's *The People's Comics* proved once again that he could rise to the challenge of rip-offs by the "straight" media, and do so effectively because he worked with his own best weapon: his art. For other cartoonists dealing with the overground media, though, responses through the comics themselves weren't enough. Sensing the partial melding of underground and "straight" sensibilities, some cartoonists sought to obtain the better finances of the "straight" media without compromising too much of their artistic integrity. This didn't always work, according to Lee Marrs: "Another tale

Opposite: Jim Janes. *Greaser Comics* No. 2. ©1972 G. DiCaprio and Jim Janes. By permission of George DiCaprio. One might call this the other side of the nostalgia trip about those "wonderful" fifties.

Left: Robert Crumb. *The People's Comics.* ©1972 R. Crumb. By permission of Robert Crumb. The death of Fritz the Cat—brought on by an overt version of the sexism of which Crumb himself is often accused.

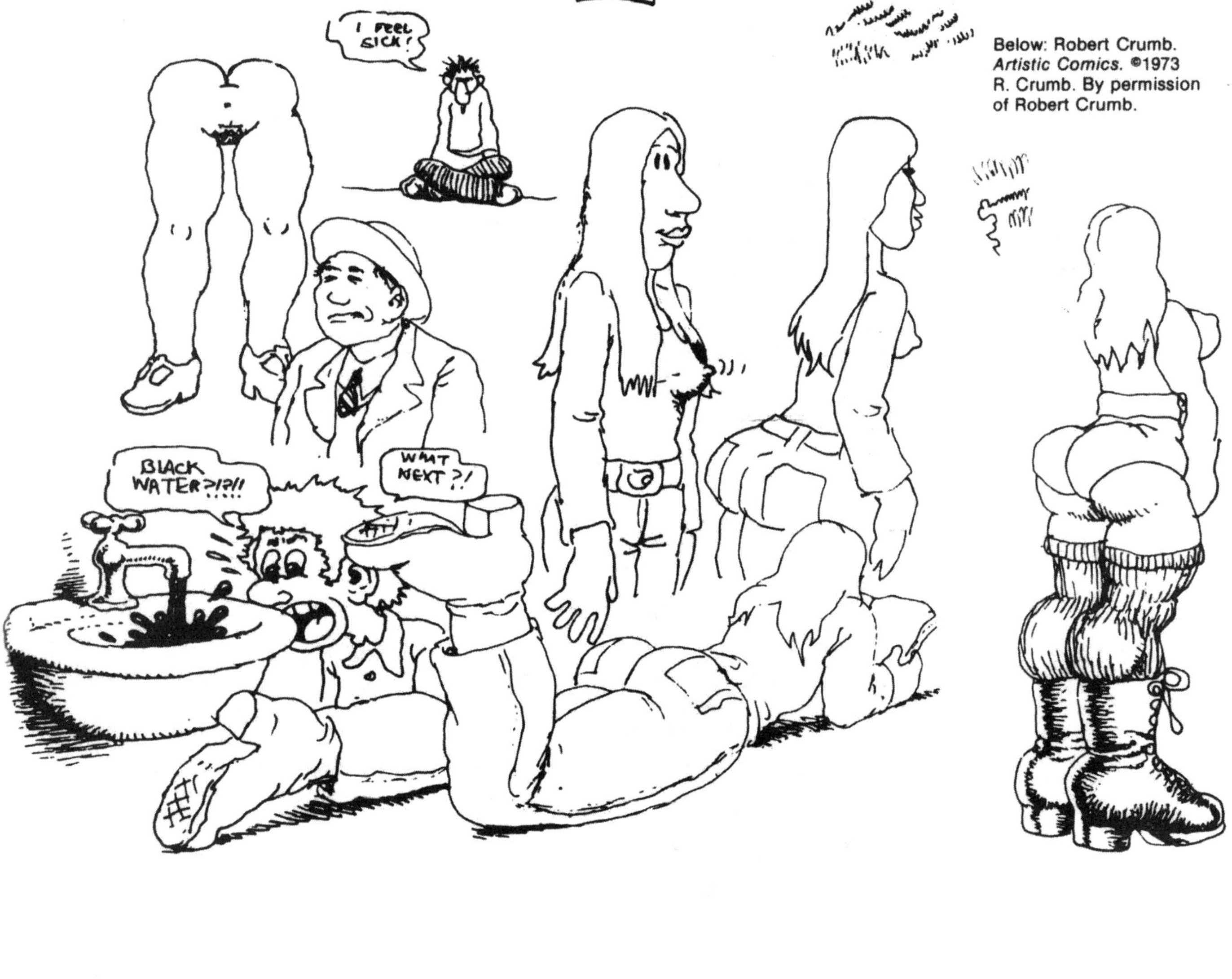

Below: Robert Crumb. *Artistic Comics.* ©1973 R. Crumb. By permission of Robert Crumb.

of '73 was the *Wimmen's Comix*-Lee-Trina-*Ms. Magazine* War. A fuck-up in several parts. Part One: *Ms.* rejected an ad that Last Gasp Eco-Funnies [see page 253] sent in for all the women's comix with a note so vague that it took days to figure out they thought we were obscene. Con-

Right: Trina. *Wimmen's Comix* No. 3. ©1974 Trina. By permission of Trina.

Far Right and Below: Two self-appraisals, with varying amounts of satire, by Robert Crumb. Both from *The People's Comics.* ©1972 R. Crumb. By permission of Robert Crumb.

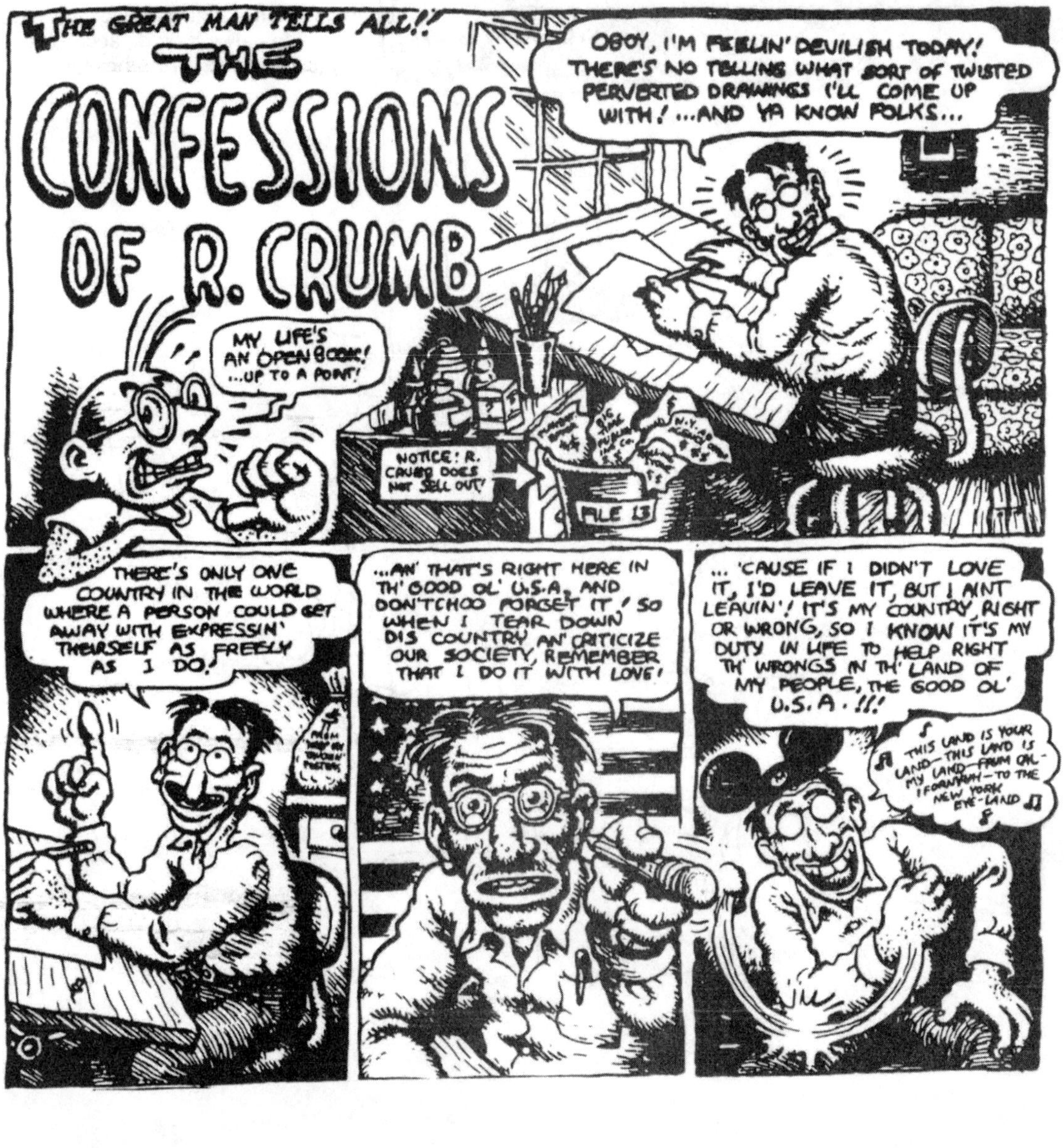

sidering the exploitative ads they *do* run, you can imagine our response. In the fall I attacked their ad department in person and, after six visits, got an ad in (you wouldn't believe the vague nonsense they handed me). Trina had stories there for months, after she had seen them in person, and finally had to threaten to sue before they sent her work back and a kill fee. I had a supertorturous fiasco with them lasting six months. They *solicited* from me stories about Pudge, Girl Blimp. For months they asked for revisions, we had long-distance conversations, etc. On and on. Finally, in a collective board meeting, using Pudge lost by one vote. I have yet to get any *concrete* answer why, even after receiving the kill fee, seeing them in person, etc. They pretend these women cartoonists just don't exist."

So while there are *signs* of a merging of sensibilities between underground and overground culture, the merger is obviously something less than complete. Mutual co-option goes on, and another cycle continues.

And then, of course, there are continuing arguments about attempted repression of the under-

UM TUT SMUT?

Bijou No. 8, our fifth anniversary issue, will be our last issue unless **you** take an active part in protesting the censorship inherent in the U.S. Supreme Court's June 1973 decision.

As you know, this decision makes it **constitutional** for individual states and / or **communities** to prohibit the sale and distribution of any "works, which taken as a whole, appeal to the prurient interest in sex, which portray sex conduct in a patently offensive way, and which, taken as a whole, do not have **serious literary, artistic, political or scientific value** " (emphasis ours.)

Previously, a work containing sexual description or depiction could only be banned if it were "utterly without redeeming social value." Now such a publication, movie, play, etc. can be banned if it fails evaluation as a "serious" work. But who is to make this evaluation? The U.S. Supreme Court specifically ruled that **no expert testimony** as to the serious value of a work in question need be presented in order for a judge and jury to declare that work **obscene** and **illegal**!

As to the portrayal of patently offensive sex conduct—what is patently offensive to **some** people may be exactly the thing **other** people are doing in the back seat of the Chevy at this very moment!

Under the old law, nobody was **forced** to view sexually oriented material. Minors were not **admitted** to X-rated movies, and were booted out of dirty bookstores, too!

The big cities with most of the states' population have fewer **delegates-per-capita** to the state legislature than do the rural communities. Urbanites, who are likely to be less "patently offended" by the media in question, are deprived by the state legislature of the option to buy such material, whereas rural dwellers, like everyone else, always had the option **not** to buy it before this decision. As this editorial is being written (July 17, 1973) there is a bill before the Illinois State Senate, for example, which would outlaw the sale of material depicting the **bare bosom.**

Still, the cities are responding to the decision with a flury of book-burning of their own. In the month since this decision was handed down, we've seen "Playboy" banned in Albemarle County, Virginia and in many other areas. "Playgirl," a magazine for women which features hazily photographed naked men with discreetly covered or shadowed pubic areas, has been banned in Cleveland and other cities.

"Paper Moon," a movie which had a **P.G.** rating, has been banned in Dallas, Texas. "Last Tango in Paris," considered by most well-known movie critics to be of serious artistic value, has been banned in Salt Lake City and other areas. "Carnal Knowledge," a Jules Feiffer / Mike Nichols Academy Award winning film which many critics considered an artistic masterpiece is now illegal in Albany, Georgia. Jack Valenti, Motion Picture Association president, says the U.S. Supreme Court decision may be a "serious blow" to the movie industry if it results in legal "harrassment" to "serious artists."

Further, the mayor of Macon, Georgia has ordered police to investigate "lascivious" books on the shelves of **school libraries!** Robert L. Bernstein, president of Random House, sees the Supreme Court decision as "a real First Amendment crisis. You can't let the publication and distribution of books be at the mercy of whim."

Remember the Nixon commission, which set out to study the effects of pornography on society and found it to be **harmless**, much to the president's embarrassment! There has been **no** study which **disproves** this conclusion; no study has linked increased crime rates with the liberalization of obscenity laws.

Recently, we heard a clergyman on a Chicago talk show say that most sex criminals have read pornography. But most sex criminals have eaten Hershey bars too...and how about all the business executives, doctors, firemen, politicians and teachers who have read pornography? It's like the 1950's when sensationalist Fred Wertham, author of garishly titled **Seduction of the Innocent** cited evidence that most criminals had read comic books as children, but ignored the fact that most law-abiding citizens had also read comic books as children!

Wertham's rantings led to a Congressional investigation of comic books which resulted in "The Good Comics Code"—a form of censorship based on the blacklisting by distributors of non-Code books.

In a country that exalts freedom of the press, it's shocking to observe our community leaders burning books for the protection of society. Outlawing sexually oriented media sets a fine precedent for outlawing other materials which might occasionally deviate from the establishment morality—like the daily newspapers, which bring us news of political scandal...

What can **you** do? If you're old enought to buy **Bijou**, you're old enough to vote, and your potential vote carries some **weight** with your state representatives. Write letters to your **state representatives** and **Congressmen** urging them to **refuse** to outlaw the sale of "hard core pornography" to adults in your state. Explain your feelings about censorship. Tell them to do what they can to seek a reversal of the U.S. Supreme Court decision, too.

If you are not sure who your state representatives and Congressmen are, you can phone the League of Women Voters in your area for this information.

Write a similar letter to your **governor**. His name and your state capital are sufficient address on the envelope. If you read in your local newspapers about your mayor or any other elected official who is seeking to ban obscenity in your community, write to him or her **too**. Your letters don't have to be typed—in fact, handwritten envelopes are usually opened first because of the numbers of typed form letters and so forth that flow into government offices. Be sincere, but, for best results, **avoid** phrases like "you fascist motherfuckers," because politicians have no sense of humor about this stuff and will assume that your snappy rhetoric is the product of a four-color glimpse of thigh.

In Bijou's five-year history we've never had a **serious** editorial until **right now**! Please, readers—don't take these words lightly! If you don't act now, a free press in American is **doomed.**

Sincerely,
The Editors of Bijou Funnies

Jay Lynch. *Bijou Funnies* No. 8. ©1973 Bijou Publishing Empire, Inc. By permission of Bijou Publishing Empire, Inc., by Jay Lynch. The editorial, appearing as the comic's inside front cover, is similar in attitudes and tone to the editorials which appeared in the E.C. Comics of the fifties, just before they went out of existence due to censorship pressure.

ground comics. Though *Zap Comix* No. 4 was at one point declared legally obscene in New York City (see Chapter 10) and in certain other jurisdictions, the Supreme Court's June 1973 ruling allowing local communities greater freedom in determining local obscenity standards made it possible to reprint and continue to distribute *Zap* No. 4 (which, in any case, had never completely disappeared from the national underground-comic market). But by and large, the underground cartoonists joined other civil-liberties-oriented groups in finding little good to say about the Supreme Court's attempt to tighten America's chastity belt. The June 1973 decision was specifically attacked on the inside front cover of *Armageddon* No. 3, and was re-

Barney Steel. *Armageddon* No. 3. ©1973 Barney Steel. By permission of Barney Steel and Last Gasp Eco-Funnies, Inc., by Ron Turner. The comic's inside front cover is unique in its combination of art for its own sake, serious sociopolitical commentary *outside* the art work, standard copyright information, and personal messages.

ferred to more obliquely in many other places. Most telling of all was an inside-front-cover editorial in *Bijou Funnies* No. 8, which made that comic—already so closely resembling the E. C. Comics of a generation earlier—seem even more like an old E. C. book. For the E. C. line carried many editorials condemning comic-book censorship during the Joe McCarthy era (see page 36), and the *Bijou* No. 8 editorial was so similar as to provide a thoroughly upsetting sense of *déjà vu*.

As the underground cartoonists came more and more frequently into contact with "straight" media, they began to use more and more of the overground techniques which, a few short years before, they had condemned. The days of "free art for the masses" died an unheralded death, as cartoonists rushed to copyright material and avoid the problems some of their earlier stands had caused them (see Chapter 11). Though uncopyrighted comics continued to emerge occasionally, these normally came only from new artists, working in places where underground comics were virtually unknown until very recently (e.g., *Swamp Fever* from New Orleans, Louisiana). The more established cartoonists were copyrighting everything, and even hiring lawyers. When the Women's Cartoonist Collective started preparing *Wimmen's Comix* No. 1 for Last Gasp Eco-Funnies, Lee Marrs says, "We got Albert Morse [who is also Robert Crumb's attorney—see Chapter 11] to help us draw up a legal contract with enough clauses to choke Owen Marshall. We fought and won to have our own editorial say on what went into the

Left: Sol Wright. *Swamp Fever.*

Below Left and Below: Two illustrations from *Morse's Funnies*, a booklet especially drawn by fourteen cartoonists for their attorney Albert Morse. Below left by Art Spiegelman. ©1974 Art Spiegelman. By permission of Art Spiegelman. Below (the cover of the book) by Robert Crumb. ©1973 R. "Hack It Out" Crumb. By permission of Robert Crumb.

book." In other cases, cartoonists who had already been careful about copyrights became more careful still, even going beyond strict legal requirements in order to make doubly sure that no one could feel his or her work was being abused or misused. Thus, Jay Lynch, who speaks for the Bijou Publishing Empire, Inc., which hold copyrights on *Bijou Funnies* material, said that he began to require both his permission *and* the permission of individual artists before reprinting could be allowed, because "I believe joint permission to be the only fair way to license reprints, 'cause I don't want to make final decisions for the other artists—even though legally it is my right as president of Bijou." This sort of attitude, unthinkable in the earlier days of underground comics, became more and more common as the seventies went on and the car-

Ted Richards. *Dopin' Dan* No. 3. ©1973 Ted Richards. By permission of Ted Richards.

Opposite: Barney Steel. *Armageddon* No. 3. ©1973 Barney Steel and Last Gasp Eco-Funnies, Inc. By permission of Barney Steel and Last Gasp Eco-Funnies, Inc., by Ron Turner.

toonists aged with them.

As the underground comics have become more conspicuous and many of their creators have begun to take on more of the trappings of many "straight" cartoonists, one interesting development has been a sense among the cartoonists of their own importance within the

larger medium of comic-book communication. As the publication date for this book approached, in fact, many cartoonists started to become every bit as concerned about their historical image as are certain politicians whom those very cartoonists often parody. Phrases like "dubious, obscure historical interest" began to be used by some cartoonists in speaking of their own early work. Other cartoonists became extremely concerned with having their "historical" comics balanced against some of their more recent material. In some cases, in which the cartoonists had shown definite and substantial growth over the years, this sort of concern made sense. For instance, Justin Green's book, *Binky Brown Meets the Holy Virgin Mary,* is cited both by Green himself and by many other cartoonists as an extremely significant work, as well as a major change in his style. This book-length, semi-autobiographical study combines serious commentary on certain kinds of American religious training with a healthy dose

Scenes from Justin Green's *Binky Brown Meets the Holy Virgin Mary.* ©1972 Justin Green. By permission of Justin Green.

Dave Geiser. *Balloon.* ©1973 Dave Geiser. By permission of Dave Geiser.

of satire. The book's serious aspect moves it beyond the religious satires of Foolbert Sturgeon and others (see Chapter 7), and also makes sequels to it unlikely: no one, including Green himself, has matched the particular combination of social commentary, social satire, and social realism of this book.

Not every cartoonist's later productions have measured up to his or her earlier ones, though, and for some cartoonists the new sense of historical self-consciousness is not a garment that fits comfortably. I have my own opinions about the improvement of certain artists and the deterioration of others over the years—but here, for once, dear reader, I don't think I'll share them with you. Cartoonists' attitudes change rapidly, after all, and so do authors'. In fact, the underground comics lend themselves especially well to changing interests and interpretations as time goes on—that's one reason the field is such a rich one. And if this book ends by giving the underground cartoonists some of the overground respectability which many have disclaimed as a goal but which many others have begun to strive for more and more strongly, then the act of your buying and reading this book may have *its* influence on the underground cartoonists in the near future! (The underground comics are a highly participational medium.)

In certain ways, the panels besprinkling this book give only a small idea of the depth and breadth of the field. Clay Geerdes' listing of the underground comics, appended to this work, gives you a chance to explore the underground comics themselves, *in toto* and in context. It's an exploration I strongly recommend. I don't think you'll be *per*verted or *sub*verted—but I think you'll be *con*verted.

"The wheel is come full circle;
I am here."
—*King Lear, V, III, 174*

Below: Denis Kitchen. *Smile* No. 2. ©1971 Krupp Comic Works, Inc. By permission of Krupp Comic Works, Inc., by Denis Kitchen.

Left: Justin Green. *Binky Brown Meets the Holy Virgin Mary*. ©1972 Justin Green. By permission of Justin Green.

Charles Dallas.
A previously unpublished drawing. ©1974 Charles Dallas. By permission of Charles Dallas. This was intended as the cover illustration for one of a series of "pirate" E.C. comic-book covers—specifically, *Shock SuspenStories* No. 19. The covers were part of a project called the Nickel Library, created by Gary Arlington of the San Francisco Comic Book Company in 1973. Each cover used the title and seal of an old E.C. comic book, but the original cover illustrations were replaced by artwork by underground cartoonists. Because of copyright problems, the project never really got off the ground. William M. Gaines, who holds all copyrights on old E.C. material, threatened a fifty-thousand-dollar law suit unless the project was stopped. Arlington complied, and the whole Nickel Library project was aborted. Nevertheless, Arlington's plan shows with unusual clarity how deeply today's underground cartoonists were influenced by the E.C. Comics of the fifties.

Afterword

Joel Beck. *The Profit.* ©1966 Joel Beck. By permission of Joel Beck.

A Kurtzmania & Cosmic Comics Consciousness

Dave Geiser. 1973 Berkeley Comix Convention program. ©1973 Dave Geiser. By permission of Dave Geiser.

Harvey Kurtzman, whose opinions on the underground comics are sprinkled liberally throughout this book, remains the single person most often cited by the underground cartoonists as a major influence on their consciousness and their style. The cartoonists' admiration for Kurtzman, though, goes back to his early days as a writer and editor of *Mad* comics—and tends to ignore the Harvey Kurtzman of today. It is, therefore, particularly revealing of the gulf between today's underground cartoonists and the people who influenced them to see how Harvey Kurtzman shows up when directly confronted with today's underground artists and their fans.

This unusual opportunity came up in June 1970, when the Alternative Media Project met at Goddard College in Plainfield, Vermont. More than a thousand self-styled "media freaks" got together to discuss ways of improving underground media and finding ways to break into the fringes of the "straight" media as well.

Below: Gilbert Shelton. *Alternative Media Comics and Stories*, an eight-page, hastily drawn book created at Goddard College's Alternative Media Project in 1970.

The last seminar was "Comics and Mass Consciousness," which was to feature Harvey Kurtzman and Gilbert Shelton and to be nominally run by your friendly neighborhood author. By the time of this seminar, the Alternative Media Project had already produced two new comics: *Alternative Media Comics and Stories*, written by Shelton and folded and collated by me (thus making me feel useful, since, if you haven't guessed, I can't even draw a straight line *with* a ruler); and *Saturday Mindfuckee Funnies*, a collaboration among Shelton, Kurtzman, and Art Spiegelman which was distributed at the comics seminar on Saturday, June 20.

Actually, this was no "seminar" in any academically accepted sense. Held at the end of three days of sex, drugs, music, and media (often, unfortunately, in that order) in the well in the basement of the Goddard College Library—with a number of people standing one floor above, looking down—the seminar was a two-hundred-person discussion group, also including several babies, a couple of dogs, and a few record and tape players. There was a multi-couple fuck-in in the center of the floor, a selection of moderately good dope being passed around, and the like. It was Guerrilla Theatre at its best and worst, simultaneously, for four solid hours. Nothing was actually accomplished, because the rhetoric tended to obscure the ideas, and the statements people made tended to get in the way of taking any action at all. But that in itself indicated something about the way these readers of underground comics saw themselves, their interests, and the cartoonists who were trying to get through to them. And it provided a rare opportunity to confront Harvey Kurtzman, whom I have elsewhere called the granddaddy of the underground comics, with the sort of family he sired. Indeed, it prompted that family to a confrontation with itself—one which I hoped would make similar future meetings more productive. That turned out to be a futile hope—for reasons which may be clear after you look over the following material.

These excerpts from "Comics and Mass Consciousness" are taken from a tape I made when I realized, very early in the proceedings, that I was neither wanted nor needed as any sort of moderator and would be free just to listen.

Man: Why do you do "Little Annie Fanny"?

Kurtzman: I . . . it brings in the loot. It's a job, and I enjoy it.

Man: Do you think it's offensive to women?

Kurtzman: If it is offensive to women, they don't tell us about it, particularly. I don't hear that it's offensive.

Woman: You're hearing it now.

Kurtzman: Well, that's the first time somebody has said that to me . . . .

Woman: Mr. Kurtzman, why don't you have Annie Fanny and her friends take over the offices of *Playboy* and show them where it's at? [*Laughter, shouts of "Right on!"*]

Kurtzman: Did she ever turn against Daddy Warbucks?

Far Left and Below Far Left: Joel Beck. *The Profit.* ©1966 Joel Beck. By permission of Joel Beck.

Left: Robert Crumb. *Snatch Comics* No. 1. ©1968 R. Cum. By permission of Robert Crumb.

[*Laughter*] I'm always looking for ideas. I'll put it down in the card index. As a matter of fact . . .

Woman: I don't think you've ever considered the fact that *Playboy* is quite a sexist publication.

Kurtzman: It's sexist all right, sure. And it intends to be.

M.J.E.: I take it you don't like that—the fact that it's sexist?

Kurtzman: I . . . I . . . I don't like to think that I have a quarrel with the Women's Liberation point of view, or *Playboy's* point of view. To me they're both extreme, and I like to feel I can tolerate them both.

Man: Let's look at the realities around here. *Playboy* is the most influential magazine for repressed middle-class men. I think that it's a beautiful vehicle for revolutionizing those people.

Man: That's bullshit about revolutionizing people. They're not going to let you, because the minute you become effective, you're offed. [*Commotion*]

Man: Why don't you tell some of us how Rip Off Press got started?

Shelton: Oh, we bought a cheap printing press and ripped off a bunch of equipment, and the artists did a bunch of artwork which we immediately started selling ourselves, and it's sort of self-perpetuating. Of course, underground comics are very small compared to *Playboy,* but we're our own bosses. We do our thing, and we can publish anything we want to. Now, artists never really get together very good as far as the community goes, except on paper. So it's a media trip instead of a community trip.

Woman: Why don't the artists get together in a community trip?

Shelton: Well, the artists . . . a lot of their life is on paper, and they're not rap artists. They don't tend to get together like some people do . . . . The question has been raised if it can be a political tool, and that gets back to the question of whether satire is good for radical politics or not, and that is a sticky question, because satire is a funny thing. Satire satirizes both sides of the question. But satire is a very strong weapon, too. We've got tremendous energy in good satirists working, but some people seem to think it hurts the Movement. That's open to question, right? Is satire good? Well, I say so, right, because if I can't work within the framework of being a satirical cartoonist, I can't get it up to do anything.

Joel Beck. *Spiffy Stories* No. 1. ©1969 The Print Mint. By permission of The Print Mint, by Bob Rita.

Man: People have fucked you over, and you should have had the courage to go on. We're starting out now. Are we supposed to go through all that shit again that you went through?

Kurtzman: No, I . . . see, there's something that happened to me and I suspect happens to a lot of people as you travel on through life. I've collected a large family, and when with my large family, I find I'm more restricted than when I was single and had no family.

Man: If you were advising someone, would you advise him to try to do something like Gilbert's doing?

Kurtzman: As a matter of fact, the underground press presents to me all kinds of exciting opportunities, and I wish that I could get back into that thing. I can't because I've got my own problems, but it seems like it's wide open for something very exciting to happen—as it is happening. . . . I do what I do from a combination of circumstances—that is, I want to do my own thing, as you say, and I try to do it

Below Left: Denis Kitchen. *Mom's Homemade Comics* No. 1. ©1969 Denis Kitchen. By permission of Denis Kitchen.

Below: Robert Crumb. *Motòr City Comics* No. 1. ©1969 R. Crumb Productions. By permission of R. Crumb Productions, by Robert Crumb.

within the limitations that I find myself in. And I constantly found a world with limitations. I haven't found any moment of my life that I've been without limitations and without some . . . . you know, there's always the Catch-22 somewhere. So I not only do what I want to do because this is exactly the way I'd like to have it, but because of external circumstances.

Jaxon. *Skull Comics* No. 3. ©1971 Irons, Sheridan, Gore, Spain, and Jaxon. By permission of Messrs. Sheridan, Gore, and Jaxon.

Man: But that's past things you're talking about. That doesn't prevent you, right now, from doing underground comics.

Kurtzman: Circumstances are still there for me. I can't work with Gilbert, because I can't support my family working for Gilbert.

Shelton: What about the idea of the Freak Brothers in *Playboy*? Is there anything wrong with that? Does that mean I'm supporting *Playboy*'s policies, or does that mean I'm slipping a revolutionary message into *Playboy*?

Woman: Do you actually think you could ever do anything political by keeping up sexist myths in *Playboy?* Even drawing cartoons for them. . . .

Man: Hey wait a second man, it doesn't matter where it appears, as long as it appears, and if it reaches a million people maybe he'll turn a million people on a little more, man.

Woman: But then you turn the page and see *Playboy*'s bunny of the month.

Man: That's the way the whole world is.

Kurtzman: I'm not sure that I know what everyone wants to speak about. I mean, you say you want to talk about cartoons. What do you want to talk about, the shape of the boxes?

Man: Tell us how you draw.

Kurtzman: Oh, you're not interested in how I—

Man: Are you a Democrat or a Republican?

Kurtzman: No political party affiliations.

Man: Really, how do you draw?

Kurtzman: Well, believe it or not, my starting point is picking something that I want to say. I've heard a lot of talk that our cartoons should be bent and twisted to make messages

Trina. *It Aint Me Babe Comix.* ©1970 Trina, Lisa Lyons, Carole, Michele, Willy Mendes, Meredith Kurtzman, and Hurricane Nancy. By permission of Mss. Trina, Willy Mendes, and Meredith Kurtzman.

Art Spiegelman. *Short Order Comix* No. 1. ©1973 Art Spiegelman. By permission of Art Spiegelman.

Below: Robert Crumb. *Motor City Comics* No. 1. ©1969 R. Crumb Productions. By permission of R. Crumb Productions, by Robert Crumb.

and do political things. I like to do my own secret political things, but I think it's the worst environment to work in when you have to conform to any kind of rules, messages, regulations—humor dies and art dies when you're working inside of restrictions. [*Applause*] As a matter of fact, the best art is totally unconditional, with the artist's talent and conscience as his own personal guide, but no conditions.

S. Clay Wilson. *Zap Comix* No. 5.

Robert Crumb. *Snatch Comics* No. 1. ©1968 R. Cum. By permission of Robert Crumb.

Man: You've said you work inside limitations. You essentially work within the system, is that right?

Kurtzman: Yeah, I work inside of my limitations.

Man: You've said that people here have great opportunities. Well, a lot of people here have children too, so I'm trying to find out what you see as the difference between what the people here are doing and what you're doing.

Shelton: Here's what happens when you do a comic strip without any limitations and without any focus. *Saturday Mindfuckee Funnies.* Some people might ask, what does this mean? See, that's the point: what's the focus? And that's the point that he brings up. I can't explain this comic strip; it just happened, in the same way that this whole discussion has been happening, without any real focal point.

Man: Well, I don't think that comic strip has a focal point.

Shelton: Right, so this comic strip expresses what's going on here.

Man: Well, I think you can work without those oppressions and still have a focus.

Shelton: Yeah, but it comes from within—it's your own personal thing, and you're just one

Below: Jim Mitchell. *Smile* No. 1. ©1971 Jim Mitchell. By permission of Krupp Comic Works, Inc., by Denis Kitchen.

person, not—

Man: What I'm trying to find out is where *we* don't have these limitations and *he* feels that he has these limitations.

Kurtzman: We all have limitations. Everybody has limitations. I mean, you have the limitations of your body, you have the limitations of your mother-in-law sometimes, you have the limitations of your front steps, where the electric light switch is, or where the water is in the well. The only time you don't have limitations is on the day you're born.

Woman: Man, if you quit *Playboy*, if you said, "Well, I'm quitting because I think it's a

Rick Veitch. *Two-Fisted Zombies* No. 1. ©1973 Veitch Brothers Enterprises. By permission of Veitch Brothers Enterprises, by Rick Veitch.

Art Spiegelman. *Funny Aminals* [*sic*] No. 1. ©1972 Art Spiegelman. By permission of Art Spiegelman.

sexist magazine". . . . We're in a revolutionary struggle, and when it happens, when the revolution comes, you're going to be crushed! And you write such funny comics, it's not *fair.*

M.J.E.: Sister, *until* it comes, where is he going to work?

Woman: Man, it's a matter of conscience. You're gonna have to decide . . . .

Kurtzman: Wait, wait. I went through this fight many years ago. I've become very familiar with it. When I was working for publishing in the very beginning, in my early days, I had a terrible conflict—it was just like yours. I found myself working with people who I considered immoral. My quarrel with them was complex, and it would be vague to you and unimportant, but nevertheless, it was my torment. Are you listening?

Woman: Yes, I am.

Kurtzman: And I had a very strong feeling about going through life squeaky clean, with my hands unsullied by dealing with people who I considered immoral. I used to talk to people about it, question people, and I slowly began to realize that my position was absolutely ridiculous, for two reasons. First of all, my assessment of what was moral and what wasn't moral was very biased; it was my own point of view. That's number one. Number two, I found that if I wanted to go through life without dealing with what I considered immorality, I couldn't work with anybody. I'd have to become an outcast on a desert island.

This last section was part of an extended debate about Women's Liberation, involving both Kurtzman and Shelton. The debate became a confrontation among the people at the seminar, not simply an attack on the values of Kurtzman or the "Establishment." In fact, what emerged from the confrontation was something like an underground generation gap. Word of the arguments spread quickly, and not everyone in the world of underground comics was pleased with what had happened. Cartoonist Trina said, "I wish there were two different names for the organization; then *they* could call themselves Hostile Women's Lib and I could call myself Friendly Women's Lib and I wouldn't have to waste so much time apologizing for *them* and saying (and hating myself for sounding so *Liberal* and *Uncle Tom*), 'we're not all like that.' I heard a bit about the Women's Lib attack on Kurtzman and Shelton. . . . I feel they were wasting their breath, and attacked the wrong people. (But I can just imagine the overreaction-type thinking that goes with being horrified by the porn in one comic and therefore hating *all* comics.)"

Spain. *The Collected Trashman.*

E.C: The Real Article

B

If the format of this book is a success, it is only because the underground cartoonists have such unique styles and approaches that the sense of their work can be put across by individual panels. This is one major respect in which the underground comics differ from their straight-line ancestors in the E.C. Comics line of the Forties and Fifties. The emphasis in the E.C. Comics, and their uniqueness, lay in the fact that even though writing and artwork were usually done by different people, there was as much emphasis on one as on the other. Thus, the stories—which were sometimes adaptations of the work of such outstanding writers as Ray Bradbury—were remarkably readable in and of themselves; the art was remarkably good; and the combination of the two had a unique power that has never since been matched (even in later works by the E.C. artists themselves).

Even when they were not adaptations of the work of fine writers, the E.C. stories, particularly the horror tales, emphasized long-line plotting to such a degree that the individual panels shown in Chapter 2 of this book give only a pale idea of the comics' power, and of their influence on the minds of so many underground cartoonists. Even a black-and-white reproduction of a full E.C. story is, in its own way (and with pun intended), a pale copy of the original stories, whose use of mood-intensifying color often added yet another element to their power. Still, a full black-and-white story is more effective in showing why the E.C. Comics influenced so many underground cartoonists than any series of individual E.C. panels can possibly be.

Here, therefore, is a complete E.C. horror story. When Bill Gaines, publisher once of the E.C. line and later of *Mad Magazine*, granted permission for use of this tale in the first edition of this book, it marked a watershed: the first appearance of a full-length E.C. horror story since the censors killed the old E.C. line in the Fifties.

This story originally appeared, in color, in *The Haunt of Fear* No. 17, January-February 1953. It was chosen for use here because it is an excellent example of the technique of E.C. horror stories, and contains a number of typical touches. The basic theme of the E.C. horror tales was revenge, usually in its most grisly form and often with supernatural tinges. All those elements are present in this story. But the E.C. writers and artists never took themselves completely seriously, even in the course of tales like this one. The tales were often "framed" by the appearance of a ghoulish host at the start and finish—the Old Witch in this case—and this framing was often done humorously, or at least wryly (as with the "dismembered" Old Witch at the end of this tale).

This story was written by Al Feldstein, based on an idea by Feldstein and Bill Gaines, and was drawn by Graham Ingels, who always signed his work "Ghastly." According to Gaines, most E.C. buffs in his experience consider Ingels to be the best artist in the horror books (an opinion which your author shares). It was art of this quality and writing of this power which went down the drain when the McCarthy-era censors managed to destroy the E.C. line. May you have your revenge on those censors, oh E.C.'s, somewhere in the happy haunting grounds!

Pages 302-309: Graham Ingels. Originally published in *The Haunt of Fear* No. 17, Jan.-Feb. 1953.

THE WITCH'S CAULDRON!
HEE, HEE! I SEE YOU'RE HORROR-HUNGRY AGAIN... BACK FOR MORE SAVORY SERVINGS OF SCREAMS FROM MY CAULDRON! WELL, GOOD! WELCOME TO THE HAUNT OF FEAR! THIS IS YOUR DELIRIUM-DIETICIAN, THE OLD WITCH, COOKING UP ANOTHER REVOLTING RECIPE! READY? GOT YOUR DROOL CUPS FASTENED UNDER YOUR DRIBBLING CHINS? GOT YOUR SHROUDS TIED NEATLY AROUND YOUR NECKS? THEN I'LL BEGIN DISHING OUT THE TERROR-TIDBIT I CALL...
HORROR WE? HOW'S BAYOU?
THE MOSS-LADEN CYPRESS TREES THAT LINE THE RUTTED BAYOU ROAD SEEM TO PART... AND AN OLD PLANTATION HOUSE, WEATHERBEATEN AND FADED, LOOMS UP IN THE CAR'S HEADLIGHT BEAMS! ITS COLUMNED PORTICO LEERS OMINOUSLY, LIKE SOME GIGANTIC FANGED MONSTER SQUATTING IN THE ROAD, BLOCKING THE AUTOMOBILE'S FURTHER PROGRESS! OFF IN THE DISTANCE A SWAMP BIRD SCREAMS INTO THE NIGHT, AS IF LAUGHING AT THE DRIVER'S DISCOMFORT...
BLAST IT! THIS ROAD ENDS HERE! BUT I'M SURE THAT SIGN BACK THERE POINTED THIS WAY...
GHASTLY
1

THE CAR DOOR SWINGS OPEN AND A YOUNG MAN STEPS OUT! HE STRIDES TOWARD THE RUN-DOWN MANSION...
THERE'S A LIGHT SHINING THROUGH ONE OF THOSE SHUTTERED WINDOWS! THAT MEANS SOMEONE'S LIVING THERE! PERHAPS THEY CAN GIVE ME DIRECTIONS...
GREY FORMS SCATTER AS THE LOST STRANGER MOUNTS THE STEPS OF THE COLUMNED PORCH...
WHEW! SWAMP RATS! UGH! HOW COULD ANYONE LIVE OUT IN THIS GOD-FORSAKEN COUNTRY?
THE LARGE BRASS DOOR-KNOCKER RESOUNDS HOLLOWLY INSIDE THE ONCE GLORIOUS HOUSE! FOOTSTEPS APPROACH AND THE HEAVY OAK FRONT DOOR CREAKS OPEN...
YES?
HOW DO YOU DO? MY NAME IS FORMAN...MAX FORMAN! I MUST HAVE MADE A WRONG TURN A FEW MILES BACK...
THE DOOR OPENS WIDE, REVEALING A SMALL, SAD-EYED, MIDDLE-AGED MAN...
COME IN, MR FORMAN! COME IN! MY! I'D GONE TO BED! I'D GIVEN UP FOR TONIGHT!
GIVEN UP? I...I DON'T UNDERSTAND!
GIVEN UP WAITING FOR SOMEONE LIKE YOU TO COME ALONG, MR. FORMAN! YOU SEE, I SWITCHED THAT SIGN DOWN THERE SO YOU'D MAKE THE TURN INTO OUR ROAD...
YOU... YOU DID THAT... ON PURPOSE! WHY?
FOR EVERETT, MR. FORMAN! EVERETT...MY BROTHER! EVERY SO OFTEN HE GETS DIFFICULT...AND I HAVE TO PROMISE HIM THINGS...
BUT WHAT'S THAT GOT TO DO WITH ME?
EVERETT IS MAD, MR. FORMAN! THAT'S WHY WE LIVE OUT HERE IN THE BAYOUS! HE IS DANGEROUS! HE IS A HOMICIDAL MANIAC...
BUT... WHY... WHY... ME? CHOKE...

EVERETT HAS A STRONG DESIRE TO KILL, MR. FORMAN! THIS DESIRE CANNOT GO UNSATISFIED FOR ANY LENGTH OF TIME! IF IT DOES... HE MAY TURN ON ME!
YOU'RE...YOU'RE JOKING! THIS IS SOME SORT OF GAG!
IF YOU WILL LOOK BEHIND YOU, YOU WILL SEE THAT THIS IS NO JOKE, MR. FORMAN!
GASP!
UH-HUHH! ...FOR EVERETT? FOR ME?
YES, EVERETT FOR YOU...
UH-HUHH! UH-HUHH!
K-KEEP AWAY...
UH-HUHH! UH-HUHH!
KEEP AWAY!
KEEP AWA-A-A EEEGGGGNHHHHH!
THE SCREAMING PROTESTS OF THE YOUNG MAN DIE IN A CHOKING GURGLE AS THE LUMBERING MANIAC'S VICE-LIKE FINGERS CLOSE AROUND HIS NECK...
UH-HUHH! UH-HUHH!
TAKE HIM AWAY, EVERETT! TAKE HIM DOWN INTO THE CELLAR! I DON'T WANT TO SEE!
THE ELDER MAN WATCHES AS HIS YOUNGER MAD BROTHER SWINGS THE PROSTRATE FORM OF THE STRANGER OVER HIS MASSIVE SHOULDERS AND MOVES OFF THROUGH THE MUSTY OLD MANSION...
I DON'T WANT TO SEE YOU DISMEMBER HIS BODY!
UH-HUHH... UH-HUHH...

LATER, THE DOOR TO THE OLD PLANTATION HOUSE OPENS AND THE ELDER BROTHER COMES OUT...
NOW TO GET RID OF THE CAR...
THE CAR LEAPS FORWARD WITH A LOUD GRINDING OF GEARS, DOWN AN OVERGROWN PATH, FINALLY STOPPING BEFORE A SHIMMERING YELLOW POOL...
THE QUICK-SAND POOL WILL SWALLOW UP ALL TRACES OF IT...
RELEASING THE EMERGENCY BRAKE, THE ELDER BROTHER LEAPS OUT, AND THE CAR ROLLS FORWARD INTO THE SUCKING BOG... SINKING SLOWLY FROM SIGHT! BEYOND, FROM THE MANSION, A SICKENING SHRIEK OF LAUGHTER ECHOES INTO THE BAYOU NIGHT...
POOR EVERETT. WELL, PERHAPS THIS WILL SATISFY HIM... FOR A WHILE, AT LEAST!
FINALLY THE CAR HAS DISAPPEARED BELOW THE SURFACE OF THE ROLLING QUICKSAND POOL! THE ELDER BROTHER MOVES BACK THROUGH THE BAYOU OVERGROWTH TO THE MANSION! EVERETT STANDS IN THE OPEN DOORWAY, BREATHING HEAVILY! HIS HANDS ARE BLOTCHED RED
I'M FINISHED, SIDNEY! COME... SEE!
N-NO, THANK YOU, EVERETT! JUST PUT WHAT'S LEFT OF HIM IN THE SACK, AS USUAL
EVERETT LUMBERS OFF AND RETURNS SHORTLY AFTER, A LARGE BLOOD-STAINED SACK SWUNG OVER HIS SHOULDERS...
HE... HE WAS A DOCTOR, SIDNEY! I FOUND HIS CARD! I DON'T LIKE DOCTORS!
THROW WHAT'S LEFT OF HIM IN THE QUICKSAND POOL, EVERETT... WITH THE OTHERS!
EVERETT'S STUPID FACE BRIGHTENS! HE GRINS IDIOTICALLY...
REMEMBER THE OTHERS, SIDNEY? THE FAT SALESMAN... AND THE WOMAN...
YES, EVERETT! I REMEMBER! GO AHEAD, NOW! IN THE QUICKSAND POOL...
THE WOMAN WAS NICE! HER FLESH WAS SO SOFT! WHEN I CUT...
EVERETT!

EVERETT SCURRIES OFF TOWARD THE QUICKSAND POOL WITH HIS GORY CARGO! SIDNEY WATCHES HIM GO! YES! THE WOMAN! SHE WAS THE FIRST! HE REMEMBERED HER...
I'M AFRAID I'VE LOST... MY WAY! COULD YOU HELP ME GET BACK TO THE... THE HIGHWAY!
UH-HUHH! UH-HUHH!
EVERETT? WHO IS IT?
I BEG YOUR PARDON, MA'AM! MY BROTHER IS NOT TOO BRIGHT! COULD I HELP YOU?
I... I WANTED TO REACH HOUMA BY DARK! I MUST HAVE TURNED OFF THE MAIN ROAD...
YOU'LL NEVER MAKE HOUMA TONIGHT, MA'AM! YOU'RE WELCOME TO STAY THE NIGHT, THOUGH! YOU CAN START OUT FRESH IN THE MORNING!
WELL, I DON'T KNOW! I WOULDN'T WANT TO IMPOSE...
YES! THE WOMAN HAD BEEN THE FIRST! DURING THAT NIGHT, EVERETT HAD GONE TO HER ROOM AND...
EEEEEE...GGHH!
HUH? WHAT WAS THAT?
THE SCREAM HAD AWAKENED SIDNEY! HE'D RUSHED TO THE WOMAN'S ROOM...
EVERETT! CHOKE...
UH-HUHH! UH-HUHH!
SIDNEY HAD THROWN THE DISMEMBERED PARTS OF THE WOMAN'S BODY INTO THE QUICKSAND POOL! THAT HAD BEEN THE BEGINNING OF IT! AFTER THAT, EVERETT HAD GOTTEN WORSE AND WORSE! AND SIDNEY REALIZED THAT HE'D HAVE TO SUPPLY HIS MAD BROTHER WITH OTHER VICTIMS TO KEEP HIM SATISFIED...
ALL RIGHT, EVERETT! ALL RIGHT! I'LL THINK OF SOMETHING!
UH-HUHH... UH-HUHH...
SO SIDNEY'D THOUGHT OF ALTERING THE DIRECTIONAL SIGN DOWN AT THE ROAD, SO WANDERERS WOULD COME TO THE MANSION...
MY NAME'S JACKSON... ANTHONY JACKSON! I'M A TRAVELING SALESMAN! I SEEM TO HAVE GOTTEN ONTO YOUR ROAD BY MISTAKE!
COME IN, MR. JACKSON! COME IN!
5

AND NOW THE DOCTOR! SIDNEY WATCHES AS EVERETT LUMBERS BACK ONTO THE PORCH CARRYING THE EMPTY SACK.
DID YOU..?
YES, SIDNEY! I... I THREW THE PIECES IN THE POOL!
COME TO BED, EVERETT!
Y-YES... SIDNEY!
SOON, THE LIGHTS BLINK OFF ONE BY ONE IN THE RAMSHAKLE OLD PLANTATION HOUSE! SIDNEY AND HIS MAD BROTHER ARE ASLEEP! BUT DOWN IN THE BAYOU, THE QUICKSAND POOL ROLLS AND QUIVERS...
BENEATH ITS SUCKING SURFACE, THE DISMEMBERED PARTS OF THREE BODIES... A WOMAN'S, A SALESMAN'S, AND A DOCTOR'S.. BUMP TOGETHER, TURNING LAZILY... MELTING.., FUSING.. REORGANIZING THEMSELVES.. UNTIL...
...A PULPY HAND REACHES INTO THE BAYOU NIGHT
A STRINGY-HAIRED ROTTED WOMAN'S HEAD BOBS TO THE SURFACE...
ANOTHER FOLLOWS.. THE PLUMP SALESMAN'S FACE APPEARS...
...AND THEN THE RECENTLY MURDERED DOCTOR'S RISES!

IN HIS BEDROOM, SIDNEY STIRS UNCOMFORTABLY IN HIS SLEEP! SUDDENLY, THE DOOR TO HIS CHAMBER BURSTS OPEN AND THREE FIGURES ARE FRAMED IN IT, SWAYING UNSTEADILY...
WHO... WHO'S THERE? EVERETT? IS THAT... YOU? I THOUGHT I LOCKED YOU... IN... YOUR... GASP...
THE FIGURES MOVE FORWARD... INTO THE LIGHT! BUT THERE IS SOMETHING STRANGELY WRONG ABOUT THE FIGURES! SIDNEY STARES IN HORROR! A WHIMPER ESCAPES FROM HIS THROAT...
NO! NO! OH, LORD...
FOR THE DISMEMBERED PARTS OF EVERETT'S THREE VICTIMS HAVE FUSED INCORRECTLY! THE WOMAN'S HEAD RESTS UPON THE SALESMAN'S TORSO...
...WHILE DOCTOR FORMAN'S HEAD RESTS UPON THE WOMAN'S TORSO...
...AND MR. JACKSON'S, THE SALESMAN'S, HEAD HAS FUSED WITH THE DOCTOR'S BODY...
THE OTHER PARTS, THE ARMS AND LEGS OF EACH, ARE EQUALLY AS CONFUSED! THE CONGLAMORATIONS MOVE FORWARD... TOWARD THE HYSTERICALLY SCREAMING SIDNEY...
CLUTCHED IN ONE OF THE MIXED-UP-FIGURE'S HANDS IS A SMALL BLACK BAG... THE KIND USED BY DOCTORS TO CARRY THEIR SHINY LITTLE SHARP INSTRUMENTS...
EEEEEEEEAAAAAAAAGGGGHHHHHHHHHH!

LOCKED IN HIS BARRED WINDOW ROOM, EVERETT LISTENS WITH GREAT PUZZLEMENT TO THE SHRIEKING THAT ECHOES THROUGH THE OLD HOUSE FOR THE NEXT TWENTY-FIVE MINUTES...
YAAAAEEEEEEEEEE!
FINALLY, THE SHRIEKING STOPS, AND ONLY A SOFT PITIFUL SOBBING IS HEARD! FROM THE BARRED WINDOW, EVERETT WATCHES AS THREE FIGURES TOTTER OUT OF THE MANSION...
...AND BACK INTO THE BAYOU TO THE QUICKSAND POOL...
SUDDENLY, A KEY RATTLES INTO THE LOCK OF THE HEAVY DOOR OF EVERETT'S ROOM! HE TURNS FROM THE BARRED WINDOW! SIDNEY, OR WHAT WAS ONCE SIDNEY BUT IS NOW NOTHING MORE THAN A CONFUSED REORGANIZATION OF SIDNEY'S DISMEMBERED BODY, STANDS BEFORE HIM... THE UPSIDE-DOWN HEAD HANGING FROM THE LEFT HIP, SOBBING... THE LEFT LEG, SEWN TO THE LEFT SHOULDER, CROOKED AWKWARDLY AROUND A MAKESHIFT CRUTCH... THE RIGHT LEG SWAYING FROM THE RIGHT SHOULDER... THE LEFT ARM, ERUPTING FROM THE NECK, GESTICULATING... AND THE RIGHT ARM SUPPORTING THE ENTIRE GRISLY SIGHT.
EVERETT! LOOK... WHAT THEY'VE... DONE TO ME!
UH-HUHH... CHOKE...
HEE, HEE! YEP, KIDDIES! EVERETT'S VICTIMS REALLY MESSED UP HIS BROTHER SIDNEY! YOU MIGHT SAY THEY GOT TOGETHER! OF COURSE, THE DOC WAS A SURGEON, SO HIS HEAD DIRECTED THE WHOLE OPERATION! WHAT A LAUGH, THOUGH! HE'D HAD NO ANAESTHETIC IN HIS BAG! SIDNEY THOUGHT IT WAS A SCREAM. WHAT HAPPENED TO SIDNEY AND EVERETT YOU ASK? OH, THEY'RE STILL DOWN THERE, DEEP IN THE BAYOUS OF LOUISIANA! NEXT TIME YOU'RE DRIVING IN THAT SECTION, JUST LOOK FOR THEM! THAT IS... IF THEY DON'T LOOK FOR YOU FIRST! AND NOW, THE VAULT-KEEPER AWAITS! SEE YOU LATER...

C Bibliography

Author's Note: Much has been written about underground comics in the years since this book was first published – but at that time, few sources on the subject existed. These are the primary ones used to research the first edition – with the original edition's annotations. Also see Chapter 11 for further early references to underground comics in "straight" publications.

Drawing of Clay Geerdes by Kim Deitch. Clay Geerdes founded the first newspaper column devoted specifically to underground comics. He started *Comix World* in 1971. It ran in *Graphic Story World*, *Wonder World*, *Changes*, the Los Angeles *Free Press*, the San Francisco *Phoenix*, the San Diego *Door*, and the Berkeley *Barb*.

Robert Crumb. *Zap Comix* No. 4.

BOOKS

Becker, Stephen D. *Comic Art in America.* New York: Simon and Schuster, 1959.

Craven, Thomas. *Cartoon Cavalcade.* New York: Simon and Schuster, 1943.

Couperie, Pierre, Horn, Maurice, et al. *A History of the Comic Strip.* New York: Crown Publishers, 1968.

Daniels, Les. *Comix: A History of Comic Books in America.* New York: Outerbridge and Dienstfrey, 1971.

Davidson, Sol. *Culture and the Comic Strip* (Ph.D. thesis). New York: New York University Press, 1969.

Feiffer, Jules. *The Great Comic Book Heroes.* New York: Bonanza Books, 1965.

Fuchs, Wolfgang and **Reitberger, Reinhold.** *Comics: Anatomy of a Mass Medium.* Boston: Little, Brown and Company, 1972.

Herdeg, Walter and **Pascal, David** (eds.). *The Art of the Comic Strip.* Zurich: The Graphis Press, 1972.

Horn, Maurice (ed.). *Seventy-Five Years of the Comics.* Boston: Boston Book and Art, 1971.

Jacobs, Frank. *The Mad World of William Gaines.* New York: Lyle Stuart, Incorporated, 1972.

Kempkes, Wolfgang. *The International Bibliography of Comics Literature.* New York: R.R. Bowker Company, 1971.

Legman, G. *Love and Death.* New York: Breaking Point, 1949. A superbly written analysis of the interrelationship between sadism and suppressed sexuality in the comics of the 1940s.

Lupoff, Dick and **Thompson, Don** (eds). *All in Color for a Dime.* New Rochelle: Arlington House, 1970.

Margolis, Jack S., and **Clorfene, Richard.** *A Child's Garden of Grass* (paperback). New York: Pocket Books, 1970. About ninety-five percent accurate, five percent put-on, and immensely readable.

Murrel, William A. *A History of American Graphic Humor* (2 vols). The Macmillan Company, 1933, 1938.

Perry, George and **Aldridge, Alan.** *The Penguin Book of Comics.* Baltimore: Penguin Books, 1967, 1971.

Rembar, Charles. *The End of Obscenity* (paperback). New York: Bantam Books, 1969. Despite the over-optimistic title, the best book for the layman on the tangles of obscenity laws.

Sheridan, Martin. *Comics and their Creators: Life Stories of American Cartoonists.* Boston: Hale Cushman and Flint, 1942.

Steranko, James. *The Steranko History of Comics* (4 vols. so far). Reading, Pennsylvania: Supergraphics, 1970, 1972.

Waugh, Coulton. *The Comics.* New York: The Macmillan Company, 1947. The first full-length study of the comic medium, and still a very fine one from the historical point of view. Analysis of trends in the comics has long since proven faulty, however, and some passages of commentary are over-optimistic and dated.

Wertham, Frederic. *Seduction of the Innocent.* New York: Rinehart and Winston, 1954.

White, David Manning, and **Abel, Robert H.** (eds.). *The Funnies: An American Idiom.* London: The Free Press of Glencoe, 1963. A collection of essays about various aspects of the comic medium.

MAGAZINE ARTICLES

Abel, Bob. "Comix of the Underground," *Cavalier,* Vol. 19, No. 5, April 1969, pp. 34 ff. The first full-scale attempt by an overground medium to study the underground comics.

Barrier, Mike. "Notes on the Underground," *Funnyworld,* No. 12, Summer 1970, pp. 5 ff. Barrier may emerge as the most important critic of the underground comics in the "straight" media.

Bonin, Robert. "The Baron of Krupp," *Insight* (the Sunday magazine of the Milwaukee *Journal*), April 29, 1973, pp. 10-13. An entertaining if somewhat superficial profile of Denis Kitchen, with emphasis on his business dealings rather than his role as a cartoonist.

Brackman, Jacob. "The International Comix Conspiracy," *Playboy,* Vol. 17, No. 12, December 1970, pp. 195 ff. Rather limited in scope and hung up on proving how relevant the field is (at the expense of failing to tell enough about it), but profusely and honestly illustrated and very well written.

Buhle, Paul. "Komix Countermedia," *Leviathan,* July/August 1969, pp. 13-17. Buhle, editor of *Radical America* magazine, analyzes the underground comics from an historical and political point of view.

Buhle, Paul. "The New Comics and American Culture," *Tri-Quarterly,* No. 23-24, Winter-Spring 1972, pp. 367-402 and 408-11. An updated look at the comics, from a later vantage point than the *Leviathan* article.

Himelstein, Jacqueline. "Why There Is No Humor in American Life Today," *National Enquirer,* Vol. 45, No. 2, September 13, 1970, pp. 18-19.

The Mad Peck. "The Legendary Comix Ripoff Ruse," *Creem,* Vol. 2, No. 18, October 1970, pp. 22-25. A witty tour through the history of cartoonists stealing other cartoonists' work, by a scholar of comic-book pornography.

Pekar, Harvey. "Rapping about Cartoonists, Particularly Robert Crumb," *Journal of Popular Culture,* Vol. 3, No. 4, Spring 1970, pp. 677-88. A pleasant, if rather superficial, set of notes about Crumb, written by a personal friend of his.

Wald, Eliot, and **Gussow, Leon.** "Eyeball Kicks," *The Chicago Seed,* Vol. 5, No. 13, pp. 14 ff. A good historical survey of the rise of underground comics, incomplete but never pretending not to be, based mainly on information supplied by Chicago-based cartoonists Jay Lynch and Skip Williamson.

Opposite: Robert Crumb. *Zap Comics* No. 6. ©1973 Apex Novelties. By permission of Apex Novelties by Don Donahue.

Robert Crumb. *Zap Comics* No. 6. ©1973 Apex Novelties. By permission of Apex Novelties, by Don Donahue.

D EPILOGUE

"Writing history is like drinking an ocean and pissing a cupful," said novelist Gustave Flaubert, and wow, does it feel that way after 20-something years and 300-something pages. Since its conception, which actually goes back considerably further than 20 years, *A History of Underground Comics* has managed to feel like pissing into the wind while also managing to piss off a fair number of the people discussed in or omitted from it – who felt that their roles should be larger, or smaller, or at any rate different.

So, one more gentle reminder: this is *a* history, no more. "God alone knows the future, but only *a* historian can alter the past," said the famously acerbic and cynical Ambrose Bierce, and this book is one alteration of a past that very definitely happened but that simply felt like life, nothing more… although certainly, for those of us who were there, like life in extraordinary times. "History never looks like history when you are living through it," according to John W. Gardner, founder of Common Cause – but the cause for which the underground cartoonists fought, or thought they were fighting, was far from common. Or felt uncommon, anyway.

Looking back at the many still-excellent examples of underground cartooning in these pages is a salutary experience, for even in our modern times – the age of the evanescent everything – it remains true that *ars longa, vita brevis* (colloquially: "art lasts; life doesn't"). The cartoonists profiled here represent most of the ones working in underground comics in the 1960s and 1970s, but by no means all of them. Another history could easily pick up where this one leaves off, and it would have its own fascinating stories to tell and wonderful art to display.

Yet there is already a sense of nostalgia about the sheer audacity of the underground cartoonists in the times chronicled in this book. A first-rate exhibit called "Underground Classics," held in 2009 at the Chazen Museum of Art at the University of Wisconsin-Madison, managed to place underground comics and cartoonists fully within the "legitimate art" world, but by the same token made the field seem frozen in time – a past that had passed. And that was in spite of presentations explaining what the cartoonists did in the years after they created the specific works on display.

The museum exhibit too was a history of underground comics, for all that it was titled "Underground Classics: The Transformation of Comics into Comix." (A fine book with the same title, by James Danky

S. Clay Wilson. *Jiz Comics.* ©1969 R. Crumb. By permission of Robert Crumb.

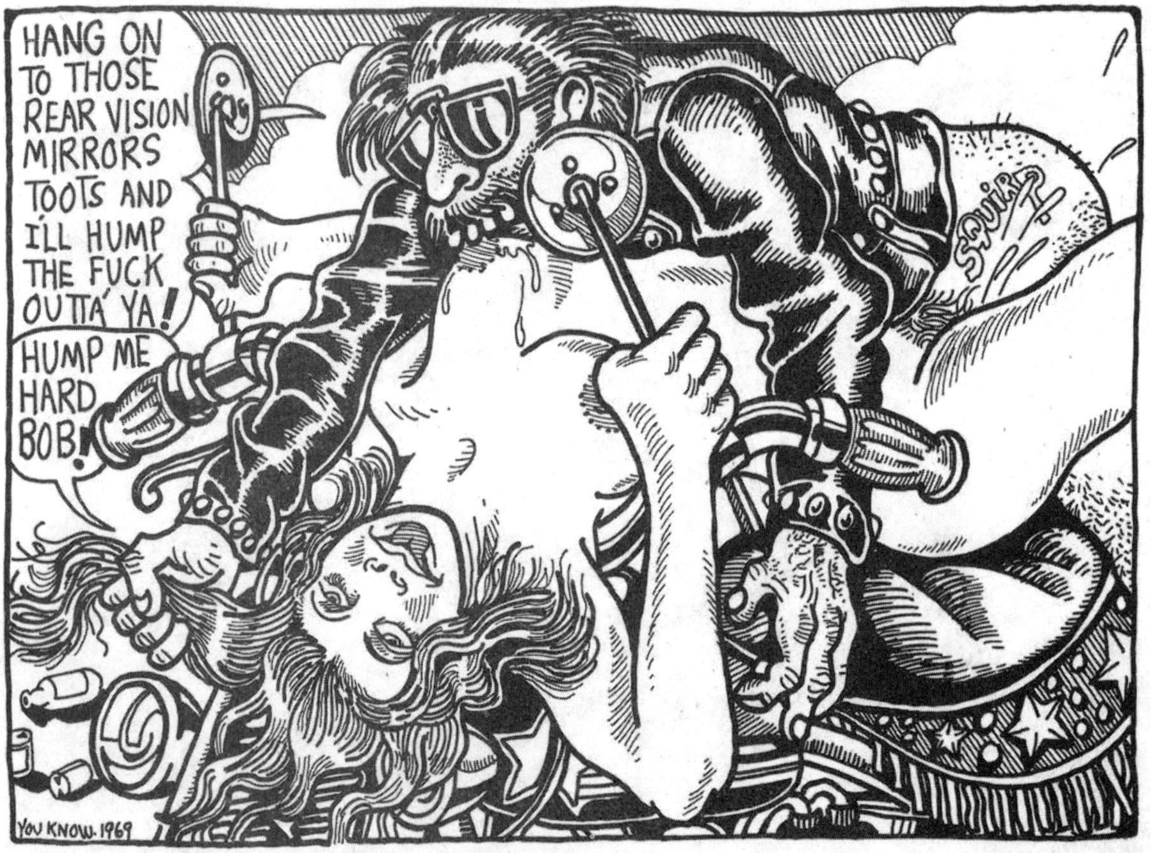

and Denis Kitchen, was subsequently published by Abrams ComicArts.) Like this history, the Chazen Museum retrospective looked at the close intermingling of the artists' lives with their work, showing clearly that Scottish essayist Thomas Carlyle knew what he was saying when he commented, "History is the essence of innumerable biographies" (although one should not always take Carlyle all that seriously: he also said, "History is a great dust heap").

The ways in which underground cartoonists branched out after the time chronicled in this book are many. Pete Poplaski, for example, became something of a chronicler himself, assembling two books on Robert Crumb's art – one of which has the words *Coffee Table* right in the title, which shows something

Robert Crumb. ***Zap Comix*** **No. 1. ©1967 R. Crumb. By permission of Robert Crumb.**

A typical Charlton Comics cover: *Space Adventures* Vol. 1, No. 13, Oct.-Nov. 1954. Charlton was one of many competitors for E.C. Comics, distinguished – if that is the right word – for combining multiple genres within each issue. Never as influential as the E.C. line, the Charlton books had inferior and inconsistent art, and the company was known for paying even less to cartoonists than the already-low rates at E.C. and elsewhere. Charlton went out of business in 1985.

Jim Pinkoski. *Spaced* No. 1. ©1974 Jim Pinkoski. By permission of Jim Pinkoski.

about the mainstreaming (at least to a limited extent) of underground cartooning. Poplaski also collaborated with none other than Will Eisner on Eisner's final book, *Expressive Anatomy.* Three cartoonists whose early works appears in these pages – Jay Lynch, John Pound and Art Spiegelman – worked on the *Garbage Pail Kids* trading-card series for bubble-gum manufacturer Topps, thus bringing to mind one of economist John Maynard Keynes' less-known pronouncements: "Most men love money and security more, and creation and construction less, as they get older." There is absolutely nothing wrong with this – Keynes' more-famous comment, "In the long run we are all dead," is worth keeping in mind – and it does not necessarily show that underground artists "sold out." Rather, it shows that they moved on – just as society did and just as Crumb's Lenore Goldberg predicted all those decades ago – ending up in a sort of confluence at a place where neither the cartoonists nor society had expected to be during the time chronicled here.

Speaking of feminists (a word never used with smash-the-state intensity nowadays), Trina Robbins, from the first a major voice for women in the underground-comics scene, went on to write some genuinely insightful studies of comics from a female perspective: *A Century of Women Cartoonists, The Great Women Super Heroes,* and *Women and Comics.* Certainly not "underground" in any meaningful sense, the books carried forward and honed themes and concerns that Robbins expressed in her own underground cartooning.

At the opposite extreme from Robbins' characters

Jay Kinney. 1973 Berkeley Comix Convention program.

Jay Kinney. *Occult Laff-Parade* No. 1. ©1973 Jay Kinney, Kim Deitch, Ned Sonntag, Justin Green, Larry Todd, Rory Hayes, and Rick Griffin. By permission of Messrs. Kinney, Deitch, Green, and Hayes.

Joel Beck. *Snarf* No. 4. ©1973 Denis Kitchen. By permission of Denis Kitchen.

was Trashman, one of the most macho and revolutionary underground protagonists of all – whose creator, Spain Rodriguez, stayed somewhat true to type over the years, to the point of producing a graphic novel in 2008 based on the life of Che Guevara. Sharon Rudahl, another of the relatively few female underground cartoonists, also went into graphic novels, creating a biography of famed anarchist Emma Goldman in graphic-novel form in 2007. Jaxon (Jack Jackson) went even more intensely into graphic novels, creating a series of well-researched and well-regarded ones about elements of the history of Texas.

Other cartoonists went where time and their own predilections, and sometimes financial necessity, took them. Richard Corben, who always had a strong science-fiction bent, produced work for *Heavy Metal* and many European publications. Tim Boxell, whose *Commies*

Robert Williams. *Zap Comix* No. 4.

from Mars No. 1 not only had SF elements but also included several comments on censorship (see pages 234-235), became a director of television and theatrical movies (*Chasing Destiny, Valley of the Heart's Delight*, etc.).

And then there are those strange comminglings that the universe, or the creative world, or the oddities of cartooning, seem to toss onto the shore of everyday life from time to time. In one of them, Bobby London of *Dirty Duck* fame (or notoriety) drew the daily *Popeye* comic strip for six years, thereby connecting with one of the oldest comic strips still extant: Popeye first appeared as a character in E.C. Segar's *Thimble Theater* in 1929. And Will Elder, an important part of the old E.C. scene (which had nothing to do with E.C. Segar!) – but who was never involved with underground cartooning – nevertheless created a brilliant and highly memorable cover for *Snarf* No. 10 in 1987. A parody of a painting that was notorious in its own time, *The Raft of the Medusa* by Théodore Géricault (1791-1824), the cover shows a plethora of countercultural types, from nubile naked women to scruffy longhaired men (one of whom is drinking from a bottle labeled "Ink"), adrift in a vast ocean in which signs such as "Head Shop" and "No Nukes" are floating, bereft of value and meaning. The makeshift sail catching

Robert Crumb. *Despair.*

Jim Osborne. 1973 Berkeley Comix Convention program.

the wind bears Porky Pig's immortal words, "That's All, Folks," as the sky ahead increasingly clouds over and the undergrounds and their creators drift toward, apparently, oblivion.

This is brilliant social commentary as well as darned good art – but so were the undergrounds in their heyday. Elder was perhaps a little too much a doomsayer, but that may depend on where one sits on the raft carrying all of us, if not forward, certainly somewhere. "History is merely a list of surprises," said Kurt Vonnegut. "It can only prepare us to be surprised yet again." Hopefully you have encountered some surprises in *A History of Underground Comics,* and hopefully you will remember, to say it for the umpteenth-and-first time, that even if it is merely *a* history, it is one that is meant well, with tremendous respect for the cartoonists as people and artists, and for what they produced.

And even if this is a history, it is one worth experiencing so as to have a better understanding of what went on in society a mere few decades ago – even if that time seems impossibly ancient in the ever-increasing pace of 21st-century life. A comment made at a time that *was* impossibly ancient is as appropriate now as it was more than 2,000 years ago. It is from Marcus Tullius Cicero: *Nescire autem quid antequam natus sis acciderit, id est semper esse puerum.* Which means: "To stay ignorant of things that happened before you were born is to remain a child." Childlike wonder is a marvelous thing. Childlike ignorance – not so much. *Ave atque vale* – hail and farewell.

Michael J. *Soft Core.* ©1973 Rob Landeros, Michael J. and Shelby. By permission of Michael J. Becker.

566

DIAMOND
IMPEACH
544

Robert Crumb. *Motor City Comics* No. 2. ©1970 R. Crumb. By permission of Robert Crumb.

MARK JAMES ESTREN is a writer, editor, TV producer and executive, venture capitalist, classical-music critic, publisher, hardware and software tester and analyst, blogger, historian, orchestra conductor, psychologist and herpetologist.

He is the only person ever to have written a book review of a Walt Kelly *Pogo* reprint, entirely in verse, for a technology publication: *High Technology Business* magazine, of which he was editor and publisher.

His study, "The Neoteny Barrier," for *Journal of Animal Ethics*, used comics and cartoons to show ways in which people react more positively to animals that exhibit anthropomorphic traits.

Among the books he has edited are *In Tune with America,* a study of music in American history, by former congressman George Nethercutt; and *Professionally Speaking*, by famed speech consultant and trainer Lilyan Wilder.

Estren was a major contributor to *In a Word: A Dictionary of Words That Don't Exist, but Ought To.* One of his entries:

Cong, noun [by shortening from Congress, a U.S. legislative organization]:

Unit of measurement of costs incurred or increased by the failure of leadership to lead. Equivalent to one billion dollars. "Far from being insulted at being dubbed 'king cong,' Congress was delighted with the new unit of measurement, since the cost of the bailout seemed much smaller when listed as 500 congs than when stated as 500 billion dollars."

Estren wrote thought-provoking and widely quoted analyses of "inner space" and the technological revolution in virtual reality for *Across the Board* magazine, and of the psychological motivations underpinning the actions of would-be presidential assassin John Hinckley for Knight-Ridder Newspapers.

He was profiled by *The Washington Post* for his years of snake presentations to young children in Virginia schools.

He created *The Insiders with Jack Anderson,* the only TV broadcast ever anchored by the muckraking columnist—a program now in the archives of the Newseum in Washington, D.C.

Mark J. Estren - markjestren.com

He also created more than 500 *Environmental Minute* segments, which he researched, wrote and anchored on national cable television.

Small wonder that *Fortune* magazine named Estren one of its "People to Watch."

When researching this book, Estren was punched in the eye by an underground cartoonist he was profiling—who then apologized and asked that his work be included (it is).

The chapter title "Into the Overground" anticipated a move that would be made by some of the top underground cartoonists—and by Estren himself. He has been executive vice president of United Press International and president of UPI Television; general manager of Financial News Network on cable television; executive producer of PBS' *The Nightly Business Report*, whose national version he created; and an executive producer for CBS and ABC News. He is a regular contributor to many publications, from *The Washington Post* to the *Bottom Line/Personal* newsletter. He has written columns, articles, commentaries and analyses for publications ranging from the alternative press (*Madison-Milwaukee Bugle-American*) to traditional community newspapers (*Bucks County [Pennsylvania] Courier-Times*) to the *Philadelphia Inquirer* and *Miami Herald.* And he studied conducting at Tanglewood Institute with Erich Leinsdorf and Leonard Bernstein.

Somewhere in there, Estren found time to earn Ph.D. degrees in English and Psychology from the University at Buffalo, where he designed and taught one of the nation's first courses in science fiction as literature—and another course called "Obscenity, Pornography and the Law." After obtaining his B.A. in English and Latin at Wesleyan University, he earned an M.S. and Pulitzer award at Columbia University's Graduate School of Journalism, where his thesis focused on "underground" media. He has also written a translation of and commentary on the complete poetry of Catullus, and a dissertation on horror in literature and psychoanalysis.

Estren says *A History of Underground Comics* makes perfect sense in this context: "I am a communicator by profession, in all available media. The interrelationship of pictures and words has always fascinated me. The underground cartoonists, at their best, were uniquely powerful communicators. That is why I resonate to their work—and to the work of their great predecessors, such as the old E.C. comics.

"The underground cartoonists created as much drama and intensity with still pictures as films and TV programs did with moving ones in the 1960s and 1970s. That's an amazing achievement—one worth looking back on with admiration even in our Internet-focused, video-saturated age.

"The best cartoonists not only had extraordinary visual impact but also had something important to say about the world they lived in, which in many ways is the one in which we still live. Some of their political references may have grown old, and some of their sexual preoccupations may seem sophomoric, but the power of the best of these comics is undiminished by time. 'Comic' means 'funny,' but it is mostly the unfunny elements of underground comics that continue to seize and hold our attention. For these still pictures to grab us and shake us up so much in these days of hyperspeed animation, quick-cut videos and ever-expanding virtual reality is truly amazing."

...ALL I WANT IS THE ANSWER, THE ANSWER!
VERY WELL, YOU FOOL!
GO FUCK YOUR SELF